Social Work Practice

Jennifer L. Bellamy • Brianna P. Lemmons
Qiana R. Cryer-Coupet • Jennifer A. Shadik
Editors

Social Work Practice with Fathers

Engagement, Assessment, and Intervention

Springer

Editors
Jennifer L. Bellamy
Graduate School of Social Work
University of Denver
Denver, CO, USA

Brianna P. Lemmons
Diana R. Garland School of Social Work
Baylor University
Waco, TX, USA

Qiana R. Cryer-Coupet
School of Social Work
Georgia State University
Atlanta, GA, USA

Jennifer A. Shadik
Department of Social Work
Ohio University
Athens, OH, USA

ISBN 978-3-031-13685-6 ISBN 978-3-031-13686-3 (eBook)
https://doi.org/10.1007/978-3-031-13686-3

This Springer imprint is published by the registered company Springer Nature Switzerland AG
The registered company address is: Gewerbestrasse 11, 6330 Cham, Switzerland

Acknowledgments

This book would not have been possible without the contributions of many of our friends and colleagues. We would like to take this opportunity to thank Janet Kim at Springer, who first approached our group to take on this project, set us on this journey, and has been so responsive and supportive along the way. We would also like to thank all the authors who said "yes" to contributing to this book, especially in the midst of a very challenging time and many other demands and opportunities. We also want to thank those who assisted us in the review process, including: Pajarita Charles, Justin Dyer, Azaliah Israel, Rebecca Kaufman, Shawna Lee, Maretta McDonald, Lisa Klein Vogel, and Carla Stover. Also, thank you to Marlene de Wilde for her copy editing assistance. Finally, we would like to thank all the fathers and families who have inspired us to take on this important work.

Contents

About the Editors

Jennifer L. Bellamy, PhD, MSSW is the associate dean for research and faculty development and professor in the Graduate School of Social Work (GSSW) at the University of Denver in Colorado. At GSSW, she teaches research courses. She earned her Bachelor of Arts in Psychology and Sociology in 1997 and her Master of Science in Social Work in 2000 from The University of Texas at Austin. Before earning her PhD, she worked as a crisis counselor at the University of Texas and served as a project coordinator for the Texas Fragile Families Initiative, a multisite demonstration project serving young, unmarried, low-income fathers. Dr. Bellamy completed her PhD at the Columbia University School of Social Work in 2006 and postdoctoral training at the George Warren Brown School of Social Work at Washington University in Saint Louis in 2008. Her current research and scholarship focuses on the engagement of fathers in child and family services and evidence-based practice in social work. She is currently the principal investigator on the Administration for Children and Families (ACF)-funded Fathers and Continuous Learning in Child Welfare (FCL) Project in partnership with Mathematica Policy Research. She is also the co-principal investigator for the ACF-funded Colorado Fatherhood Project in partnership with the Colorado Office of Early Childhood. Dr. Bellamy is the co-developer of the Dads Matter-HV and the Nurturing Dads and Partners (NDAP) Program.

Brianna P. Lemmons, PhD, MSW is an assistant professor in the Garland School of Social Work at Baylor University, where she teaches research courses at the undergraduate and graduate levels. She earned her Bachelor of Arts in Psychology in 2000 from Spelman College and her Master of Social Work in 2006 from Howard University. Before earning her PhD, she worked as an aftercare program coordinator at Sasha Bruce Youthwork, Inc. in Washington, DC. Dr. Lemmons completed her PhD and postdoctoral training at Howard University School of Social Work in 2015 and 2016, respectively. Her current research and scholarship focuses on predictors of Black father involvement with children, the impact of Black father involvement on child development, social work practice with fathers, and the integration of fatherhood content into social work education programs. She currently serves as part of an expert working group for the REFRAME Project (Race Equity for Fatherhood, Relationship, and Marriage Programs to Empower Black Families) with AMEF Associates and as part of a technical working group for the FRAMING Project (Fatherhood, Relationships, and Marriage – Illuminating the Next Generation of Research) with Mathematica Policy Research. In her spare time, she enjoys exercising, baking, crafting, volunteering, and traveling.

Qiana R. Cryer-Coupet, PhD, MSW is an associate professor of social work in the Andrew Young School of Policy Studies at Georgia State University. Prior to this appointment, she taught in the human behavior and research methods sequences of the MSW program at North Carolina State University. Dr. Cryer-Coupet earned her Bachelor of Arts in psychology from Illinois Wesleyan University, her MSW from the University of Maryland-Baltimore, and her PhD from the Jane Addams College of Social Work at the University of Illinois-Chicago. Dr. Cryer-Coupet's direct practice included work with families engaged in kinship care at Uhlich Children's Advantage Network and with adolescents in residential treatment for substance use disorders at Chestnut Health Systems. Her research practice included work as a field researcher for Chapin Hall at the University of Chicago. Dr. Cryer-Coupet's program of research explores the impacts of parenting practices on child, adolescent, and family well-being. Her current projects examine family trauma in relation to paternal experiences with substance use disorders, incarceration, racial discrimination, and economic instability. Her work has been funded by the Fatherhood Research and Practice Network and HRSA. Dr. Cryer-Coupet has served on technical work groups with Mathematica Policy Research for the Fathers and Continuous Learning in Child Welfare Project and the KEEP Fathers Engaged Project.

Jennifer A. Shadik, PhD, MSW, LISW-S is an associate professor in the Department of Social Work at Ohio University. She also serves as the coordinator for Athens Undergraduate Social Work Programs and as the director of studies for the Honors Tutorial College's social work program. She teaches practice courses at the undergraduate and graduate levels. Dr. Shadik earned her Bachelor of Arts in Psychology from Kalamazoo College and her Master of Social Work, with a concentration in clinical social work, from Western Michigan University. She earned her PhD in social work from Virginia Commonwealth University in 2014. Her practice background involved working with families in a variety of settings. She spent 6 years working with parents at high risk or who had maltreated a child at Greater Richmond SCAN (Stop Child Abuse Now). Other direct practice experience included delivering intensive, in-home family preservation services and providing outpatient therapy for children, teens, and their families. Her current research and scholarship focuses on fathering, child welfare, and sibling violence. She has received funding from the Fatherhood Research and Practice Network. She was licensed in Virginia as an LCSW for over 20 years and is currently a licensed independent social worker in Ohio.

Contributors

Angelica Alonso, MA University of Maryland, College Park, MD, USA

Jeffrey D. Ball, JD La Mesa, CA, USA

Aaron Banman, PhD, LCSW University of Nebraska at Omaha, Omaha, NE, USA

Jennifer L. Bellamy, PhD, MSW Graduate School of Social Work, University of Denver, Denver, CO, USA

Clinton Boyd Jr, PhD Fathers, Families & Healthy Communities, Chicago, IL, USA

Natasha J. Cabrera, PhD University of Maryland, College Park, MD, USA

Yu Chen, BA University of Maryland, College Park, MD, USA

Qiana R. Cryer-Coupet, PhD, MSW School of Social Work, Georgia State University, Atlanta, GA, USA

Grace Y. Dennis, BA Department of Psychology and Neuroscience, Baylor University, Waco, TX, USA

Kimberly A. Dent, MA Ohio Commission on Fatherhood, Ohio Department of Job and Family Services, Columbus, OH, USA

Rachel Ghosh, BA University of Maryland, College Park, MD, USA

Stephen M. Gibson, MS Virginia Commonwealth University, Richmond, VA, USA

McKenzie N. Green, PhD Virginia Commonwealth University, Richmond, VA, USA

Geoffrey L. Greif, PhD, LCSW-C University of Maryland, Baltimore, Baltimore, MD, USA

Justin S. Harty, PhD, MSW, LCSW Arizona State University, Phoenix, AZ, USA

Brianna P. Lemmons, PhD, MSW Diana R. Garland School of Social Work, Baylor University, Waco, TX, USA

S. Alexa McDorman, BA University of Maryland, College Park, MD, USA

Branden A. McLeod, PhD, MSW University of Illinois Chicago, Chicago, IL, USA

Daniel P. Miller, PhD Boston University, Boston, MA, USA

Lenna Nepomnyaschy, PhD Rutgers University, New Brunswick, NJ, USA

Armon R. Perry, PhD University of Louisville, Louisville, KY, USA

Ann M. Ream, MSW, LSW Summit County Children Services, Akron, OH, USA

Latrice S. Rollins, PhD, MSW Morehouse School of Medicine, Atlanta, GA, USA

Terrance Ruth, PhD North Carolina State University, Raleigh, NC, USA

Jennifer A. Shadik, PhD, MSW, LISW-S Department of Social Work, Ohio University, Athens, OH, USA

Kevin Shafer, PhD, MA Brigham Young University, Provo, UT, USA

Miriam G. Valdovinos, PhD University of Denver, CO, USA

Nigel Vann, MA National Responsible Fatherhood Clearinghouse, Dunwoody, GA, USA

Chapter 1
Introduction

Jennifer L. Bellamy, Jennifer A. Shadik, Brianna P. Lemmons, and Qiana R. Cryer-Coupet

Overall Framing

This book is written for social workers who are working for the equitable inclusion of fathers in social services, research, and policies. This includes social work students, instructors, researchers, and practitioners in both micro and macro practice. Unfortunately, for many years, child and family services, criminal justice, education, and other systems and providers have not sufficiently attended to the needs and experiences of fathers. Many fathers have been excluded, forgotten, or treated as a less important part of the family system compared to mothers and maternal family members. This is particularly so for low-income fathers as well as racially and ethnically minoritized fathers. The field of social work, along with other related professions and disciplines, has made strides in recent years to demonstrate through a mounting body of research that engaging fathers in services is critical to the well-being of children, mothers, extended family members, communities, and fathers themselves. Similarly, increasing efforts are being made to engage fathers more

J. L. Bellamy
University of Denver, Graduate School of Social work, Denver, CO, USA
e-mail: Jennifer.Bellamy@du.edu

J. A. Shadik
Department of Social Work, Ohio University, Athens, OH, USA
e-mail: Shadik@ohio.edu

B. P. Lemmons
Diana R. Garland School of Social Work, Baylor University, Waco, TX, USA
e-mail: Brianna_Lemmons@baylor.edu

Q. R. Cryer-Coupet (✉)
School of Social Work, Georgia State University, Atlanta, GA, USA
e-mail: qcryercoupet@gsu.edu

J. L. Bellamy et al. (eds.), *Social Work Practice with Fathers*,
https://doi.org/10.1007/978-3-031-13686-3_1

successfully in programs and service systems; and research is beginning to describe the benefits of doing so.

The editors of this book are all women who have come to recognize the need for, and the lack of, equitable attention to fathers in social work. Social work is a female-dominated field, which some suggest has contributed to the poor engagement of fathers in social services—particularly in those systems and programs that are largely staffed by women. While women have an important role to play in supporting father engagement, we felt it critical to bring the voices of men and fathers to this text. Therefore, the editors invited a group of authors diverse in terms of race, ethnicity, and gender to contribute to this text. We invited them to draw upon their expertise and experiences in multiple fields to present a relevant snapshot of current theory, literature, and research on assessment, engagement, and intervention practices with fathers. Some are researchers and academics; others are policy makers, administrators, and service providers.

Every chapter follows a similar format, including an introduction, background, and context, followed by conceptual framing, recommended approaches, resources, and discussion questions designed to spark additional reflection and insight from readers. Some chapter authors have more expertise in providing services at the micro and mezzo levels, some work on programs and policies at the macro level, and some are researchers and educators. Due to the substantive expertise, identities, and experiences of the authors, the framing, perspective, and voice for each chapter will differ. The provision of equitable father-inclusive services is not the task of one of us alone but requires a fundamental shift in social service systems and the way we all work together as social workers to serve fathers in research, policy, and practice.

Defining Parenting, Fathering, and Co-Parenting

It is important to define what we mean by *parenting*, *fathering*, and *co-parenting*. Defining these terms is more complicated than it might seem at first as they are not used consistently throughout the field or in the literature describing fathers and fathering. From classic anthropological and human development perspectives, parenting is often defined as a primary mechanism of socialization, that is, a primary means of training and preparing children to meet the demands of their environments and take advantage of the opportunities within those environments (National Academies of Science, Engineering, and Medicine, 2016). For this book, we take a broad view of parenting activities, from more direct caretaking activities (e.g., feeding, clothing, monitoring) to more indirect forms of parenting (e.g., contributing to decision making about education, health, and other activities), financial contributions, and emotional support.

This book employs a similarly broad view of fathers and fathering and does not limit fathers to only those men who have a biological relationship to children. Our definition of a father includes those who identify as male and are engaged in a parenting role for one or more children. Men become designated as fathers through their association with women who are mothers, through behaving in a parental manner, or through a legal or administrative act (Eichler & McCall, 1992). Male caretakers with varying kinds of relationships with their biological children and with other family members are included (Strug & Wilmore-Schaeffer, 2003). Fathers include men who are married, cohabitating, divorced, or separated; single fathers with custody of children; and young, unwed fathers (Featherstone, 2001). Noncustodial fathers (fathers who do not have legal custody of their children) may be divorced, separated, never-married, or absent fathers. This could include a broad range of fathers including fathers of adopted children and those who are fathering from afar, such as those who are incarcerated or live away from their families due to military service, work, or disability.

Finally, co-parents are broadly defined as well. Although single father-headed households comprise one of the fastest-growing demographic categories in the United States (U.S. Census Bureau, 2020), most fathers do not parent on their own. Co-parents include a wide variety of other adults with whom fathers share parenting responsibilities and from whom they receive support in parenting. This book is guided by Feinberg's (2002) framework of co-parenting, which includes four components: (1) co-parenting support; (2) childrearing agreement/disagreement; (3) division of duties, tasks, and responsibilities; and (4) management of interactional patterns. Broadly defining these terms is important as it makes space for the diversity of cultures, structures, socioeconomic realities, and other bio-psycho-social dimensions that shape families, fathers, and parenting. Although all chapters in this book are framed within these broad definitions, authors may highlight one or more specific dimensions of parenting, fathering, or co-parenting, depending on the focus of each.

Engagement of Fathers in Social Work Practice

The engagement of fathers in social work practice is an ethical imperative. Although social workers and service systems, historically, have not always engaged fathers well, social workers have an ethical responsibility to work with men who are playing a parenting role. The National Association of Social Workers' (NASW) Code of Ethics states, "Social workers' primary goal is to help people in need and to address social problems" (NASW, 2021, Ethical Principles, para. 3). Fathers need support and face a variety of social problems which social workers are well positioned to address. For example, becoming a father is a challenging transition that is accompanied by changes in role, identity, and responsibility. This can be stressful, and some fathers have additional challenges in navigating this transition because of their service system involvement, experiences, identities, resources, or relationships. Fathers, like mothers, may need assistance with parenting as they navigate family and co-parenting relationships, seek to balance education and employment with family demands, and learn how to support and care for their children as their developmental needs change over time. For this reason, this book also uses a developmental and family systems perspective to aid in our understanding of how to better serve fathers. Fathers are not just embedded in families; their experiences are also shaped by the many service systems with which they interact. Service systems like early childhood and education have important roles to play in supporting fathers, but unfortunately, they struggle to engage men as parents. Other systems, such as child welfare and child support, have historically been more punitive in their approach to fathers. Social workers in these service systems have a critical role to play in shifting practices, policies, and organizational cultures away from barriers to father engagement and toward becoming promoters of father engagement.

The NASW Code of Ethics (2021) also states, "Social workers challenge social injustice" (Ethical Principles, para 6). Most social work texts and courses do not include fathers (Brown et al., 2009); and social work education programs tend to neglect many issues related to men's needs and the interventions to help them (Baum, 2016). The editors of this book were trained as social workers in a variety of schools and now serve as faculty in social work programs at diverse institutions. We received very little training at the master's level on how to work with men and fathers, and when men and fathers were included in our training, it was often from a deficit perspective and focused more often on the risks they pose rather than on their strengths and the assets they can be to their families and communities. Our hope is that this book helps to shift that narrative in training and in the field and increases social workers' competencies in how to better assess, engage, and serve diverse fathers, and to do so with a more balanced and strengths-based approach. Furthermore, the available research on fathers and fathering is considerably less than that which is focused on mothers (Shapiro & Krysik, 2010). This inequity in research is also a social justice issue. If we do not have an adequate evidence base on how to work with fathers, our efforts to optimally serve them are diminished and inequities may be further amplified. For this reason, this book also includes a chapter on increasing the engagement of fathers in research.

As is the case for many people with whom social workers work, fathers face injustices as they seek to go to school, work, access needed services, and be there for their families. For example, many non-resident fathers who want to stay involved in the lives of their children face challenges in gaining access to them, in part due to the structure and the policies of child support service systems that were initially created to collect money from divorced fathers. More recently, child support has made efforts to strengthen both the capacity of fathers to contribute financially to their families and their relationships with their children. Because of dominant cultural beliefs that have historically emphasized a father's financial contributions and a mother's contributions in the direct care of children, many policies in child support and other systems still reflect similar gender inequities and assumed gender roles. Single fathers, for example, do not have access to the same social benefits and resources as single mothers (Haworth, 2019).

This book not only aligns with the ethical principles of social workers but also seeks to provide practical guidance to social workers to increase their competence in working with fathers. Social work ethics direct us to work with all clients, in their best interests, not pick and choose who we work with based on preference. Social work ethics also direct us to work within our competence. If you are a social worker working in education, health, mental health, child welfare, child support, early childhood, child support, criminal justice, or many other spaces, you are going to encounter fathers. There are very few social work roles that are solely female serving. And yet, we have found that many of our colleagues in practice and in social work education are uncertain of how to work with fathers.

Until recently, there have been limited evidence-supported interventions available to the field, and few best practices that social workers could draw upon to guide their work with fathers. Fortunately, this is changing. Now, we have not only research on the ways in which fathers matter to children, families, service outcomes, and communities but also mounting research on effective engagement, assessment, and intervention practices with fathers. These three areas form the major sections of this book.

Overview of the Structure of the Book

The engagement chapters of this book use an ecological approach, placing fathers in the context of their own well-being and that of their families and communities, as well as the service systems and contexts within which they live. Fathers are a highly diverse group, and we seek to call particular attention to issues of diversity, including race, ethnicity, immigration status, and sexual orientation throughout this book. Chapter 2 provides a historical overview of the engagement of fathers in human service systems and the barriers to engagement, as well as guides and frameworks that can be used to engage fathers in social work practice. The next two chapters explore father engagement from micro (Chap. 3) and macro perspectives (Chap. 4), with more details and applied examples of father engagement at these levels of practice. Chapter 5 is focused on father engagement in research. Father engagement in research has been a persistent challenge, but recent studies and strategies explore how fathers can be successfully recruited and included in research.

The two assessment chapters in this book take a multidimensional approach to assessing fathers in a more holistic and balanced way than has historically been the case. Unfortunately, fathers are often assessed primarily for the risks they bring to families and communities, including interpersonal violence and criminal justice. Sometimes, these risks are used as an argument to not work with them. While some fathers do present such risks, most fathers, even those in higher-risk groups such as child welfare-involved families, do not. Even when fathers do present risks to families and communities, these concerns are even more reason to offer them support and interventions. All fathers need to also be assessed for their goals, strengths, needs, and family roles. The chapters on assessment provide guidance on how to implement strong assessment practices with fathers. Chapter 6 provides guidance on comprehensive assessment with fathers in the context of their families; the assessment of father involvement and the quality of fathering he provides his children is also discussed. Chapter 7 describes approaches to assessing the "father friendliness" of programs and organizations.

The largest section of this book is dedicated to intervening with fathers in different service contexts. Although many of the values and principles articulated in each of the chapters are the same, (i.e., attention to diversity, ecological complexity, research evidence, and holistic approaches) each intervention context described is unique and brings to our attention important and specific considerations. Each of these chapters provides an overview of the intervention context and the nature of the work with fathers in those contexts and provides guidance to readers on suggested interventions and practices. The section on interventions includes Chapters 8, 9, 10, 11, 12, 13, 14, 15, and 16. Chapter 8 provides a broad intervention overview that touches on multiple systems and father involvement, and the remaining chapters focus on intervening with fathers in the context of public policy, criminal justice, child welfare, education, early childhood, child support, and interpersonal violence. Finally, this book contains useful appendices to assist instructors and students.

Guidance for Instructors

In our experience, few schools of social work offer courses specifically dedicated to fathers, and we hope that this book serves as an impetus to develop such courses across programs. This book can also be integrated into existing social work courses, including practice courses, courses on diversity, equity and inclusion, research courses, and courses on human behavior in the social environment. For example, courses dedicated to assessment may find the assessment chapters particularly useful; and, similarly, courses focused on specific service systems may incorporate the relevant intervention chapters focused on their system of interest. In addition, each chapter concludes with discussion questions that can be used by instructors to facilitate live discussions, online discussion boards, or reflective assignments. In addition, we have included some resources to support the use of this book in social work training. These include a table describing the Social Work Grand Challenges related to fathers and fathering, including relevant examples from the literature (see Appendix B). This book also touches on multiple competencies from the Council on Social Work Education (CSWE); in Appendix C, we included a table with competencies and linkages to fatherhood content throughout the book. Appendix D includes syllabi maps for Human Behavior in the Social Environment (HBSE), practice, research, and policy courses with sample objectives and assignments. The book also contains policy and practice reflection exercises (see Appendices E and F). We have also included six case vignettes to assist in course discussions, reflections, and application of material from the book (see Appendix G).

Complementary Texts

There are many important texts dedicated to fathers, which we encourage the readers to also review and apply in their work. Some are related to interventions (Fagan & Pearson, 2021), Black fathers (Johnson, 2010; Rollins, 2021), and the role of fathers in children's development (Lamb, 2004). These and other resources are included at the end of each chapter and within a suggested resource guide in Appendix H of this book. What the field lacked, in our opinion, was a comprehensive, practical, and research-informed text on working with fathers aimed specifically at social work practitioners, educators, and students—and that is what we have aimed to deliver with this book.

Conclusion

We know that fathers provide benefits to children and families. This is an important argument for increased attention to them in the field of social work. But, fathers are also deserving of support, opportunities, and services that promote their well-being in their own right. Including fathers in research and services is a critical social justice issue that, when left inadequately addressed, has broad-reaching consequences for children, families, communities, and fathers. We hold a shared vision for equitable father-inclusive engagement, assessment, and intervention practices across the many service systems where social workers serve families and communities. To be successful in realizing this vision, we must be specific and intentional about the service needs and experiences of minoritized and marginalized fathers. The intersecting identities of fathers must be integrated across all these efforts. It is our hope that this text will spur continued discussion on, and discernable improvements in, how fathers are approached in the classroom and in research and practice settings.

References

Baum, N. (2016). The unheard gender: The neglect of men as social work clients. *British Journal of Social Work, 46*, 1463–1471. https://doi.org/10.1093/bjsw/bcv074

Brown, L., Callahan, M., Strega, S., Walmsley, C., & Dominelli, L. (2009). Manufacturing ghost fathers: The paradox of father presence and absence in child welfare. *Child and Family Social Work, 14*, 25–34. https://doi.org/10.1111/j.1365-2206.2008.00578.x

Eichler, M., & McCall, M. (1992). Clarifying the legal dimensions of fatherhood. *Canadian Journal of Family Law, 11*, 197.

Featherstone, B. (2001). Putting fathers on the child welfare agenda. *Child & Family Social Work, 6*(2), 179–186.

Feinberg, M. E. (2002). Coparenting and the transition to parenthood: A framework for prevention. *Clinical Child and Family Psychology Review, 5*(3), 173–195.

Fagan, J., & Pearson, J. (Eds.). (2021). *New research on parenting programs for low-income fathers*. Routledge.

Haworth, S. (2019). A systematic review of research on social work practice with single fathers. *Practice, 31*(5), 329–347.

Johnson, W. E. (2010). *Social work with African American males: Health, mental health, and social policy*. OUP.

Lamb, M. E. (Ed.). (2004). *The role of the father in child development*. Wiley.

National Academies of Sciences, Engineering, and Medicine. (2016). *Parenting matters: Supporting parents of children ages 0–8*. The National Academies Press. https://doi.org/10.17226/21868

National Association of Social Workers. (2021). *Code of ethics*. https://www.socialworkers.org/about/ethics/code-of-ethics/code-of-ethics-english

Rollins, L. S. (Ed.). (2021). *Engaging and working with African American fathers: Strategies and lessons learned*. Routledge.

Shapiro, A., & Krysik, J. (2010). Finding fathers in social work research and practice. *Journal of Social Work Values & Ethics, 7*(1), 1–8.

Strug, D., & Wilmore-Schaeffer, R. (2003). Fathers in the social work literature: Policy and practice implications. *Families in Society: The Journal of Contemporary Human Services, 84*, 503–511.

U.S. Census Bureau. *America's families and living arrangements: 2020*. Available at: https://www.census.gov/data/tables/2020/demo/families/cps-2020.html. Accessed 15 Sept 2021.

Part I
Engagement

Chapter 2
Framing Father Engagement

Brianna P. Lemmons, Grace Y. Dennis, and Latrice S. Rollins

Introduction

This chapter provides an in-depth examination of the concept of *father engagement* in human service systems. Specifically, it will begin by offering an overview of five key events that have led to an increased focus on father engagement in human services (see Fig. 2.1). It will then discuss definitions of father engagement as well as guides and frameworks that can be used to engage fathers in practice. This chapter will conclude by discussing some key barriers to father engagement and offer best practices and recommendations for effectively engaging fathers in human services.

Background and Context

The Evolution of Fathering Roles in the United States

Societal perceptions of fathering roles are largely shaped by demographic, social, economic, political, and historical trends. As a result, defining fatherhood and responding to the question of what it means to be a father are complicated and

B. P. Lemmons (✉)
Diana R. Garland School of Social Work, Baylor University, Waco, TX, USA
e-mail: Brianna_Lemmons@baylor.edu

G. Y. Dennis
Department of Psychology and Neuroscience, Baylor University, Waco, TX, USA
e-mail: Grace_Dennis@baylor.edu

L. S. Rollins
Morehouse School of Medicine, Atlanta, GA, USA
e-mail: lrollins@msm.edu

J. L. Bellamy et al. (eds.), *Social Work Practice with Fathers*,
https://doi.org/10.1007/978-3-031-13686-3_2

Fig. 2.1 Five key events leading to a focus on father engagement in human services

society continues to grapple with them (Livingston & McAdoo, 2007; Parke, 2000; Tamis-LeMonda, & Cabrera, 1999). From generation to generation, our expectations surrounding the fathering role change (Hammond et al., 2011). Day and Lamb (2004) describe social scientists' conceptualizations of fatherhood and the role of fathers in families as a "moving target" (p. 2).

Pleck and Pleck (1997) provide a comprehensive review of the shifts that have taken place in the ideals of fatherhood over time in the United States. While recognizing the racial and cultural diversity that exists in fatherhood ideals among Americans, these authors examined the changes that have taken place in the dominant culture's understanding of and expectations for fatherhood. These ideals are defined as "a set of implicit rules about what constitutes a good father" (Pleck & Pleck, 1997, p. 34). During the colonial period (1600–1800), the cultural ideal of fatherhood among European Americans was that of a *stern patriarch, moral guide, and teacher*. However, in the conversion from an agrarian to an industrialized state and socioeconomic societal order (1801–1900), it shifted to a *breadwinner and economic provider* (Pleck & Pleck, 1997).

Furthermore, between 1900 and 1970, the idealized role became that of a *sex role model*, with a particular focus on the man's ability to model appropriate behaviors for their male children (Lamb, 2010; Pleck & Pleck, 1997). Pleck and Pleck (1997) suggest that this change in focus was related to the inability of fathers to fulfill the provider role due to the Great Depression in the 1930s, when the unemployment rate among White and Black men (in the northern region of the United States) was 24.9% and 38.9%, respectively (Conner, 2011). Additionally, in the 1970s and 1980s, as women entered the labor force at a rapid pace, the focus shifted from sex role model to *the new nurturant father*. Fathers were increasingly urged to co-parent along with their wives and partners and take an active role in caregiving responsibilities (Lamb, 1997, 2010). Doherty et al. (1998) introduce yet another shift in society's definition of good fathering, which also emerged in the 1990s and carried over into the 2000s as a result of welfare reform and an increasing focus within society on reversing the trend toward father absence—*the responsible father* (Mincy & Pouncy, 2004).

Social scientists and policymakers have tended to emphasize some roles more than others (Lamb, 2010), despite the literature rejecting the notion of singular fathering roles and recognizing that men function in a variety of capacities when caring for their children (Lamb, 2010; Tamis-LeMonda & Cabrera, 1999). Undeniably, some aspects of fathering, such as the provider role, have remained predominant from decade to decade. Furthermore, it should be noted that these ideals of fatherhood largely apply to the dominant European American culture and to married parents and their biological children (Lamb, 2010; Pleck & Pleck, 1997). As noted by Conner (2011), "the norms used to determine successful fathering tend to reflect a Eurocentric, middle class bias" (p. 3). Greater clarity is brought to our understanding of fatherhood by considering its meaning across diverse cultural groups and the extent to which these meanings converge with or diverge from the dominant cultural motif. Below, we discuss several trends within the United States that have resulted in the *responsible fatherhood* movement and the evolution of this movement across time.

The Responsible Fatherhood Movement

The responsible fatherhood movement has been the catalyst for increasing father engagement in human service systems within the United States. It is an outgrowth of social, cultural, political, and historical factors such as: (1) shifting demographic trends toward higher rates of divorce, non-marital childbearing, and lower rates of marriage, (2) a rise in single female-headed homes, (3) increases in father absence, and as a result, (4) increases in poverty and economic instability among single mothers, and (5) rising welfare participation rates. Many of these societal trends were utilized by policymakers and the public to construe a "crisis" within the American family structure—namely, the fall of the nuclear family. Such portrayals have had a tremendous impact on the development of social welfare policies, many of which are targeted at low-income fathers and families of color (Lemmons & Johnson, 2019; Tamis-LeMonda & Cabrera, 1999), who are often pathologized or viewed as social deviants due to their non-traditional approaches to family formation and maintenance (McDonald, 2020).

The combination of these factors led to major shifts in welfare reform and child support policies in the United States. As noted by Battle (2018), "since 1974, the U.S. federal government has passed more than 30 pieces of legislation related to child support" (p. 443). Deeply embedded within welfare reform and child support policies is a great deal of rhetoric related to the issue of responsible fatherhood, with much of the discourse centered around the moral problems of poverty, deadbeat dads, and the need for greater economic provision for children (Battle, 2018). Given the higher rates of non-marital childbearing and single-female-headed households within the African American community, Black non-custodial fathers and single Black mothers have been at the center of the debate on welfare reform, child support policies, and the responsible fatherhood movement.

Overview of Federal Initiatives to Promote Responsible Fatherhood

A number of federal initiatives were implemented in the 1990s to promote responsible fatherhood (Mincy & Pouncy, 2004), which is described as "every father taking responsibility for a child's intellectual, emotional, and financial well-being…being present in the child's life, actively contributing to a child's healthy development, sharing economic responsibilities, and cooperating with a child's mother in addressing the full range of a child's and family's needs" (The White House, 2012, p. 2). The general goal of such initiatives is to increase the positive involvement (both financially and emotionally) of fathers in the lives of their children and families, by offering a broad array of social services (i.e., job training and placement, mediation services, conflict resolution, parenting classes, support groups, paternity establishment, marriage promotion, pregnancy prevention, assistance with child support arrearage, etc.) to support men in their role as fathers and help them take full responsibility for their children (Anderson et al., 2002; Carlson & McLanahan, 2004; Holmes et al., 2020; Mincy & Pouncy, 2004; Solomon-Fears, 2013). Over time, these initiatives have served a diverse group of men. However, the primary target group has most often been low-income, non-custodial, unmarried fathers who often struggle to meet their child support obligations (Anderson et al., 2002; Bernard et al., 1999; Coley, 2001; Mincy & Pouncy, 2004). Since their inception, these initiatives have received both congressional and presidential attention (Solomon-Fears, 2013), beginning with the administration of former President William ("Bill") Clinton and the 106th Congress (1999–2000). Although responsible fatherhood legislation was passed by the House of Representatives during the 106th, 107th, and 108th Congresses, this legislation died in the Senate (Solomon-Fears, 2013). In 2000, during Clinton's second term, he introduced the *New Responsible Fatherhood Initiative to Promote Work and Boost Child Support Payments* (Weaver, 2012). As the name suggests, the goal of this new initiative was to promote work, child support payment, and responsible fatherhood.

The George W. Bush and Obama administrations continued the work of former President Clinton in responsible fatherhood promotion. For example, over the course of his presidency, former President Bush allocated several million dollars in the federal budget (from FY 2002 to FY 2008) to the promotion of fatherhood initiatives to strengthen the role of fathers in families. He also extended competitive grants to faith-based and community organizations serving unemployed and low-income fathers and their families (Solomon-Fears, 2011, 2013). In the beginning of his administration, former President Obama proposed increasing (from $150 million to $500 million) and redirecting funds toward what he termed the Fatherhood, Marriage, and Families Innovation Fund, which he believed would serve as a "catalyst for innovative service models that integrate a variety of service streams" (Solomon-Fears, 2013, p. 20). However, this proposal was not passed by the House or Senate (Solomon-Fears, 2013). He went on to propose several other father- and family-focused initiatives over the course of his tenure, some of which were supported and others not.

The Trump administration budget also continued to include funding for responsible fatherhood initiatives through FY 2020 (Child & Family Research Partnership, 2017; Tollestrup, 2018). In 2020, 58 fatherhood grants totaling approximately $59 million were awarded (Administration for Children and Families, 2020). The Biden administration has justifiably been focused on the economy and the COVID-19 pandemic. However, the administration's American Families Plan and American Rescue Plan could be expanded to support fatherhood programming as a means to address child poverty (Seinfeld, 2021).

State and local fatherhood initiatives have also proliferated across the United States. The National Responsible Fatherhood Clearinghouse maintains a program map that can help with identifying state and local fatherhood initiatives and resources (https://www.fatherhood.gov/program-map). In the early manifestations of the responsible fatherhood movement, there was increased attention on father absence, which gave birth to the emergence of responsible fatherhood initiatives across the United States (Klempin & Mincy, 2011). However, today, the field is in place of reflection. Specifically, attention has shifted from program proliferation and implementation to program efficacy, effectiveness, and impact (Holmes et al., 2020; Klempin & Mincy, 2011). In addition, greater consideration has been given to how participation in responsible fatherhood programs shapes and constructs marginalized fathers' identities (Randles, 2020). However, one of the most pressing concerns today has been the engagement of fathers within human service systems.

A Rising Focus on Father Engagement in Human Services

In October 2018, the U.S. Department of Health and Human Services, Administration for Children and Families, issued an information memorandum (IM) to all ACF programs. The purpose of this IM was to:

> ...strongly encourage all human agencies including agencies, courts, offices of enforcement, offices of public assistance, offices of child care, Head Start programs and family and youth services programs to work together across governments to jointly create and maintain an environment that prioritizes as a critical factor in strengthening families and adopt approaches to enhance paternal involvement in all family support and related programs (U.S. Department of Health & Administration for Children and Families, , p. 1). 2018

The IM also highlights the benefits of father engagement, underscores the linkage between agency commitment to father engagement and improved outcomes for children and families, and provides some promising practices for promoting and sustaining meaningful father engagement within and across ACF human service agencies. The message sent through this memorandum was key in elevating the conversation regarding the treatment of fathers within governmental and non-governmental human service programs and organizations across the United States. Despite the increased attention toward fathers within human service systems, the social work profession has struggled to engage fathers effectively.

The Social Work Profession and the Father Engagement Imperative

The Council on Social Work Education (CSWE) is the national association representing social work education in the United States. CSWE has adopted a competency-based education approach that is outlined in its Educational Policy and Accreditation Standards (EPAS), which is updated on an annual basis. This approach involves assessing students' ability to demonstrate the nine competencies identified in the educational policy and standards. Social work professionals are charged with effectively engaging people at all levels of society, including fathers. In other words, reluctance on the part of social work practitioners to engage fathers in practice results in their voices being omitted from the process of making decisions that could potentially improve their life outcomes.

Furthermore, as per EPAS 2022, competency #6 suggests that "social workers understand that engagement is an ongoing component of the dynamic and interactive process of social work practice with, and on behalf of individuals, families, groups, organizations, and communities" (p. 6). As noted in Pfitzner et al. (2017), "the starting point of any intervention lies with engagement" (p. 537). Thus, it is important to consider ways to improve engagement with fathers in the helping process. The generalist education approach taken within most social work education programs has explicitly included a focus on the needs of women and mothers, with less attention being given to issues facing men and fathers. According to CSWE's 2019 Annual Survey of Social Work Programs, the vast majority of social work students at BSW and MSW levels are female (Table 2.1). Thus, the social work profession will remain female dominant in the foreseeable future. Studies have noted that many men who do seek services report feeling that helping professionals are ill-equipped to improve their mental health (Shafer & Wendt, 2015) and lack an understanding of the emotional, physical, interpersonal, and family problems they face (Baum, 2016). Studies have also noted gaps in father-worker perceptions that imply misunderstandings in the helping process (Huebner et al., 2008). Some have attributed such gaps to a neglect of focus on unique male characteristics in social work education (Baum, 2016; Shafer & Wendt, 2015).

For example, due to socialization processes and gender-based societal norms associated with masculinity, mental health issues among men are easily masked and often go undetected. Thus, intentional and gender-specific education and training

Table 2.1 Gender breakdown in social work education programs (2019)

	BSW ($n = 450$)	MSW ($n = 304$)
Male	12.4%	13.0%
Female	85.8%	85.6%
Unknown	1.8%	1.2%
Other	0%	0.1%

Source: 2019 Statistics on Social Work Education in the United States (CSWE, 2019)

can assist the next generation of social workers to effectively engage this population. All in all, as family structures continue to grow increasingly complex, there is a need for greater emphasis on engaging fathers in social work education, research, and practice. The following section discusses frameworks and practice guides that can be applied to enhance work with fathers, both in human service systems generally, and within the social work profession, specifically.

Definitions, Practice Guides, and Frameworks for Engaging Fathers in Human Services

Increased attention to the need to improve father engagement within human service agencies also necessitates definitions that clearly delineate the term "father engagement" and specify what this constitutes at program, organization, and systems levels. While the term can have different meanings across a wide variety of sectors, it is generally defined as the "purposeful inclusion of fathers (including biological, social, resident, non-resident, and stepfathers) in program services and activities with the objective of improving outcomes for fathers, children, and families" (Selekman & Holcomb, 2021, p. 2). Table 2.2 provides an overview of the most commonly cited frameworks for father engagement. Common across all three frameworks is the notion that father engagement efforts must be multi-level and rooted in systemic, cultural, and contextual factors to achieve effectiveness. Finally, several practice guides provide insights that can be helpful for practitioners in their efforts to effectively engage fathers (see "Practice Guides" under the resources section of this chapter). On the opposite end of the spectrum, it is also important to consider some of the factors that have been associated with barriers to father engagement.

Barriers to Father Engagement in Human Services

Program and Provider-Based Barriers

A significant barrier to father engagement is how human service organizations are organized (McAllister et al., 2004). Organizations being designed to primarily serve mothers instead of servicing both parents equally is one major barrier to father engagement, as they may not involve fathers adequately or address their specific needs (Sandstrom et al., 2015b). Fathers may also be further deterred by programming that does not adequately relate to them (Sandstrom et al., 2015b; Pfitzner et al., 2017). Previous research has linked lower levels of engagement to fathers' perceptions of programs as "not for them" (Sandstrom et al., 2015b).

Table 2.2 Father engagement frameworks

Name of framework	Overview of framework	Components of framework
Three-phase temporal model of father engagement Pfitzner et al. (2017)	This framework conceptualizes engagement as a multi-level systems approach that occurs in three stages: "getting," "keeping," and "engaging." This model is grounded in the extant parental engagement literature—particularly the work of Moran et al. (2004)—and takes into consideration five categories of factors that operate on different levels to impact engagement.	Five factors: Practical factors Relational factors Cultural and contextual factors Strategic factors Structural factors
Father competency framework Rollins (2021)	This framework is specific to engaging African American fathers in organizations. Within this framework, Rollins (2021) suggests that there are three categories of competencies that are necessary for implementing father-inclusive practices within practice settings.	Three Competencies: Knowledge Skills Mindset
Father engagement in human services framework Child Welfare Information Gateway (2021). Selekman & Holcomb (2021)	This is one of the only known frameworks that provides specific guidance on father engagement within human service systems. It postulates that efforts to promote and support father engagement should occur on multiple levels within human service systems.	Three Levels: Program Level Organization Level Systems Level

Generally, programs that are focused on mothers regard them as the principal client (Sandstrom et al., 2015a, b). Therefore, staff may form stronger relationships with mothers and inadvertently exclude fathers (Sandstrom et al., 2015b. These unilateral relationships increase the risk of gatekeeping (Sandstrom et al., 2015b), which occurs when mothers, as primary clients, impede fathers' involvement with children (Sandstrom et al., 2015a, b). In some programs, fathers are intentionally excluded from the helping process at the mother's discretion (Sandstrom et al., 2015b). Other programs entrust mothers with the responsibility of encouraging father participation in program activities. However, personal factors such as the quality of the co-parenting relationship or perceptions of parenting competence may influence a mother's decision to reach out (Sandstrom et al., 2015b).

An additional barrier to engagement on the provider level is the lack of training or expertise in serving fathers (Pfitzner et al., 2017). Research demonstrates that staff may hold biases about men and their role as parents , with some believing that fathers are incompetent caretakers or are not interested in utilizing resources (Sandstrom et al., 2015b). Negative beliefs about fathers have been linked to decreased assistance and support from staff (Pfitzner et al., 2017; Sandstrom et al., 2015b).

Finally, to effectively engage fathers, it is essential to understand how their circumstances can impact their capacity for engagement (Roggman et al., 2002). Fathers may work hours that are non-traditional (e.g., graveyard shift) or unpredictable and many programs hold fixed hours that prevent fathers from participating (Sandstrom et al., 2015b). Transportation, another barrier to engagement, is especially relevant to non-resident fathers or fathers with limited public transportation options (Sandstrom et al., 2015a, b).

Personal Paternal Barriers to Father Engagement

Additional barriers may also exist on a personal level. Father engagement in human service systems can be affected by strained or fragile co-parenting relationships (McAllister et al., 2004; Sandstrom et al., 2015a, b). A mother may oppose paternal involvement due to beliefs about the father's parenting capabilities, concerns about his behavior, relationship tension, or because she wishes to be the sole participant in programming (Sandstrom et al., 2015b). These situations are commonly seen when parents are separated or not romantically involved (Sandstrom et al., 2015a, b).

The negative attitudes and beliefs fathers hold about themselves are a further obstacle to their engagement in services (Sandstrom et al., 2015b). In some studies, fathers frequently reported low levels of parenting self-efficacy or doubts regarding their competence as caregivers (Sandstrom et al., 2015b). Such doubts were especially common in fathers who believed they were inadequate financial contributors to their families (McAllister et al., 2004). Other personal barriers to engagement include fathers' beliefs about Child Protective Services (CPS) and other government programs (Sandstrom et al., 2015a, b). Even fathers who were not fearful of government interference still reported concerns about being judged due to their experiences in other government programs (Sandstrom et al., 2015b).

Finally, circumstantial barriers are prevalent among vulnerable populations of fathers. For example, fathers experiencing homelessness, monetary strain, a lack of social support, health problems (physical or mental), and other stressors may find it difficult to be fully engaged in programs and services (Carbone et al., 2004). These fathers may experience difficulties in concurrently meeting their personal needs while also meeting program expectations and demands (Carbone et al., 2004).

Best Practices and Recommendations for Engaging Fathers in Human Services

With the recent shift in the systemic understanding of father inclusion, many organizations are now aiming to increase their rates of father engagement (Harris Professional Development Network, 2021). The following set of best practices and

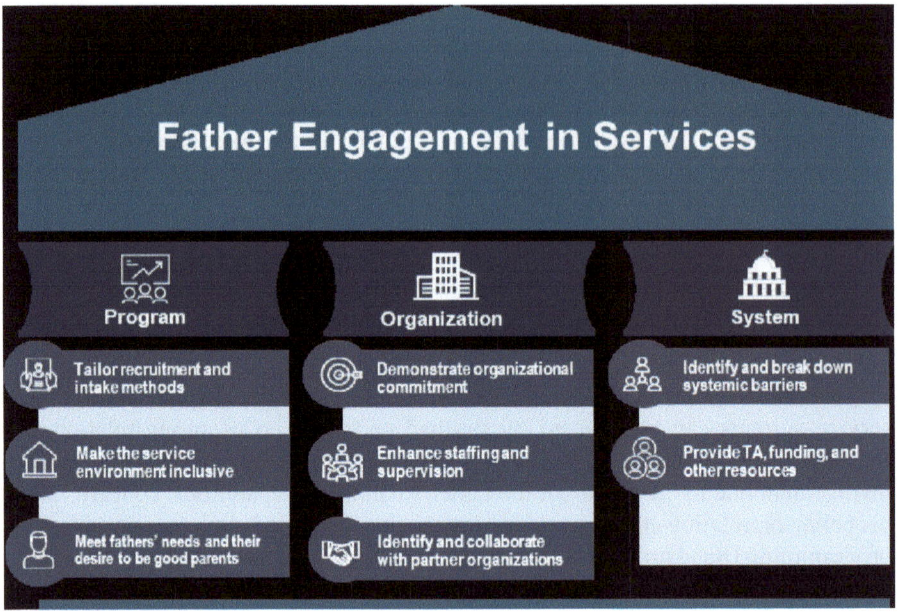

Fig. 2.2 Approaches to father engagement in human services (Selekman & Holcomb, 2021)

recommendations are organized around the framework offered by the U.S. Department of Health and Human Services, Office of the Assistant Secretary of Planning and Evaluation/Mathematica (See Table 2.2 and Fig. 2.2).

Program Level Practices

Recruitment Strategies

Community Engagement

Many programs experience difficulties with recruiting and engaging fathers (Child and Family Research Partnership, 2014). One strategy to recruit fathers involves program staff contacting agencies that frequently serve fathers in their community (Selekman & Holcomb, 2021). Relevant programs include child support offices, parole offices, halfway homes, family courts, schools, school districts, and health clinics (Child and Family Research Partnership, 2019; Selekman & Holcomb, 2021). Program staff can also initiate contact at locations that fathers visit for recreational or practical purposes, for example, grocery stores, children's sporting events, barbershops, after-school programs, hospitals after childbirth, childcare programs, and family homes during home visits (Selekman & Holcomb, 2021).

Direct Invitations

When initiating engagement, an effective strategy is to offer a simple and direct invitation. These direct invitations can strengthen fathers' perceptions of inclusiveness (Child and Family Research Partnership, 2019). Such direct interactions relay to fathers that they are welcome within an organization and there are services unique to them (Child and Family Research Partnership, 2019). In these invitations, program staff can emphasize the importance of father involvement for healthy child development and family well-being (Watson, 2011).

Utilize Word of Mouth

In contrast to direct invitations, word of mouth is a recruitment strategy that does not require targeted interaction. Mothers are commonly utilized as a point of contact for father engagement (Sandstrom et al., 2015a, b). Programs can discuss the importance of involving fathers in services with mothers to encourage them to invite fathers to participate (Sandstrom et al., 2015a). Selekman & Holcomb (2021) suggest that previously involved fathers can also be utilized as "outreach specialists" to recruit fathers.

Provide Incentives and Practical Assistance

Father engagement in programming can also be encouraged through incentives (Casey Family Programs, 2019; Child and Family Research Partnership, n.d.) such as formula, children's clothing, or diapers. This can be an expensive strategy, but costs can be offset by donations and grant funding (Child and Family Research Partnership, 2019). Additionally, to aid in the recruitment process, programs should highlight and make accessible services that address fathers' immediate and most practical needs. For example, the National Fatherhood Initiative (2015) recommends providing aid in areas where fathers often experience the greatest challenges, such as child visitation, educational attainment, and job acquisition.

Retention Strategies

Programs that serve fathers commonly experience difficulties with attrition (National Responsible Fatherhood Clearinghouse, 2019), but this can be mitigated by providing fathers with the accommodations necessary for overcoming potential obstacles to attendance (Sandstrom et al., 2015a, b). For example, fathers may benefit from flexible service hours, transportation accommodations, meals, or childcare during programming. Additionally, it is recommended that programs be understanding of and empathetic toward fathers' absences or lapses in attendance (National

Responsible Fatherhood Clearinghouse, 2019). Furthermore, organizations should be mindful of the length of services as not all fathers can participate in prolonged programming (Child and Family Research Partnership, n.d.).

Creating a Father-Inclusive Environment

Physical Environment

When considering the physical inclusiveness of an environment, programs should attend to several aspects. For example, it is important for programs to display visible and positive representations of fathers or male caretakers on posters, photographs, or print materials found within the organization (Child and Family Research Partnership, 2019; Martinez et al., 2013; U.S. Department of Health and Human Services, 2013). Programs should also examine any current materials for negative or dismissive portrayals of father inclusion (U.S. Department of Health and Human Services, 2013). The U.S. Department of Health and Human Services (2013) also recommends that programs incorporate décor and furniture that are considerate of male clients, for example, including chairs or couches that accommodate larger-sized individuals. The installation of diaper-changing stations in men's restrooms is another enhancement to program environments that promotes father-inclusiveness (Child and Family Research Partnership, 2019).

Social Environment

In conjunction with the physical environment, an organization's social climate can also facilitate father engagement (Child and Family Research Partnership, 2019; Martinez et al., 2013; U.S. Department of Health and Human Services, 2013). One way to do so is to develop a concrete plan that begins with an assessment of organizational readiness to engage fathers and the current practices and processes for including fathers in services (Child and Family Research Partnership, 2019). Attempts at father engagement should be welcoming and convey judgment-free messages (Child and Family Research Partnership, 2019). In addition, communication with fathers should consider their individuality, cultural beliefs, and any previous experiences that could impede their engagement (U.S, Department of Health and Human Services, 2013). Programs should center communication around both parents, demonstrating to fathers that they are equal co-parents with a significant role in their child's development. Fathers should be invited to share comments or suggestions on the inclusiveness of the program environment (U.S. Department of Health and Human Services, 2013) and provide recommendations for program activities or general program services (Watson, 2011). Finally, programs can also invite fathers to take on official leadership roles, such as policy council or board members (U.S. Department of Health and Human Services, 2013).

Father Responsive Programming

Program Flexibility

Organizations should be flexible with the services they offer and engage fathers according to their capacity to participate (Fontaine et al., 2017). Programs can achieve flexibility by tailoring their services to the specific needs of fathers or providing supplementary services according to the father's needs (Child and Family Research Partnership, 2014). Increasing flexibility in programming is necessary for supporting participants across a diversity of settings and contexts (Fontaine et al., 2017). One strategy that some programs employ is offering a variety of services and activities, which helps to meet fathers where they are and increases the chances of engaging them at all levels (Fontaine et al., 2017).

Father-Specific Services

Programs should prioritize services and educational materials that emphasize parenting practices specific to fathers (Martinez et al., 2013), as many fathers take on gender-specific parenting roles that traditional mother-focused programming may not address (Child and Family Research Partnership, 2014). By providing curricula specific to fathers, programs may increase their levels of engagement (Sandstrom et al., 2015b). Examples of key issues to address include assistance with co-parenting, financial management, and general child development and disciplinary practices (Child and Family Research Partnership, 2014). Collaborative group activities are also suggested for improving father engagement (Sandstrom et al., 2015a, b), as they allow fathers to set goals, form peer relationships with experienced or new fathers, and form stronger relationships with staff. Programs should encourage fathers to share feedback on their program experiences to facilitate productive group sessions (Child and Family Research Partnership, 2014). This feedback can then be used to inform the future implementation of program activities (U.S. Department of Health and Human Services, 2013).

Co-Parenting Relationships

Tense co-parenting relationships can be a barrier to father engagement (Sandstrom et al., 2015a, b). Some programs report that they struggle to help fathers establish healthy co-parenting relationships (Sandstrom et al., 2015b). Handling these challenges inappropriately can result in the exclusion of fathers from programs and services (Sandstrom et al., 2015a, b). To mitigate this barrier to father engagement, it is recommended that programs provide parents with resources on conflict avoidance strategies such as mediation or parallel parenting (Child and Family Research Partnership, 2019). In addition, programs should be mindful that the role of co-parent can extend to any adult (i.e., grandparents or extended family members) that takes on significant caregiving responsibilities for a child (U.S. Department of Health and Human Services, 2013). Thus, these individuals may also be key resources in resolving conflict and fully engaging fathers in services.

Organization-Level Practices

Staff Training

Negative perceptions are a significant barrier to father engagement (Sandstrom et al., 2015b). Biases can include judgments about how fathers look, communicate, parent, or their family dynamics (U.S. Department of Health and Human Services, 2013). Staff biases can be addressed through organization-wide training on the importance of father engagement and how to properly engage fathers (Selekman & Holcomb, 2021). Programs should provide a safe space for staff to examine any stereotypes or negative perceptions they hold about fathers (U.S. Department of Health and Human Services, 2013). By addressing these biases, staff are better able to develop strong relationships with fathers (U.S. Department of Health and Human Services, 2013).

Program Assessments

Before establishing programming for fathers, conducting a father-friendly assessment is recommended. Father-friendliness is defined as the degree to which an organization's operations encourage father involvement in the services and programs it offers (National Fatherhood Initiative, 2016). The National Fatherhood Initiative offers a tool that can be used by organizations to assess their degree of father friendliness (https://www.fatherhood.org/ffcu). The topic of father friendliness is discussed in greater detail in Chap. 7 of this book.

Utilizing Community Partnerships

Fathers have a wide variety of needs that may not be addressed by the services of one organization (Child and Family Research Partnership, 2018; Fontaine et al., 2017). Therefore, it is important for organizations to utilize resources within the community (Child and Family Research Partnership, 2019) and attempt to form non-traditional or creative partnerships to better serve and engage fathers (OPRE Final Implementation, 2017). Examples of organizations that programs can seek partnerships with include higher education institutions, school districts, hospitals, health centers, mental health organizations, human service agencies, banks, or faith-based organizations (U.S. Department of Health and Human Services, 2013). Programs can also utilize resources within the community, such as parks, libraries, and museums to achieve their goals (U.S. Department of Health and Human Services, 2013).

Furthermore, community referrals from program staff can be used to address any unmet needs (Child and Family Research Partnership, 2019), such as legal assistance (Child and Family Research Partnership, 2019). Many fathers struggle to navigate the legal system, especially when dealing with matters of child support, paternity, child custody, and visitation rights (Child and Family Research Partnership, 2019; Martinez et al., 2013). By utilizing partnerships and referrals across organizations, programs can create a more comprehensive support system for fathers (U.S. Department of Health and Human Services, 2013).

Systems-Level Practices

Employing a Community-Based Participatory Approach

A key factor in introducing successful systems-level changes is engaging the affected community from the outset and continuing engagement throughout the process of program development (i.e., planning, development, adoption, implementation, and evaluation of supportive policies and practices). Fathers and the communities they represent should be included in the work to identify and break down systemic barriers (Child Welfare Information Gateway, 2021). The Child and Family Research Partnership (2018) proposes a framework for evidence-based, systems-level change to support father engagement, which includes working with fathers and community partners throughout five phases: (1) identify community partners and agree on specific measurable goals that will support father engagement, (2) identify facilitators and barriers for each goal and how partners can contribute, (3) develop evidence-based strategies to assess and measures changes, (4) measure short-term progress, and (5) measure progress toward overall goals. This framework emphasizes the importance of fathers' voices as complementary to research and practice in an effort to create systems-level change.

Engaging in Policy Review

Historically, policies that drive social programs have been more supportive of motherhood than fatherhood (Harris & Melter, 2014; Tamis-LeMonda & Cabrera, 1999). Thus, organizations should assess their policies and procedures to determine the level of father friendliness (National Fatherhood Initiative, 2016). Additionally, as recommended in the ACF memorandum mentioned previously, child and family-serving agencies must work together to prioritize father engagement, which includes aligning policies that affect fathers across programs (Administration for Children and Families, 2020; Child Welfare Information Gateway, 2021).

Providing Resources for Infrastructure and Capacity Building in Fatherhood Program

Even though some federal funding has been dedicated to supporting fatherhood programming, more funding, technical assistance, and capacity building for organizations, communities, researchers, and practitioners to engage fathers are needed to create systems-level change. Each year, the federal government invests billions of dollars in programs for mothers and children. For example, over $5 billion a year is spent on the Special Supplemental Nutrition Program for Women, Infants, and Children (WIC), and only .2% of this amount is spent on federal fatherhood initiatives (Seinfeld, 2021). Systems-level changes to support father engagement can also be achieved with more funding to assess the impact of fatherhood initiatives. The more evidence there is to demonstrate the positive outcomes of these initiatives, the more likely it is that policymakers will provide funding to continue these efforts. Additionally, providing technical assistance would increase the capacity of communities and organizations to collect data that provides evidence of the effectiveness of father engagement efforts. Increased funding and technical assistance combined have the potential to drive meaningful systems change for fathers (Pearson, 2018).

Conclusion

This chapter provided a historical overview of the key events that have led to an increased focus on father engagement in human services. This overview is critical to understanding the current state of father engagement in human service systems and which practices and policies are needed to more effectively engage fathers. It also provided an in-depth examination of the concept of father engagement in human service systems and offered models and frameworks that can be applied to encourage more father-inclusive practices, which can lead to more positive outcomes for fathers, children, and families.

A comprehensive overview of program/provider and personal barriers to father engagement, along with the best practices and recommendations on program, organization, and systems levels for mitigating them, was also given. What is common at all levels is the need to meaningfully engage fathers and the communities they represent to achieve the most optimal outcomes for children, families, and societies.

Discussion Questions

1. Despite the rising focus on father engagement in this country, social work professionals continue to be challenged in their attempts to engage fathers. Given what you have learned from this chapter, what steps do you believe need to be taken to change this dynamic?
2. Considering the various challenges with father engagement discussed in this chapter, which do you anticipate being the greatest obstacles in your own practice with fathers? How can you work to overcome these obstacles in order to better engage the fathers you serve?
3. This chapter discusses several barriers to father engagement that occur at the program, organization, and systems levels. How do you think social workers' personal barriers get in the way of their work with fathers? What do you think can be done to address this?

Resources

Books

Johnson, W. E. (Ed.). (2010). *Social work with African American males: Health, mental health, and social policy*. Oxford University Press. 10.1093/acprof:oso/9780195314366.001.0001

- Mazza, C., & Perry, A. R. (Eds.). (2017). *Fatherhood in America: Social work perspectives on a changing society*. Charles C Thomas, Publisher, LTD.
- Pearson, J., & Fagan, J. (Eds.). (2021). *New research on parenting programs for low-income fathers*. Routledge/Taylor & Francis Group.
- Rollins, L. S. (Ed.). (2020). *Engaging and working with African American fathers: Strategies and lessons* (1 Edition). Routledge Books.

Websites

Father Engagement in Human Services https://www.mathematica.org/publications/father-engagement-in-human-services

- Engaging Fathers and Paternal Family Members https://www.childwelfare.gov/topics/famcentered/engaging/fathers/
- Father Engagement Academy https://academy.fatherhood.org/
- The Fatherhood Engagement Certificate Training https://academy.fatherhood.org/courses/father-engagement-certificate

- KEEP Fathers Engaged https://www.mathematica.org/projects/key-programmatic-elements-of-father-engagement-to-promote-self-sufficiency

Child Welfare Information Gateway Webpage: Supporting Fatherhood at the Community and Individual Levels https://www.childwelfare.gov/topics/preventing/promoting/fatherhood/community/#community

Case Studies

Father Engagement in Substance Use Disorder Treatment Programs: ForeverDads https://aspe.hhs.gov/reports/foreverdads-case-study

- Father Engagement in Healthy Start Programs: Northeast Florida Healthy Start Coalition Fatherhood PRIDE https://aspe.hhs.gov/reports/fatherhood-pride-case-study
- Father Engagement in Family Nutrition and Health Programs: California WIC Association https://aspe.hhs.gov/reports/cwa-case-study

Multimedia (Podcasts, Webinars, & Videos)

How Fatherhood Programs Support Fathers During the Pandemic https://www.mathematica.org/blogs/how-fatherhood-programs-supported-dads-during-the-pandemic

- A Conversation About Engaging Young Fathers in Human Services https://vimeo.com/622579372
- Engaging Fathers https://eclkc.ohs.acf.hhs.gov/video/engaging-fathers
- Fatherhood Connection Webinar Series https://eclkc.ohs.acf.hhs.gov/family-engagement/article/fatherhood-connection-webinar-series
- Child Welfare Information Gateway Podcast Series (Episodes 6, 7, and 8) https://www.childwelfare.gov/more-tools-resources/podcast/
- Advancing Racial Equity in Fatherhood Programs https://www.mathematica.org/blogs/advancing-racial-equity-in-fatherhood-programs

Practice Guides

KEEP Practice Guide for Centering Fathers in Human Services Programming to Increase Participation https://aspe.hhs.gov/reports/practice-guide-centering-fathers

- Best Practice Guide for Engaging Non-Resident Fathers https://fatherhood.gov/sites/default/files/resource_files/e000002615.pdf

- Best Practice Guide for Engaging Fathers: Ohio Department of Job & Family Services https://fatherhood.ohio.gov/Portals/0/Revised%20FINAL_JFS-01444%20Best%20Practice%20Guide%20for%20Fathers%20(online).pdf
- CalSWEC Father Engagement and Father Involvement Toolkit https://calswec.berkeley.edu/toolkits/father-engagement-and-father-involvement-toolkit
- Engaging Fathers in the Early Years: A Practitioner's Guide https://www.tandfonline.com/doi/abs/10.1080/09503153.2014.889417?journalCode=cpra20
- Head Start Early Childhood Learning and Knowledge Center: Birth to 5 Father Engaging Guide https://eclkc.ohs.acf.hhs.gov/family-engagement/birth-5-father-engagement-guide/birth-5-father-engagement-guide

References

Administration for Children and Families. (2020). *$119 million in Healthy Marriage and Responsible Fatherhood grants awarded by HHS' Administration for Children and Families.*. https://www.acf.hhs.gov/media/press/2020/119-million-healthy-marriage-and-responsible-fatherhood-grants-awarded

Anderson, E. A., Kohler, J. K., & Letiecq, B. L. (2002). Low-income fathers and "responsible fatherhood" programs: A qualitative investigation of participants' experiences. *Family Relations, 51*, 148–155. https://doi.org/10.1111/j.1741-3729.2002.00148.x

Battle, B. P. (2018). Deservingness, deadbeat dads, and responsible fatherhood: Child support policy and rhetorical conceptualizations of poverty, welfare, and the family. *Symbolic Interaction, 41*(4), 443–464. https://doi.org/10.1002/symb.359

Baum, N. (2016). The unheard gender: The neglect of men as social work clients. *British Journal of Social Work, 46*, 1463–1471. https://dx.doi.org/10.1093%2Fbjsw%2Fbcv074

Bernard, S., & Knitzer, J. (1999). *Map and track: State initiatives to encourage responsible fatherhood.* https://academiccommons.columbia.edu/doi/10.7916/d8-mmkq-f665

Carbone, S., Fraser, A., Ramburuth, R., & Nelms, L. (2004). Breaking cycles, building futures. *Promoting inclusion of vulnerable families in antenatal and universal early childhood services. Melbourne, Victorian Government Department of Human Services.*

Carlson, M. J., & McLanahan, S. S. (2004). Early father involvement in fragile families. In R. D. Day & M. E. Lamb (Eds.), *Conceptualizing and measuring father involvement* (pp. 241–271). Lawrence Erlbaum Associates Publishers.

Casey Family Programs. (2019). How can we better engage fathers in prevention? https://www.casey.org/engaging-fathers-prevention/

Child and Family Research Partnership. (2013). Involving fathers in home visiting programs:

Child and Family Research Partnership. (2014). Increasing father participation in home visiting: Lessons from mothers (Policy Brief B.001.0514). https://childandfamilyresearch.utexas.edu/sites/default/files/CFRPBrief_B0010514_MothersAboutFatherParticHV.pdf

Child and Family Research Partnership. (2017). Federal, state, and local efforts supporting.

Child and Family Research Partnership. (2018). Transforming Communities for Fathers through.

Child and Family Research Partnership. (2019). Implementing Services for Fathers (Policy Brief B.043.0819). https://childandfamilyresearch.utexas.edu/sites/default/files/ImplementingServicesforFathersBrief.pdf

Child and Family Research Partnership. (n.d.). *Tips for retaining fathers in programs* [Infographic]. Child and Family Research Partnership. https://childandfamilyresearch.utexas.edu/sites/default/files/TipsforRetainingFathersinProgramsOnePager.pdf

Child Welfare Information Gateway. (2021). *Family engagement: Partnering with families to improve child welfare outcomes.* U.S. Department of Health and Human Services, Administration for Children and Families, Children's Bureau. https://www.childwelfare.gov/pubPDFs/f_fam_engagement.pdf

Coley, R. L. (2001). (In)visible men: Emerging research on low-income, unmarried, and minority fathers. *A merican Psychologist, 56(9), 743–753.* https://doi.org/10.1037/0003-066X.56.9.743

Conner. (2011). African descended fathers: Historical considerations. In M. E. Conner & J. L. White (Eds.), *Black fathers: An invisible presence in America* (2nd ed., pp. 3–19). Routledge Taylor and Francis Group.

Day, R. D., & Lamb, M. E. (2004). Conceptualizing and measuring father involvement: Pathways, problems, and progress. In R. D. Day & M. E. Lamb (Eds.), *Conceptualizing and measuring father involvement* (pp. 1–15). Lawrence Earlbaum, Publishers.

Doherty, W. J., Kouneski, E. F., & Erickson, M. F. (1998). Responsible fathering: An overview and conceptual framework. *Journal of Marriage and Family, 60*, 277–292. https://doi.org/10.2307/353848

Fontaine, J., Cramer, L., Kurs, E., Paddock, E., Eisenstat, J., Levy, J., & Hussemann, J. (2017). *Final implementation findings from the Responsible Fatherhood Reentry Projects* (OPRE Report #2017–05). Washington, DC: Office of Planning, Research and Evaluation, Administration for Children and Families, U.S. Department of Health and Human Services. https://www.acf.hhs.gov/sites/default/files/documents/opre/final_implementation_report_508.pdf

Ghate, D., Shaw, C., & Hazel, N. (2000). *Engaging fathers in preventive services: Fathers and family centres.* York Publishing Services. https://citeseerx.ist.psu.edu/viewdoc/download?doi=10.1.1.627.9246&rep=rep1&type=pdf

Hammond, P. H., Caldwell, C. H., Brooks, C., & Bell, L. (2011). Being there in spirit, fire, and mind: Expressive roles among nonresidential African American fathers. *Research on Social Work Practice, 21*, 308–318. https://doi.org/10.1177/1049731510383441

Harris Professional Development Network Fatherhood Engagement Committee. (2021, January). *The power of fathers: A concept paper on fatherhood, father engagement, and early childhood.* Harris Professional Development Network. https://www.irvingharrisfdn.org/wp-content/uploads/2021/01/Father-Engagement-Concept-Paper-FINAL.pdf

Harris, K., & Metler, D. (2014). Transforming responsible fatherhood practice and policy: Bringing scalability, sustainability, and measurability to father involvement and family strengthening. *Childrens' Voice, 23*(1) https://www.cwla.org/responsible-fatherhood/

Holmes, E. K., Egginton, B. R., Hawkins, A. J., Robbins, N. L., & Shafer, K. (2020). Do responsible fatherhood programs work? A comprehensive meta-analytic study. *Family Relations, 69*(5), 967–982. https://doi.org/10.1111/fare.12435

Huebner, R. A., Werner, M., Hartwig, S., White, S., & Shewa, D. (2008). Engaging fathers: Needs and satisfaction in child protective services. *Administration in Social Work, 32*, 87–103. https://doi.org/10.1300/J147v32n02_06

Klempin, S., & Mincy, R. B. (2011). Tossed on a sea of change: A status update on the responsible fatherhood field. *Center for Research on Fathers, Children, and Family Well-Being at the Columbia University School of Social Work.* http://crfcfw.columbia.edu/files/2012/09/OSF-Fatherhood-Survey_Final-Report_9.25.12_SK_RM.pdf

Lamb, M. E. (1997). Fathers and child development: An introductory overview and guide. In M. E. Lamb (Ed.), *The role of the father in child development* (3rd ed., pp. 1–18). Wiley.

Lamb, M. E. (2010). How do fathers influence children's development? Let me count the ways. In M. E. Lamb (Ed.), *The role of the father in child development* (5th ed., pp. 1–26). Wiley.

Lemmons, B. P., & Johnson, W. E. (2019). Game changers: A critical race theory analysis of the economic, social, and political factors impacting Black fatherhood and family formation. *Social Work in Public Health, 34*, 86–101. https://doi.org/10.1080/19371918.2018.1562406

Livingston, J. N., & McAdoo, J. L. (2007). The role of African American fathers in the socialization of their children. In H. Pipes McAdoo (Ed.), *Black families* (4th ed., pp. 219–237). Sage Publications.

Martinez, K. J., Rider, F., Cayce, N. A., Forssell, S. L., Poirier, J. M., Hunt, S. R., Crawford, G., & Sawyer, J. O. (2013). *A guide for father involvement in systems of care*. Technical Assistance Partnership for Child and Family Mental Health. https://wvsystemofcare.org/wp-content/uploads/2013/03/Guide-for-Father-Involvement-in-SOCs-TAP-2011.pdf.

McAllister, C. L., Wilson, P. C., & Burton, J. (2004). From sports fans to nurturers: An Early Head Start program's evolution toward father involvement. *Fathering, 2*(1), 31–59. https://doi.org/10.3149/fth.0201.31

McDonald, M. (2020). Child support enforcement as social control: Black fathers and multi-partner fertility. In *Introduction to Africana demography* (pp. 47–78). Brill.

Mincy, R. B., & Pouncy, H. W. (2004). The responsible fatherhood field: Evolution and goals. In C. S. Tamis-LeMonda & N. Cabrera (Eds.), *Handbook of father involvement: Multidisciplinary perspectives* (pp. 555–597). Lawrence Earlbaum, Publishers.

Moran, P., Ghate, D., Van Der Merwe, A., & Policy Research Bureau. (2004). *What works in parenting support? A review of the international evidence*. DfES Publications. https://dera.ioe.ac.uk/5024/1/RR574.pdf

National Fatherhood Initiative. (2015). *7 steps to starting a successful fatherhood program* [E-book]. National Fatherhood Initiative. https://www.fatherhood.org/start-fatherhood-program-ebook

National Fatherhood Initiative. (2016). *Father friendly checkup*. https://www.fatherhood.org/ffcu.

National Responsible Fatherhood Clearinghouse. (2019). *Program attendance and retention*. U.S. Department of Health & Human Services. https://www.fatherhood.gov/sites/default/files/resource_files/nrfc_tipcard_source_508_0.pdf

Parke, R. D. (2000). Father involvement: A developmental psychological perspective. *Marriage and Family Review, 29*, 43–58. https://doi.org/10.1300/J002v29n02_04

Pearson, J. (2018). *State approaches to including fathers in programs and policies dealing with children and families*. https://www.frpn.org/asset/frpn-research-brief-state-approaches-including-fathers-in-programs-and-policies-dealing

Pfitzner, N., Humphreys, C., & Hegarty, K. (2017). Research review: Engaging men: A multi-level model to support father engagement. *Child & Family Social Work, 22*(1), 537–547. https://doi.org/10.1111/cfs.12250

Pleck, E. H., & Pleck, J. H. (1997). Fatherhood ideals in the United States: Historical dimensions. In M. E. Lamb (Ed.), *The role of the father in child development* (3rd ed., pp. 33–48). Wiley.

Roggman, L. A., Boyce, L. K., Cook, G. A., & Cook, J. (2002). Getting dads involved: Predictors of father involvement in Early Head Start and with their children. *Infant Mental Health Journal, 23*, 62–78. https://doi.org/10.1002/imhj.10004

Randles, J. (2020). Role modeling responsibility: The essential father discourse in responsible fatherhood programming and policy. *Social Problems, 67*(1), 96–112. https://doi.org/10.1093/socpro/spy027

Rollins, L. S. (2021). Conclusion: Moving to father inclusive services. In L. S. Rollins (Ed.), *Engaging and working with African American fathers* (pp. 132–146). Routledge. https://doi.org/10.4324/9780429278389

Sandstrom, H., Healy, P., Gearing, M., & Peters, M. (2015a). *Serving young fathers in home visiting programs* (OPRE Report #2015–105). Office of Planning, Research and Evaluation. https://www.urban.org/sites/default/files/publication/76126/2000539-Serving-Young-Fathers-in-Home-Visiting-Programs-Highlights-from-a-Research-Study.pdf

Sandstrom, H., Gearing, M., Peters, H., Heller, C., Healy, O., & Pratt, E. (2015b). *Approaches to father engagement and fathers' experiences in home visiting programs* (OPRE Report #2015–103). Office of Planning, Research and Evaluation. https://www.urban.org/sites/default/files/publication/76116/2000537-Approaches-to-Father-Engagement-and-Fathers-Experiences-in-Home-Visiting-Programs.pdf

Seinfeld, J. (2021). *We are leaving fathers out of this important discussion*. https://www.cnn.com/2021/04/30/opinions/investing-in-fathers-to-tackle-child-poverty-seinfeld/index.html

Selekman, R., Holcomb, P. (2021, September 17.) *Father Engagement in Human Services [Infographic]. Mathematica.* https://aspe.hhs.gov/sites/default/files/2021-09/e-3-infographicstrategy-list.pdf

Shafer, K., & Wendt, D. (2015). Men's mental health: A call to social workers. *Social Work, 60*, 105–112. https://doi.org/10.1093/sw/swu061

Solomon-Fears, C. (2011). *Non-marital childbearing: Trends, reasons, and public policy interventions. Diane Publishing.*

Solomon-Fears, C. (2013). *Fatherhood initiatives: Connecting fathers to their children.* https://ecommons.cornell.edu/xmlui/bitstream/handle/1813/78260/CRS_Fatherhood_Initiatives.pdf?sequence=1

Tamis-LeMonda, C., & Cabrera, N. (1999). Perspectives on father involvement: Research and policy. *Society for Research in Child Development, 13*, 1–25. https://www.srcd.org/sites/default/files/file-attachments/spr13-2.pdf

The White House (2012). *Promoting responsible fatherhood every father taking responsibility for his child's intellectual, emotional, and financial well-being.*

Tollestrup, J. (2018). *Fatherhood initiatives: Connecting fathers to their children..* https://www.everycrsreport.com/files/20180501_RL31025_d272263c13d-b2796443862a3861a0f6960286fb6.pdf.

U.S. Department of Health and Human Services. (2013). *Head Start father engagement birth to five programming guide.* U.S. Department of Health and Human Services, Administration for Children and Families, Office of Head Start. https://www1.nyc.gov/assets/acs/pdf/hoot_mail/HEADSTART_Father_Engagement.pdf

U.S. Department of Health & Human Services, Administration for Children and Families. (2018). *Integrating approaches that prioritize and enhance father engagement.* https://www.acf.hhs.gov/sites/default/files/documents/ofa/acffatherhoodim_final.pdf

Watson, J. (2011). *OFA Promoting Responsible Fatherhood Grant: Summary of lessons learned.* Parents as Teachers National Center, Inc. https://static1.squarespace.com/static/56be46a6b6aa60dbb45e41a5/t/584598693e00be2980f29371/1480956010036/OFA_PromotingResp.pdf

Weaver, J. D. (2012). The first father: Perspectives on the president's fatherhood initiative. *Family Court Review, 50*(2), 297–309. https://doi.org/10.1111/j.1744-1617.2012.01453.x

Chapter 3
Engaging Individual Fathers From a Developmental and Family Systems Perspective

Brianna P. Lemmons, Qiana R. Cryer-Coupet, Jennifer A. Shadik, and Jennifer L. Bellamy

Introduction

A review of the scholarly literature focused on the experiences of fathering and being fathered suggests that the meaning of fatherhood and the way fathering is carried out varies widely among individuals, families, and communities and evolve over time for any given father. This chapter provides an overview of factors that impact father and family engagement from life course and family systems perspectives. Fathering, like other roles in life, is impacted by developmental stage and life experience as well as the context in which the role is carried out. A great deal of the literature describing issues of development and fathering focuses on the role of fathers in shaping child development. While the relationship between fathers and child development is important, this chapter is focused on fathers' own development and how that shapes practitioners' engagement with them in systems, organizations, and programs. *Family systems theory* is often used to frame and describe *father involvement* within families, but this theoretical framework is also important for

B. P. Lemmons
Diana R. Garland School of Social Work, Baylor University, Waco, TX, USA
e-mail: Brianna_Lemmons@baylor.edu

Q. R. Cryer-Coupet (✉)
School of Social Work, Georgia State University, Atlanta, GA, USA
e-mail: qcryercoupet@gsu.edu

J. A. Shadik
Department of Social Work, Ohio University, Athens, OH, USA
e-mail: Shadik@ohio.edu

J. L. Bellamy
University of Denver, Graduate School of Social work, Denver, CO, USA
e-mail: Jennifer.Bellamy@du.edu

J. L. Bellamy et al. (eds.), *Social Work Practice with Fathers*,
https://doi.org/10.1007/978-3-031-13686-3_3

understanding *father engagement* in programs, organizations, and systems. Father involvement with families is linked to father engagement in systems, as fathers with differing levels or types of involvement in their families may require different types of services and engagement approaches. This chapter examines the diverse experiences of fathers across varying contexts related to age, educational attainment, relationship status, socioeconomic status, culture, and family structure and how this relates to their engagement in services.

Background and Context

As the research on fathers and fathering has developed over the years, it has become much more nuanced in its reflection of the diversity of experiences represented among men who play parenting roles. Much of the early research describing fathers focused on *cis-gender*, married fathers who were biologically related to and living with the children they were parenting. This work also tended to focus on fathering in White, middle-class families. Early studies of fathers and fathering also predominantly focused on father involvement, specifically on clarifying their contributions to family and child well-being. It took some time to build an evidence base that clearly indicated that fathers, regardless of characteristics such as race, income, or residential status, make important and unique contributions to children and families. The question of whether fathers matter to children, families, and communities has been answered. It is clear that if social workers want to promote a myriad of positive outcomes for families, they must engage fathers (e.g., Allport et al., 2019; Guterman, et al., 2018; Lundahl et al., 2008).

The question has now turned to how best to engage fathers in programs, organizations, and service systems. Although all fathers are important, they are not a monolithic group. Fathering is shaped by various factors such as age, race, ethnicity, socio-economic status, residential status, family relationships, and intersecting identities. For example, data from the Fragile Families and Child Well-Being national study and others demonstrate how each of these factors shape involvement (e.g., Castillo et al., 2011). In general, this research suggests that co-residential fathers are more frequently involved with their children, likely because they have more opportunities to do so. Non-resident fathers face unique barriers to involvement that relate to the lack of access to their children in daily life and also to the higher likelihood that they face stressors related to family relationships and income. In general, older fathers tend to be more involved with their children than younger fathers; they are more likely to have the income, education, and life stability that make it easier for them to be, and remain, involved.

For these reasons, we take a developmental and family systems approach to describing engagement with individual fathers. We are also careful to attend to the intersecting identities that shape fathers' experiences. A great deal of research has examined the complex interplay of race and gender on service access, engagement, and quality (e.g., Manuel, 2018). Research suggests that fathers face a number of barriers to engagement, including gendered notions of mental health, parenting, and family roles that are reflected in the biases of professionals and the structure of systems (Shafer & Bellamy, 2016). In some child and family serving systems, such as child welfare, men and fathers have been historically labeled as "dangerous", "absent", or "unimportant" (Bellamy, 2009), and these deficit narratives can be amplified for young fathers, low-income fathers, and racially and ethnically minoritized fathers. If we are to successfully engage fathers, we need to take a balanced and holistic approach that acknowledges the potential and importance of every father and addresses the specific constellation of challenges they each face. Services should be targeted to the development needs, family structures, and identities of fathers but also responsive to the diversity represented within subgroups of fathers.

Conceptual Framing

In this chapter, we use a life course or developmental perspective to organize our discussion of father engagement and illustrate how family systems and intersecting racial, ethnic, and other identities influence individual fathers' access to, and the quality of their engagement in, services, programs, organizations, and service systems. We start with briefly explaining family systems theory and how this theory applies to fathers.

Family Systems Theory

Family systems theory applies principles of *general systems theory* to the study of the family as an organized system. These principles dictate that families have properties of: (a) wholeness and order, whereby the whole is greater than the sum of its parts and cannot be understood simply from the combined characteristics of each part; (b) a hierarchical structure, whereby systems are composed of subsystems that are systems in and of themselves; and (c) adaptive self-stabilization/self-organization, wherein the family system can adapt to challenges in the environment by making changes to the internal working of the system (Cox & Paley, 1997, 2003; Wilson, 1989).

Recent work argues that research on parenting should include a family systems approach, which allows researchers and practitioners to understand the behaviors of both parents as well as how their individual and combined behaviors impact their child's development (Cabrera et al., 2018). Children do not exist in a vacuum; the family systems perspective reminds us of the importance of understanding that influence can come from multiple individuals within the family system, that influence can be bidirectional (i.e., parent to child and child to parent), and that researchers and practitioners should consider individual family members as well as the whole family as a group. Historically, much of the parenting literature has focused on mothers' impact on child development, while some newer scholarship includes a focus on the influence of fathers. The many social, demographic, and economic changes in the last half century make the exclusive focus on mothers as parents a poor representation of the majority of children's experiences (Cabrera et al., 2000).

Life Course Theory

The study of the life course crosses several fields, including sociology, psychology, history, aging, social work, human development, and family studies (Elder et al., 2007). The theory provides a general framework for relating history to social pathways and developmental trajectories across the lifespan. It situates human development and aging within a contextualist perspective, taking into consideration how historical time and place, as well as relations with societal systems, can shape life patterns and trajectories. In addition, central to life course theory is the notion that human development is contextualized by social pathways that are contingent upon opportunities and constraints within societal structures and culture (Elder, 1998).

Furthermore, the theory also maintains the importance of attending to age distinctions, specifically age-related life transitions and the timing of such shifts (Elder, 1998). This perspective helps to locate individuals and families in time and history and considers how certain age-related patterns may impact development at different times. The core tenets of life course theory (as articulated in Elder, 1998) include the following: (a) historical time and place, or that the life course of individuals is embedded within and shaped by history and place-based experiences; (b) timing in lives, or that the developmental impact of life transitions is contingent on the timing in which they occur in one's life; (c) linked lives, or that lives are lived interdependently and influenced by a network of social relationships, and such connections extend across generations and serve as channels for socialization and social control; and (d) human agency, or that individuals have the ability to construct their own life course through choices and actions. However, the theory also acknowledges that all choices and actions are made within the context of larger structural and environmental dynamics that leave some with the ability to fully exercise human agency and freely select the paths they take, and others with limited abilities to do so. This theory is particularly relevant to the engagement of individual fathers as it provides a basis for understanding their unique needs at different stages of development and how to situate such needs within the proper context, taking into consideration historical time, place, social relationships, key life transitions, and various constraints that bear on choices and actions.

Teen Fathers

Developmental Considerations and Unique Needs

Adolescence is a period of increased independence and is often accompanied by dramatic shifts in physical, psychological, and social development (Finch & Bacon, 2015). In this section, we speak specifically to the early adolescent or teenage years. Just like their peers, teen parents are still developing in multiple domains. Many of them are still in school or may just be entering their first employment experiences.

This developmental stage is both exciting and challenging. Navigating the teenage years with the additional responsibilities and shifts in roles associated with parenting is particularly complex. For example, teen fathers have reported that stressors related to parenting can negatively impact school attendance and performance (Finch & Bacon, 2015). Teen fathers may struggle with trying to complete their education while providing financial support and spending time with their children. Parenthood is a stressful time for most parents but is especially so for teens who are undertaking parenthood while still maturing, which can impact relationships with their children and co-parents.

Teen fathers tend to experience multiple risk factors, some of which are linked to taking on the complexities and challenges of fathering at their developmental stage. Such risks include low family income (Xie et al., 2001), a history of maltreatment (Devault, 2014), depression (Lee et al., 2012), antisocial behavior (Fagot et al., 1998), and a difficult or absent relationship with their own father (Kiselica & Kiselica, 2014). Despite the challenges, many young parents report counterbalancing the stereotypes and barriers they face with developing a positive self-concept as a parent, focusing on the benefits and lessons of parenting, and seeing parenting as a catalyst or motivator for positive life changes (Conn et al., 2018).

Family Systems and Involvement

The family systems of teen fathers are unique and often complex. Several factors are correlated with greater involvement of teen fathers with their children, including higher levels of social support and a strong co-parenting relationship (Fagan & Lee, 2011). However, most teen fathers do not co-reside with their child's mother when their child is born (SmithBattle et al., 2019). Many of them live with their own parents and are unmarried. When teen fathers do not share a home with their children, they may have fewer opportunities to participate in caregiving activities (Futris & Schoppe-Sullivan, 2007). Furthermore, *visitation* and involvement with their child may be limited by the child's mother and her family, which has been referred to as *maternal gatekeeping* (SmithBattle et al., 2019). In some cases, teen fathers report challenges with access to their child due to difficulties with providing financial support (Saleh et al., 2005). Many teen fathers have a low income and may not be able to maintain *child support* payments or regularly contribute financially to their families. Such lack of access can lead to difficulties in building or maintaining a relationship with their child.

Engagement

For service providers seeking to work with teen fathers, these considerations shape service engagement in many ways. To begin with, teen fathers are more difficult to identify than teen mothers, particularly when they are unmarried and non-residential, which presents challenges for engagement (Harding et al., 2020). Furthermore, many service systems do not properly or intentionally assess teen fathers or their needs as parents. It is possible that many systems may indeed serve teen fathers, but if they are not assessed for issues related to fatherhood or impending fatherhood, these needs may remain invisible to the system. In addition, stereotypes and stigma can negatively impact teen fathers and their service utilization (Devault, 2014; Kiselica et al., 1998). Fathers report ageism or labeling and marginalization because of their young age (Conn et al., 2018). Those who are young, low-income, and minoritized are often stereotyped as negligent or irresponsible (Winstanley et al., 2002). Additional stereotypes may be assigned to specific groups of teen fathers. For example, Mexican-origin teen fathers have been stereotyped as being domineering or controlling of their female partners (Parra-Cardona et al., 2008). These biases may reduce or limit service providers' efforts to engage with them effectively. Alternatively, programs and staff that are welcoming to teen fathers can counter these stereotypes and embody a strengths-based perspective that can help to increase engagement, thereby retaining them in services and strengthening families (SmithBattle et al., 2019).

Fathering in Adulthood

The period of adulthood is broad, and within this developmental stage, fathers may have different needs. Adulthood ranges from late adolescence (18–25 years) through middle age (45–65 years). This section will highlight two important subgroups of fathers within this age group: (1) first-time fathers and (2) fathers who have children with more than one co-parent. Specifically, we will address their unique developmental and family systems needs as well as other characteristics that may impact their experiences as fathers, along with developmentally appropriate ways to engage them in the service delivery process.

First-Time Fathers

Developmental Considerations and Unique Needs

Many fathers become parents for the first time in early adulthood. Numerous studies have documented the transformative impact of the transition to fatherhood on adult male development (Eggebeen et al., 2010) and have acknowledged this transition as a critical period in men's lives (Bakermans-Kranenburg et al., 2019). Becoming a father is an important developmental milestone and life course transition for men that impacts numerous life domains (Bakermans-Kranenburg et al., 2019; Torche & Rauf, 2021); and most men will experience this milestone sometime in their lifetime.

Men may have gender-specific needs as they make the transition to fatherhood. One set of factors to consider is role and identity transitions, many of which are influenced by social and cultural factors. Upon assuming the role of father, men begin to consider the saliency of this role and often experience a reconceptualization or restructuring of their identity (Baldwin et al., 2018; Strauss & Goldberg, 1999). Studies have shown that upon the transition to fatherhood, men are often faced with a number of prescribed behavioral requirements and expectations that emerge not only on a societal level but also from within the family system (i.e., from partners, parents, friends, and communities). Such expectations are often related to norms and values about work-life balance, gender roles, involvement in child-care, and the provision of emotional and financial support (Bakermans-Kranenburg et al., 2019; Eggebeen et al., 2010; Singley & Edwards, 2015). These expectations play a powerful role in shaping the identity and experiences of first-time fathers.

Another set of factors to consider is psychological factors. Research has well documented the impact of the transition to fatherhood on men's mental health, which is described by some fathers as an "emotional roller coaster" (Asenhed et al., 2014). Specifically, the emotional changes (i.e., pressures to be a good father, fears of becoming a father, insecurities, and feelings of unpreparedness), complexities, and demands associated with becoming a new father have been linked to both anxiety and depression (Philpott & Corcoran, 2018; Silva, Pinto, & Martins, 2021). Approximately 10% of new dads experience mental health difficulties (Chin et al., 2011). In addition, although the topic of depression among new fathers has been understudied, depression and other types of mental distress have been found to be more common among this group compared to the general male population (Chin et al., 2011). Some of the unique needs of this group of fathers center around assistance with managing the new expectations that come with the role of father; navigating competing demands and challenges with balancing work and fatherhood; and cultivating spaces where emotions and mental health needs related to the transition to fatherhood can be explored (Baldwin et al., 2018).

Family Systems and Involvement

Aside from the impact that becoming a new father can have on the life course and development of adult men, it is also important to consider the consequences of this experience for the family system as a whole. Becoming a new father can lead men to increase intergenerational and extended family interactions in an effort to best meet the needs of their children (Knoester & Eggebeen, 2006). In addition, new fathers may experience significant lifestyle changes or a deterioration in their relationship with partners as well as competing challenges and responsibilities (i.e., balancing work and the role of father; Baldwin et al., 2018). The emotional adjustment that comes with being a new father can also impact the well-being of the family system.

Engagement

Social work practitioners should make an effort to engage first-time fathers in ways that promote a smoother transition into fatherhood and the most optimal outcomes for the family system (Bakermans-Kranenburg et al., 2019). Specifically, practitioners should keep in mind that emotional needs are likely to change from the prenatal to postnatal period. Thus, engagement efforts will likely need to be different at each phase. Particular attention should be given to assessing for postpartum depression, which is often overlooked among fathers (Singley & Edwards, 2015). Furthermore, many fathers have reported dissatisfaction with the limitations of formal support services available to expectant fathers (i.e., lack of father-centered supports and services, lack of father-centered information on fathering, and feelings of exclusion from the birthing process; Carlson, Edleson, & Kimball, 2014). Thus, a key strategy for engaging first-time fathers is to expand and tailor support and services in ways that are specific to their unique needs and experiences.

Fathers with Multiple Partners and Households

Developmental Considerations and Unique Needs

The structure of families in the United States has evolved over time, and the number of fathers who have children with multiple partners and different households has increased. Fatherhood is no longer carried out predominantly in the context of a single marriage with two parents and biologically related children. Carlson and Furstenberg (2006) note that, "today a significant fraction of adults have (or will have) biological children by more than one partner" (p. 718). This phenomenon is referred to by some authors as *multiple partner fertility* (Carlson & Furstenberg, 2006; Turney & Carlson, 2011; Monte, 2019) or *multi-partner fertility*.

In general, having children with more than one partner is not a new phenomenon (Guzzo & Furstenberg, 2007; Monte, 2019). However, rates of fathering with multiple partners and the overall fertility patterns among men are difficult to capture (Bart Stykes & Guzzo, 2019; Guzzo, 2014; Monte, 2017). For example, paternity is not always clear or known to parents, and most fathers do not take paternity tests. Furthermore, estimates vary considerably depending on the data source, population, and analytical sample. Estimates provided by Guzzo (2014) suggest that the rate of fathering children with multiple partners among men in the United States varies from 14% to 17% and increases with age.

The likelihood of having a child with more than one partner is higher among some marginalized groups of men, which often contributes to further disadvantage (Guzzo & Furstenberg, 2007; Manlove et al., 2008). For example, Black, Hispanic, young (Manlove et al., 2008), and low-income men (Guzzo & Furstenberg, 2007) are more likely to have children with more than one partner (Manlove et al., 2008). In addition, men who experience instability as children (Logan et al., 2006), have a first sexual experience at a young age (Logan et al., 2006; Manlove et al., 2008), have children outside of marriage or cohabitation (Manlove et al., 2008), and have a history of incarceration (Carlson & Furstenberg, 2006; Logan et al., 2006) are also more likely to have children with more than one partner.

Other large shifts in U.S. demography include high rates of divorce and declines in marriage. Data from the U.S. Census Bureau (2020) reveal persistent marital dissolution rates. In 2019, for every 1000 women aged 15 or older, the U.S. Census (2020) recorded an average of 7.6 divorces. Research also indicates that men experience higher rates of *repartnering* following divorce in comparison to women (Brown et al., 2019; Livingston, 2014; Payne, 2018). A range of factors can influence the likelihood of repartnering after the experience of separation or divorce (Vanassche et al., 2015). For example, divorced fathers who care full-time for minor children are less likely to repartner than childless divorcees (Vanassche et al., 2015). Younger children and their associated responsibilities could make finding and building a relationship with a new partner more challenging (Ivanova et al. 2013; Meggiolaro & Ongaro, 2008; Poortman, 2007), given that they generally require more attention from their parents (Ivanova et al., 2013).

When one or both partners have children from former relationships and form a family, these are referred to as *stepfamilies* or *blended families*. The literature is somewhat inconsistent in the use of these terms but in some instances, a blended family refers specifically to families with both biological and non-biological children (i.e., children from a former relationship as well as children shared by both parents). These families can vary significantly in structure, organization, and expectations (Sweeney, 2010) and have been characterized by parents as difficult to navigate (Ganong & Coleman, 2004).

Family Systems and Involvement

Aspects related to fathering with multiple partners and across households can have a great influence on family systems and father involvement (Koster et al., 2020). For example, the repartnering of either parent following divorce has been associated with lower levels of father involvement (McGene & King, 2012) due to the demands of co-parents, new partners, stepchildren, or any new children from repartnered relationships (Koster et al., 2020). Furthermore, the literature has extensively documented the impact of having children with multiple partners on family systems (Guzzo, 2014). For example, while mothers tend to live with all of their children regardless of how many partners they may have children with, fathers who have children with more than one partner are more likely to endure highly complex family configurations which often involve parenting multiple sets of children across different households (Carlson & Furstenberg, 2006). Such complexity can lead to ambiguity in family roles and boundaries. Additionally, the quality of interactions with children can vary widely, with quality tending to be highest with co-resident children (Guzzo, 2014). Though most fathers in complex families attempt to parent all children to some degree, research has shown that the most intense involvement tends to occur with the children of one mother (Tach et al., 2014). Overall, fathering with multiple partners and across households has been linked to increased economic stress (Monte, 2011), diminished financial resources, and paternal depression, impacting the financial well-being and stability of the entire family or multiple families (Bronte-Tinkew et al., 2009).

Engagement

Given all of the challenges that men who have children with more than one partner contend with, it is important to also consider strategies for engaging them and best meeting their needs in social work practice. Social work practitioners who work with divorced and repartnered fathers should center their engagement around promoting healthier stepfamily or blended family systems (Ganong & Coleman, 2004). The process of repartnering can be challenging for all members of a family. Therefore, practitioners should also assist repartnered families with exploring the complex feelings and experiences they may encounter due to changes in their family dynamics (Ganong & Coleman, 2004).

In addition, practitioners should support fathers as they navigate common challenges related to repartnering, such as strained or difficult co-parenting relationships (Bernstein, 2006). Other areas for intervention include improving communication between family members, educating fathers and their families on repartnered or stepfamily dynamics (Ganong & Coleman, 2004), and helping fathers and their families develop healthy expectations for each other (Adler-Baeder, et al., 2010). To promote the well-being of fathers who have children with multiple partners as well as their families, social work practitioners' engagement efforts should be focused on addressing various aspects of family and environmental instability as well as economic stressors (Petren, 2017).

Older Fathers and Grandfathers

Developmental Considerations and Unique Needs

Fathering as an older adult is a topic that has been under examined among researchers. The epidemiological literature describes the period of advanced paternal age as beginning between 35 and 40 years of age (Andersen & Urhoj, 2017). Research on advanced paternal age suggests that there are several potential risks to the offspring of men who reproduce during this period of life, with risk increasing with age. These risks include fetal mortality via miscarriage or stillbirth, the development of childhood cancers and neurodevelopment concerns, and the development of other congenital syndromes and abnormalities, with risks for each of these outcomes ranging from weak to strong respectively (Andersen & Urhoj, 2017). Mutations in the aging reproductive germ cells are thought to contribute to the development of these negative outcomes. As such, public health researchers across the world have noted the importance of offering genetic testing and fertility counseling for fathers of advanced paternal age, particularly those over the age of 40 (Bray et al., 2006).

In addition to conception among older fathers, scholars have investigated the health and well-being of older single fathers and older custodial grandfathers. In Whitley and Fuller-Thomson's (2017) study of older fathers and grandfathers, both older single fathers and older custodial grandfathers faced health challenges at higher rates than men of the same age in the general population. Overall, custodial grandfathers reported poorer health outcomes than did older single fathers. Some of the concerns reported by grandfathers included chronic health issues such as heart attacks, diabetes, and Chronic Obstructive Pulmonary Disease (COPD). In contrast, older single fathers reported a higher incidence of mental health concerns and experiences with obesity than did older custodial grandfathers. Formal social support from doctors, social workers, and other community-based resources are important for ensuring the well-being of both groups of fathers and the children in their care. Informal social support from family, friends, and neighbors is also important for these fathers, as parenting stress may contribute to further declines in physical and mental health.

Family Systems and Involvement

Family structure and household composition are two factors that may impact the physical, mental, and socioeconomic well-being of older fathers and grandfathers. For example, according to research by Keene et al. (2012), older custodial grandfathers are less likely to experience financial hardship if they are married or live in a three-generation household. Similarly, the nature of the relationship between older fathers and their adult children may cause fathers to reflect on the costs and rewards of parenting over time (Stelle & Sheehan, 2011). If fathers perceive the costs to outweigh the rewards, they may experience angst, which could have a negative impact on their physical and mental health. On the other hand, building on Erickson's Psycho-Social Stages of Development, research has also explored the role of *generativity* among older fathers, finding that parenting or grandparenting can be a means for contributing to and expressing concern and care for the next generation (Stelle & Sheehan, 2011) and providing a second chance for reconciling difficult pasts (Roy & Lucas, 2006), both of which can enhance psychological well-being.

Engagement

Differentiated engagement efforts are needed, depending on the type of fathering in which older men are partaking. For older custodial grandfathers, social work practitioners may seek to engage their clients in support groups for grandparents raising grandchildren. These groups have shown efficacy at reducing negative outcomes for grandparents and the children in their care (Chan et al., 2019). For older single fathers, engagement strategies should reflect the specific experience of single fathering (i.e., by choice, divorce, widower). Strategies should be tailored to reduce challenges encountered by men of advanced paternal age. One example might include providing respite services so that older fathers have opportunities to socialize with peers who are no longer raising children. Tools for engaging older fathers of adult children should take a family-centered approach and seek to engage the adult children in intervention services as support for the fathers, particularly for those who may not seek help from formal systems of care.

Recommended Strategies and Practices

The successful engagement of fathers in services requires intentional strategies for recruitment and retention as well as attention to services that address fathers' unique needs. We offer some additional strategies and practices that are helpful in considering engaging fathers, including targeting services based on developmental considerations, bringing services to fathers where they are, and ensuring services are relevant to each father. Once fathers are recruited into services, some tools such as genograms and eco-mapping can be very helpful in better understanding fathers' experiences and contexts from a systems perspective. An overview of each of these tools is reviewed below.

Target Services Developmentally

Strategies to engage teen fathers include many of the same approaches used with older fathers. However, their developmental stage and needs must be taken into consideration. For example, given that teen fathers are often living with their own parents, have not completed their education, and are still developing in multiple realms, they may benefit from specialized services, and their own caregivers likely need to be engaged in services to support them as fathers as well. Services focused on housing, education, job training, parenting, and co-parenting can particularly benefit this subgroup of fathers. Key findings from research focused on fathers in their teens and early twenties emphasizes the importance of engaging new fathers early in their fatherhood journey, approaching young fathers as capable of and interested in being effective parents, individualizing services, and giving young fathers choices; these factors are key to engaging them in services (Davies, 2016).

Another important window of opportunity for engagement is the birth of a first child. According to data from the Fragile Families and Child Well-Being study, most fathers, even those who are not married, are involved with their children through the first year of life (Carlson & McLanahan, 2003). Some researchers have referred to the birth of a first child as the "magic moment" (McLanahan et al., 2010), and it may represent a particularly opportune time to engage fathers. Some fathers have indicated that their child's birth was a turning point in their lives, resulting in healthier life choices (Shadik & O'Connor, 2016).

Bringing Services to Fathers

Fathers may struggle to engage in services that require them to travel or take time away from their other commitments. One engagement strategy that can help reduce these barriers is to bring services to where fathers already are. For example, many expectant fathers attend prenatal ultrasound appointments with their partners, and these appointments may be an opportunity to engage men in positive relationship or parenting interventions at a very early stage (Walsh et al., 2014). Other studies have found that engaging fathers in other perinatal services, including doula services and home visiting, can support ongoing engagement and involvement (e.g., Bellamy et al., in press; Thullen et al., 2014). Seeking out fathers where they are, including schools, places of employment, and organizations and systems from which they are already receiving services as well as places of community, recreation, and leisure activities are all fruitful opportunities for engagement.

Genograms

Social workers often use *genograms* to better understand individuals and their families. A genogram is a graphic depiction of, typically, three generations of the family. They can be fairly basic, with births, deaths, marriages, and lines indicating relationship quality, or, alternatively, quite intricate, involving trauma, cut-offs between family members, behavioral health issues, and abuse. Genograms can provide an overview of the family and help practitioners see multigenerational issues and patterns (Collins et al., 2010).

Social workers can engage fathers to be actively involved in the creation of the genogram, demonstrating their perspectives on their family are an important part of the process. Constructing the genogram is a cooperative process and helps build rapport (Collins et al., 2010). Some fathers have complex family configurations; this is often the case with fathers who have children with multiple partners. Constructing a genogram that includes a father's relationships with each of his children as well as his co-parents helps the practitioner understand the quality and types of relationships. Dyer et al. (2018) found constructing genograms with incarcerated fathers was beneficial for understanding a father's connections and the affective relationships between himself and his children. When working with fathers, it is important to understand his relationships with all of his children as he may have differing needs related to each child (Shadik, 2020). Creating a genogram helps practitioners rapidly engage with fathers and ensure that a broad range of his strengths and needs are understood.

Ecomaps

An *ecomap* is another tool that can help practitioners engage fathers in services. The ecomap is a graphic representation of an aspect of individual and family life, representing relationships with individuals, organizations, and systems outside the family. Use of an ecomap allows practitioners to understand the quality of the relationships between individuals and those they interact with (Collins et al., 2010). An ecomap may capture a father's relationships with his workplace or school, co-parents, friends, church, support group, court system, and the school or daycare his child attends. While constructing the ecomap, the social worker asks questions to understand if the father's relationships with these individuals and systems are one-sided, if both sides invest similar energy and resources, and whether healthy boundaries exist in the relationship.

Rempel et al. (2007) found ecomaps were helpful for developing a relationship with caregivers and recognizing potential resources within their social network. Holtslander (2005) suggests constructing an ecomap with families in the postpartum period to highlight stressors, sources of support, and other agencies the individual and family work with. If a father's social support network is limited, he may be able to identify the people and agencies he would like to build a relationship with, so the creation of a second, future-oriented ecomap may be helpful. Further, the construction of an ecomap may help social workers better understand the relational factors impacting the father's involvement in services. For instance, a father who is balancing caretaking responsibilities for several children residing in different homes with different mothers may be challenged to attend programming. Development of the ecomap may also highlight resources such as social fathers, who do not appear on official paperwork but play an important role in caregiving. Creating an ecomap can be enlightening, increase engagement, and assist in the recognition of strengths and challenges of each father.

Conclusion

Successfully engaging individual fathers requires attention to both their developmental stage and the family systems and contexts of which they are a part. Fathers are a diverse group with many different characteristics, identities, and needs. By targeting engagement strategies to the needs of individual fathers, social workers can increase fathers' access to and benefit from a variety of services and programs that can help them be the best fathers they can be.

Resources

Teen Fathers

- The Fatherhood Project – https://www.thefatherhoodproject.org/teen-dads-forgotten-parent
- National Fatherhood Initiative – https://www.fatherhood.org/championing-fatherhood/what-to-do-when-teen-boys-become-fathers
- National Responsible Fatherhood Clearinghouse – https://www.fatherhood.gov/for-programs/young-fathers

Older Fathers and Grandfathers

- Generations United – https://www.gu.org

Genograms

- Butler, J. F. (2008). The family diagram and genogram: Comparisons and contrasts. *The American Journal of Family Therapy*, 36(3), 169–180. https://doi.org/10.1080/01926180701291055
- Watts-Jones, D. (1997). Toward an African American genogram. *Family Process*, *36*(4), 375–383. https://doi.org/10.1111/j.1545-5300.1997.00375.x
- Kuehl, B. P. (1995). The solution-oriented genogram: A collaborative approach. *Journal of Marital and Family Therapy*, *21*(3), 239–250. . https://psycnet.apa.org/doi/10.1111/j.1752-0606.1995.tb00159.x

Eco Mapping

- McCormick, K. M., Stricklin, S., Nowak, T. M., & Rous, B. (2008). Using eco-mapping to understand family strengths and resources. *Young Exceptional Children*, *11*(2), 17–28. https://doi.org/10.1177/1096250607311932

- Harold, R. D., Mercer, L. R., & Colarossi, L. G. (1997). Eco maps: A tool to bridge the practice-research gap. *Journal of Sociology & Social Welfare*, *24*, 29–44. https://scholarworks.wmich.edu/jssw/vol24/iss4/4?utm_source=scholarworks.wmich.edu%2Fjssw%2Fvol24%2Fiss4%2F4&utm_medium=PDF&utm_campaign=PDFCoverPages

Discussion Questions

1. How might the social support needs of custodial grandfathers differ from the social support needs of adolescent fathers?
2. What are the potential benefits and challenges of constructing a genogram with a teen father?
3. What is your current field program or agency doing well to engage fathers in services?
4. What could be improved about the way your field program or agency is engaging fathers in services from a family systems or life course perspective?
5. What qualities or perspectives should staff members embody to enhance engagement with developmentally diverse fathers?

References

Adler-Baeder, F., Russell, C., Kerpelman, J., Pittman, J., Ketring, S., Smith, T., Lucier-Greer, M., Bradford, A., & Stringer, K. (2010). Thriving in stepfamilies: Exploring competence and well-being among African American youth. *Journal of Adolescent Health, 46*(4), 396–398. https://doi.org/10.1016/j.jadohealth.2009.10.014

Allport, B. S., Solomon, B. S., & Johnson, S. B. (2019). The other parent: An exploratory survey of providers' engagement of fathers in pediatric primary care. *Clinical Pediatrics, 58*(5), 555–563. https://doi.org/10.1177/0009922819829032

Andersen, A. M. N., & Urhoj, S. K. (2017). Is advanced paternal age a health risk for the offspring? *Fertility and Sterility, 107*(2), 312–318. https://doi.org/10.1016/j.fertnstert.2016.12.019

Åsenhed, L., Kilstam, J., Alehagen, S., & Baggens, C. (2014). Becoming a father is an emotional roller coaster – An analysis of first-time fathers' blogs. *Journal of Clinical Nursing, 23*(9–10), 1309–1317. https://doi.org/10.1111/jocn.12355

Bakermans-Kranenburg, M. J., Lotz, A., Alyousefi-van Dijk, K., & van IJzendoorn, M. (2019). Birth of a father: Fathering in the first 1,000 days. *Child Development Perspectives, 13*(4), 247–253. https://doi.org/10.1111/cdep.12347

Baldwin, S., Malone, M., Sandall, J., & Bick, D. (2018). Mental health and wellbeing during the transition to fatherhood: A systematic review of first time fathers' experiences. *JBI Database of Systematic Reviews and Implementation Reports, 16*(11), 2118. https://doi.org/10.11124/jbisrir-2017-003773

Bart Stykes, J., & Guzzo, K. B. (2019). Multiple-partner fertility: Variation across measurement approaches. In *Analytical family demography* (pp. 215–239). Springer. https://doi.org/10.1007/978-3-319-93227-9_10

Bellamy, J. L. (2009). A national study of male involvement among families in contact with the child welfare system. *Child Maltreatment, 14*, 255–262. https://doi.org/10.1177/1077559508326288

Bellamy, J. L., Phillips, J., Speer, R., Harty, J., Banman, A., Guterman, N. B., & Morales-Mirque, S. (in press). Strategies to enhance father engagement in home visiting: Results from a qualitative study of Dads Matter-HV. *Journal for the Society for Social Work and Research*. https://doi.org/10.1086/720010

Bernstein, A. (2006). Re-visioning, restructuring, and reconciliation: Clinical practice with complex postdivorce families. *Family Process, 46*, 67–78. https://doi.org/10.1111/j.1545-5300.2006.00192.x

Bray, I., Gunnell, D., & Smith, G. D. (2006). Advanced paternal age: How old is too old? *Journal of Epidemiology & Community Health, 60*(10), 851–853. https://doi.org/10.1136/jech.2005.045179

Bronte-Tinkew, J., Horowitz, A., & Scott, M. E. (2009). Fathering with multiple partners: Links to children's well-being in early childhood. *Journal of Marriage and Family, 71*(3), 608–631. https://doi.org/10.1111/j.1741-3737.2009.00622.x

Brown, S. L., Lin, I.-F., Hammersmith, A. M., & Wright, M. R. (2019). Repartnering following gray divorce: The roles of resources and constraints for women and men. *Demography, 56*, 503–523. https://doi.org/10.1353/dem.2006.0021

Cabrera, N., Tamis-LeMonda, C. S., Bradley, R. H., Hofferth, S., & Lamb, M. E. (2000). Fatherhood in the twenty-first century. *Child Development, 71*, 127–136. https://doi.org/10.1111/1467-8624.00126

Cabrera, N. J., Volling, B. L., & Barr, R. (2018). Fathers are parents, too! Widening the lens on parenting for children's development. *Child Development Perspectives, 12*(3), 152–157. https://doi.org/10.1111/cdep.12275

Carlson, J., Edleson, J. L., & Kimball, E. (2014). First-time fathers' experiences of and desires for formal support: A multiple lens perspective. *Fathering, 12*(3), 242–261. https://doi.org/10.3149/fth.1203.242

Carlson, M. J., & Furstenberg, F. F., Jr. (2006). The prevalence and correlates of multipartnered fertility among urban US parents. *Journal of Marriage and Family, 68*(3), 718–732. https://doi.org/10.1111/j.1741-3737.2006.00285.x

Carlson, M. J., & McLanahan, S. S. (2003). Early father involvement in fragile families. In R. D. Day & M. E. Lamb (Eds.), *Conceptualizing and measuring father involvement* (pp. 241–271). Routledge. https://doi.org/10.4324/9781410609380

Castillo, J., Welch, G., & Sarver, C. (2011). Fathering: The relationship between fathers' residence, fathers' sociodemographic characteristics, and father involvement. *Maternal and Child Health Journal, 15*(8), 1342–1349. https://doi.org/10.1007/s10995-010-0684-6

Chan, K. L., Chen, M., Lo, K. M. C., Chen, Q., Kelley, S. J., & Ip, P. (2019). The effectiveness of interventions for grandparents raising grandchildren: A meta-analysis. *Research on Social Work Practice, 29*(6), 607–617. https://doi.org/10.1177/1049731518798470

Chin, R., Hall, P., & Daiches, A. (2011). Fathers' experiences of their transition to fatherhood: A metasynthesis. *Journal of Reproductive and Infant Psychology, 29*(1), 4–18. https://doi.org/10.1080/02646838.2010.513044

Collins, D., Jordan, C., & Coleman, H. (2010). *An introduction to family social work* (3rd ed.). Cengage.

Conn, B. M., de Figueiredo, S., Sherer, S., Mankerian, M., & Iverson, E. (2018). "Our lives aren't over": A strengths-based perspective on stigma, discrimination, and coping among young parents. *Journal of Adolescence, 66*, 91–100. https://doi.org/10.1016/j.adolescence.2018.05.005

Cox, M. J., & Paley, B. (1997). Families as systems. *Annual Review of Psychology, 48*(1), 243–267. https://doi.org/10.1146/annurev.psych.48.1.243

Cox, M. J., & Paley, B. (2003). Understanding families as systems. *Current Directions in Psychological Science, 12(5), 193–196.* https://doi.org/10.1111/1467-8721.01259

Guterman, N. B., Bellamy, J. L., & Banman, A. (2018). Promoting father involvement in early home visiting services for vulnerable families: Findings from a pilot study of "Dads matter". *Child Abuse & Neglect, 76*, 261–272. https://doi.org/10.1016/j.chiabu.2017.10.017

Davies, L. (2016). Are young fathers 'hard to reach'? Understanding the importance of relationship building and service sustainability. *Journal of Children's Services, 11*(4), 317–329. https://doi.org/10.1108/JCS-03-2016-0007

Devault, A. (2014). Commentary on the complicated worlds of adolescent fathers: Implications for clinical practice, public policy, and research. *Psychology of Men & Masculinity, 15*(3), 275–277. https://doi.org/10.1037/a0037341

Dyer, W. J., Day, R. D., & Wiley, A. R. (2018). Jailed fathers and family complexity. *Social Work Research, 42*(3), 210–222. https://doi.org/10.1093/swr/svy015

Eggebeen, D. J., Dew, J., & Knoester, C. (2010). Fatherhood and men's lives at middle age. *Journal of Family Issues, 31*(1), 113–130. https://doi.org/10.1177/0192513x09341446

Elder, G. H., Jr. (1998). The life course as developmental theory. *Child Development, 69*(1), 1–12.

Elder, G., Johnson, M., & Crosnoe, R. (2007). The emergence and development of life course theory. In J. T. Mortimer & M. J. Shanahan (Eds.), *Handbook of the life course* (pp. 3–19). Springer Science & Business Media.

Fagan, J., & Lee, Y. (2011). Do coparenting and social support have a greater effect on adolescent fathers than adult fathers? *Family Relations, 60*, 247–258. https://doi.org/10.1111/j.1741-3729.2011.00651.x

Fagot, B. I., Pears, K. C., Capaldi, D. M., Crosby, L., & Leve, C. S. (1998). Becoming an adolescent father: Precursors and parenting. *Developmental Psychology, 34*(6), 1209–1219. https://doi.org/10.1037/0012-1649.34.6.1209

Finch, J. P., & Bacon, K. M. (2015). Teen fathers: Implications for school counselors. *Michigan Journal of Counseling Research, Theory, and Practice, 42*(1), 4–12. https://doi.org/10.22237/mijoc/1441065660

Futris, T. G., & Schoppe-Sullivan, S. J. (2007). Mothers' perceptions of barriers, parenting alliance, and adolescent fathers' engagement with their children. *Family Relations, 56*, 258–269. https://doi.org/10.1111/j.1741-3729.2007.00457.x

Ganong, L., & Coleman, M. (2004). *Stepfamily relationships: Development, dynamics, and interventions*. Kluwer Academic/Plenum. https://doi.org/10.1007/978-1-4419-9112-6

Guzzo, K. B., & Furstenberg, F. F. (2007). Multipartnered fertility among American men. *Demography, 44*(3), 583–601. https://doi.org/10.1353/dem.2007.0027

Guzzo, K. B. (2014). New partners, more kids: Multiple-partner fertility in the United States. *The Annals of the American Academy of Political and Social Science, 654*(1), 66–86. https://doi.org/10.1177/0002716214525571

Harding, J. F., Zief, S., Farb, A., & Margolis, A. (2020). Supporting expectant and parenting teens: New evidence to inform future programming and research. *Maternal and Child Health Journal, 24*(Suppl 2), S67–S75. https://doi.org/10.1007/s10995-020-02996-2

Holtslander, L. (2005). Clinical application of the 15-minute family interview: Addressing the needs of postpartum families. *Journal of Family Nursing, 11*(1), 5–18. https://doi.org/10.1177/1074840704273092

Ivanova, K., Kalmijn, M., & Uunk, W. (2013). The effect of children on men's and women's chances of re-partnering in a European context. *European Journal of Population, 29*(4), 417–444. https://doi.org/10.1007/s10680-013-9294-5

Lee, Y., Fagan, J., & Chen, W. Y. (2012). Do late adolescent fathers have more depressive symptoms than older fathers? *Journal of Youth and Adolescence, 41*(10), 1366–1381. https://doi.org/10.1007/s10964-011-9717-8

Lundahl, B. W., Tollefson, D., Risser, H., & Lovejoy, M. C. (2008). A meta-analysis of father involvement in parent training. *Research on Social Work Practice, 18*(2), 97–106. https://doi.org/10.1177/1049731507309828

Keene, J. R., Prokos, A. H., & Held, B. (2012). Grandfather caregivers: Race and ethnic differences in poverty. *Sociological Inquiry, 82*(1), 49–77. https://doi.org/10.1111/j.1475-682x.2011.00398.x

Kiselica, M. S., Gorczynski, J., & Capps, S. (1998). Teen mothers and fathers: School counselor perceptions of service needs. *Professional School Counseling, 2*(2), 146–152.

Kiselica, M. S., & Kiselica, A. M. (2014). The complicated worlds of adolescent fathers: Implications for clinical practice, public policy, and research. *Psychology of Men & Masculinity, 15*(3), 260–274. https://doi.org/10.1037/a0037043

Knoester, C., & Eggebeen, D. J. (2006). The effects of the transition to parenthood and subsequent children on men's well-being and social participation. *Journal of Family Issues, 27*(11), 1532–1560. https://doi.org/10.1177/0192513x06290802

Koster, T., Poortman, A.-R., van der Lippe, T., & Kleingeld, P. (2020). Parenting in postdivorce families: The influence of residence, repartnering, and gender. *Journal of Marriage Family, 83*, 498–515. https://doi.org/10.1111/jomf.12740

Livingston, G. (2014). *Four-in-ten couples are saying 'I do,' again*. Pew Research Center. https://www.pewresearch.org/social-trends/2014/11/14/four-in-ten-couples-are-saying-i-do-again/

Logan, C., Manlove, J., Ikramullah, E., & Cottingham, S. (2006). Men who father children with more than one woman: A contemporary portrait of multiple-partner fertility. *Child Trends Research Brief, 10*. https://www.fatherhood.gov/sites/default/files/resource_files/e000000495.pdf

Manlove, J., Logan, C., Ikramullah, E., & Holcombe, E. (2008). Factors associated with multiple-partner fertility among fathers. *Journal of Marriage and Family, 70*(2), 536–548. https://doi.org/10.1111/j.1741-3737.2008.00499.x

Manuel, J. I. (2018). Racial/ethnic and gender disparities in health care use and access. *Health Services Research, 53*(3), 1407–1429. https://doi.org/10.1111/1475-6773.12705

McGene, J., & King, V. (2012). Implications of new marriages and children for coparenting in nonresident father families. *Journal of Family Issues, 33*(12), 1619–1641. https://doi.org/10.1177/0192513x12437150

McLanahan, S., Garfinkel, I., Mincy, R. B., & Donahue, E. (2010). Introducing the issue. *The Future of Children, 3–16*. https://www.jstor.org/stable/20773692

Meggiolaro, & Ongaro, F. (2008). Repartnering after marital dissolution: Does context play a role? *Demographic Research, 19*, 1913–1934. https://doi.org/10.4054/demres.2008.19.57

Monte, L. M. (2019). Multiple-partner fertility in the United States: A demographic portrait. *Demography, 56*(1), 103–127. https://doi.org/10.1007/s13524-018-0743-y

Monte, L. M. (2017). *Multiple partner fertility research brief.* US Department of Commerce, Economics and Statistics Administration, US Census Bureau. https://www.census.gov/content/dam/Census/library/publications/2017/demo/p70br-146.pdf

Monte, L. M. (2011). The chicken and the egg of economic disadvantage and multiple partner fertility: Which comes first in a sample of low-income women. *The Western Journal of Black Studies, 35*(1), 53–67. https://www.proquest.com/docview/1018071255?pq-origsite=gscholar&fromopenview=true.

Parra-Cardona, J. R., Sharp, E. A., & Wampler, R. S. (2008). "Changing for my kid": Fatherhood experiences of Mexican-Origin teen fathers involved in the justice system. *Journal of Marital and Family Therapy, 34*(3), 369–387. https://doi.org/10.1111/j.1752-0606.2008.00078.x

Payne, K. K. (2018). Change in the U.S. remarriage rate, 2008 and 2016. https://www.bgsu.edu/ncfmr/resources/data/family-profiles/payne-change-remarriage-rate-fp-18-16.html

Petren, R. E. (2017). Paternal multiple partner fertility and environmental chaos among unmarried nonresident fathers. *Journal of Social Service Research, 43*(1), 100–114. https://doi.org/10.1080/01488376.2016.1235069

Philpott, L. F., & Corcoran, P. (2018). Paternal postnatal depression in Ireland: Prevalence and associated factors. *Midwifery, 56*, 121–127. https://doi.org/10.1016/j.midw.2017.10.009

Poortman, A. R. (2007). The first cut is the deepest? The role of the relationship career for union formation. *European Sociological Review, 23*(5), 585–598. https://doi.org/10.1093/esr/jcm024

Silva, C., Pinto, C., & Martins, C. (2021). Transition to fatherhood in the prenatal period: A qualitative study. *Ciência & Saúde Coletiva, 26*, 465–474. https://doi.org/10.1590/1413-81232021262.41072020

Rempel, G. R., Neufeld, A., & Kushner, K. E. (2007). Interactive use of genograms and ecomaps in family caregiving research. *Journal of Family Nursing, 13*(4), 403–419. https://doi.org/10.1177/1074840707307917

Roy, K. M., & Lucas, K. (2006). Generativity as second chance: Low-income fathers and transformation of the difficult past. *Research in Human Development, 3*(2–3), 139–159. https://doi.org/10.1080/15427609.2006.9683366

Saleh, M. F., Buzi, R. S., Weinman, M. L., & Smith, P. B. (2005). The nature of connections: Young fathers and their children. *Adolescence, 40*(159), 513–523.

Shadik, J. A., & O'Connor, M. K. (2016). Fathering and child maltreatment: Building theory to enhance treatment interventions. *Social Work Research, 40*(4), 213–224. https://doi.org/10.1093/swr/svw016

Shadik, J. A. (2020). Fathering and child maltreatment: Understanding the impact of fluidity in fathers' lives. *Journal of Family Social Work, 23*(3), 257–276. https://doi.org/10.1080/10522158.2020.1725794

Shafer, K., & Bellamy, J. L. (2016). Focusing on men and fathers: A challenge for social work research and practice. *Social Work Research, 40*(4), 199–202. https://www.jstor.org/stable/24899407

Singley, D. B., & Edwards, L. M. (2015). Men's perinatal mental health in the transition to fatherhood. *Professional Psychology: Research and Practice, 46*(5), 309. https://doi.org/10.1037/pro0000032

SmithBattle, L., Phengnum, W., Shagavah, A. W., & Okawa, S. (2019). Fathering on tenuous ground: A qualitative meta-synthesis on teen fathering. *MCN: The American Journal of Maternal/Child Nursing, 44*(4), 186–194. https://doi.org/10.1097/NMC.0000000000000536

Stelle, C. D., & Sheehan, N. W. (2011). Exploring paternal maturity in the relationships between older fathers and adult children. *The International Journal of Aging and Human Development, 72*(1), 45–65. https://doi.org/10.2190/ag.72.1.c

Strauss, R., & Goldberg, W. A. (1999). Self and possible selves during the transition to fatherhood. *Journal of Family Psychology, 13*(2), 244. https://doi.org/10.1037/0893-3200.13.2.244

Sweeney, M. (2010). Remarriage and stepfamilies: Strategic sites for family scholarship in the 21st century. *Journal of Marriage and Family, 72*(3), 667–684. https://doi.org/10.1111/j.1741-3737.2010.00724.x

Tach, L., Edin, K., Harvey, H., & Bryan, B. (2014). The family-go-round: Family complexity and father involvement from a father's perspective. *The Annals of the American Academy of Political and Social Science, 654*(1), 169–184. https://doi.org/10.1177/0002716214528655

Thullen, M. J., McMillin, S. E., Korfmacher, J., Humphries, M., Bellamy, J. L., Henson, L., & Hans, S. (2014). Father participation in a community-doula home-visiting intervention for young, African American mothers. *Infant Mental Health Journal, 35*(5), 422–434. https://doi.org/10.1002/imhj.21463

Torche, F., & Rauf, T. (2021). The transition to fatherhood and the health of men. *Journal of Marriage and Family, 83*(2), 446–465. https://doi.org/10.1111/jomf.12732

Turney, K., & Carlson, M. J. (2011). Multipartnered fertility and depression among fragile families. *Journal of Marriage and Family, 73*(3), 570–587. https://doi.org/10.1111/j.1741-3737.2011.00828.x

U.S. Census Bureau. (2020). U.S. Marriage and Divorce Rates by State: 2009 & 2019 [Infographic]. *The United States Census Bureau.* https://www.census.gov/library/visualizations/interactive/marriage-divorce-rates-by-state-2009-2019.html

Vanassche, S., Corijn, M., Matthijs, K., & Swicegood, G. (2015). Repartnering and childbearing after divorce: Differences according to parental status and custodial arrangements. *Population Research and Policy Review, 34*(5), 761–784. https://doi.org/10.1007/s11113-015-9366-9

Walsh, T. B., Davis, R. N., Palladino, C. L., Romero, V. C., & Vijay Singh, M. D. (2014). Moving up the "magic moment": Fathers' experience of prenatal ultrasound. *Fathering, 12*(1), 18–37. https://doi.org/10.3149/fth.1201.18

Whitley, D. M., & Fuller-Thomson, E. (2017). The health of the nation's custodial grandfathers and older single fathers: Findings from the behavior risk factor surveillance system. *American Journal of Men's Health, 11*(6), 1614–1626. https://doi.org/10.1177/1557988315621604

Wilson, M. N. (1989). Child development in the context of the Black extended family. *American Psychologist, 44*(2), 380–385. https://doi.org/10.1037/0003-066X.44.2.380

Winstanley, M. R., Meyers, S. A., & Florsheim, P. (2002). Psychosocial correlates of intimacy achievement among adolescent fathers-to-be. *Journal of Youth and Adolescence, 31*(2), 91–100. https://doi.org/10.1023/A:1014093308760

Xie, H., Cairns, B. D., & Cairns, R. B. (2001). Predicting teen motherhood and teen fatherhood: Individual characteristics and peer affiliations. *Social Development, 10*(4), 488–511. https://doi.org/10.1111/1467-9507.00177

Chapter 4
Engaging Fathers Within Programs, Organizations, and Systems

Kimberly A. Dent, Ann M. Ream, and Jennifer L. Bellamy

Introduction

Parent, family, and community programs, organizations, and systems can serve to either help or hinder father engagement. Engagement is about motivating and empowering fathers and their families to recognize their strengths, needs, and resources and to take an active role in making changes for the better. Ongoing engagement in a genuinely supportive relationship with a father helps to maintain the ability of fathers and families to work toward positive change. Recognizing and respecting that fathers count as much as mothers in parenthood is paramount, and when fathers are considered true partners in their children's lives, it is to the benefit of the children. Finding unique ways to engage and support fathers should be an equal if not more of a top priority in practice as engaging and supporting mothers.

In this chapter, we explore the multi-level factors that impact the ability of programs, organizations, and systems to successfully engage fathers. We draw on the existing research as well as the collective experience of the first two authors in leadership and service provision. The two lead authors for this chapter have long-standing experience in program administration and service delivery in Ohio. Kimberly Dent brings over 23 years of government experience to the fathers and

K. A. Dent
Ohio Commission on Fatherhood, Columbus, OH, USA
e-mail: Kimberly.Dent@jfs.ohio.gov

A. M. Ream
Summit County Children Services, Akron, OH, USA
e-mail: Ann.Ream@summitkids.org

J. L. Bellamy (✉)
University of Denver, Graduate School of Social Work, Denver, CO, USA
e-mail: Jennifer.Bellamy@du.edu

J. L. Bellamy et al. (eds.), *Social Work Practice with Fathers*,
https://doi.org/10.1007/978-3-031-13686-3_4

families she serves, and Ann Ream has been employed at Summit County Children Services (SCCS) for nearly 30 years.[1]

Historically, fathers have not been as involved as mothers in many systems, including child welfare, early childhood services, and child support. This chapter is designed to assist systems, organizations, and programs to identify how they can increase their multi-level, equitable, and ongoing approaches to father engagement. Although many examples in this chapter are drawn from child welfare because of the experiences of the primary authors, the principles of father engagement across different services and systems are similar. For a variety of reasons, child welfare practice has been unkind to fathers, oftentimes even ignoring their existence. They have been referred to as ghosts, unseen and assumed missing (Brown et al., 2009). Involving fathers in child welfare case plans has not always been common practice within the public system, and often these fathers are not engaged in supportive services.

Background and Context

National Policy Context

Processes and policies over the decades provide important background and context for understanding the engagement (or disengagement) of fathers in systems and programs at the national level. Over 80 years ago, public assistance rules and other government benefit programs like the Aid to Families with Dependent Children

[1] Kimberly Dent is currently the executive director of the Ohio Commission on Fatherhood, Ohio Department of Job and Family Services. She brings over 23 years of government experience to the fathers and families she serves in Ohio. The Ohio Commission on Fatherhood provides funding to Responsible Fatherhood programs throughout the state and makes policy recommendations. During her time with the government, Ms. Dent has served in various capacities in the local and state child support programs such as a child support caseworker at the local level, a program consultant, a business analyst and a human services program administrator in County Services, Policy as well as Outreach, Education and Grants Management units at the State Office of Child Support. Ms. Dent has also served as a commissioner on the Ohio Commission on Fatherhood, representing the Ohio Department of Job and Family Services Director.

The second author, Ann Ream has been employed at Summit County Children Services for nearly 30 years. Her responsibilities at the agency have included protective services social worker, family meeting coordinator and facilitator, supervisor of the family meeting unit, supervisor of the paid placement unit, Protective Services Department director and her current position as the department director of community relations. Ms. Ream has also played a pivotal role in bringing team decision-making meetings to the agency. In addition, Ms. Ream has chaired the agency's Father Factor initiative which has promoted the engagement of fathers in child welfare. This work became the catalyst for the development of a best practice guide for the state of Ohio on strategies to improve identifying, locating, and engaging fathers and paternal family members in child welfare. Ms. Ream has served as a Governor appointee as a Commissioner for The Ohio Commission on Fatherhood for over 6 years.

(AFDC) were provided to low-income mothers with children, if there was no father or "man" in the home. This policy incentivized single-mother heads of households. Both parents found themselves in situations where difficult decisions were made to shelter, clothe, and feed their children at the cost of keeping men as parents out of the home. In 1975, Congress enacted the Child Support Program under Title D of the Social Security Act. The IV-D Program was designed to locate absent parents (primarily men), establish paternity, set child support orders, and collect on those orders. The main purpose of the Child Support Program was to collect payments from non-custodial or non-residential parents of children receiving cash assistance. Payments were collected to reimburse the state for AFDC and the later iteration of that policy called Temporary Assistance to Needy Families (TANF).

These are examples of policies that cast the father as an "absent parent" with the sole obligation of providing financial support to the child or reimbursing the state for money received by the caretaker of his child. Child support programs were given authority to suspend driver's licenses and professional licenses, intercept federal tax refunds, intercept bank accounts, suspend passports, and sentence the non-custodial parent to jail or prison time for non-payment of support. This practice also contributed to the mass incarceration of low-income African American fathers, who were overrepresented among low-income nonresidential fathers (Brito, et al., 2020). What is more, these fathers continued to incur debt while incarcerated, leaving them thousands of dollars in arrears and pushing them out of employment (Holzer et al., 2005). These federal programs and practices shaped larger cultural narratives about fathers that were reflected in other service systems, organizations, and programs that were largely designed to serve mothers. For example, the major evidence-based home visiting programs developed in the United States were designed for mothers (Bellamy et al., 2020).

In 2005, under the Bush administration, Health and Human Services, Administration for Children and Families, and the Office of Family Assistance offered grants to states and non-profit organizations to promote healthy marriage and fatherhood. These 5 year grants were funded by TANF, and the fourth cohort of these Healthy Marriage Responsible Fatherhood (HMRF) grants continue to help states and local communities provide low-income fathers with the services and resources to become better parents and co-parents. Government agencies and family-serving organizations continue to recognize the importance of engaging and empowering fathers, especially those in marginalized communities. Just as the earlier policies—focused on mothers as parents and treating fathers as absent or simply financial resources—shaped state and local programs and broader system responses to fathers, the HMRF's investment in fatherhood programs and research in the late 1990s and early 2000s began to shift the narrative toward father inclusion. More efforts to engage and serve fathers in fatherhood programs and other service systems have emerged alongside mounting research that demonstrated fathers' contributions to child and family well-being. These shifts were followed by the implementation of a variety of initiatives on the state and local levels as well.

For example, in 2011 the Ohio Commission on Fatherhood (OCF) launched the first ever Ohio County Fatherhood Initiative, which included collaborations and coordinated services between community leaders. Participating counties received training, including how to conduct a needs and assets assessment in their communities, guidance, and assistance on how to implement a community action plan on fatherhood. The OCF provided training at no cost to the counties, each receiving a one-time $10,000 implementation grant to begin or continue fatherhood programs in their county. The leadership teams brought together stakeholders in a variety of service systems, including a combination of county commissioners or state representatives; family or domestic relations judges; directors of child support; directors of child welfare; leaders of local faith-based entities or businesses; community fathers; and corrections representatives from jail or community corrections.

Changing Roles of Fathers in the Family

Although mothers continue to provide the majority of direct childcare, fathers—including young, low-income, nonresident fathers—are more involved than has sometimes been assumed or portrayed in the literature or popular culture (Perry et al., 2012). Fathers have become increasingly involved in the socialization (Bianchi & Milkie, 2010) and direct care of children in recent years (Jones & Mosher, 2013). According to the National Fatherhood Initiative (NFI) millennial, fathers view parenting as an essential part of their identity (National Fatherhood Initiative, 2019). In addition to shifts in father involvement in caring for children, newer generations do not tend to marry as often as previous generations, making unmarried and nonresidential fathers a large group. Although family demographics, calls for father engagement, and parenting practices have evolved over time, service systems have not kept pace with these changes.

Barriers to Father Engagement

Biases

Caseworker bias regarding father involvement is one of the most widely researched barriers to father participation in child welfare case planning (Baum, 2017). Caseworkers often take for granted the mother's connection to the child and require that fathers demonstrate their relationship to the child (Rosenberg, 2006). Caseworker biases may also be amplified because of the gendered nature of the human services and social work fields. For example, about 90% of master's level social workers identify as female (CSWE, 2018). In our experience, caseworkers may not even realize that they hold these biases and bring them into their work with fathers. In trainings and meetings, we have heard caseworkers and supervisors describe having negative personal experiences with men and fathers and that these biases shape their work. For example, when examining the differential rates of father engagement practices in Ohio, one supervisor disclosed their self-assessed bias against fathers. This supervisor went on to say that their biases existed related to their feelings about their father as well as their former spouse. Their life experience included abuse as a child and a dysfunctional abusive marital relationship, and these negative experiences spilled over into their work with fathers.

By failing to acknowledge a present and engaged father in that child's life, these biases can unintentionally contribute to the trauma the children involved with service systems experience. If the caseworker has a negative bias toward the child's father, they may not acknowledge the father in the case plan and exclude him from supportive services to help him gain custody of his child. Ignoring that relationship further traumatizes the child.

Unfortunately, fathers have been stereotyped as "absent," "not involved," and "sperm donors;" these and other similar derogatory descriptions can be reflected not just in staff interactions with fathers but also in program eligibility rules, assessment tools, physical environments, and other places. An important part of father engagement in programs, organizations, and systems is acknowledging and addressing the biases of the individuals who work within these systems and how these biases can be reflected in the written and unwritten organizational policies and practices.

Failure to Identify, Locate, and Communicate with Fathers

In some systems, fathers are not consistently identified or located. If a father is not "known" to a system, he cannot be engaged. For example, child welfare caseworkers may not seek to identify a father until his rights are in the process of being terminated, or caseworkers may not work to include incarcerated fathers in child welfare cases. This is so even though research indicates that family engagement in incarceration, specifically father and child engagement, reduces recidivism (La Vigne et al., 2008). Just as child welfare caseworkers may not seek to work with fathers, men involved in the criminal justice system may not be treated as parents and may not have access to programming or opportunities to build or maintain relationships with their children. One of the authors worked with a juvenile corrections facility that wanted to improve their support of young fathers but had never counted how many fathers they had in custody. These problems are not limited to these large systems. Child and family serving programs may similarly not seek to identify or communicate with fathers. For example, one study found that one-third of fathers had no contact with their child's preschool teacher, and that lack of contact increased to over 50% in kindergarten. The same study found that father-school communication occurred at a rate of 10% of family-school communication with other caregivers (Rimm-Kaufman & Zhang, 2005).

Leadership, Supervision, and the Organizational Culture

The problem of father engagement is not one that rests with caseworkers alone. The caseworkers may not have been trained and supervised to work with fathers and father engagement, or the culture and leadership of the agency or office may be focused on mothers and maternal relatives. If father engagement is not explicitly and intentionally targeted in systems, organizations, and programs, fathers are not likely to be successfully engaged; it must be built into leadership, supervision, and organizational culture. In our experience, caseworkers and human services professionals are pulled in many different directions, and they face many competing demands. If father engagement is not well understood by system, organization, or program leadership and continuously emphasized as a priority, it is likely to be set aside when other pressing, important, and time-consuming tasks take precedence (e.g., Agosti et al., 2021). Leaders play an important role in setting the organizational priorities, policies, and messaging that shape the culture related to father engagement and can be barriers when they do not consistently center father engagement in their work.

Exclusion of Fathers in Tools, Data Systems, and Evaluation Practices

Because many programs and systems were set up when parenting and parenting services were primarily focused on mothers as parents, many parenting assessments, forms, and data systems do not include fathers or more than one parent. For example, a recent study of the engagement of fathers and paternal relatives in child welfare found that although child welfare data systems sought to track father identification, location, and participation in services to use continuous quality improvement to increase father engagement, they were not designed to collect data about fathers and could not be easily adapted to do so (Fung et al., 2021). Many standardized instruments designed to measure the important aspects of parenting were similarly developed for mothers and may not work as well for fathers. In other cases, tools may be designed only for biologically related or married fathers. Some efforts, including those by the Fatherhood Research and Practice Network (FRPN), have sought to not only develop father-specific measures but also tools appropriate for use with nonresidential fathers and fathers parenting children of various ages. In home visiting, for example, home visitors report rarely using standardized assessment tools with fathers (Bellamy et al., in press).

Policy Context

The final barrier we would like to highlight is the policy context. As we described earlier in this chapter, throughout the twentieth and early twenty-first centuries, most local, state, and federal benefits targeted custodial families to provide a safety net for the family. US social welfare policy has traditionally focused on supporting "single" custodial parents, typically mothers, and children, ignoring noncustodial parents who are contributing financially and emotionally to the support of their children. This social policy was based on a definition of family as "custodial parent(s) and their children," assuming, we presume, that the custodial parent would engage the noncustodial parent if appropriate. One of the consequences of this policy has been the creation of financial and service inequities between mothers and fathers in a child's life. Service systems, organizations, and programs must work within the policy context but they can also work to implement father-inclusive policies and pursue advocacy efforts to change policies that present barriers to father engagement.

Conceptual Framing

Continuous and Multi-level Engagement

Involving the father and his family early on, continuously, and through multiple service systems, organizations, and programs will help to ensure the best outcomes for children, mothers, and fathers. Now more than ever, it is critical that government systems, including child protective services agencies, education, healthcare, and criminal justice, realize the importance not only of including fathers in the development of, and positive measured outcomes for, children but also of implementing strategies that support these results. Decades of research have informed society that healthy, responsible, and supportive fathers yield positive outcomes for their children as they develop into adults (e.g., Cano et al., 2019; McWayne et al., 2013; Sarkadi et al., 2008). The contribution of fathers begins at, or even before, conception. Mothers-to-be certainly experience healthier birth outcomes with the existence of a support system, especially the father of the child (e.g., Braun et al., 2017). Early and ongoing strategies to engage fathers over the course of their fathering career are vital for the relational foundation between parents and their infants. Programs, organizations, and systems need to be built on the assumption that fathers want to be involved in their children's lives by having a loving and caring relationship with them, and that this relationship is lifelong.

In a recent interview with the NFI, the first author of this chapter said:

> The most important thing for organizations to understand, when it comes to serving fathers effectively, is that most fathers want to be there for their children. Do not stereotype and judge fathers as non-factors and unimportant to their children. Remember that effective services for fathers contribute to the foundation of healthier, more resilient families and better developed children. Many fathers did not have a father or positive male role model in their lives while growing up; therefore, they, too, are trying to learn what a good father looks like and how to be that for their children. Meet them where they are in a non-judgmental way. Programming for fathers is not cookie-cutter. Fathers require different supports, education, and resources during various stages of their journey as dads.

Strengths-Based Approach

A strengths-based approach emphasizes self-determination and strengths. This is an approach that should be applied when involving and engaging fathers. Fathers play a central role in the positive development of their young children and influence an array of critical family outcomes. For example, infant mortality and racial disparities in infant mortality decrease significantly when a father is engaged and empowered to participate in protecting his child, particularly through the first year of his child's life (Alio et al., 2011). Highlighting fathers' strengths as parents helps to counter the historical deficits that many systems have put upon them. Fathers who are positively involved contribute to family well-being by contributing economically (Tamis-LeMonda et al., 2004), supporting mother-infant attachment quality (Hossain et al., 1994), promoting academic achievement (Jeynes, 2015), and reducing adverse outcomes in children such as aggression, delinquency, depression, and anxiety (Amato & Gilbreth, 1999).

Research indicates fathers play an important role in the lives of their children, in part, because they are not mothers (Pruett, 1998). Some research, such as Doucet (2006), shows that the playful interactions between caregiving fathers and their children differ from the playful interactions between mothers and their children; men tend to be more sports-oriented and physical, for example (Doucet, 2006). Each gender teaches something essential to the child, with mother care being more repetitive and rhythmic and father care being less predictable and more playful (Pruett, 1998). Fathers provide protection, economic support and serve as male role models, and children are impoverished developmentally when they are deprived of their father's love.

While positive fathering contributes to child and family well-being, it is also true that children whose fathers engage in negative parenting behaviors are more likely to evidence conduct problems, as well as conduct problems such as aggressive and disruptive behaviors (e.g., Stormshak et al., 2000). Furthermore, negative relationship behaviors between mothers and fathers—such as interpersonal violence—have been linked with aggression, depression, and cognitive delays in children (Shipman et al., 1999; Sousa et al., 2011). Using a strengths-based approach does not mean that we ignore these risks but rather that we thoughtfully assess fathers' contributions to families in a balanced way to assess family service needs more fully, support fathers' strengths, and intervene to provide services and supports when paternal risks are identified, just as we do with mothers.

Recommended Strategies and Practices

Leadership, Training, and Supervision

The best practice of engaging fathers will begin to expand within a system, organization, or program once efforts are required from both the top-down and bottom-up. These efforts need to move beyond recommendations and encouraged best practices, which tend to be viewed as optional in practice, to explicit policies and procedures. This can start with training on fathers and father engagement. Caseworkers who are engaged in child and family serving systems certainly need this training, but many different system stakeholders and other professionals and paraprofessionals can also benefit. For example, courts and guardian ad litems, or court-appointed special advocates, play a critical role in child welfare; their training should also include the importance of a father in the life of a child.

In order to establish a relationship and successfully engage with fathers, caseworkers and practitioners must be aware of their biases about fathers and fatherhood. It is likely that most people establish their views about fathers based on their own life experiences, or for practitioners, perhaps by their professional involvement with a father. Being aware of biases enables the practitioner to do self-checks throughout their involvement with fathers to ensure they are not impacting their work.

Earlier in this chapter, we described a supervisor who had personal experiences and biases that were getting in the way of their successful engagement of fathers. That supervisor recognized their personal biases and worked hard to ensure they did not permeate into their professional practice and ultimately negatively impact child outcomes in the cases in their unit. Through training, awareness, and acknowledgment, the supervisor was able to address their biases against fathers and improve their practice and supervisory skills.

Training and work on biases is not a "one and done" approach. Supervisors need to cue caseworkers to attend to fathers in families and address father-engagement in supervision practices through tracking and evaluating father-engagement efforts and requiring the inclusion of fathers on all tools, in family communications, and in family meetings.

Efforts to Identify and Locate Fathers

In order to engage fathers in systems, organizations, and programs, efforts must first be made to identify and locate them. For example, some states, such as Ohio, implement family engagement activities that include father-child interaction. Child welfare caseworkers and child support staff must continue to identify, locate, and engage fathers in case plans even when fathers have been incarcerated. In some states and counties, systems such as Ohio's Child Support Enforcement Tracking System (SETS) are beginning to share information to support efforts to locate and identify fathers (Fung et al., 2021). If a dad is incarcerated when his child becomes child-welfare involved, it is imperative that he is notified and possibly added to the child welfare case plan or the paternal family should be engaged in the process. The current Ohio Department of Rehabilitation and Correction (ODRC) director has an interest in determining how caseworkers can engage with a father when he is incarcerated. The director is making efforts to change practice so that fathers labeled as "unavailable" due to incarceration are instead approached as "available" and efforts are made to engage them if not in person, then through video conferences or phone calls. Too often, a father is not informed until after the child has been placed with other kin or placed in the foster care system. The Office of Families and Children (OFC), Ohio Department of Job and Family Services (ODJFS), plan to meet with leadership at ODRC to discuss how ODRC staff at the prisons can better assist with in-person visits with incarcerated fathers.

Another important way of making sure these partnerships are successful in ensuring that policy keeps up with changes in societal needs, for example, changing monthly in-person prison visits to virtual visits. Because of COVID-19, many prisons will not allow visitors, but this should not impede the caseworker from connecting with a father while he is incarcerated.

Creating a Multi-level Culture of Father Inclusion

Systems, organizations, and programs can use many different approaches to create a culture of father inclusion. For example, at Summit County Children Services (SCCS), a child welfare-providing organization in Ohio, they have empowered male staff, who are supported by the organization to engage and build an ongoing rapport with fathers visiting their children. These visits are important for strengthening fathers' parenting skills and reunification and help to promote bonding and attachment. This deliberate attention to fathers and demonstration that staff value men as parents increased father participation in parenting time during visits. Communicating with fathers, greeting them, supporting them throughout the visit, and encouraging them to come back for their next scheduled visit have been successful.

Inter-system collaboration is another important approach given how many families are served by the same intersecting systems. For example, the OCF is currently working with Passages Fatherhood Program in Cleveland, Ohio to fund a fatherhood practitioner position at the Cuyahoga County Public Children Services Agency. As part of the Public Children Services Association of Ohio (PCSA), this practitioner will be tasked with building trust among the caseworkers as well as engaging and empowering the fathers on their caseloads. Other child welfare jurisdictions have used strategies such as making supervised visitation spaces more home-like and welcoming and offering services to fathers during visits (Fung et al., 2021).

Continuous Efforts at Improvement and Assessment

Engaging and involving fathers and their family members is vital for father engagement. All programs, organizations, and systems should examine their assessment and reassessment of barriers practices to determine what might be precluding fathers from being viewed as a parent and an important resource to their families. A needs assessment should be conducted when working with and engaging fathers as it can help generate optimum opportunities to partner with fathers throughout their involvement. Exploring different strategies such as continuous quality improvement (e.g., Fung et al., 2021) to engage fathers is recommended as this is not a one-size-fits-all approach.

An important aspect of continuous improvement efforts is collecting data from fathers themselves. For example, Table 4.1 from the Ohio Commission on Fatherhood's Annual Report depicts the services requested by fathers when discussing their individual fathering goals. One point worth noting is that they were interested in learning how to become better fathers by enrolling in fatherhood classes taught by practitioners using various evidence-based or evidence-informed fatherhood curricula recognized by the OCF. Data to help identify barriers, needs, and ideas for systems, organization, and program improvements can be collected from fathers using surveys, focus groups, or interviews.

Fathers' needs and engagement should also be assessed and reassessed. For example, in the Dads Matter-HV intervention, if at the initial assessment it is determined that the father is not in the right place to engage due to domestic violence concerns or other risks, other services and referrals are used to reassess the father rather than dismissing him from inclusion (Bellamy et al., 2020).

Shifting the Policy Frame

Mr. Steve Killpack from the Ohio Practitioners' Network for Fathers and Families (OPNFF) proposes addressing the historical focus on single parents (primarily mothers) by defining the term "family" through the eyes and hearts of the children (personal communication, n.d.). Children simply see parents, not custodial or noncustodial parents. If we are truly committed to building a safety net around them, it is imperative that we design a social policy that engages and supports both the custodial and noncustodial parents and their respective families as both parents provide for their children financially, spiritually, and emotionally.

For example, when the client is the child rather than the custodial parent, the financial benefits follow the child whether they are with their mother, father (or both), or a kinship caregiver. This change in policy from custodial parent to child

Table 4.1 Services requested by fathers

What are the top areas where you need help?	
Interested in participating in a fatherhood class	889 (40%)
Need help with child support	390 (18%)
Need help seeing my child(ren)	436 (20%)
Need help with employment	448 (20%)
Expecting a child and need help preparing	60 (3%)

Ohio commission on fatherhood's annual report state fiscal year 2021 would allow the extension of TANF job and education benefits and earned income tax credit for noncustodial fathers or kinship caregivers who are financially and emotionally involved with the child, like those offered to single custodial mothers. In addition, access to school records as well as medical records would then be available to both parents. Current access to these services is only available to the mother in situations where the parents are unmarried. If the client is the child, programs and service systems can focus on supporting both parents to cooperate on behalf of the shared child rather than struggle with each other over access to the child and financial resources. In addition, schools can provide records to both parents in a child's life, engaging both parents and their families in the child's education.

Adding Programming and Father-Inclusive Spaces

In some systems and organizations, additional programming aimed specifically at fathers may be needed. For example, the OCF funds Dads2B, a program associated with Moms2B, a motherhood program focused on eliminating infant mortality in two Ohio counties. Expectant moms and dads connect during "Sister/Brother Circle" and are encouraged to ask questions and communicate successes and challenges. Fathers then step away with the project director of Dads2B and his staff and are provided pertinent information in a space where they can connect as expectant and new fathers. The topics of focus are based on healthy birth outcomes and supporting their wives, fiancées, girlfriends, or parent-partners, and protecting their infants during the first year of life. When fathers are engaged and given the opportunity to be involved with their children's lives, they can and often do make substantial contributions. Fathers need to be viewed as a parent on equal footing as mothers, not as backup plans for their child, and both parents need consistent information regarding safe sleep practices, breastfeeding, smoking cessation, and safe birth spacing.

Child welfare agencies have also been utilizing family decision-making models to make decisions as a team while optimizing family strengths. These meetings are one of the most effective ways to help children and involve their families, friends, community members, and professionals in critical decision-making related to child safety and placement. The organization and process are also viewed as transparent in partnering with families and the community from a strengths-based perspective. Involving fathers, including nonresidential and/or alleged fathers, in these meetings is important as they can be a support to the mother and child emotionally, financially, physically, and spiritually. Child welfare families are an important example, but other service systems, including healthcare and education, also use family meetings to facilitate important processes and decisions. For example, individualized education program meetings for children include parents. The father can be an additional resource option as the team, including the father, makes plans to ensure the child's well-being. It is essential for the caseworker or practitioner to assess the dynamics of the relationship between the father and mother as well as the father and child to best engage fathers in these meetings.

All family meetings, regardless of the model adhered to or system in which they are implemented, need to factor in fathers as they play an important part in the assessment and ongoing case process. Family meetings bring together the parents, family, extended family, the youth, if appropriate, and others in the family's social support network to make decisions regarding how to ensure the safety and well-being of the child. These meetings, led by a trained facilitator, are based on the family's strengths and can help the family develop a sense of hope and broaden their circle of support, both formal and informal, promoting family and cultural connections.

Father Engagement Collaboratives and Committees

Another effective practice is the creation of collaboratives or committees of diverse stakeholders tasked with improving father engagement in systems, organizations, and programs. While working on a 5-year-old child and family services plan (CFSR), the ODJFS and county partners recognized that Ohio counties struggled to identify, locate, and engage fathers and the paternal relatives of children involved in the child welfare system. ODJFS formed the Engaging Fathers Subcommittee, which included representatives from the OFC, the OCF, and county child welfare agencies of varying sizes and locations. The members of the subcommittee were dedicated to supporting child welfare agencies as they worked to help fathers and paternal relatives cultivate important and lasting connections with their children. A Best Practice Guide for Engaging Fathers: A Toolkit for Children Services Staff was developed, which contains suggestions for ways agencies can include fathers earlier and more effectively in each case in order to ensure the best outcomes for children. The committee acknowledged that child welfare agencies practice with varying levels and expectations of paternal engagement and that changing agency culture takes time and consistent effort as it is a large-scale undertaking. Included in the guide is an assessment tool for agency readiness in developing a fatherhood program.

There are several items on the assessment tool that can help change the organizational culture related to fathers. Encouraging father involvement through organizational support and shared values is key to moving the needle toward culture change; one way of doing this is to include the subject of fathers in all staff, division, and department meetings. It is also important that staff recognize that fathers and mothers parent differently. In practice, it means ensuring that father involvement is discussed in all case conferences, team meetings, decisions, and case planning reviews. Having consistent father-friendly visual reminders to include and engage fathers is essential, such as father-specific flyers and brochures and having changing stations in the men's restrooms. Changing culture is not a mandate but a movement. The Best Practice Guide is intended to be used by all child welfare agencies regardless of where they are in the process of fatherhood program development and practice.

In conclusion, when programs, organizations, and service systems engage, empower, and partner with the whole family, child outcomes will improve and children are more likely to thrive. Fathers must be considered as essential contributors to the family. Improving the levels of engagement with fathers across systems has a positive impact on children, which is invaluable. Promoting responsible fatherhood is much cheaper than paying for the consequences of father absence or exclusion. When fathers acquire the skills they need to be responsible fathers, children are better off and better positioned to build their own strong families. Families are better off because of a father's love, care, and emotional and financial support, and taxpayer dollars are saved as families are more likely to be well functioning and self-sufficient.

Resources

- A Best Practice Guide for Engaging Fathers: A Toolkit for Children Services Staff: Best Practice Guide for Fathers (online).
- Best Practice Guide for Engaging Fathers: A toolkit for Children Services Staff
- http://fatherhood.ohio.gov/Portals/0/Revised%20FINAL_JFS-01444%20Best%20Practice%20Guide%20for%20Fathers%20(online).pdf
- Fatherhood Research & Practice Network – www.frpn.org
- www.ParentsAsTeachers.org
- The Ohio Commission on Fatherhood – www.fatherhood.ohio.gov

Discussion Questions

1. How should caseworker training address negative stereotypes and biases about fathers?
2. What does successful father engagement in your system, organization, or program look like?
3. What data would be important to track to improve father engagement in your service system, organization, or program?
4. What community partners outside of your organization are important to include in training and other efforts to increase father engagement?
5. What can leaders do to set the tone and expectation that fathers are continuously engaged using a strengths-based approach?

References

Agosti, J., Bellamy, J. L., Burton, L., Graves, A. M., Lau, C., & Mahoney, J. (2021). A breakthrough series on engaging fathers and paternal relatives in child welfare: A system response to COVID-19 and racial unrest. *Journal of the Society for Social Work and Research, 12*(3), 437–444. https://www.journals.uchicago.edu/doi/10.1086/715214

Alio, A. P., Mbah, A. K., Kornosky, J. L., Wathington, D., Marty, P. J., & Salihu, H. M. (2011). Assessing the impact of paternal involvement on racial/ethnic disparities in infant mortality rates. *Journal of Community Health, 36*(1), 63–68. https://doi.org/10.1007/s10900-010-9280-3

Amato, P. R., & Gilbreth, J. G. (1999). Nonresident fathers and children's well-being: A meta-analysis. *Journal of Marriage and Family, 61*(3), 557–573. https://doi.org/10.2307/353560

Baum, N. (2017). Gender-sensitive intervention to improve work with fathers in child welfare services. *Child & Family Social Work, 22*(1), 419–427. https://doi.org/10.1111/cfs.12259

Bellamy, J. L., Harty, J., Guterman, N., Banman, A., Morales-Mirque, S., & Massey Combs, K. (2020). *The engagement of fathers in home visiting services: Learning from the Dads Matter-HV study*, Fatherhood Research and Practice Network Report. https://www.frpn.org/asset/frpn-grantee-report-the-engagement-fathers-in-home-visiting-services-learning-the-dads-matter.

Bianchi, S. M., & Milkie, M. A. (2010). Work and family research in the first decade of the 21st century. *Journal of Marriage and Family, 72*(3), 705–725. https://doi.org/10.1111/j.1741-3737.2010.00726.x

Braun, J. M., Messerlian, C., & Hauser, R. (2017). Fathers matter: Why it's time to consider the impact of paternal environmental exposures on children's health. *Current Epidemiology Reports, 4*(1), 46–55. https://doi.org/10.1007/s40471-017-0098-8

Brito, T. L., Pate, D., & Wong, J. S. (2020). *Negotiating race and inequality in family court*. IRP Focus, Institute for Research on Poverty.

Brown, L., Callahan, M., Strega, S., Walmsley, C., & Dominelli, L. (2009). Manufacturing ghost fathers: The paradox of father presence and absence in child welfare. *Child & Family Social Work, 14*(1), 25–34. https://doi.org/10.1111/j.1365-2206.2008.00578.x

Cano, T., Perales, F., & Baxter, J. (2019). A matter of time: Father involvement and child cognitive outcomes. *Journal of Marriage and Family, 81*(1), 164–184. https://doi.org/10.1111/jomf.12532

CSWE (Council on Social Work Education). (2018). *2017–2018 annual report*. Council on Social Work Education.

Doucet, A. (2006). 'Estrogen-filled worlds': Fathers as primary caregivers and embodiment. *The Sociological Review, 54*(4), 696–716. https://doi.org/10.1111/j.1467-954X.2006.00667.x

Fung, N., Bellamy, J., Abendroth, E., Mittone, D., Bess, R., & Stagner, M. (2021). *A seat at the table: Piloting continuous learning to engage fathers and parental relatives in child welfare*, OPRE Report # 2021–62, Washington, DC: Office of Planning, Research, and Evaluation, Administration for Children and Families, U.S. Department of Health and Human Services.

Holzer, H. J., Offner, P., & Sorensen, E. (2005). Declining employment among young black less-educated men: The role of incarceration and child support. *Journal of Policy Analysis and Management: The Journal of the Association for Public Policy Analysis and Management, 24*(2), 329–350. https://doi.org/10.1002/pam.20092

Hossain, Z., Field, T., Gonzales, J., & Malphurs, J. (1994). Infants of depressed mothers interact better with their nondepressed fathers. *Infant Mental Health Journal, 15*(4), 348–357. https://doi.org/10.1002/1097-0355(199424)15:4<348::AID-IMHJ2280150404>3.0.CO;2-Y

Jeynes, J. H. (2015). A meta-analysis: The relationship between father involvement and student academic achievement. *Urban Education, 5*(4), 387–423. https://doi.org/10.1177/0042085914525789

Jones, J., & Mosher, W. D. (2013). *Fathers' involvement with their children: United States, 2006–2010 (National Health Statistics Reports No. 71)*. Retrieved from https://pubmed.ncbi.nlm.nih.gov/24467852/

La Vigne, N. G., Davies, E., & Brazzell, D. (2008). *Broken bonds: Understanding and addressing the needs of children with incarcerated parents*. Urban Institute.

McWayne, C., Downer, J. T., Campos, R., & Harris, R. D. (2013). Father involvement during early childhood and its association with children's early learning: A meta-analysis. *Early Education & Development, 24*(6), 898–922. https://doi.org/10.1080/10409289.2013.746932

National Fatherhood Initiative. (2019). *Father facts 8*. National Fatherhood Initiative.

The Ohio Commission on Fatherhood – www.fatherhood.ohio.gov.
Perry, A. R., Harmon, D. K., & Leeper, J. (2012). Resident Black fathers' involvement: A comparative analysis of married and unwed, cohabitating fathers. *Journal of Family Issues, 33*(6), 695–714. https://doi.org/10.1177/0192513X11428125
Pruett, K. D. (1998). Role of the father. *Pediatrics, 102*(Supplement_E1), 1253–1261.
Rosenberg, J. (2006). *The importance of fathers in the healthy development of children.* U.S. Department Health and Human Services, Administration for Children and Families, Administration on Children, Youth and Families, Children's Bureau, Office of Child Abuse and Neglect.
Sarkadi, A., Kristiansson, R., Oberklaid, F., & Bremberg, S. (2008). Fathers' involvement and children's developmental outcomes: A systematic review of longitudinal studies. *Acta Paediatrica, 97*(2), 153–158. https://doi.org/10.1111/j.1651-2227.2007.00572.x
Shipman, K. L., Rossman, B. R., & West, J. C. (1999). Co-occurrence of spousal violence and child abuse: Conceptual implications. *Child Maltreatment, 4*(2), 93–102. https://doi.org/10.1177/1077559599004002002
Sousa, C., Herrenkohl, T. I., Moylan, C. A., Tajima, E. A., Klika, J. B., Herrenkohl, R. C., et al. (2011). Longitudinal study on the effects of child abuse and children's exposure to domestic violence, parent-child attachments, and antisocial behavior in adolescence. *Journal of Interpersonal Violence, 26*(1), 111–136. https://doi.org/10.1177/0886260510362883
Stormshak, E. A., Bierman, K. L., McMahon, R. J., & Lengua, L. J. (2000). Parenting practices and child disruptive behavior problems in early elementary school. *Journal of Clinical Child Psychology, 29*(1), 17–29. https://doi.org/10.1207/S15374424jccp2901_3
Tamis-LeMonda, C. S., Shannon, J. D., Cabrera, N. J., & Lamb, M. E. (2004). Fathers and mothers at play with their 2- and 3-year-olds: Contributions to language and cognitive development. *Child Development, 75*(6), 1806–1820. https://doi.org/10.1111/j.1467-8624.2004.00818.x

Chapter 5
Engaging Fathers in Research and Evaluation

Qiana R. Cryer-Coupet and Stephen M. Gibson

Introduction

This chapter will provide an overview of factors that have impacted fathers' engagement in social work research and evaluation using a historical lens. Traditionally, more research has focused on mothers' parenting practices and their outcomes than that of fathers. As has been argued by social work scholars, we frame the relative exclusion and underrepresentation of fathers as a social justice issue (McAdoo, 1993; Shafer & Bellamy, 2016). Using the *Just Practice framework* (Finn & Jacobson, 2003) as a guide, we explore strategies for enhancing the inclusion of diverse perspectives from an array of fathers in research and evaluation. We contend that clear and intentional communication, prolonged partnership, and ethical research and evaluation protocols are all methods for improving father engagement in social work research. In this chapter, *program evaluation* is defined as "social work research that is conducted … to assess social programs" (Engel & Schutt, 2017, p. 344). As such, the terms social work research and evaluation are used interchangeably throughout the chapter.

Q. R. Cryer-Coupet (✉)
School of Social Work, Georgia State University, Atlanta, GA, USA
e-mail: qcryercoupet@gsu.edu

S. M. Gibson
Department of Psychology, Virginia Commonwealth University, Richmond, VA, USA
e-mail: gibsons4@vcu.edu

J. L. Bellamy et al. (eds.), *Social Work Practice with Fathers*,
https://doi.org/10.1007/978-3-031-13686-3_5

Background and Context

In 1990 Greif and Bailey posed the question: *Where are the fathers in social work literature?* In their review of five of the top social work journals over a period of 27 years, they found a scant literature base focused on the roles, outcomes, and engagement of fathers. Further, the literature that was present focused primarily on fathers as absent, abusers, or entangled in legal, relational, or economic battles (Greif & Bailey, 1990). They believed several factors contributed to the limited research and focus on deficits, including the logistical difficulty of reaching some fathers, stereotypical masculinity narratives, which may have precluded fathers from being present in spaces where families were recruited for research, and privilege being given to mothers' voices by nature of their family caregiving roles. Given the lack of a holistic focus on fathers, Grief and Bailey proposed a research agenda for the field of social work that focused on exploring the changing patterns of fatherhood.

Greif and Greif (1997) revisited the question of the presence of fathers in social work research less than a decade later. In their updated review, they noted an increase in content focused on fathers and a shift away from content predominantly focused on absence and abuse. As such, social work scholars were then beginning to focus on an expanded conceptualization of fathering, which included explorations of fathers as nurturers and multifaceted caregivers. The updated review did note, however, a remaining gap in the literature related to marginalized fathers, such as those from the LGBTQ community (Greif & Greif, 1997).

In the early 2000s, other scholars expanded the interrogation of father-focused literature in social work journals. For example, Strug and Wilmore-Schaeffer (2003) reviewed 118 articles that were written about fathers in major social work journals from 1977 to 2000. Their findings suggest that the literature was often focused on White, middle-class, married, and residential fathers. As such, only 28% of the articles in their review focused on the experiences and needs of noncustodial fathers, who lack primary oversight of their children's day-to-day care. Additionally, only 6% of the articles contained content about single fathers. In terms of cultural diversity, the review found that Black fathers were overrepresented in articles that focused on father absence, there was only one article that focused on the roles of Hispanic fathers, and no articles examined the experiences of Asian fathers (Strug & Wilmore-Schaeffer, 2003). In subsequent years, social work researchers have continued to highlight the underrepresentation of fathers in research, particularly within top social work journals (Shafer & Bellamy, 2016; Shapiro & Krysik, 2010). As scholars reflect on the subpopulations of fathers whose voices are important to engage in future research, they highlight the need to recruit and retain low-income and working-class fathers, minoritized fathers, immigrant fathers, single fathers, fathers of children with identified health and mental health needs, and fathers who are themselves experiencing health and mental health challenges (Guendelman et al., 2018; Mogro-Wilson et al., 2019; Nicholas et al., 2020; Walsh et al., 2020).

While calling for increased engagement of fathers in social work research, scholars have also noted difficulties in recruiting fathers. As such, various recruitment barriers may contribute to the underrepresentation of fathers as participants in family-based research (Cassano et al., 2006; Costigan & Cox, 2001; Mitchell et al., 2007) compared to mothers. One potential reason for this low participation is the perception that fathers are unavailable and often uninterested in participating in research. For instance, Cassano et al. (2006) suggested that, in comparison to mothers, fathers are more difficult to recruit, which reflects the historical frame of fathers as a "hard-to-reach" population (O'Brien, 2007). Some scholars also suggest that psychological and relationship barriers may be factors that impact father engagement in research. For example, some fathers may find the subject of the research interview to be emotionally triggering; for others, participating in interviews in close proximity to their partner or child's caregiver may mean they are not as forthcoming as they would be if interviewed alone (Macfadyen et al., 2011). As we will outline in this chapter, additional barriers to fathers' participation in research include issues related to maternal gatekeeping, lack of awareness regarding the purpose or significance of the research, and rigid scheduling imposed by researchers.

Conceptual Framing—Just Practice Framework

The historic under-engagement of fathers in social work research and evaluation practice is a social justice issue. This section outlines a critical social justice perspective that can be used to interrogate and enhance the inclusion of fathers in family research and evaluation. Finn and Jacobson (2003) developed the Just Practice framework (JPF) to challenge social workers to engage in practices that prioritize social justice. The framework supports an engaged practice approach that encourages people to interrogate everyday contradictions and restrictions that often serve as barriers to social justice and hope. As such, the framework pushes social workers to explore the social construction of reality from multiple perspectives. Finn and Jacobson (2003) outline five key themes that are inherent to Just Practice: meaning, history, power, context, and possibility. Below, we apply these concepts to the engagement of fathers in social work research and evaluation.

Meaning

According to Finn and Jacobson (2003), "meaning is often defined as the purpose or significance of something. All human beings are meaning makers" (p. 70). As such, it is important for social work researchers and evaluators to understand the meaning that men ascribe to fatherhood. For example, researchers have found that among low-income Black and Latino fathers who participate in responsible fatherhood programs, the meaning they ascribe to their fatherhood roles is often connected to their paternal behavior and interactions with their children. As such, for those who value being present and involved fathers, attending a fatherhood program may be important for them because it supports their ability to enhance the quality of their parenting (Randles, 2020). Understanding these values can help to shape recruitment, engagement, and retention efforts in family research. Similarly, researchers and evaluators are tasked with helping fathers make meaning of the research in which they are engaged or being asked to engage, and to clearly understand the purpose and value of research and its potential risks and benefits. This can be accomplished by implementing streamlined protocols that prioritize clear and open communication with fathers about the nature of the work and its value (Davidson et al., 2017).

History

As outlined in the framework, "attention to history moves us beyond here-and-now pragmatism and creates spaces for the examination of the structures, practices, and assumptions that have shaped our present circumstances" (Finn & Jacobson, 2003, p. 70). Mistrust regarding research participation is often rooted in the collective memory of ethical violations, particularly among men from minoritized communities (Randolph et al., 2018). For example, Cochran (1997) highlights the negative research-community impacts that were created because of researcher deception in the Tuskegee syphilis study with Black men in Alabama. Further, mistrust of public policy research was also created by the mischaracterization of deficits within Black family structures, particularly pertaining to the roles of fathers, as noted in the federally supported Moynihan Report. Additionally, Cochran (1997) purports that research products such as the Bell Curve Theory of Intelligence, which posits that Black individuals are inherently less intelligent than Whites, also harm the credibility of social science research among minoritized communities. Acknowledging the harm of deceitful and dismissive practices helps researchers build partnerships with fathers to better understand and protect their rights as participants in research and evaluation. Using informed consent documents to provide clear statements about participant rights throughout the research process and contact information for obtaining post-study updates are methods that can be employed to attend to negative research-community history.

Power

Closely related to the concept of history, the Just Practice framework highlights the importance of dismantling power imbalances. "Social justice work calls on us to ask how power is created, produced, legitimized, and used and to understand how relations of power influence the nature of social work practice" (Finn & Jacobson, 2003,

p. 71). When considering fathers' decisions to engage in research and evaluation, the questions of who is assessing the need for the research, developing the focus of the research, and framing the interpretation of findings highlight potential power imbalances within the researcher-father relationship. In working to address imbalances of power, especially among historically marginalized fathers, participatory action research frameworks hold remarkable possibilities for moving the field forward.

According to Rubin and Babbie (2016), by using a participatory action research approach, "the researcher serves as a resource to those being studied, as an opportunity for them to act effectively in their own interest ... the participants define their problems, define the remedies desired, and take the lead in designing the research that will help them realize their aims" (p. 309). In accordance with this approach, research is a tool not only for knowledge production but also for supporting critical consciousness (i.e., critical reflection, critical agency, and critical action). Braye and McDonnell (2013) highlight some of the difficulties of employing a truly participatory model within a university-community research partnership with young fathers in the United Kingdom. In their study, young fathers were trained in skills necessary to be qualitative researchers. Following training, the fathers developed interview guides, conducted interviews with other young fathers, and analyzed and interpreted findings. Braye and McDonald (2013) describe shifts in the power balance at various points of the research process, particularly related to interviewing styles and data quality. Acknowledgment of discomfort with shifting power by the university-researchers and the father-researchers led to discussions about the true possibility of eliminating power imbalances in participatory research. Noting these limitations, other scholars have relied on community-based research approaches that prioritize the synergetic strengths of community stakeholders and university researchers when developing and evaluating research efforts with fathers (Julion et al., 2018).

Context

When considering the vast array of paternal identities, it is important to consider the context of fathering as an important factor shaping engagement in research. "Context can be thought of as the set of circumstances and conditions that surround and influence particular events and situations"'(Finn & Jacobson, 2003, p. 70). Therefore, one's identity as a resident or nonresident father, racially minoritized father, teen father, single father, or LGBTQIA PLUS_SPI father, and many other possible intersecting identities impact the context for recruitment, engagement, and retention in research and evaluation efforts. For example, researchers are required to obtain parental consent and child/adolescent assent when engaging in research with individuals under the age of 18 (Engel & Schutt, 2017). As such, when seeking to recruit adolescent fathers, researchers have to include the teen's parent or guardian during the informed consent process. Researchers may also consider engaging the parent or guardian as a participant as well. This approach may help an adolescent father and his family to develop a stronger rapport with the research team. See Dallas (2009) for an exemplary study that employed this technique in acknowledgment of the unique context of adolescent fatherhood.

Possibility

The final theme of the JPF pushes us to consider the possibilities that can emerge by centering social justice in our research and evaluation practice with fathers. "A sense of possibility enables us to look at what has been done, at what can be done, and at what can exist" (Finn & Jacobson, 2003, p. 71). Scholars have outlined the various challenges of conducting research with fathers, which include identifying nonresident fathers, recruiting fathers when there is tension within the caregiver-father relationship, connecting with fathers who have varying work schedules, cultural or language barriers, and difficulty determining equitable incentive structures (Mitchell et al., 2007). When envisioning possibilities for research with fathers, the issue of determining a research incentive structure for incarcerated fathers comes up. Many states have policies in place that prohibit or limit the use of monetary research incentives for inmates (Smoyer et al., 2009). Considering this issue from a social justice perspective necessitates developing solutions with the incarcerated fathers themselves, as those closest to the issue are closest to the solution (Martin, 2017). In prior research with this subpopulation, innovative solutions such as sending monetary incentives to the inmate's children or family have been employed (Smoyer et al., 2009).

Recommended Strategies and Practices

Recruiting, maintaining, and sustaining research relationships with fathers remains a perennial challenge. Below, we offer strategies to overcome known barriers to recruiting and retaining fathers in social work research and evaluation. Each strategy is informed by the Just Practice framework.

Strategy 1: Community Advisory Board

JPF Themes to Consider: Power, History, Possibility

"Nothing about us without us" is a mantra made popular by disability advocates (Charlton, 1998) and is applicable when considering the role of fathers in social work research and evaluation. We espouse that fathers are key participants who should be involved in all aspects of research and evaluation planning. One

recommended strategy for ensuring this level of engagement is the development of a community and scientific advisory board. Prior to launching a study, researchers can assemble a group of community and scientific or substantive experts to assess needs, strategize design approaches, pilot instruments, and solicit wisdom regarding recruitment techniques. In instances where prolonged engagement is built into the study design, this group should be consulted at every phase to ensure ethical engagement and troubleshoot solutions to problems that may arise over the course of the study. In cases where researchers do not have the resources (e.g., pilot/small projects) to develop and maintain an advisory board, fathers can be consulted individually or research teams can host small events where preliminary proposals or research findings are shared with stakeholders to gather feedback before moving forward.

Strategy 2: Word of Mouth

JPF Themes to Consider: Meaning, Context, Power

Word of mouth is a traditional form of recruiting, one benefit of which is that community liaisons or key informants primarily spread and share the information regarding the study. Community liaisons are often trusted people that fathers in the community respect. As such, these individuals help fathers identify the value of research participation and decipher the context in which participation may not be in the community's best interest. For example, important community liaisons for Black/African American fathers are often barbers, so one key strategy employed when recruiting in barbershops is connecting and maintaining a strong, positive relationship with the barbers. Barbers have a trusted role in the community and may hold several roles, including peer educator, mentor, and confidant. Coaches, school social workers/counselors, teachers, and clergy may serve in similar roles within community settings. As such, identifying and building a positive relationship with community liaisons is a vital process for recruiting fathers via a word-of-mouth recruiting strategy. For instance, Julion et al. (2018) describe using a tripartite method to engage community partners "built on reciprocated respect and trust, shared power, and mutual gain" (p. 422) prior to even securing funding for their work. As such, the research team worked with the community liaisons early in the project conception phase to build bonds that supported their relationship during funding processes, study development, recruitment, and data collection.

Fathers from the targeted subpopulation should also be considered to join the research team. Using a community participatory approach, researchers could hire fathers to assist with recruitment, data collection, and dissemination of findings. By capitalizing on the shared experiences of new fathers, for example, this approach has been successful for engaging fathers in breastfeeding education initiatives (Stremler & Lovera, 2004).

Strategy 3: Face-to-Face Contact

JPF Themes to Consider: Meaning and Context

Making face-to-face contact with fathers is vital for researchers when recruiting fathers. Mitchell et al. (2007) suggests that, in comparison to phone calls, face-to-face visits provide a unique opportunity for fathers to learn about and discuss the study in more depth. Face-to-face visits are perceived as more personal than flyers and offer an opportunity for fathers to meet the researchers and begin building a relationship, which allows researchers to comfortably address the various concerns that can affect a father's decision to participate in a study and allows fathers to hear how important and valued their participation is. In particular, Ibrahim and Sidani (2014) found that more personal contact, like face-to-face visits, greatly increase participation among ethnically minoritized groups. Adderley-Kelly and Green (2005) emphasized the need for training culturally competent staff to interact with potential participants from diverse ethnic and racial backgrounds.

Mitchell et al. (2007) outlined the importance of a "convincing pitch", which includes conveying a positive attitude, expressing sincere gratitude for time and participation, and answering any questions, to increase fathers' participation. Researchers should also stress that a good recruitment pitch will encompass two main themes: eagerness to hear the father's perspective and confirming that all information collected will be *confidential* and *invaluable* (Mitchell et al., 2007). As effective as face-to-face visits are, an ongoing challenge for researchers is finding appropriate places to meet with fathers. Appropriate spaces include those that are not difficult to access and do not make fathers feel unwelcome or uncomfortable. For example, some fathers may not feel comfortable coming to university lab spaces that may identify the reason for their visit to campus (Smoyer et al., 2014), particularly when interviewing about sensitive subjects such as the impacts of fathers' risk-taking behaviors on father-child interactions and outcomes. Researchers have used telephone interviews to accommodate fathers' schedules or the desire to be interviewed from their homes. This approach, along with recent advances such as Zoom interviews, are often convenient and cost effective. However, limitations to this approach include the potential for technical glitches and the loss of body-language-related data with audio-only calls. Scholars who have found success interviewing fathers via the telephone note the importance of training telephone interviewers in rapport building. When done properly, fathers have appreciated the ease and anonymity of the non-face-to-face option (Kirsch & Brandt, 2002). Community buildings such as barbershops, churches, libraries, and community centers have been successful places in which to recruit minoritized fathers (Jones et al., 2009; Mason, 2005). In an overview of their recruitment strategies among fathers of pre-adolescent sons, Doyle et al. (2016) noted a high response rate following their face-to-face and community-based recruitment efforts. Such reports signal that many fathers are interested in participating in research, and it is up to researchers and evaluators to consider meaningful ways to increase opportunities for fathers to do so.

Strategy 4: Engagement Through Online and Text Communication

JPF Themes to Consider: Context and Possibility

To overcome low participation and the hefty cost of using traditional media recruiting strategies (e.g., print, radio, and television advertising), contemporary recruitment strategies include the use of online platforms (e.g., social media, online survey panels, and other internet-based sources) to recruit participants (Leach et al., 2019). When asked for strategies to increase father participation in research, a group of fathers endorsed the use of social media and online recruitment platforms over the use of more traditional recruitment techniques (Davidson et al., 2017). Researchers have found that when employing online recruitment strategies, it is more effective to target ads to fathers, as opposed to targeting ads more generally toward parents. Additionally, in terms of cost, Facebook, Craigslist and ResearchMatch have yielded more engagement than outlets such as parenting magazines and postal mail (Yaremych & Persky, 2022).

In addition to incorporating online recruitment techniques, SMS or mobile text messaging strategies offer multiple benefits for retention. Hayward et al. (2021) have noted the utility of text-based messaging for recruiting and retaining low-income fathers in a fatherhood program and subsequent evaluation. As such, using text messaging as a retention tool offers real-time interactions with participants. Researchers have noted that this approach is effective for maintaining interactions with participants who are typically hard to research (Fletcher et al., 2017).

Utilizing multiple modes of participant communication (i.e., email, social media, text-based messaging) may also improve recruitment by providing protection from public engagement and scrutiny, particularly for studies involving sensitive subject matter (see Ladeiras-Lopes et al., 2020). Within this context, online communication via social media and social networking sites enables investigators to increase their outreach to the targeted population by overcoming accessibility barriers (e.g., geographical locations). Challenges may exist however, in relation to protecting the confidentiality of personal information in the online space. While there is little research exploring the comparative effectiveness of social media and other internet-based platforms for recruiting fathers, social networking sites have proven to be an integral tool when recruiting other marginalized and diverse populations (see Akard et al. 2015; Watkins et al., 2017).

As researchers and evaluators seek continued innovation with father engagement, online crowdsourcing of participants via services such MTurk and Qualtrics Panels has increased (for an example, see Cryer-Coupet et al., 2020). Scholars note that the use of such services allows for the recruitment of diverse groups of fathers across a number of domains (i.e., race, socioeconomic status, household structure, geographic representation) and may decrease traditional barriers to engagement such as travel, scheduling, and incentive structure. As such, after securing institutional review board approval, recruitment and incentives are often handled by the panel service. This decreases advertising time and costs and may also circumvent the administrative burdens related to the types of incentives that can be offered for research participation. However, there are potential pitfalls with online crowdsourcing related to lower levels of reliability and validity with online self-report measures (Parent et al., 2017).

Strategy 5: Outreach Through Local Organizations and Natural Groups

JPF Themes to Consider: Power, History, Context

Targeting community infrastructures such as barbershops, gyms, social clubs, and religious institutions offers various avenues for identifying, recruiting, and retaining fathers for research studies as these spaces provide access to natural groups and social networks. While the idea of using natural groups for the recruitment of fathers is an under-explored approach, some studies have shown it has great promise. To reduce the barriers related to historical mistrust, some researchers choose to host recruitment events in culturally revered and trustworthy spaces such as churches, community centers, neighborhood schools, and other community-based organizations. While several of these contexts have shown promise for recruiting minoritized women and children, there has been less success in connecting with and recruiting men, specifically fathers.

Prior research has identified barbershops and sporting events as vital recruitment venues when targeting men due to men's lower church attendance compared to women (Saunders et al., 2015). Beyond relying upon barbers as community liaisons when using the word-of-mouth approach mentioned above, researchers must consider the meaning ascribed to the physical and emotional space the barbershop embodies. Historically, barbershops have been labeled within the Black/African American community as a cultural asset, holding various purposes such as: (1) an organizing space for social movements (Mawdsley, 2015), (2) a forum for in-depth discussions on current events ranging from political banter to celebrity gossip (Friedman, 2001), and (3) a safe space in which to share and process cultural and gender-related experiences (Alexander, 2003). Given these functions, intervention researchers are increasingly relying on barbershops as key venues for recruiting men and implementing health behavior programs (Randolph et al., 2017). Interventions in this area have spanned health-related issues including asthma, diabetes, cancer, heart health, sexual health, smoking, and nutrition (Browne et al., 2006), and researchers are noting the favorable uptake of health messaging in barbershop settings (Cowart et al., 2004). Given that some barbershops have a distinct history as a public space where men can socialize without the intrusion of outsiders, researchers must take care to develop authentic relationships with shop owners and clients before engaging in explicit recruitment.

Additional sites for father recruitment based on natural groups include school-based groups such as parent teacher associations, exercise groups such as running clubs, social clubs such as fraternal organizations, libraries, and support groups based on social identities. Recruiting via natural groups pairs well with snowball sampling techniques (i.e., a non-probability sampling technique where research participants recruit additional respondents from their network), as members of the group who develop trusting relationships with the researchers are more likely to share recruitment materials with members of their group. Researchers who employ this strategy must, however, be cautious of network size and clusters as well as the potential impacts of network biases when analyzing data and interpreting findings. For example, when utilizing snowball sampling, researchers have little control over who respondents will recruit to participate. As such, the variability of respondents' attitudes, knowledge, and behavior may be limited as respondents may have shared experiences with the phenomenon of interest (Illenberger & Flötteröd, 2012). In the case of research with fathers, snowball samples may include an overrepresentation of fathers who have strong social ties or are more likely to endorse help-seeking behaviors. Researchers can adjust for this bias by limiting the number of respondents in a given network or cluster.

Strategy 6: Recruitment Support and Gatekeeping

JPF Themes to Consider: Power, Context, Possibility

A breadth of research has demonstrated that mothers and other co-parents often serve as "gatekeepers" of fathers' participation in family research (Allen & Hawkins, 1999; Mitchell et al., 2007; Sherr et al., 2006). In addition to serving as gatekeepers, mothers, historically the primary participants in studies of family life, and other relatives have also supported fathers' engagement in research, often serving as recruiters for their involvement (Dallas, 2009; Reichman et al., 2001). As such, researchers have interviewed mothers then sought to engage fathers by either asking mothers to share the study information with the father or by asking the mother to report on paternal behaviors relevant to the study. A father's subsequent engagement or representation in the study has often been strongly dictated by the status of the father-mother relationship. In instances where a mother shares a favorable co-parenting relationship with a father, she may be more willing to invite or encourage the father to participate in the research. For instance, Walsh et al. (2021) outlined how making first contact with an expectant mother increased the chance that expectant fathers would participate in a qualitative exploration of fathers' perspectives on prenatal care. In cases where there is a strained co-parenting relationship, the mother may be unlikely to share study information with the father or more likely to report unfavorable parenting practices on the father's behalf. To overcome some of these gatekeeping dilemmas, Doyle et al. (2016) suggest asking mothers and other co-parents to provide the father's contact information to diminish the burden and need to answer on his behalf. This includes discussing best potential times to contact fathers to recruit them directly. In their effort to avoid maternal and other co-parent gatekeeping, some researchers have begun to prioritize research designs that begin with fathers as the entry point to the family.

Strategy 7: Father-Friendly Research Design

JPF Themes to Consider: Meaning, Context, Power, History, Possibility

To recruit and retain fathers in research, intentional design strategies must be implemented, and, in some cases, unique accommodations offered to meet participant needs. Traditional research incentives such as paying participants for their time, providing meals during in-person interviews, and offering childcare are options that have been used in family research and can be implemented to support father engagement. Additional father-friendly designs should consider issues related to fathers' work schedules, transportation options, and other family responsibilities. For example, Dilworth-Anderson and Williams (2004) found that flexible scheduling approaches (e.g., drop-in interview appointments) offer solutions for participants who cannot meet during rigid timeslots selected by the research team. Additionally, flexible scheduling may benefit fathers who have parenting responsibilities in multiple households and thus may have limited free time. Phares (1996) also offers practical engagement suggestions such as paying attention to methods for reducing fathers' total time commitment to the study. Taking this approach might entail scheduling research interviews at a father's home or a community-based location of his choosing, which does not require travel to the research lab. Sharing recruitment materials in community locations that fathers frequent daily may also increase the likelihood of paternal engagement. These locations include daycare centers, after-school centers, grocery stores, and public transportation hubs. Other approaches might include giving fathers the option to choose the data collection approach that is easiest for them, whether by paper, telephone, smartphone, computer, or in-person. Given research design innovations during the COVID-era, research teams may also consider conducting study activities virtually via a web-conferencing platform.

For those fathers who are willing to travel to participate in research, providing monetary compensation for gas reimbursement may be a fruitful recruitment tool. For those without access to a car, consider ordering and covering the cost of a ride share (i.e., Uber or Lyft). Innovation in the research incentive structure may also be required. For example, when engaging with incarcerated, deported, or deployed fathers, consider donating research incentives (i.e., cash, gift cards, or books) to the children from whom they are physically separated. When developing father-focused interventions, consider developing a component that includes their children (Caldwell et al., 2004). In addition to addressing childcare concerns, this approach also provides family-level support.

To support Black fathers who might be suspicious of the research enterprise, Cochran (1997) recommends the use of focus groups that include Black fathers with similar experiences. This approach may help to foster a welcoming and supportive environment for data collection. Riley (2014) explores the utility of joint interviews. Interviewing fathers and their children together may reduce barriers to engagement and help fathers feel more comfortable.

When engaging fathers in longitudinal studies, it is important to collect multiple forms of contact information in case the father's information changes over time. These contacts could include the name and telephone numbers of three people who would always know how to contact the father (i.e., close family or friends), a primary and secondary email address, social media handles, and current address. To maintain engagement with the father between interviews, collect information such as the father's birthday, favorite leisure activity, and most important holiday. The research team can use this information to send birthday wishes, tips about upcoming events of interest, or season's greetings. Sharing study updates through the mail or via emails or text may assist with keeping the father interested in participation and the outcomes of the research.

Conclusion

Engaging fathers in social work research and evaluation is vital for ensuring the needs of fathers and families are adequately met. Without the voices of fathers, social work intervention lacks an important perspective and is thus at risk of neglecting assets within the family system that can support the development and maintenance of strong and healthy families. In addition to prioritizing efforts to include fathers in research, there must be a focus on socially just father engagement. The JPF and engagement strategies outlined in this chapter provide researchers and evaluators with a toolkit for working with fathers to improve the landscape of family research.

Resources and Additional Reading

- Researchmatch.org is a nonprofit program funded by the National Institutes of Health that seeks to connect potential participants with active researchers.
- Bauer, M. E., & Giles, A. R. (2020). Where are all the gay fathers? Reflections on recruiting gay fathers as participants in leisure research. *Leisure Studies*, *39*(3), 454–462. https://doi.org/10.1080/02614367.2019.1684979
- Denzmore, P., Dilorio, C., & McCarty, F. (2005). The PATIENCE Model: An approach to recruiting African American fathers and sons for behavioral research studies. *Challenge Online*, 11(2), 38–54.

- Julion, W., Sumo, J. N., Schoeny, M. E., Breitenstein, S. M., & Bounds, D. T. (2021). Recruitment, retention, and intervention outcomes from the Dedicated African American Dad (DAAD) study. *Journal of Urban Health, 98*(2), 133–148. https://doi.org/10.1007/s11524-021-00549-8
- Keys, E. M., Norris, J. M., Cameron, E. E., Bright, K. S., Tomfohr-Madsen, L. M., & Benzies, K. M. (2019). Recruitment and retention of fathers with young children in early childhood health intervention research: A systematic review and meta-analysis protocol. *Systematic Reviews, 8*(1), 1–8. https://doi.org/10.1186/s13643-019-1215-1
- Mogro-Wilson, C., Hayes, C., Loomis, A. M., Drake, A., Martin-Peele, M., & Fifield, J. (2018). Supporting recruitment and retention of young African-American and Hispanic fathers in community-based parenting interventions research. *Advances in Social Work, 18*(4), 1068–1084. https://doi.org/10.18060/22293
- Vollmer, R. L., Adamsons, K., & Mobley, A. R. (2019). Recruitment, engagement, and retention of fathers in nutrition education and obesity research. *Journal of Nutrition Education and Behavior, 51*(9), 1121–1125. https://doi.org/10.1016/j.jneb.2019.07.006
- Wigfall, V. G., Brannen, J., Mooney, A., & Parutis, V. (2013). Finding the right man: Recruiting fathers in inter-generational families across ethnic groups. *Qualitative Research, 13*(5), 591–607. https://doi.org/10.1177/1468794112446109

Discussion Questions

1. What are some strengths and weaknesses of using social media platforms to recruit fathers for research?
2. How might snowball sampling be used to recruit participants for a study about father engagement?
3. Consider the program where you are currently employed, volunteering, or completing your field placement. Who are the key stakeholders who would need to be consulted before developing a father-focused program evaluation plan?
4. Select one tenet from the Just Practice framework. How could this tenet inform the development of a father-focused research project?
5. Consider various circumstances that may cause a father to parent from afar (i.e., employment opportunity, immigration status, incarceration, military deployment). What strategies would you implement to engage a geographically distant father in research?

References

Adderley-Kelly, B., & Green, P. M. (2005). Strategies for successful conduct of research with low-income African American populations. *Nursing Outlook, 53*(3), 147–152. https://doi.org/10.1016/j.outlook.2005.03.004

Akard, T. F., Wray, S., & Gilmer, M. (2015). Facebook ads recruit parents of children with cancer for an online survey of web-based research preferences. *Cancer Nursing, 38*(2), 155. https://doi.org/10.1097/NCC.0000000000000146

Alexander, B. K. (2003). Fading, twisting, and weaving: An interpretive ethnography of the Black barbershop as cultural space. *Qualitative Inquiry, 9*(1), 105–128. https://doi.org/10.1177/1077800402239343

Allen, S. M., & Hawkins, A. J. (1999). Maternal gatekeeping: Mothers' beliefs and behaviors that inhibit greater father involvement in family work. *Journal of Marriage and the Family*, 199–212. https://doi.org/10.2307/353894

Braye, S., & McDonnell, L. (2013). Balancing powers: University researchers thinking critically about participatory research with young fathers. *Qualitative Research, 13*(3), 265–284. https://doi.org/10.1177/1468794112451012

Browne, M. C., Ford, A. F., & Thomas, S. B. (2006). Take a health professional to the people: A community outreach strategy for mobilizing African American barber shops and beauty salons as health promotion sites. *Health Education and Behavior, 33*(4), 425–432. https://doi.org/10.1177/1090198106288199

Caldwell, C. H., Wright, J. C., Zimmerman, M. A., Walsemann, K. M., Williams, D., & Isichei, P. A. (2004). Enhancing adolescent health behaviors through strengthening non-resident father–son relationships: A model for intervention with African-American families. *Health Education Research, 19*(6), 644–656. https://doi.org/10.1093/her/cyg078

Cassano, M., Adrian, M., Veits, G., & Zeman, J. (2006). The inclusion of fathers in the empirical investigation of child psychopathology: An update. *Journal of Clinical Child and Adolescent Psychology, 35*(4), 583–589. https://doi.org/10.1207/s15374424jccp3504_10

Charlton, J. I. (1998). *Nothing about us without us*. University of California Press.

Cochran, D. L. (1997). African American fathers focus on the family: A group approach to increasing visibility in research. *Social Work with Groups, 20*(3), 75–88. https://doi.org/10.1300/J009v20n03_06

Costigan, C. L., & Cox, M. J. (2001). Fathers' participation in family research: Is there a self-selection bias? *Journal of Family Psychology, 15*(4), 706–720. https://doi/10.1037/0893-3200.15.4.706

Cowart, L. W., Brown, B., & Biro, D. J. (2004). Educating African American men about prostate cancer: The Barbershop Program. *American Journal of Health Studies, 19*(4), 205–213.

Cryer-Coupet, Q. R., Dorsey, M. S., Lemmons, B. P., & Hope, E. C. (2020). Examining multiple dimensions of father involvement as predictors of risk-taking intentions among Black adolescent females. *Children and Youth Services Review, 108*. https://doi.org/10.1016/j.childyouth.2019.104604

Dallas, C. M. (2009). Interactions between adolescent fathers and health care professionals during pregnancy, labor, and early postpartum. *Journal of Obstetric, Gynecologic & Neonatal Nursing, 38*(3), 290–299. https://doi.org/10.1111/j.1552-6909.2009.01022.x

Davison, K. K., Charles, J. N., Khandpur, N., & Nelson, T. J. (2017). Fathers' perceived reasons for their underrepresentation in child health research and strategies to increase their involvement. *Maternal and Child Health Journal, 21*(2), 267–274. https://doi.org/10.1007/s10995-016-2157-z

Dilworth-Anderson, P., & Williams, S. W. (2004). Recruitment and retention strategies for longitudinal African American Caregiving Research. *Journal of Aging and Health, 16*(5_suppl), 137S–156S. https://doi.org/10.1177/0898264304269725

Doyle, O., Weller, B. E., Daniel, S. S., Mayfield, A., & Goldston, D. B. (2016). Overcoming barriers to fathers' participation in clinically relevant research: Recommendations from the field. *Social Work Research, 40*(4), 1–5. https://doi.org/10.1093/swr/svw015

Engel, R. J., & Schutt, R. K. (2017). *The practice of research in social work*. SAGE Publications.

Finn, J. L., & Jacobson, M. (2003). Just practice: Steps toward a new social work paradigm. *Journal of Social Work Education, 39*(1), 57–78. https://doi.org/10.1080/10437797.2003.10779119

Fletcher, R., May, C., Kay Lambkin, F., Gemmill, A. W., Cann, W., Nicholson, J. M., et al. (2017). SMS4dads: Providing information and support to new fathers through mobile phones–a pilot study. *Advances in Mental Health, 15*(2), 121–131. https://doi.org/10.1080/18387357.2016.1245586

Friedman, E. (2001). Haircut. *The American Scholar, 60*, 433–439.

Greif, G. L., & Bailey, C. (1990). Where are the fathers in social work literature? *Families in Society, 71*(2), 88–92. https://doi.org/10.1177/104438949007100204

Greif, G. L., & Greif, J. L. (1997). Where are the fathers in social work literature? Revisiting the question. *Families in Society, 78*(4), 433–435.

Guendelman, S., Nussbaum, J., Soliday, A., & Lahiff, M. (2018). Hispanic immigrant father involvement with young children in the United States: A comparison with US-Born Hispanic and White non-Hispanic Fathers. *Maternal and Child Health Journal, 22*(8), 1118–1126. https://doi.org/10.1007/s10995-018-2496-z

Hayward, R. A., McKillop, A. J., Lee, S. J., Hammock, A. C., Hong, H., & Hou, W. (2021). A text messaging intervention to increase engagement and retention of men in a community-based father involvement program. *Journal of Technology in Human Services, 39*(2), 144–162. https://doi.org/10.1080/15228835.2020.1841070

Ibrahim, S., & Sidani, S. (2014). Strategies to recruit minority persons: A systematic review. *Journal of Immigrant and Minority Health, 16*(5), 882–888. https://doi.org/10.1007/s10903-013-9783-y

Illenberger, J., & Flötteröd, G. (2012). Estimating network properties from snowball sampled data. *Social Networks, 34*(4), 701–711. https://doi.org/10.1016/j.socnet.2012.09.001

Jones, R. A., Steeves, R., & Williams, I. (2009). Strategies for recruiting African American men into prostate cancer screening studies. *Nursing Research, 58*(6), 452. https://doi.org/10.1097/NNR.0b013e3181b4bade

Julion, W. A., Sumo, J. N., & Bounds, D. T. (2018). A tripartite model for recruiting African-Americans into fatherhood intervention research. *Public Health Nursing, 35*(5), 420–426. https://doi.org/10.1111/phn.12411

Kirsch, S. E. D., & Brandt, P. A. (2002). Telephone interviewing: A method to reach fathers in family research. *Journal of Family Nursing, 8*(1), 73–84. https://doi.org/10.1177/107484070200800105

Ladeiras-Lopes, R., Baciu, L., Grapsa, J., Sohaib, A., Vidal-Perez, R., Bohm, A., et al. (2020). Social media in cardiovascular medicine: a contemporary review. *European Heart Journal-Digital Health, 1*(1), 10–19. https://doi.org/10.1093/ehjdh/ztaa004

Leach, L. S., Bennetts, S. K., Giallo, R., & Cooklin, A. R. (2019). Recruiting fathers for parenting research using online advertising campaigns: Evidence from an Australian study. *Child: Care, Health and Development, 45*(6), 871–876. https://doi.org/10.1111/cch.12698

Mason, S. E. (2005). Offering African Americans opportunities to participate in clinical trials research: How social workers can help. *Health & Social Work, 30*(4), 296–304. https://doi.org/10.1093/hsw/30.4.296

Mawdsley, S. E. (2015). Black barbers and the civil rights movement. *Reviews in American History, 43*(4), 647–651. https://doi.org/10.1353/rah.2015.0087

Martin, G. E. (2017). Those closest to the problem are closest to the solution. *The Appeal.*. https://theappeal.org/those-closest-to-the-problem-are-closest-to-the-solution-555e04317b79/

Macfadyen, A., Swallow, V., Santacroce, S., & Lambert, H. (2011). Involving fathers in research. *Journal for Specialists in Pediatric Nursing, 16*(3), 216–219. https://doi.org/10.1111/j.1744-6155.2011.00287.x

McAdoo, J. L. (1993). The roles of African American fathers: An ecological perspective. *Families in Society, 74*(1), 28–35. https://doi.org/10.1177/104438949307400103

Mitchell, S. J., See, H. M., Tarkow, A. K., Cabrera, N., McFadden, K. E., & Shannon, J. D. (2007). Conducting studies with fathers: Challenges and opportunities. *Applied Development Science, 11*(4), 239–244. https://doi.org/10.1080/10888690701762159

Mogro-Wilson, C., Loomis, A. M., Hayes, C., & Rojas, R. (2019). Emerging bicultural views of fatherhood: Perspectives of Puerto Rican fathers. *Advances in Social Work, 19*(2), 311–328. https://doi.org/10.18060/22581

Nicholas, D., Beaune, L., Belletrutti, M., Blumberg, J., Ing, S., Rapoport, A., & Barrera, M. (2020). Engaging fathers in pediatric palliative care research. *Journal of Social Work in End-of-Life & Palliative Care, 16*(1), 42–56. https://doi.org/10.1080/15524256.2019.1703877

O'Brien, M. (2007). Making fathers count: Methodological dilemmas and emerging solutions. *Applied Development Science, 11*(4), 245–246. https://doi.org/10.1080/10888690701762167

Parent, J., Forehand, R., Pomerantz, H., Peisch, V., & Seehuus, M. (2017). Father participation in child psychopathology research. *Journal of Abnormal Child Psychology, 45*(7), 1259–1270. https://doi.org/10.1007/s10802-016-0254-5

Phares, V. (1996). Conducting nonsexist research, prevention, and treatment with fathers and mothers: A call for a change. *Psychology of Women Quarterly, 20*(1), 55–77. https://doi.org/10.1111/j.1471-6402.1996.tb00665.x

Randles, J. (2020). The means to and meaning of "being there" in responsible fatherhood programming with low-income fathers. *Family Relations, 69*(1), 7–20. https://doi.org/10.1111/fare.12376

Randolph, S., Coakley, T., & Shears, J. (2018). Recruiting and engaging African-American men in health research. *Nurse Researcher, 29*(2), 8–12. https://doi.org/10.7748/nr.2018.e1569

Randolph, S. D., Pleasants, T., & Gonzalez-Guarda, R. M. (2017). Barber-led sexual health education intervention for Black male adolescents and their fathers. *Public Health Nursing, 34*(6), 555–560. https://doi.org/10.1111/phn.12350

Reichman, N. E., Teitler, J. O., Garfinkel, I., & McLanahan, S. S. (2001). Fragile families: Sample and design. *Children and Youth Services Review, 23*(4–5), 303–326. https://doi.org/10.1016/S0190-7409(01)00141-4

Riley, M. (2014). Interviewing fathers and sons together: Exploring the potential of joint interviews for research on family farms. *Journal of Rural Studies, 36*, 237–246. https://doi.org/10.1016/j.jrurstud.2014.09.003

Rubin, A., & Babbie, E. R. (2016). *Empowerment series: Essential research methods for social work*. Cengage Learning.

Saunders, D. R., Holt, C. L., Le, D., Wang, M. Q., Slade, J. L., Savoy, A., Muwwakkil, B., Williams, R., Whitehead, T. L., & Naslund, M. J. (2015). Recruitment and participation of African American men in church-based health promotion workshops. *Journal of Community Health, 40*(6), 1300–1310. https://doi.org/10.1007/s10900-015-0054-9

Shafer, K., & Bellamy, J. L. (2016). Focusing on men and fathers: A challenge for social work research and practice. *Social Work Research, 40*(4), 199–202. https://doi.org/10.1093/swr/svw020

Shapiro, A. F., & Krysik, J. (2010). Finding fathers in social work research and practice. *Journal of Social Work Values and Ethics, 7*(1), 1–8.

Sherr, L., Davé, S., Lucas, P., Senior, R., & Nazareth, I. (2006). A feasibility study on recruiting fathers of young children to examine the impact of paternal depression on child development. *Child Psychiatry & Human Development, 36*, 295–309. https://doi.org/10.1007/s10578-005-0004-3

Smoyer, A. B., Blankenship, K. M., & Belt, B. (2009). Compensation for incarcerated research participants: Diverse state policies suggest a new research agenda. *American Journal of Public Health, 99*(10), 1746–1752. https://doi.org/10.2105/AJPH.2008.148726

Smoyer, A. B., Rosenberg, A., & Blankenship, K. M. (2014). Setting the stage: Creating study sites that promote the safety and dignity of research participants. *Social Work Research, 38*(3), 178–183. https://doi-org.prox.lib.ncsu.edu/10.1093/swr/svu019

Stremler, J., & Lovera, D. (2004). Insight from a breastfeeding peer support pilot program for husbands and fathers of Texas WIC participants. *Journal of Human Lactation, 20*(4), 417–422. https://doi.org/10.1177/0890334404267182

Strug, D., & Wilmore-Schaeffer, R. (2003). Fathers in the social work literature: Policy and practice implications. *Families in Society, 84*(4), 503–511. https://doi.org/10.1606/1044-3894.145

Watkins, D. C., Allen, J. O., Goodwill, J. R., & Noel, B. (2017). Strengths and weaknesses of the young Black men, masculinities, and mental health (YBMen) Facebook project. *American Journal of Orthopsychiatry, 87*(4), 392–401. https://doi.org/10.1037/ort0000229.supp. (Supplemental).

Walsh, T. B., Carpenter, E., Costanzo, M. A., Howard, L., & Reynders, R. (2021). Present as a partner and a parent: Mothers' and fathers' perspectives on father participation in prenatal care. *Infant Mental Health Journal, 42*(3), 386–399. https://doi.org/10.1002/imhj.21920

Walsh, T. B., Davis, R. N., & Garfield, C. (2020). A call to action: Screening fathers for perinatal depression. *Pediatrics, 145*(1). https://doi.org/10.1542/peds.2019-1193

Yaremych, H. E., & Persky, S. (2022). Recruiting fathers for parenting research: An evaluation of eight recruitment methods and an exploration of fathers' motivations for participation. *Parenting*, 1–33. https://doi.org/10.1080/15295192.2022.2036940

Part II
Assessment

Chapter 6
Assessment with Fathers: Recognizing Strengths, Challenges, and Contexts

Jennifer A. Shadik and Kevin Shafer

Introduction

This chapter begins by discussing the importance of fathers and why their involvement in their children's lives is so important. The content focuses on understanding the ways fathering is currently assessed and limitations to these approaches. While social workers are trained that assessment is a multifaceted and ongoing process, standard assessments can fall short when working with fathers. This chapter focuses on two primary areas related to assessment. The first relates to assessing father involvement and the quality of fathering he provides his children; the second involves the need for a comprehensive assessment to consider specific areas that are relevant for fathers, including personal and relational factors as well as external and contextual factors. By understanding the relevant factors impacting fatherhood, practitioners will better understand areas to assess and the need for thorough, strengths-based, and father-friendly assessments.

J. A. Shadik (✉)
Department of Social Work, Ohio University, Athens, OH, USA
e-mail: Shadik@ohio.edu

K. Shafer
Sociology, Brigham Young University, Provo, UT, USA
e-mail: kevin_shafer@byu.edu

J. L. Bellamy et al. (eds.), *Social Work Practice with Fathers*,
https://doi.org/10.1007/978-3-031-13686-3_6

Background and Context

Why Fathering Matters

Research on and assessment of father involvement is a relatively recent development in parenting research. For many years, researchers did not include fathers in their work on parenting, did not link paternal involvement to child outcomes, and generally ignored the positive contributions fathers make to families. Much of this was rooted in the belief, pervasive in Western cultures, that fathers did little to facilitate child development. Instead, the focus was on mothers, who typically spend far more time with children than fathers and who were viewed as responsible for children's well-being, health, development, and cognitive advancement. While the number of parenting studies focused on or including fathers remains comparatively small, there has been a major growth in the number of studies addressing father involvement. Many of these studies focus on the influence of fathers on child outcomes, providing tangible evidence that men are critical to understanding child development.

Fathers help infants actively explore their environments, react to complex stimuli, and have a strong, positive influence on their ability to trust others (Palkovitz et al., 2014). By 6 months, for example, babies with involved fathers score higher on the Bayley Scales of Infant Development, a standardized test used to map the developmental trajectory of small children (Lamb, 2010). Other developmentally important skills, like resilience and secure attachments, are also commonly instilled by fathers at early ages (Cabrera et al., 2018). As children get older, developmental trajectories continue to be positively influenced by fathers, as is their behavior. A voluminous literature demonstrates that children's behavior is positively impacted by the father-child relationship (Twamley et al., 2013). Children with warm and responsive fathers tend to experience fewer internalized problems, like depressive symptoms, negative emotions, and impulsivity than children with less engaged dads (Allen & Daly, 2002; Coates & Phares, 2019; Day & Padilla-Walker, 2009; Dermott, 2008; Twamley et al., 2013). These problems tend to be less common because fathers can help their children manage negative emotions. Scholarship assessing the effects of fathering on children's externalizing behavior tends to focus on adolescence, an age when delinquency and deviance are most likely. These studies illustrate that fathers can help protect against problematic externalizing behavior, including illegal substance abuse, truancy, stealing, and drinking (Allen & Daly, 2002). Involved fatherhood appears to protect children and adolescents against a host of issues, including physical and mental health problems, poor psychosocial adjustment, and behaviors that could put one's health and well-being at risk.

Although fathers spend substantially less time on educational tasks than mothers, they still positively influence their children in this domain (Palkovitz et al., 2014). The effects of paternal engagement on cognitive competence and functioning can be demonstrated as early as 6 months of age (Allen & Daly, 2002; Jones, 2004). When dads help with school work and other educational tasks, their kids tend to get better grades and scores on standardized tests, are more likely to participate in extracurricular activities, attend school more regularly, and frequently graduate high school (McBride et al., 2005a). These positive influences may be rooted in fathers' providing more cognitively stimulating home environments. Moreover, children may also benefit from having two parents that emphasize education and provide clear and consistent expectations about school (Jeynes, 2015). Notably, it is unlikely that the relationship between cognitive outcomes and fathering is the result of selection—a phenomenon where positive child outcomes are associated with the same factors that predict paternal involvement in child education. Involved fathers help their children cognitively and academically regardless of their own educational attainment, the educational attainment of their mother, the child's racial/ethnic background, the father's residential status, or family income (McBride, Schoppe-Sullivan et al., 2005b; McWayne et al., 2013).

There are also clear benefits of high-quality fathering for children's social well-being, including pro-social behavior, executive functioning, positive self-regard, and courteous comportment (Dermott, 2008). Fathers can help their children choose positive friendships, have closer relationships, and be well-regarded by adults and their peers. Moral development and attachment styles are also associated with fathering behaviors (Palkovitz et al., 2014; Torres et al., 2014). Many of these social benefits may be the result of unique parenting practices by fathers that encourage healthy risks, distinct types of interaction, and adaptation to unique or challenging situations (Kuo et al., 2018; Palkovitz et al., 2014).

Why Fathering Should Be Assessed

The benefits to children of fathering are diverse, beginning from an early age and continuing through adulthood. Given these advantages, it is critical to help fathers understand how they are doing, the sources of strength in their parenting, and potential areas for improvement. There are several reasons to do so. First, a social justice perspective necessitates the assessment of fathering. It is critical to "help fathers take on positive family roles" (Shafer & Bellamy, 2016, p. 200). Social services overtly burden women and mothers, and working to integrate fathers, via assessment, into the discussion can help alleviate these issues. However, fathers need the tools to become increasingly engaged in families—facilitating change in the expectations, burdens, and overly restrictive gender boundaries that constrict both mothers and fathers. Doing more to help fathers, understanding their strengths and weaknesses, and addressing their needs can also help alleviate the discrimination and sexism commonly associated with womanhood, motherhood, and the link between the two.

Second, the assessment of fathering behavior, how fathers interact with children, and father-co-parent relationship quality can help eliminate the stigmas associated with social and therapeutic services among men and fathers. Bellamy (2009), for example, shows that many child welfare workers describe fathers as "dangerous," "absent," and "unimportant." Men often report that they feel misunderstood, unwanted, and distrusted by helping professionals (Rochlen et al., 2010). The use of assessment tools and a broader assessment focus can help facilitate a better client-provider relationship by showing fathers that they are taken seriously and are viewed as important contributors to family life and by helping them identify their strengths and the areas that could be further improved.

Third, social workers have an ethical obligation to competently assess clients. Assessment is the foundation of social work practice and is taught at both undergraduate and graduate levels. Assessment is expected to encompass client challenges and strengths at the micro, mezzo, and macro levels while considering human diversity (Kirst-Ashman & Hull, 2015). Assessment involves collecting pertinent information about the client, including their problems and strengths, and provides the basis for intervention. When it is incomplete or neglects clients' challenges or strengths, we do a disservice to clients and limit our ability to intervene effectively. Relatedly, assessment tools have substantial utility for practitioners. Standardized assessments and well-designed assessment tools help practitioners understand fathers across multiple dimensions, such as involvement in care, warmth toward children, disciplinary style, and emotional support, generating a complete picture of what a particular father does.

Conceptual Framing

Approaches to Assessing Fathering

Scholars have used several approaches, measures, theories, assumptions, and conceptual frameworks to assess father involvement. While there are some positives associated with using diverse approaches to understand how fathers interact with their children, it also means that there is no single accepted framework to assess men's involvement in parenting in the literature. Given men's increased engagement in both expressive and instrumental parenting (Petts et al., 2018), for example, there are debates about whether to measure men's involvement with children using gender-neutral measures of parenting (Fagan et al., 2014) or gender-specific measures of fathering (Palkovitz et al., 2014). Gender-neutral measures suggest that parenting is best conceptualized as a set of attitudes about child rearing, the behaviors focused on meeting the emotional and physical needs of children, and the skills necessary to address these needs. Such an approach suggests that parenting by both mothers and fathers should be measured similarly because of the increasing convergence in the socially informed responsibilities and expectations associated with motherhood and fatherhood. Counterarguments to this approach emphasize differences in how mothers and fathers parent children—differences rooted in gender socialization and gendered behavioral expectations—even though gendered parenting behaviors are frequently directed at similar developmental goals.

The best available evidence suggests that even the most egalitarian different-gender couples engage in gendered parenting. Fathers are more likely than mothers, for example, to engage in physical, imaginative, unconventional, and rough-and-tumble play (Schoppe-Sullivan & Fagan, 2020). Mothers and fathers also confer different resources to their children, including unique forms of social and human capital (Eggebeen, 2013). Significant debate around the potential sources of these gendered behaviors persists. Evidence for biologically-rooted differences between mothers and fathers is virtually non-existent (Palkovitz et al., 2014). Instead, social differentiation seems far more plausible, including early childhood socialization, gender differences in how individuals engage with their social environments, persistent gendered expectations in parenting behavior, and institutional reinforcement of "separate spheres."

Contemporary fathering expectations, distinctive influences on children, and interpretative differences around maternal and paternal parenting behavior suggest that our approach to studying and evaluating father involvement should not starkly contrast from how we conceptualize and operationalize mothering. At the same time, the assessment of fathering must remain sensitive to the competing expectations of breadwinning, family order, discipline, caregiving, and emotional availability that define modern fatherhood (Petts et al., 2018). In other words, both historical and contemporary expectations should be reflected in the assessment of fathering behavior. As norms about fathering continually evolve toward more emotionally supportive parenting and engagement in caregiving, traditional roles remain central to how fathers evaluate themselves and how they are evaluated by others (Schoppe-Sullivan & Fagan, 2020). A keen awareness of social forces such as gendered norms, inequalities at home and at work, and the influence of social policies and institutions is necessary to better understand fathering and, subsequently, evaluation. Ultimately, assessment must examine the myriad of expectations around fathering, acknowledging that both contemporary and traditional responsibilities are valuable and reliable predictors of the paternal influences on child and family well-being, development, and health.

Quantitative approaches to assessing father involvement have evolved over the past several decades. Many initial assessments, rooted in an era of American cultural politics which considered divorce and single parenthood as crises to blame for many social ills and data that lacked detailed information on fathering behavior, focused on the paternal presence (McLanahan et al., 2013). Such assessments are problematic for several reasons, but two issues stand out. First, a robust literature shows that many non-residential fathers are highly engaged in the lives of their children (Jensen & Shafer, 2013; Jones & Mosher, 2013), and many children raised without a co-residential father still have fathers and father figures who are consistently present and provide significant support (Edin & Nelson, 2013). A focus on paternal residence glosses over these patterns. Second, a focus on presence tends to play into racist notions about the "absent Black father" despite the fact that residential and non-residential Black fathers are, on average, more involved than their respective White counterparts (Jones & Mosher, 2013). Acknowledging these issues, other measurement strategies have been proposed to capture fathering behavior. One alternate strategy is to assess the quantity of time fathers spend parenting their children. Such an approach typically asks fathers to use detailed time diaries to keep track of what they do, when they do it, and with whom. These measures provide details about the time fathers spend on child-related tasks relative to other tasks, like paid work, but do little to quantify fathers' participation in specific behaviors that have proven beneficial for children, co-parents, and fathers alike.

A second, preferable, alternative is to measure fathering quality. Such assessments are built on a better understanding of which aspects of paternal engagement have the largest impact on child development and well-being. Initial measures of quality were rooted in several assumptions: (1) mothers act as primary parents and fathers are primarily responsible for breadwinning, discipline, and sometimes helping with childcare; (2) White middle- and upper-class standard North American family norms; and (3) family norms and expectations remain static (Fagan et al., 2014). As a result, the first measures of fathering quality ignored diverse family forms and often included a blend of gender-specific and gender-neutral ideas about parenting. Doing so ignored important variabilities in father involvement, particularly among low-income and Black, Indigenous, and people/persons of color (BIPOC) families, who are more likely to embrace egalitarian gender roles in response to economic necessity and the marginalization that limited access to significant social resources (Coontz, 2016).

Recent multidimensional conceptualizations around father involvement have led to assessment strategies that better integrate diversity and the shifts in parental roles. Pleck's (2010, 2012) expanded model of father involvement addresses five dimensions of behavior: (1) emotional availability and social support; (2) responsibility for the care and development of children; (3) warmth through hugging, praise, and other loving behaviors; (4) monitoring children's activities and communication; and (5) caregiving, play, and the inclusion of children into routine activities. Notably, this latter category can be thought of as consisting of two distinct subcategories: behaviors where fathers directly interact with their children and non-interactive, indirect actions that benefit their children—like advocating for a child or scheduling their activities. An alternative multidimensional approach suggests that we should consider a broad constellation of what fathers do across a number of instrumental, expressive, and developmental domains (Hawkins et al., 2002; Hawkins & Palkovitz, 1999). Some broader conceptualizations capture a range of parenting behaviors in men, including those that are traditionally associated with the paternal role, traditional maternal responsibilities, and gender-neutral parenting behaviors. For example, the 26-item Inventory of Father Involvement considers a myriad of paternal behaviors across traditional and contemporary norms and expectations around fathering (Hawkins et al., 2002).

Marginalized Fathers

It is critical to consider marginalized fathers when assessing paternal involvement. To be clear, our understanding of fathering is based largely on American, middle-class, married, White samples and their associated values. Racial and ethnic differences in family life are influenced by social structures that are racialized and limit access to resources among many groups of fathers, including BIPOC fathers, immigrant fathers, rural fathers, and many other groups of fathers from historically marginalized or structurally disadvantaged groups (Marsiglio et al., 2005). All are important assessment contexts deserving of considerable thought and attention. Unfortunately, our chapter cannot cover all these groups and the particular issues each faces. As a result, we address several common issues in the assessment of fathering. The lessons from the groups discussed here may prove valuable for thinking through the issues faced by other groups of marginalized or disadvantaged fathers.

Race affects parenting behaviors in numerous ways. A particularly prominent example of differences between White and BIPOC parents relates to the parental disciplinary techniques commonly employed by the two groups. In response to racism, discrimination, and other structural disadvantages, Black parents are far more likely to spank misbehaving children than White parents. These parenting patterns develop in response to marginalization and oppression that demands compliance, often with life and death consequences (Lee & Alschul, 2015; McWayne, et al., 2018). Therefore, parents react in rational ways to disproportionately severe consequences of non-conformity for marginalized and oppressed racial and ethnic minorities by socializing their children to consider the serious threats that exist within institutions. At the same time, these processes help BIPOC parents help their children develop a strong racial identity, making them aware of racialized structures and spaces and providing them with the strategies necessary to navigate race, discrimination, and bias over the life course (Manning, 2019).

Despite clear evidence of structural racism, commentators and political figures often blame fathers for the persistent social problems commonly experienced in BIPOC communities. In the United States, more than 70% of Black births are to unmarried women, and Black children are disproportionately likely to be raised in single-parent homes (Martin, et al., 2018). In some circles, poor analyses of basic statistics have led to racist tropes about the "absent Black father" and victim blaming for a host of social ills. These conclusions lack context and ignore the systemic issues that impact nearly every aspect of life in Black America. Black Americans are six times more likely to be incarcerated than their White counterparts because of policing and sentencing disparities that target the Black community (Nellis, 2016). Differences in drug crime statistics are particularly telling. Black men and women make up 12.5% of drug users in the United States, but more than one-third of individuals incarcerated for a drug offense are Black (Mitchell & Caudy, 2015). Poverty, joblessness, and other structural issues are epidemic in minority communities, and family instability is a symptom of these systemic issues, not a cause. Moreover, the concept of fatherlessness is an ill-defined one. Studies that rely on a dichotomous proxy for fatherlessness reify politically and socially problematic ideas about BIPOC communities. Jones and Mosher (2013) found, for example, that both residential and non-residential Black fathers engage in more caregiving, spend more time with their children, and provide more emotional support than their White counterparts. A failure to account for systemic issues and an overreliance on mean differences based on unfair comparisons make the family structure a proxy for race and suggest that problems in the BIPOC community would improve if only they would get married and then have children. These arguments are methodologically and theoretically sloppy because they ignore social structure.

These same conceptual issues are prominent with non-biological and non-residential fathers as well. Stepfathers, by and large, are different from biological fathers in several ways and tend to be marginalized. Despite their ubiquity, stepfamilies remain ungoverned by social norms, are rarely institutionalized in the same ways that biologically intact families are, and can be disregarded by others because of their unique family circumstances (Jensen et al., 2017; Jensen & Shafer, 2013). Expectations around this role are often unclear, and members of the same family can have contradictory ideas about what stepfamilies should do. Many biological mothers expect residential stepparents to take on the roles and responsibilities of a biological parent. Stepparents, particularly stepfathers, often see themselves as akin to a supportive relative, and only a few see themselves like a biological parent. Stepchildren typically want stepparents to be supportive and friendly but are hesitant to accept their authority or attempt to change the family culture (Campbell & Winn, 2018; Fine & Kurdek, 1994; King, 2009). The ambiguous roles and responsibilities associated with stepfathering are rarely reflected in evaluative measures.

Positive stepparent-stepchild relationships can alleviate common problems in stepfamilies such as maladjustment, psychological stress, difficulties getting along with peers and family members, behavioral issues, and poor academic performance (Dunn, 2002; Stewart, 2007). Good stepparent-stepchild relationships are rooted in warmth, positive control, and emotional support (Coleman et al., 2013; Ganong & Coleman, 2004); such fathering behaviors increase family cohesiveness and ease the tumultuous transition into stepfamily life (Jensen & Shafer, 2013; Stewart, 2007). These behaviors also encourage children in stepfamilies to communicate more openly and help them feel understood by both their residential biological parent and residential stepparent (Martin et al., 1999). Conversely, the inability to develop a warm relationship with the stepparent can lead to divided loyalties within the stepfamily, which may be the strongest predictor of adolescent stress (Lutz, 1983). These family processes can have important effects on the developmental trajectories, health, and well-being of children. For example, stepfather relationship quality is positively associated with the mental health of stepchildren, even into emerging adulthood (Jensen et al., 2017). In contrast, many stepfathers try to take on an authoritarian parenting role—particularly when they attempt to make new rules, become the disciplinarian, and want to change the family culture (Golish, 2003). Perhaps unsurprisingly, stepchildren typically react poorly to these attempts (MacDonald & DeMaris, 2002). In fact, qualitative studies have shown that overstepping the disciplinary expectations of stepchildren often leads to high levels of family conflict and the view that the stepparent is illegitimate (Hetherington & Kelly, 2002; Kinniburgh-White et al., 2010).

Recommended Assessment Approaches

For the assessment process to be useful, it must be thorough. Focusing on fathering strengths and challenges is essential to understanding how and where to intervene. This section discusses the need for a comprehensive assessment. It covers the importance of including fluidity in fathering assessment, including relevant contexts such as child factors, marital status, residential status, and co-parenting relationships. Finally, a father-friendly assessment is discussed.

Need for Comprehensive and Strengths-Based Assessment

Palkovitz and Hull (2018) developed a *resource theory of fathering* to incorporate the dimensions of fathering diversity. They discuss five dimensions of diversity: personal resources, interpersonal resources, contextual resources, father-child relationships, and resource management. This theory helps highlight the varied experiences of fathers, the importance of asking them about their situation, and recognizes that each father has different resources, challenges, and contexts. A thorough assessment using these dimensions can help social workers better understand the experiences and needs of the fathers they work with.

Social workers often work with families experiencing challenges such as family violence, mental health, substance use, poverty, or some combination of these factors. In each of these situations, the social worker must comprehensively assess the risks, strengths, and protective factors, as well as external resources, to effectively intervene. By utilizing a strengths-based and thorough assessment process, practitioners will likely gather more complete information while enhancing engagement and rapport with fathers.

Assessments that start from a *deficit perspective* are off-putting to fathers and may miss essential information. Research has identified that fathers are often viewed as unimportant or a risk (Bellamy, 2009; Zanoni et al., 2013). Unmarried fathers are often viewed through a lens of stereotypes, deficits, and dysfunction (Marczak et al., 2015). If the goal of assessment is to gain key information on the father, including his strengths and needs, it must start from a position of assets and possibility. Scourfield (2014) emphasizes the importance of respectful and empathetic communication toward fathers and an individualized assessment. When we recognize existing strengths, it stands to reason that fathers are more likely to feel seen and respected, increasing the likelihood that they will engage in services. At the same time, practitioners can identify and address challenges, building on the capabilities the father has already exhibited.

Fathers have indicated the importance of cultivating an environment where they feel welcome (Spjeldnes et al., 2020). Many programs were created for mothers without specific attention given to the unique needs and preferences of fathers. Creating programs that are specifically geared to the needs of fathers may improve engagement in services (Lee et al., 2016). More recent research has focused on training providers to provide services to fathers (Scourfield, 2014) and has indicated the importance of providers being caring and empathetic (Lee et al., 2016; Spjeldnes et al., 2020) and helping fathers feel understood rather than judged (Tully et al., 2017).

In child welfare services, there is often limited engagement with fathers. Scourfield (2014) notes that many child welfare staff are women, they may have limited training on engaging fathers in services, and agencies may have limited expectations related to working with fathers. The tendency to dichotomize fathers as either a risk or an asset (Maxwell et al., 2012) ignores the reality that humans are complex and their contributions to the child and family may include both risks and assets. In their work on child welfare practice, Zanoni et al. (2013) emphasize the risks to children when fathers are not involved in assessment and services. They identify risks to children when abusive fathers are not engaged in services as well as risks when nurturing and protective fathers are excluded. Additionally, when conducting comprehensive assessments, practitioners are reminded that fathers (like mothers) often have a combination of strengths and challenges (Panter et al., 2014).

One area that is often overlooked and underdiagnosed is paternal depression. Previous research suggests perinatal depression is experienced by 4 to 25% of men (Carlberg et al., 2018; Edward et al., 2019), yet current measurement tools may fall short when assessing depression in men (Goodman, 2004). Since depression in men may present differently than in women, Magovcevic and Addis (2008) developed the Masculine Depression Scale, an instrument to help assess depression in men. Paternal depression has negative consequences for the father's functioning, the parental relationship, and the emotional and behavioral well-being of children (Bruno et al., 2020). Assessing paternal depression during pregnancy and throughout the child's life allows providers to intervene as early as possible. Chung et al. (2021) found that parental self-efficacy buffered negative effects of paternal depression in a sample of low-income fathers of children receiving Head Start and Early Head Start services. Providers who are aware of a father's depression can treat it and work to enhance areas such as *parental self-efficacy*, which may help limit the negative impact on family relationships.

Incorporating Fluidity in Fathering into Assessment

Fatherhood is often viewed as fixed; it is important to remember that fathering is a fluid concept. Fathers change over time as they gain new knowledge, their children move into different developmental stages, and their contexts shift. Not only do fathers and their children change over time, but "the availability, the 'flow,' and the balance of fathering resources are understood to change over time" (Palkovitz & Hull, 2018, p. 187). This section will focus on how fluidity should be considered in the assessment, particularly related to marital/partner status, living arrangements, co-parenting, contextual factors, and factors related to individual children. Dubowitz

(2009) emphasizes the importance of the *ecological framework* and the need to assess a father's involvement, roles, and his relationships with family members. Thus, ongoing assessment is critical due to this fluidity in fathering.

According to Roy (2014), "Fathering is dynamic and emergent" (pp. 319–320). To help fathers, social workers must resist the urge to make decisions based solely on past information. Research by Zanoni et al. (2014) found some fathers reported that their workers did not believe that they had changed, particularly related to substance use and prior criminal activity. Within the social work profession, core values include the importance of social justice, integrity, and dignity and worth of the person (National Association of Social Workers, 2021). Therefore, listening to those we work with, believing change is possible, and providing fair and nondiscriminatory services are required. Fathering is complex and shaped by men's families, finances, and social supports (Perry & Lewis, 2016; Shadik & O'Connor, 2016); therefore, assessment approaches must take these factors into account.

The quality of a father's relationship with his children may vary considerably. Much of the literature on fathers focuses on one point in time or a father's relationship with only one of his children, making it easy to overlook changes and complexities (Shadik, 2020). Fathers may have greater knowledge of and skills at certain stages of child development and less in others. While asking about only one child saves time, it ignores the complexity of parenting multiple children (Fagan & Kaufman, 2015a, b). The transactional model considers the interplay of child characteristics and the environment, which includes the parents (Sameroff & Fiese, 2000). Parenting is bidirectional, with children impacting parents and parents impacting children. It is shortsighted to assume a father's relationship with one child represents his parenting of all his children. There may be contextual factors that impact his parenting, including child characteristics, geographical distance, and the co-parenting relationship.

Many intake forms ask about marital status, which may not provide enough information about a father's current life. Given the decreasing marriage rates (U.S. Census Bureau, 2020) and the high rates of *multi-partner fertility* (Guzzo & Furstenberg, 2007) and social fathering (Dubowitz, 2009), it is important to understand a father's current relationships with his partner and the children he cares for. It is also important to understand the demands of time and finances, whether a child is currently living with their father or not. Children may live with their father for certain times of the year, or this may vary based on the needs of the child, mother, or father (Shadik & O'Connor, 2016). By staying open to the idea that children may reside with their mother, father, or another relative at various times, practitioners are more likely to ask specific questions to understand the unique situation of each family. Practitioners should inquire about all of a father's children, not just those that currently reside with him.

Fathering is closely tied to co-parenting relationships. Earlier research on co-parenting focused primarily on middle-class families who were married or divorced; this focus left co-parenting within nonresidential, nonmarried, and low-income families largely unexplored (Fagan & Kaufman, 2015a, b). Given the frequency of multi-partner fertility, it is important to assess the father's relationship with all his children's mothers. With the higher rates of nontraditional family structures, some fathers co-parent with multiple mothers. They may have different communication and relationship qualities with each mother. Mothers have identified co-parenting challenges such as communication, respect, incarceration, and substance use (Perry et al., 2020). Researchers have identified co-parenting challenges for unmarried nonresidential fathers related to *maternal gatekeeping*, undermining, and challenges regarding new romantic partners (Fagan & Kaufman, 2015a, b). Practitioners must ask about all co-parenting relationships as some may be healthier and others more problematic, and the quality of any of these relationships may change over time. It is likely that managing relationships with multiple mothers adds to a father's stress. It is important to assess dimensions of the co-parenting relationship such as communication, collaboration, and cooperation (McHale & Negrini, 2018), as these factors impact children and adults.

Father involvement can vary over time. This is often impacted by residential status, marital status, and challenges such as incarceration, mental health, and substance use (Castillo et al., 2011; Solis et al., 2012). Historically, most data on father involvement relies on reports from the mother, even when she was not present to witness the involvement (Charles et al., 2018). Further, father involvement has often been viewed dichotomously—fathers were either present or absent (see Day & Lamb, 2004; Gadsden et al., 2004). Many fathers who do not reside with their children are actively involved, so a more nuanced view would allow recognition of varied types of involvement and contributions.

There are various factors which can impact father involvement. Roberts et al. (2014) conducted a qualitative study to understand the supports and barriers that impact the fatherhood role. They found obtaining fatherhood guidance, receiving emotional support, and having a good relationship with the children's mothers were key factors in facilitating good fathering. Fagan (2020) conducted a study with low-income nonresident fathers and found similar factors were key to higher levels of father involvement. These included receiving encouragement from family and friends; valuing their status as fathers; and lower levels of maternal gatekeeping. Some of these factors may be present in a father's existing relationships; however, many fathers would benefit from more information and support to enhance these factors. Previous literature has identified that fathers are often unaware of existing fatherhood resources and their purpose (Lee et al., 2016; Tully et al., 2017). Enhancing public awareness of fatherhood programs and their aims may increase participation rates and help fathers see the benefits for them and their children.

It is important to consider the number of children, their living arrangements, and the individual requirements of each child to assess needs and intervention approaches for fathers. To accurately assess current needs, both the past and present must be considered. If the father was incarcerated or struggling with substance use during part of the child's life, addressing these factors may be important to current family functioning. Do any of the children have specific medical or learning needs? A father may struggle with parenting teenagers but excel at parenting a toddler. Asking questions about these specifics will help ensure a comprehensive assessment, which will help practitioners identify appropriate interventions.

Father-Friendly Assessment of Father Involvement

Contemporary fathers are more nurturing toward and emotionally invested in their children than previous generations (Pleck, 2012). Although there is broad agreement among sociologists, family scientists, and other social scientists on this trend, there is less consensus on how to conceptualize and operationalize father involvement. Many measures of fathering are comparable to measures of mothering, which may emphasize paternal deficits (Marsiglio & Roy, 2012). While substantial gender inequities in family life persist, a measurement that fails to account for paternal strengths may not reflect the transformation in the paternal role over time (Hawkins & Dollahite, 1997; Marsiglio & Roy, 2012) and becomes problematic. Finally, commonly used measures of father involvement tend to reflect both traditional fathering roles and contemporary expectations that men be engaged in emotional and instrumental parenting tasks. Using a multidimensional approach to father involvement is recommended.

Contemporary fathering expectations are such that the measurement of father involvement should not starkly contrast with maternal parenting. At the same time, however, fathering behaviors should be examined with theoretical sensitivity toward men's historical involvement in particular tasks and how that involvement is meaningful given persistent, although shifting gendered roles and expectations. For example, continually evolving norms of contemporary fatherhood increasingly emphasize emotionally supportive parenting. In this vein, measures like warmth, which refers to displays of loving and affectionate behavior and engagement in routine activities, being emotionally available, and providing social support are included. At the same time, fathers have traditionally been viewed as responsible for family order and have taken on the disciplinary role. Measures of positive control, which reflect awareness about where children are, what they are doing, and providing constructive corrective action when necessary, and harsh discipline or physically and emotionally abusive responses to child misbehavior, reflect these more traditional paternal roles. Studies have consistently shown that high levels of warmth, engagement, and positive control have significant and positive effects on child outcomes, independent of maternal behavior (Barton et al., 2015; Jeynes, 2015; McLanahan et al., 2013). Thus, while these measures demonstrate sensitivity toward current conceptualizations of the paternal role, there is also evidence that these behaviors are valuable and reliable predictors of child health, well-being, and development as well.

There are some issues that researchers and practitioners should keep in mind when assessing paternal involvement. It is critical that services and providers comprehend what fathers are doing in their homes and with their children alongside potential changes in their behavior because of programs and services. As a result, assessment cannot be divorced from programs or services. First, we must realize that fathers often have competing demands on their time—including employment, financial difficulties, and time crunches—which can manifest in the assessment process. For example, fathers may be reluctant to take long complicated surveys. The

Table 6.1 Potential areas of assessment and associated measures that are commonly used

Content area	Potential measures
Involvement	Father involvement and nurturant fathering scales Relationship with the child questionnaire Fatherhood research and practice network fathers' engagement measure
Co-parenting	Parenting alliance measure Fatherhood research and practice network Co-parenting Relationship scale Coparenting across family structures scale
Father-child relationship quality	Child-parent relationship scale Parent-child relationship scale

second author worked with a California-based fatherhood program where an analysis of the surveys taken by more than 1000 fathers in the program noted that assessments lasting more than 20 minutes tend to increase the dropout rate substantially. As a result, assessors should be judicious in the questions that they ask, not get overly complicated in their questionnaires, and think about what it is they are interested in assessing. The use of pre-existing measures can help programs and providers thread the needle between assessing a broad range of behaviors in necessary detail while accounting for needs like simplicity and brevity that are often required among the populations being served. Table 6.1 provides some areas of potential assessment and commonly used measures that address these conceptual areas. The provided measures do a good job of assessing fathers across numerous family structures while being aware of issues such as gendered norms, inequalities, and structural constraints on fathers. While this list is not fully comprehensive, it does provide a number of possibilities that service providers could use in their assessment of fathers.

Second, we should be careful about the stereotypes we maintain about fathers, particularly those related to seeing their potential and realizing that many are willing to participate in research. Research indicates that social workers often perceive fathers negatively (Nygren et al., 2019), and fathers report feeling that they are not given the same benefit of the doubt as mothers and that some agencies have an "anti-dad" environment (Lee et al., 2016; Shadik & O'Connor, 2016). Therefore, it is important that the assessment process is thorough and encompasses strengths, challenges, and progress. Many scholars and practitioners believe that men and fathers are reluctant to participate in programs and assessments (Shafer & Bellamy, 2016), but there is little empirical basis for this claim. Survey research response rates with fathers hover near national averages, (Shafer et al., 2019) and response rates in fatherhood program assessment tend to be relatively high (Dyer et al., 2018). Perhaps most telling are the qualitative studies that include both mothers and fathers. For example, qualitative interviews conducted in Detroit by Dayton et al. (2019) took longer, on average, with fathers than mothers—suggesting that many fathers are waiting to be asked about their lives, their challenges, and their paternal role. Yet harmful stereotypes about men and fathers persist both inside and outside the research community.

Pearson (2020) highlights many of the challenges and lessons learned around delivering programs to fathers and the challenges encountered in the assessment process—noting the difficulty in a Fatherhood Research and Practice Network (FRPN) research brief of engaging some fathers in surveys and focus groups. The issues raised included the lack of incentives, cultural competence, and the lack of baseline data to understand the needs and issues facing fathers. Practitioners might think about including fathers in advisory capacities, understanding the unique ecological barriers and opportunities that exist in certain locations. Cultural awareness of the populations served by practitioners is also necessary. Earlier, we noted that there is significant fluidity in fathering. Assessment should also consider differences across race/ethnicity, social class, sexuality, living arrangements, and child characteristics if it is to be highly effective with as many fathers as possible. Finally, it may prove beneficial to get "buy in" from fathers from the beginning of programs and other practice settings. To this end, convincing fathers about the importance of assessment, its personal value to them, and its greater value to understand the myriad strengths and challenges fathers face can improve assessment processes.

Resources

- Fatherhood Research and Practice Network (FRPN) – scales and measures related to assessment:
  - FRPN Fathers' Engagement Measures: https://www.frpn.org/asset/frpn-research-measure-fathers-engagement-english-and-spanish-versions-available
  - FRPN Coparenting Relationship Scales: https://www.frpn.org/asset/frpn-research-measure-coparenting-relationship-scale-english-and-spanish-measures-available
- Father Involvement and Nurturant Fathering Scales: https://journals.sagepub.com/doi/10.1177/0013164403258453
- Child-Parent Relationship Scale (CPRS): https://education.virginia.edu/faculty-research/centers-labs-projects/castl/measures-developed-robert-c-pianta-phd
- Fatherhood Institute. United Kingdom-based website with information and resources related to fatherhood: http://www.fatherhoodinstitute.org/

Discussion Questions

1. Are intake and assessment forms at your agency designed with fathers in mind?
2. What is one change you could make to enhance the assessment process at your agency for fathers?

3. How might adopting some of the changes discussed in this chapter positively impact mothers and children as well as fathers?
4. How can you assess fathers in a way that reflects the diversity of your clients?
5. What are some potential challenges your organization might face to engage fathers in assessment?

References

Allen, S. M., & Daly, K. (2002). The effects of father involvement: A summary of the research evidence. *Newsletter of the Father Involvement Initiative – Ontario Network*, 1–11.

Barton, A. W., Beach, S. R. H., Kogan, S. M., Stanley, S. M., Fincham, F. D., Hurt, T. R., & Brody, G. H. (2015). Prevention effects on trajectories of African American adolescents' exposure to interparental conflict and depressive symptoms. *Journal of Family Psychology, 29(2), 171–179.* https://doi.org/10.1037/fam0000073

Bellamy, J. L. (2009). A national study of male involvement among families in contact with the child welfare system. *Child Maltreatment, 14*, 255–262. https://doi.org/10.1177/1077559508326288

Bruno, A., Celebre, L., Mento, C., Rizzo, A., Silvestri, M. C., De Stefano, R., Zoccali, R. A., & Muscatello, M. R. A. (2020). When fathers begin to falter: A comprehensive review on paternal perinatal depression. *International Journal of Environmental Research and Public Health, 17*(4), 1139. https://doi.org/10.3390/ijerph17041139

Cabrera, N. J., Volling, B. L., & Barr, R. (2018). Fathers are parents, too! Widening the lens on parenting for children's development. *Child Development Perspectives, 12*(3), 152–157. https://doi.org/10.1111/cdep.12275

Campbell, C. G., & Winn, E. J. (2018). Father-daughter bonds: A comparison of adolescent daughters' relationships with resident biological fathers and stepfathers: Stepfathers and stepdaughters. *Family Relations, 67*(5), 675–686. https://doi.org/10.1111/fare.12342

Carlberg, M., Edhborg, M., & Lindberg, L. (2018). Paternal perinatal depression assessed by the Edinburgh Postnatal Depression Scale and the Gotland Depression Scale: Prevalence and possible risk factors. *American Journal of Men's Health, 12*(4), 720–729. https://doi.org/10.1177/1557988317749071

Castillo, J., Welch, G., & Sarver, C. (2011). Fathering: The relationship between fathers' residence, fathers' sociodemographic characteristics, and father involvement. *Maternal and Child Health Journal, 15*, 1342–1349. https://doi.org/10.1007/s10995-010-0684-6

Charles, P., Spielfogel, J., Gorman-Smith, D., Schoeny, M., Henry, D., & Tolan, P. (2018). Disagreement in parental reports of father involvement. *Journal of Family Issues, 39*(2), 328–351. https://doi-org.proxy.library.ohio.edu/10.1177/0192513X16644639

Chung, G., Smith, Q., Frey, J., & Lanier, P. (2021). Associations between depression and parenting of fathers in Head Start and parental self-efficacy as a protective factor. *Children and Youth Services Review, 120*, 1–9. https://doi.org/10.1016/j.childyouth.2020.105758

Coates, E. E., & Phares, V. (2019). Pathways linking nonresident father involvement and child outcomes. *Journal of Child and Family Studies, 28*(6), 1681–1694. https://doi.org/10.1007/s10826-019-01389-6

Coleman, M., Ganong, L. H., & Russell, L. T. (2013). Resilience in step-families. In D. Becvar (Ed.), *Handbook of family resilience* (pp. 85–103). Springer.

Coontz, S. (2016). *The social origins of private life: A history of American families, 1600–1900. Verso Books.*

Day, R. D., & Lamb, M. E. (2004). Conceptualizing **and measuring father involvement: Pathways, problems, and progress. In R. D. Day & M. E. Lamb (Eds.),** *Conceptualizing and measuring father involvement. Lawrence Erlbaum Associates.* https://doi.org/10.4324/9781410609380

Day, R. D., & Padilla-Walker, L. M. (2009). Mother and father connectedness and involvement during early adolescence. *Journal of Family Psychology, 23*(6), 900–904. https://doi.org/10.1037/a0016438

Dayton, C. J., Brown, S., Goletz, J., Hicks, L., Barron, C., Sperlich, M., & Smith-Darden, J. (2019). Pathways to parenting: Predictors of prenatal bonding in a sample of expectant mothers and fathers exposed to contextual risk. *Journal of Child and Family Studies, 28*(4), 1134–1144. https://doi.org/10.1007/s10826-019-01343-6

Dermott, E. (2008). *Intimate fatherhood: A sociological analysis*. Routledge.

Dubowitz, H. (2009). Commentary on fathers and children and maltreatment: Relationships matter most. *Child Maltreatment, 14*, 291–293. https://doi.org/10.1177/1077559509339389

Dunn, J. (2002). The adjustment of children in stepfamilies: Lessons from community studies. *Child and Adolescent Mental Health, 7*(4), 154–161. https://doi.org/10.1111/1475-3588.00028

Dyer, W. J., Fagan, J., Kaufman, R., Pearson, J., & Cabrera, N. (2018). Self-perceived coparenting of nonresident fathers: Scale development and validation. *Family Process, 57*(4), 927–946. https://doi.org/10.1111/famp.12331

Edin, K., & Nelson, T. J. (2013). *Doing the best I can: Fatherhood in the inner city*. University of California Press.

Edward, K., Giandinoto, J., Stephenson, J., Mills, C., Mcfarland, J., & Castle, D. J. (2019). Self-screening using the Edinburgh post natal depression scale for mothers and fathers to initiate early help seeking behaviours. *Archives of Psychiatric Nursing, 33*(4), 421–427. https://doi.org/10.1016/j.apnu.2019.05.007

Eggebeen, D. J. (2013). Do fathers uniquely matter for adolescent well-being? In W. B. Wilcox & K. K. Kline (Eds.), *Gender and parenthood: Biological and social scientific perspectives* (pp. 249–270). Columbia University Press.

Fagan, J. (2020). Associations between low-income nonresident fathers' parenting identity and involvement with their children. *Psychology of Men & Masculinities, 22*(3), 433–442. https://doi.org/10.1037/men0000295

Fagan, J., Day, R. D., Lamb, M. E., & Cabrera, N. J. (2014). Should researchers conceptualize differently the dimensions of parenting for fathers and mothers? *Journal of Family Theory & Review, 6*(4), 390–405. https://doi.org/10.1111/jftr.12044

Fagan, J., & Kaufman, R. (2015a). Co-parenting relationships among low-income, unmarried parents: Perspectives of fathers in fatherhood programs. *Family Court Review, 53*(2), 304–316. https://doi.org/10.1111/fcre.12152

Fagan, J., & Kaufman, R. (2015b). Reflections on theory and outcome measures for fatherhood programs. *Families in Society, 96*(2), 133–140. https://doi.org/10.1606/1044-3894.2015.96.19

Fine, M. A., & Kurdek, L. A. (1994). Parenting cognitions in stepfamilies: Differences between parents and stepparents and relations to parenting satisfaction. *Journal of Social and Personal Relationships, 11*(1), 95–112.

FRPN Research Brief: Implementation & Lessons Learned from the FRPN State Planning Grant Initiative. Fatherhood Research and Practice Network (n.d.). https://www.frpn.org/asset/frpn-research-brief-implementation-lessons-learned-the-frpn-state-planning-grant-initiative

Gadsden, V. L., Fagan, J., Ray, A., & Davis, J. E. (2004). Fathering indicators for practice and evaluation: The Fathering Indicators Framework. In R. D. Day & M. E. Lamb (Eds.), *Conceptualizing and measuring father involvement* (pp. 385–415). Erlbaum.

Ganong, L. H., & Coleman, M. (2004). *Stepfamily relationships: Development, dynamics, and interventions*. Springer U.S. http://public.ebookcentral.proquest.com/choice/publicfullrecord.aspx?p=3073682

Golish, T. D. (2003). Stepfamily communication strengths—Understanding the ties that bind. *Human Communication Research, 29*(1), 41–80. https://doi.org/10.1111/j.1468-2958.2003.tb00831.x

Goodman, J. H. (2004). Paternal postpartum depression, its relationship to maternal postpartum depression, and implications for family health. *Journal of Advanced Nursing, 45*(1), 26–35. https://doi.org/10.1046/j.1365-2648.2003.02857.x

Guzzo, K. B., & Furstenberg, F. F. (2007). Multipartnered fertility among American men. *Demography, 44(3), 583–601.*

Hawkins, A. J., Bradford, K. P., Palkovitz, R., Christiansen, S. L., Day, R. D., & Call, V. R. A. (2002). The inventory of father involvement: A pilot study of a new measure of father involvement. *The Journal of Men's Studies, 10*(2), 183–196. https://doi.org/10.3149/jms.1002.183

Hawkins, A. J., & Dollahite, D. C. (1997). *Generative fathering: Beyond deficit perspectives*. Sage Publications.

Hawkins, A. J., & Palkovitz, R. (1999). Beyond ticks and clicks: The need for more diverse and broader conceptualizations and measures of father involvement. *The Journal of Men's Studies, 8*(1), 11–32. https://doi.org/10.3149/jms.0801.11

Hetherington, E. M., & Kelly, J. (2002). *For better or for worse: Divorce reconsidered.* Norton.

Jensen, T. M., & Shafer, K. (2013). Stepfamily functioning and closeness: Children's views on second marriages and stepfather relationships. *Journal of Social Work, 58*(2), 127–136. https://doi.org/10.1093/sw/swt007

Jensen, T. M., Shafer, K., & Holmes, E. K. (2017). Transitioning to stepfamily life: The influence of closeness with biological parents and stepparents on children's stress. *Child & Family Social Work, 22*(1), 275–286. https://doi.org/10.1111/cfs.12237

Jeynes, W. H. (2015). A meta-analysis: The relationship between father involvement and student academic achievement. *Urban Education, 50*(4), 387–423. https://doi.org/10.1177/0042085914525789

Jones, J., & Mosher, W. D. (2013). *Fathers' involvement with their children: United States, 2006–2010 National Health Statistics Reports*, 71. https://www.cdc.gov/nchs/data/nhsr/nhsr071.pdf.

Jones, K. (2004). Assessing psychological separation and academic performance in nonresident-father and resident-father adolescent boys. *Child and Adolescent Social Work Journal, 21*(4), 333–354. https://doi.org/10.1023/B:CASW.0000035220.56477.19

King, V. (2009). Stepfamily formation: Implications for adolescent ties to mothers, nonresident fathers, and stepfathers. *Journal of Marriage and Family, 71*, 954–968. https://doi.org/10.1111/j.1741-3737.2009.00646.x

Kinniburgh-White, R., Cartwright, C., & Seymour, F. (2010). Young adults' narratives of relational development with stepfathers. *Journal of Social and Personal Relationships, 27*(7), 890–907. https://doi.org/10.1177/0265407510376252

Kirst-Ashman, K. K., & Hull, G. H. (2015). *Understanding generalist practice* (7th ed.). Cengage.

Kuo, P. X., Volling, B. L., & Gonzalez, R. (2018). Gender role beliefs, work–family conflict, and father involvement after the birth of a second child. *Psychology of Men & Masculinity, 19*(2), 243–256. https://doi.org/10.1037/men0000101

Lamb, M. E. (2010). How do fathers influence children's development? Let me count the ways. In M. E. Lamb (Ed.), *The role of the father in child development* (5th ed., pp. 1–26). Wiley.

Lee, S. J., Hoffman, G., & Harris, D. (2016). Community-based participatory research (CBPR) needs assessment of parenting support programs for fathers. *Children and Youth Services Review, 66*, 76–84. https://doi.org/10.1016/j.childyouth.2016.05.004

Lee, S. J., & Altschul, I. (2015). Spanking of young children: Do immigrant and U.S.-born Hispanic parents differ? *Journal of Interpersonal Violence, 30(3), 475–498.* https://doi.org/10.1177/0886260514535098

Lutz, P. (1983). The stepfamily: An adolescent perspective. *Family Relations, 32*(3), 367–375. https://doi.org/10.2307/584614

MacDonald, W. L., & DeMaris, A. (2002). Stepfather-stepchild relationship quality: The stepfather's demand for conformity and the biological father's involvement. *Journal of Family Issues, 23*(1), 121–137. https://doi.org/10.1177/0192513X02023001006

Magovcevic, M., & Addis, M. E. (2008). The Masculine Depression Scale: Development and psychometric evaluation. *Psychology of Men & Masculinity, 9*(3), 117–132. https://doi.org/10.1037/1524-9220.9.3.117

Manning, A. (2019). The age of concerted cultivation: A racial analysis of parental repertoires and childhood activities. *Du Bois Review, 16(1), 5–35.* https://doi.org/10.1017/S1742058X19000080

Marczak, M. S., Becher, E. H., Hardman, A. M., Galos, D. L., & Ruhland, E. (2015). Strengthening the role of unmarried fathers: Findings from the Co-Parent Court Project. *Family Process, 54*(4), 630–638. https://doi.org/10.1111/famp.12134

Marsiglio, W., & Roy, K. (2012). *Nurturing dads: Social initiatives for contemporary fatherhood.* Russell Sage Foundation.

Marsiglio, W., Roy, K., & Fox, G. L. (2005). *Situated fathering: A focus on physical and social spaces.* Rowman & Littlefield Publishers.

Martin, M. M., Anderson, C. M., & Mottet, T. P. (1999). Perceived understanding and self-disclosure in the stepparent-stepchild relationship. *The Journal of Psychology, 133*(3), 281–290. https://doi.org/10.1080/00223989909599741

Maxwell, N., Scourfield, J., Featherstone, B., Holland, S., & Tolman, R. (2012). Engaging fathers in child welfare services: A narrative review of recent research evidence. *Child & Family Social Work, 17(2), 160–169.* https://doi.org/10.1111/j.1365-2206.2012.00827.x

McBride, B. A., Brown, G. L., Bost, K. K., Shin, N., Vaughn, B., & Korth, B. (2005a). Paternal identity, maternal gatekeeping, and father involvement. *Family Relations, 54*(3), 360–372. https://doi.org/10.1111/j.1741-3729.2005.00323.x

McBride, B. A., Schoppe-Sullivan, S. J., & Ho, M.-H. (2005b). The mediating role of fathers' school involvement on student achievement. *Journal of Applied Developmental Psychology, 26*(2), 201–216. https://doi.org/10.1016/j.appdev.2004.12.007

McHale, J. P., & Negrini, L. S. (2018). How the assumption of a coparenting frame will transform social work practice with men and fathers. *Social Work Research, 42*(1), 9–21. https://doi.org/10.1093/swr/svx024

McLanahan, S., Tach, L., & Schneider, D. (2013). The causal effects of father absence. *Annual Review of Sociology, 39*, 399–427. https://doi.org/10.1146/annurev-soc-071312-145704

McWayne, C., Downer, J. T., Campos, R., & Harris, R. D. (2013). Father involvement during early childhood and its association with children's early learning: A meta-analysis. *Early Education and Development, 24*(6), 898–922. https://doi.org/10.1080/10409289.2013.746932

Mitchell, O., & Caudy, M. S. (2015). Examining Racial Disparities in Drug Arrests. *Justice Quarterly, 32(2), 288–313.* https://doi.org/10.1080/07418825.2012.761721

National Association of Social Workers. (2021). *NASW code of ethics*. Author. https://www.socialworkers.org/About/Ethics/Code-of-Ethics.

Nellis, A. (2016). The color of justice: Racial and ethnic disparity in state prisons. The Sentencing Project.

Nygren, K., Walsh, J., Ellingsen, I. T., & Christie, A. (2019). What about the fathers? The presence and absence of the father in social work practice in England, Ireland, Norway, and Sweden – A comparative study. *Child & Family Social Work, 24*, 148–155. https://doi.org/10.1111/cfs.12592

Palkovitz, R., & Hull, J. (2018). Toward a resource theory of fathering. *Journal of Family Theory & Review, 10*, 181–198. https://doi.org/10.1111/jftr.12239

Palkovitz, R., Trask, B. S., & Adamsons, K. (2014). Essential differences in the meaning and processes of mothering and fathering: Family systems, feminist and qualitative perspectives. *Journal of Family Theory & Review, 6*, 406–420. https://doi.org/10.1111/jftr.12048

Panter, B. C., Burgess, A., Eggerman, M., McAllister, F., Pruett, K., & Leckman, J. F. (2014). Practitioner review: Engaging fathers – Recommendations for a game change in parenting interventions based on a systematic review of the global evidence. *Journal of Child Psychology & Psychiatry, 55*(11), 1187–1212. https://doi-org.proxy.library.ohio.edu/10.1111/jcpp.12280

Pearson, J. (2020). FRPN research brief: Implementation and lessons learned from the FRPN state planning grant initiative. Fatherhood Research & Practice Network. https://fatherhood.gov/sites/default/files/resource_files/FRPN_PlanningInitiatives_FullReport_042120_FA.pdf

Perry, A., & Lewis, S. (2016). Leaving legacies: African American men discuss the impact of their fathers on the development of their own paternal attitudes and behavior. *Journal of Family Social Work, 19(1), 3–21.*

Perry, A. R., Rollins, A., & Perez, A. (2020). *Fatherhood & Coparenting.* Fatherhood Research & Practice Network Grantee Report. https://www.frpn.org/asset/frpn-grantee-report-fatherhood-coparenting

Petts, R. J., Shafer, K., & Essig, L. (2018). Does adherence to masculine norms shape fathering behavior? *Journal of Marriage and Family, 80*(3), 704–720. https://doi.org/10.1111/jomf.12476

Pleck, J. H. (2010). Paternal involvement: Revised conceptualization and theoretical linkages with child outcomes. In M. E. Lamb (Ed.), *The role of the father involvement in child development* (pp. 58–93). Wiley.

Pleck, J. H. (2012). Integrating father involvement in parenting research. *Parenting, 12*, 243–253. https://doi.org/10.1080/15295192.2012.683365

Roberts, D., Coakley, T. M., Washington, T. J., & Kelley, A. (2014). Fathers' perspectives on supports and barriers that affect their fatherhood role. *SAGE Open, 4*(1), 1–10. https://doi.org/10.1177/2158244014521818

Rochlen, A. B., Paterniti, D. A., Epstein, R. M., Duberstein, P. R., Willeford, L. C., & Kravitz, R. L. (2010). Barriers in diagnosing and treating men with depression: A focus group report. *American Journal of Men's Health, 4*(2), 167–175. https://doi.org/10.1177/1557988309335823

Roy, K. (2014). Fathering from the long view: Framing personal and social change through life course theory. *Journal of Family Theory & Review, 6(4), 319–335.* https://doi.org/10.1111/jftr.12050

Sameroff, A. J., & Fiese, B. H. (2000). Models of development and developmental risk. In C. Zeanah Jr. (Ed.), *Handbook of infant mental health* (2nd ed., pp. 3–19). Guilford Press.

Scourfield, J. (2014). Improving work with fathers to prevent child maltreatment. *Child Abuse & Neglect, 38*, 974–981. https://doi.org/10.1016/j.chiabu.2014.05.002

Schoppe-Sullivan, S. J., & Fagan, J. (2020). The evolution of fathering research in the 21st century: Persistent challenges, new directions. *Journal of Marriage and Family, 82*(1), 175–197. https://doi.org/10.1111/jomf.12645

Shadik, J. A. (2020). Fathering and child maltreatment: Understanding the impact of fluidity in fathers' lives. *Journal of Family Social Work, 23*(3), 257–276. https://doi.org/10.1080/10522158.2020.1725794

Shadik, J. A., & O'Connor, M. K. (2016). Fathering and child maltreatment: Building theory to enhance treatment interventions. *Social Work Research, 40*(4), 213–224. https://doi.org/10.1093/swr/svw016

Shafer, K., & Bellamy, J. L. (2016). Focusing on men and fathers: A challenge for social work research and practice. *Social Work Research, 40*(4), 199–202. https://doi.org/10.1093/swr/svw020

Shafer, K., Fielding, B., & Holmes, E. K. (2019). Depression, masculine norm adherence, and fathering behavior. *Journal of Family Issues, 40*(1), 48–84. https://doi.org/10.1177/0192513X18800782

Solis, J. M., Shadur, J. M., Burns, A. R., & Hussong, A. M. (2012). Understanding the diverse needs of children whose parents abuse substances. *Current Drug Abuse Reviews, 5*(2), 135–147. https://dx.doi.org/10.2174%2F1874473711205020135

Spjeldnes, S., Shadik, J. A., Ruhil, A., Kloepfer, D., & Bell, Z. (2020). *Fatherhood programs: Factors associated with retention, completion, and outcomes report.* Fatherhood Research & Practice Network Grantee Report. https://www.frpn.org/asset/frpn-grantee-report-fatherhood-programs-factors-associated-retention-completion-and-outcomes

Stewart, S. D. (2007). *Brave new stepfamilies: Diverse paths toward stepfamily living*. Sage Publications.

Torres, N., Veríssimo, M., Monteiro, L., Ribeiro, O., & Santos, A. J. (2014). Domains of father involvement, social competence and problem behavior in preschool children. *Journal of Family Studies, 20*(3), 188–203. https://doi.org/10.1080/13229400.2014.11082006

Tully, L. A., Piotrowska, P. J., Collins, D. A. J., Mairet, K. S., Black, N., Kimonis, E., Hawes, D. J., Moul, C., Lenroot, R. K., Frick, P. J., Anderson, V., & Dadds, M. R. (2017). Optimising child outcomes from parenting interventions: Fathers' experiences, preferences, and barriers to participation. *BMC Public Health, 17*(550), 1–14. https://doi.org/10.1186/s12889-017-4426-1

U.S. Census Bureau. (2020). *2009 and 2019 American Community Survey 1-year estimates.* https://www.census.gov/library/stories/2020/12/united-states-marriage-and-divorce-rates-declined-last-10-years.html

Twamley, K., Brunton, G., Sutcliffe, K., Hinds, K., & Thomas, J. (2013). Fathers' involvement and the impact on family mental health: Evidence from Millennium Cohort Study analyses. *Community, Work & Family, 16*(2), 212–224. https://doi.org/10.1080/13668803.2012.755022

Zanoni, L., Warburton, W., Bussey, K., & McMaugh, A. (2013). Fathers as 'core business' in child welfare practice and research: An interdisciplinary review. *Children and Youth Services Review, 35*(7), 1055–1070. https://doi.org/10.1016/j.childyouth.2013.04.018

Zanoni, L., Warburton, W., Bussey, K., & McMaugh, A. (2014). Are all fathers in child protection families uncommitted, uninvolved, and unable to change? *Children and Youth Services Review, 41*, 83–94. https://doi.org/10.1016/j.childyouth.2014.03.014

Chapter 7
Organizational "Father-Friendliness" Assessments

Nigel Vann and Armon R. Perry

Introduction

As interest in the role that fathers play in their children's growth and development has increased over the last 30 to 40 years, so too has the number of programs that provide supportive services for fathers (Vann, 2021). Many of these programs have been stand-alone community initiatives, generally funded only on a short-term basis through public or private grants. Other programs have been embedded in established social service organizations that provide general parent support services such as Head Start, Healthy Start, and Home Visiting. Regardless of program type and funding source, research concludes that many of these programs struggle to maintain consistent services through leadership and staffing changes. Literature has provided some guidance on the promising practices, recommending that programs provide barrier-reducing program support, maintain flexible hours of operation, and encourage staff to talk with fathers rather than automatically engaging mothers exclusively (Cowan et al., 2007). In addition to adopting these practices, research has also concluded that assessing the *father friendliness* of the host organization is an important step in understanding the effectiveness of services. This has led to the development of father-friendliness assessments to guide practitioners, program administrators, and researchers in their efforts to better understand how programs are perceived by fathers.

N. Vann (✉)
National Responsible Fatherhood Clearinghouse, Silver City, NM, USA
e-mail: nigelvann@msn.com

A. R. Perry
Kent School of Social Work and Family Science, University of Louisville, Louisville, KY, USA
e-mail: arperr01@louisville.edu

J. L. Bellamy et al. (eds.), *Social Work Practice with Fathers*,
https://doi.org/10.1007/978-3-031-13686-3_7

To help advance the state of knowledge in this area, this chapter provides an overview of father-friendliness assessment tools and discusses how agency leaders and staff can utilize these tools to ensure that their programs and places of operation are welcoming and supportive of fathers in terms of geographical location, physical environment, staff training, and programming. This chapter concludes with a discussion of how father-friendliness assessments can guide adaptations to policies and services to better serve fathers.

Background and Context

Social service organizations have traditionally worked mainly with mothers and children. As a consequence, many struggle to effectively engage with fathers. This practice dates back to the so-called "man-in-the-house" rules that authorized social workers to make unannounced visits to their clients' homes. If signs of a man's presence were found, the family would lose their eligibility for public assistance (Simon, 2020). This pathologizing and problematizing of fathers later manifested in benign neglect, in which fathers were just ignored or simply not considered as viable caregiving options. For example, early childhood programs, in particular, have tended to be mother-centered and likely to equate the term *parent* with *mother* (Fagan & Iglesias, 1999; Levine, 1993). Research has shown that staff in these programs often hold negative attitudes toward men and assume that fathers do not have the capacity to be positively involved with and supportive of their children (Fagan, 1996; Garinger & McBride, 1995; Levine, 1993; McAllister et al., 2004; McBride et al., 2001).

Most recently, research has found that some staff may stereotype men and make assumptions that restrict their willingness and ability to engage with fathers. For example, they may assume that fathers do not want to talk about emotional matters, are unlikely to engage in activities with their infant children, and are not invested in their children's healthy growth and development. In an article describing the results of a maternal and child health program's fatherhood needs assessment, Perry et al. (2016) found that Healthy Start staff were reluctant to work with fathers, were not intentional about scheduling time to meet with them, and were not likely to connect with fathers who did not initiate contact with program officials. In some cases, these negative attitudes were grounded in previous negative or apathetic experiences with fathers. In other cases, staff attitudes stemmed from experiences with their own fathers or other men in their personal lives. The authors concluded that program staff had generally not received training on the importance of father involvement in the lives of children, had not been given the opportunity to reflect on their own early childhood experiences, or had not been shown strategies to include fathers in program activities. Brewsaugh et al. (2018) examined child welfare workers' sexism and beliefs about father involvement in a survey of 490 frontline child protective service workers. Their results revealed that participants with less sexist beliefs had more positive views of father involvement and were less likely to report a preference for working exclusively with mothers. In agreement with previous research, the authors concluded that staff needed the training to increase their knowledge of the importance of father involvement and their comfort in providing services to men.

> *Because program efforts to involve fathers depend on staff members' attitudes about and behaviors toward involving fathers with young children, it is critical to find meaningful ways to assess attitudes and behaviors that either hinder or support the father friendliness of a program.*
>
> (White et al., 2011)

Promising Practices for Engaging Fathers

Even though gendered stereotypes about whether men are worthy enough to participate in safety net programs persist in contemporary society (Perry, 2020), there is a growing literature, both domestic (Fagan & Pearson, 2019) and international (Anderson et al., 2019), offering guidance for engaging fathers in social service programs. Bronte-Tinkew et al. (2007) conducted a review of several fatherhood program studies and found that programs were more likely to produce positive outcomes if they were creative with their outreach and recruitment, used teaching methods that focused on fathers as individuals, and were appropriate for and respectful of the fathers' cultural backgrounds. Perhaps most importantly, programs that selected staff who believed in the importance of providing support for fathers were more likely to be welcoming and engaging to men.

Other promising practices have come from comparisons of the father-engagement efforts of the Head Start and Early Head Start programs (Fagan, 1996, 1999; Raikes et al., 2005), which found that the most successful programs allowed time to design and implement father-specific programs, recruited fathers as classroom volunteers, and trained staff to be sensitive to fathers' social and emotional needs. McAllister et al. (2004) suggested that before trying to adopt new activities, organizations should first focus on developing new ways of thinking about father engagement. These suggestions included understanding that staff can build relationships with fathers just as they do with mothers, engaging in a reflective and self-critical approach to program services, providing opportunities for program management and staff to evaluate and learn from their own experiences as well as incorporate the perspectives of participating parents, applying program approaches and principles to work with fathers to the same degree that such approaches and principles are applied to work with mothers, and ensuring that all program staff develop an understanding of father involvement as a key aspect of their work with program families.

The U.S. Department of Health and Human Services' Healthy Marriage Responsible Fatherhood (HMRF) funding mechanism has also produced tips to inform program planning. Zaveri et al. (2015) focused on the design and implementation of fatherhood initiatives. Their findings indicated that programs were better able to connect with fathers when they used data about the target population to develop content and services to address specific needs. It was recommended that programs employ staff who had the ability to connect with fathers or had experiences similar to those of fathers so they could serve as role models for them. The authors encouraged program developers to cultivate partnerships with child support agencies to facilitate positive outcomes for nonresident fathers and use evaluation data to monitor performance benchmarks and inform refinements to service delivery. Finally, programs were encouraged to offer cohort-based services and incentives to promote participation.

Behrmann and Brennan (2020) went beyond the initial engagement of fathers and leveraged data from the Building Bridges and Bonds (B3) project to provide tips for sustaining engagement in programs. These tips covered strategies for inside and outside the program. More specifically, the inside tips included making a positive first impression, creating a comfortable environment, building a thoughtful program structure, and incorporating hands-on learning. Efforts outside of the program included providing assistance to address basic needs, working with fathers to respond to competing demands, and making it easier to attend programming by addressing logistical problems. The authors also recommended using program data to monitor and refocus program efforts and incorporate participants' perspectives and experiences into program decision making.

More recently, Abendroth et al. (2021) shared findings from six child welfare teams participating in the Fathers and Continuous Learning in Child Welfare project related to engaging fathers during the COVID-19 pandemic. The brief considers the consequences of pandemic lockdowns and prohibitions on face-to-face interaction and details how moving to virtual services created new challenges for those without the requisite technology. Some teams were able to creatively navigate these challenges, including the use of Title IV-E funds to buy tablets for fathers. Other strategies included social distancing practices like buying lawn chairs and hosting socially distanced events in local parks, as well as making use of text messaging and conference call options to deliver programming and maintain communication. As a result of the reductions in travel time to in-person meetings, program staff were more available to connect with fathers. Staff also reported that fathers were more receptive to virtual meetings and appeared less intimidated by them than the in-person alternatives. As a result, several improvements were reported, including higher attendance by fathers, fewer meeting cancellations, improved father-social worker relationships, and greater caregiver involvement in cases.

Avellar et al. (2020) published an interim report for the 2015 cohort of HMRF grantees. The report focused on program operations data from July 2016 to March 2019, a period when over 30,000 fathers were enrolled. Grantees reported using myriad strategies to recruit participants into their responsible fatherhood programs. These strategies were divided into two categories: advertising/outreach and recruitment methods. The most-used advertising activities were presentations for community partners, word of mouth, flyers, and social-media marketing. The most often used recruitment methods were on-site recruitment at community agencies, referrals from community agencies, phone or mail outreach, and street outreach.

Home visiting research has also contributed to the promising practices literature on engaging fathers. In a recent brief, Bellamy (2020) states that despite the evidence of their effectiveness in producing positive outcomes and reducing the risk of child maltreatment, many studies suggest that home visiting outcomes fade over time. Therefore, increasing father engagement in home visiting has been posited as a strategy to extend the program benefits for participating families. Drawing on observations from the Dads Matter Home Visiting intervention, Bellamy debunks several misconceptions about fathers, including erroneous assumptions that engaging fathers will negatively impact an organization's ability to serve mothers and beliefs that most fathers are absent or present risks of domestic violence. In addition to citing research countering these notions, the brief also outlines four key principles to guide the engagement of fathers in home visiting services: (1) engaging fathers at the inception of the service delivery process, (2) training all staff on how to create an atmosphere that facilitates father engagement, (3) consistently seeking out opportunities to engage fathers, and (4) leveraging agency leaders' influence to reinforce the culture of father engagement.

In sum, there has been a significant increase in the attention paid to father involvement over the past 30 years, as a result of which there is now more interest in programs designed to help fathers take more active roles in their children's lives. As the literature on father engagement promising practices has developed, organizational father friendliness and the tools used to assess it have taken on more significance than ever before. To contribute to the state of knowledge in this area, the subsequent sections of this chapter are dedicated to discussing father-friendliness assessments, reviewing several of the more frequently used father-friendliness instruments, and offering recommendations for practitioners and organizations interested in serving fathers and their families.

> *The most successful programs are those which create an ongoing "culture of father-friendliness" based on staff awareness of the value of a father-friendly atmosphere, efforts to create and maintain a welcoming environment for fathers as parents, and specific activities that invite fathers and father figures to be meaningfully involved in their children's lives and the programs that support them.*
>
> (White et al., 2011)

Elements of Effective Parenting Programs and Strategies for Increasing Program Participation and Retention

Studies indicate that parenting interventions benefit from approaches that give greater priority to fathers' participation, such as:

- Starting with the expectation that fathers will participate.
- Using content and activities that are relevant for fathers.
- Scheduling sessions at times that are convenient.

(Committee on Supporting the Parents of Young Children, 2016)

Recommended Assessment Approaches

There are a number of father-friendliness assessment tools available online or on request. In this section, we offer some tips to guide you through a general assessment process, provide an overview of four popular tools, look at some common assessment categories, and suggest some initial questions to develop a quick impression of how father-friendly a specific organization might be.

General Father-Friendly Assessment Process

No matter which tool you choose to use, or if you decide to create your own, there are some commonalities to assess and examine. For example, all organizations will want to consider whether their reception area and intake procedures are designed with fathers in mind, whether their staff are knowledgeable and trained to work with fathers, whether their program services are sufficient to meet the needs of fathers, and whether the services were developed with input from fathers. From an organizational standpoint, it is also important to assess the extent to which the organization has made a commitment to engaging fathers. For instance, does father engagement appear in the organization's strategic plan, are there policies prescribing father engagement, are specific staff dedicated to working with fathers, and do program evaluation protocols include father-specific metrics?

Father-Friendliness Assessment Tools

In selecting an assessment tool, one of the first questions to ask is, "Who is going to participate in the assessment process?" To ensure that input is considered from a variety of stakeholders, we recommend a team approach that involves at least one organization decision maker, staff representing various job positions (e.g., receptionist, direct service providers, managers), and parents (fathers and mothers) who have participated in programs or services provided by the organization. Unless a significant number of fathers have been served before, we recommend inviting other community fathers to provide input. You may also want to include the perspectives of board members and community partners. We recommend a three-phase assessment process:

1. Ask each team member to respond to all relevant assessment questions independently.
2. Tabulate the responses and identify areas where there are strengths and those where improvement is needed.
3. Discuss and develop short-term and long-term plans to sustain strengths and improve father friendliness in the identified areas.

Depending on the specific assessment tool used, the team will respond to a series of questions in up to seven categories. After completing the assessment questionnaires, responses should be tabulated and the team convened to discuss priorities that need to be addressed. The goal is to identify categories or areas that need improvement and then develop action plans to increase the father friendliness of the organization.

The following four tools are representative of the types of questions that should be considered during any assessment of an organization's father friendliness. (See Table 7.1 for an overview of the general categories covered, and the Resources section for more information on each tool).

Father-Friendliness Organizational Self-Assessment and Planning Tool (FFOSAP)

Developed in 1999 by Pamela Wilson and Nigel Vann for the National Head Start Association and the National Partnership for Community Leadership (NPCL), this tool was updated in 2000 based on feedback from early users and is still available for free download via the National Responsible Fatherhood Clearinghouse (www.fatherhood.gov). The FFOSAP includes 58 questions designed to measure father friendliness in seven categories: Organizational Support, Position and Reputation in the Community, Policies and Procedures, Staffing, Program Services, Physical Environment, and Communication and Interaction (including staff attitudes). There are a few shorter adaptations available.

Table 7.1 Comparison of four assessment tools by categories and number of questions

FFOSAP		FFCU		FIP (abbreviated version)		DFF	
4-item Likert		Likert		1 to 5 score		Likert	
Organizational support	5	Leadership development	27	Organizational philosophy	4	Staff attitudes	7
Community reputation	4	Organizational development	15	Physical environment	4	Staff bias	7
Agency policies and procedures	7	Environment	12	Program content	4	Staff behaviors	6
Staffing	14	Staffing	23	Staff training	4	Organizational attitudes	6
Services	12	Program development	34	Policies and procedures	4	Organizational behaviors	8
Physical environment	7	Community engagement	34	Marketing strategies	4		
Communication and attitudes	9			Outreach efforts	3		
Total Questions	**58**		**145**		**27**		**34**

Users of the tool are asked to score each question on a 4-point scale, where 1 = "Haven't even thought about it," 2 = "We've started to think about this, but haven't made much progress," 3 = "We've made some good efforts but still have some work to do," and 4 = "We have successfully completed this step." By tabulating all responses of 1, 2, and 3, the team can indicate areas that require action steps.

Father Friendly Check-Up (FFCU)

The FFCU was developed by the National Fatherhood Initiative in 2000 and has since been evaluated and updated through various iterations. It was most recently updated in 2020 and is available online from the NFI (www.fatherhood.org), along with the option of follow-up assistance. The FFCU includes 145 questions across four broad domains: Leadership Development, Organizational Development (including Environment and Staffing), Program Development, and Community Engagement. Responses are scored on a Likert scale from 1 (strongly agree) to 5 (strongly disagree), and a scoring chart is provided to help identify where action steps are required. Some adaptations are available.

Assessment Guide on Father Inclusive Practices (FIP)

FIP was developed by Neil Tift for the National Practitioners Network Fathers and Families in 2000. Abbreviated and full versions are now available, with training, through Paternal Instincts, Inc. FIP covers seven categories: Organizational Philosophy, Physical Environment, Program Content, Staff Training, Policies and Procedures, Marketing Strategies, and Outreach Efforts. There are 130 questions in the full version and 27 in the abbreviated version. Responses are scored on a 1 to 5 Likert scale, ranging from "never" to "consistently."

The Dakota Father-Friendly Assessment (DFF)

The DFF was developed and tested in 2011 by Joseph White, Sean E. Brotherson, Adam Galovan, Erin Holmes, and Jennifer Kampmann. Copies of the questionnaire and more information are available from the first two authors. The original DFF had 55 questions designed to measure five domains (Organizational Attitudes, Organizational Behaviors, Staff Attitudes, Staff Behaviors, and Staff Bias). However, through a process known as factor analysis, the authors examined the data from the response patterns and reduced the number of questions to 34 to make the DFF more efficient and manageable. Responses are scored on a Likert scale from 1 (strongly agree) to 5 (strongly disagree).

Common Assessment Categories and Sample Questions

There are some general categories and questions to consider in any father-friendliness assessment. The following is a sample based on our review of the literature and commonly used assessment questions.

1. *Organizational location and community reputation*
   - Do fathers see the organization as a place they can come for assistance?
   - Can they easily get to the facility (e.g., is it on a bus line or other public transportation route)?
   - Do community members and program providers think of the organization as a good resource for fathers?
   - Do local media call on the organization for information about fathers?
2. *Leadership and organizational support*
   - Does the organization have a mission statement that recognizes the importance of father involvement and clearly mentions support services for fathers?
   - Do the organization's budget priorities reflect a commitment to serving fathers?
   - Are board members and organization decision makers committed to providing services for fathers?
3. *Policies and procedures*
   - Do intake forms ask for information about both parents? Do they ensure that staff have contact information for mothers and fathers?
   - Do agency policies include ways to assess situations where one parent may not want the other involved, and help parents resolve differences with the best interests of the child in mind?
   - Can program hours be adjusted to accommodate the time constraints of working fathers?
4. *Physical environment*
   - Does the physical environment have a general feel that is inviting to men/fathers?
   - Do images and language in brochures or posters represent all types of families in the community? Do the materials include positive images of fathers and children?
   - Is there an area with materials directed at fathers or where fathers can gather for group meetings?
   - Is there a diaper-changing deck in the men's bathroom?
   - Is there a designated place where fathers and children can interact?

5. *Staffing*

   - Does the organization hire service delivery staff who are empathic to the lived experiences of fathers and reflect the culture and demographics of fathers served?
   - Are male staff available to work with fathers, especially in the area of recruitment? Have specific staff been designated to work with fathers?
   - Are staff aware of research on the importance of father involvement in the lives of children?
   - Are staff aware of issues faced by low-income men/fathers?
   - Do staff have the skills to engage with fathers and earn their confidence and respect?

6. *Staff training*

   - Do all staff receive initial and ongoing training to ensure they understand the importance of father involvement in child development?
   - Are all staff trained to recognize unconscious biases that may impact their work?
   - Are all staff trained in best practices for father-engagement?
   - Are staff aware of community resources they can refer fathers to?
   - Do staff receive ongoing training and support to help with any personal issues they may face?

7. *Program services*

   - Do fathers have opportunities to help design and provide feedback on program services for fathers?
   - Are services delivered at times that are convenient for fathers to participate? Are virtual options available?
   - Are program curricula designed specifically for fathers, not parents in general?
   - Do group sessions include activities and materials that appeal to fathers?
   - Are services available (internally or through community referrals) to help fathers who may need to deal with issues such as child support, co-parenting, employment, legal assistance, mental health, or substance abuse?

8. *Communication*

   - Are written communications (letters, newsletters, etc.) addressed to both parents and sent separately if the parents do not live together?
   - Do staff interact with fathers in a style that demonstrates respect, empathy, and high expectations?
   - Do staff avoid language that may be divisive or stereotyping by gender, race, or culture (e.g., do they avoid comments such as "babysitting" in reference to fathers spending time with their children)?
   - Do marketing materials, brochures, websites, and other communication materials convey positive messages to fathers?

Evaluating Results of the Assessment and Implementing Changes

Once your team has completed its assessment, it is time to tabulate responses, identify areas in which the organization is performing well, and highlight areas that may need improvement. Then, working with the same team and possibly additional staff, fathers, or decision makers, it is time to develop short-term and long-term plans to increase staff knowledge and understanding, sustain strengths, and address the areas that need improvement. During both the assessment and planning stages, it is important to include fathers and their input. At a minimum, this could be done by recruiting community fathers who are demographically similar to those the organization serves. An even better fit might be to solicit feedback from past or present participants.

Programs often need time to evolve, so do not expect change overnight. Begin by setting manageable goals that can be implemented in the first 2 to 6 months. Programs can also set longer-term goals with associated benchmarks and measurable outcomes, but during the first 6 months, the focus should be on the short-term goals, adjusting as necessary, and building for the future.

The following are examples of some short-term action steps to consider:

- Make sure posters and brochures feature pictures of fathers and/or include the word "father."
- Ensure that all forms of communication with families address both parents.
- Make sure all program materials are inclusive of diverse cultures, languages, and families.
- Change program entry/intake forms to include information on fathers.
- Ensure that the physical space is welcoming and inclusive for the whole family.
- Train all staff on the importance of father involvement and how to foster a culture of father engagement.
- Provide training that includes a review of situational barriers that fathers may face and opportunities for all staff to reflect on their personal attitudes and behaviors along with any potential biases.
  - This should include reflection on their relationship with their own fathers and the impact of this and other life experiences on their personal and professional attitudes and behaviors.
- Plan and implement programming designed for fathers and invite their feedback.

Recommendations and Considerations

Assessing an organization's father friendliness is an important step in its ability to effectively recruit and retain fathers in program services. In addition to identifying and administering a father-friendliness assessment tool and evaluating the data that

Suggested Staff Training Topic: Situational Barriers Faced by Many Fathers

As discussed earlier in this chapter, one way to enhance the father friendliness of organizations is to ensure that all staff understand the range of issues that their prospective clients may face. For instance, many fathers face barriers connected to:

- Past trauma, often connected to the absence of their own father or other negative childhood experiences.
- Relationship problems, which may lead to "maternal gatekeeping" whereby mothers actively discourage father involvement.
- Restricted employment opportunities that undermine their ability to fulfill a traditional provider role for their children.
- High rates of incarceration, particularly among African American men.
- Media images that may undermine their confidence in their value as fathers.
- Lack of social capital that limits their ability, and opportunities, to be exposed to new and different experiences and perspectives.

emerge from it, we offer other father-engagement recommendations. First, recognize that fathers tend to parent differently than mothers, so they should not be expected to parent like mothers. Related to this recommendation is the reality that there is no widely accepted social script for fathering behavior. This is particularly true of nonresident fathers. Therefore, there is a lot of variability in fathers' parenting knowledge, skill, and efficacy. Organizations should be prepared to meet fathers where they are and exhibit patience and grace as they gain experience.

Second, organizations should be certain to consult with participating fathers to ensure that their involvement is measured in ways that reflect fathers' thoughts, ideas, and values, not just their attendance and participation in agency programming. This is important as previous research (Levine, 1993) has documented the ways in which reports of program effectiveness can be negatively impacted by misalignment between program evaluation data collection protocols and the target populations' lived experiences. To avoid this, care must be taken to select measures that are not only psychometrically sound but that also capture the parenting repertoires of participating fathers.

Finally, organizations must make a real commitment to engaging fathers. This means that engaging and serving fathers permeates every facet of the organization. Father-engagement efforts should be included in the strategic planning process so they can be appropriately resourced and evaluated. Programs and services must be developed with fathers in mind so that the synergy between their interests and needs can be catalyzed and leveraged. Organization leaders and administrators must be intentional about making sure fathers are valued and seen as assets with the capacity for making positive contributions to their family's functioning. They must also ensure that adequate training is provided to staff so they can become comfortable in engaging and serving fathers. In doing so, the organizational culture will become warm and welcoming, and fathers will see it as a place and space where they can learn and grow. Most importantly, by creating a father-friendly atmosphere, fathers will be better positioned to positively contribute to the healthy growth and development of their children.

Resources

Father-Friendliness Assessment Tools

- *Father-Friendliness Organizational Self-Assessment and Planning Tool (FFOSAP)*: https://www.fatherhood.gov/research-and-resources/father-friendliness-organizational-self-assessment-and-planning-tool.
- *Adaptations of FFOSAP*
  - Enhancing Organizational Father Friendliness – adapted by Strategies Center at Youth for Change (2012). Presented in matrix format with select questions from all seven NHSA categories.
  - Father-Friendliness Organizational Self-Assessment – 22-item questionnaire adapted from the NHSA tool by Cowan, Cowan, Pruett, Pruett, & Wong, with additional items drawn from *The Assessment Guide on Father Inclusive Practices*, which was developed for the National Practitioners Network for Fathers and Families.
  - Father-Friendliness: WIC Program Assessment Tool – Available for download at https://www.dadsandkidshealth.com, a website hosted by William Marsiglio. The WIC Program Assessment Tool considers four of the NHSA categories: Physical Environment, Communication, Staffing/Human Resources, Program Services.
- *Father Friendly Check-Up (FFCU)*: https://www.fatherhood.org/ffcu.
- *Adaptations of FFCU*
  - Father Friendly Check-Up for Child WelfareChild welfare Agencies and Organizations (National Fatherhood Initiative, American Humane Association, and American Bar Association Center on Children and the Law, 2011).
  - Father Friendly Check-Up TM For Child Protective Courts (National Fatherhood Initiative and American Bar Association, 2011).

- *Assessment Guide on Father Inclusive Practices (FIP)*
  - Abbreviated and full versions are available, with training, through Paternal Instincts, Inc (neiltift@yahoo.com, 480-334-3022).
- *Dakota Father Friendly (DFF) Assessment*
  - Information available from Joseph White (Foundation for Family Life, http://fflut.org, 801-750-5398) and Sean Brotherson (North Dakota State University, Sean.Brotherson@ndsu.edu).
- *Additional Resources*
- Mazza, C., & Perry, A.R. (2017). Fatherhood in America: Social work perspectives on a changing society – a sourcebook for practitioners that includes a section on fatherhood service delivery, with chapters on culturally competent practice with fathers, measuring father involvement, and a review of responsible fatherhood programs and their gaps.
- Texas Fatherhood Resource Hub – Making Your Organization Father-Friendly.
- U.S. Department of Health and Human Services, Administration for Children and Families, Office of Head Start, National Center on Parent, Family, and Community Engagement. (2020). Birth to Five Father Engagement Programming Guide. https://eclkc.ohs.acf.hhs.gov/family-engagement/birth-5-father-engagement-guide/download-birth-5-father-engagement-guide.

Discussion Questions

1. Identify a policy or practice at your organization that may inhibit father engagement and participation. How could this policy or practice be improved so that it is more father-friendly?
2. Is there evidence that your organization's administration has made a commitment to engaging fathers?
3. What is your organization's historical reputation related to father friendliness? What is it doing to improve it?
4. How can organizations include fathers in their strategic planning, program development, and evaluation efforts?
5. How does an organization address staff reluctance or hostility toward engaging fathers without alienating them?

References

Abendroth, E., Bellamy, J., Mittone, D., Bess, R., & Stagner, M. (2021). *Opening up possibilities: Father engagement lessons during the COVID-19 public health emergency*. OPRE Report 2021-82. Washington, DC: Office of Planning, Research, and Evaluation, Administration for Children and Families, U.S. Department of Health and Human Services. https://www.acf.hhs.gov/opre/report/opening-up-possibilities-father-engagement-lessons-during-covid-19-public-health

Anderson, V., Burn, M., Collins, D. A. J., Dadds, M. R., Doyle, F. L., Frick, P. J., Hawes, D. J., Jiang, Y., Kimonis, E. R., Lechowicz, M. E., Lenroot, R. K., Moul, C., Piotrowska, P. J., & Tully, L. A. (2019). Enhancing father engagement in parenting programs: Translating research into practice recommendations. *Australian Psychologist, 54*, 83–39. https://doi.org/10.1111/ap.12361

Avellar, S., Stanczyk, A., Aikens, N., Stange, M., & Roemer, G. (2020). *The 2015 Cohort of healthy marriage and responsible fatherhood grantees: Interim Report on Grantee Programs and Clients, OPRE Report 2020-67*, Washington, DC: Office of Planning, Research and Evaluation, Administration for Children and Families, U.S. Department of Health and Human Services. https://www.acf.hhs.gov/sites/default/files/documents/opre/interim_report_on_2015_hmrf_grantees_508.pdf

Bellamy, J. (2020). *Engaging fathers in home visiting programs*. [Information Brief.] National Responsible Fatherhood Clearinghouse. www.fatherhood.gov/research-and-resources/engaging-fathers-home-visiting-program

Behrmann, R. & Brennan, E. (2020). *Inside, outside, round and round: Sustaining engagement in responsible fatherhood programs*. OPRE Report 2020-34. Washington, DC: Office of Planning, Research, and Evaluation, Administration for Children and Families, U.S. Department of Health and Human Services. https://www.acf.hhs.gov/opre/report/inside-outside-round-and-round-sustaining-engagement-responsible-fatherhood-programs

Brewsaugh, K., Masyn, K. E., & Salloum, A. (2018). Child welfare workers' sexism and beliefs about father involvement. *Children and Youth Services Review, 89*, 132–144. https://doi.org/10.1016/j.childyouth.2018.04.029

Bronte-Tinkew, J., Carrano, J., Allen, T., Bowie, L., Mbawa, K., & Matthews, G. (2007) *Elements of promising practice for fatherhood programs: Evidence-based research findings on programs for fathers*. [NRFC Research Brief]. National Responsible Fatherhood Clearinghouse. https://www.fatherhood.gov/research-and-resources/elements-promising-practice-fatherhood-programs-evidence-based-research-findings

Committee on Supporting the Parents of Young Children. (2016). Elements of effective parenting programs and strategies for increasing program participation and retention (chapter in National Academies of Sciences, Engineering, and Medicine. *Parenting matters: Supporting parents of children ages 0-8.* The National Academies Press. https://doi.org/10.17226/21868

Cowan, C. P., Cowan, P. A., Pruett, M. K., & Pruett, K. (2007). An approach to preventing coparenting conflict and divorce in low-income families: Strengthening couple relationships and fostering fathers' involvement. *Family Process, 46*, 109–121. https://doi.org/10.1111/j.1545-5300.2006.00195.x

Fagan, J. (1996). Principles for developing male involvement programs in early childhood settings: A personal experience. *Young Children, 51*(4), 64–71. https://eric.ed.gov/?id=EJ523415

Fagan, J. (1999). *Predictors of father and father figure involvement in pre-kindergarten Head Start.* National Center on Fathers and Families. https://www.fatherhood.gov/research-and-resources/predictors-father-and-father-figure-involvement-pre-kindergarden-head-start

Fagan, J., & Iglesias, A. (1999). Father involvement program effects on fathers, father figures, and their Head Start children: A quasi-experimental study. *Early Childhood Research Quarterly, 14*(2), 243–269. https://doi.org/10.1016/S0885-2006(99)00008-3

Fagan, J., & Pearson, J. (2019). State efforts to support the engagement of nonresident fathers in the lives of their children. *Families in Society: The Journal of Contemporary Social Services, 100*(4), 392–408. https://doi.org/10.1177/1044389419874172

Garinger, J., & McBride, B. A. (1995). Successful parental involvement strategies in prekindergarten at-risk programs: An exploratory study. *The School-Community Journal, 5*, 59–77. https://eric.ed.gov/?id=EJ517780

Levine, J. A. (1993). Involving fathers in Head Start: A framework for public policy and program development. *Families in Society: The Journal of Contemporary Social Services, 74*, 4–19. https://doi.org/10.1177/104438949307400101

McAllister, C., Wilson, P., & Burton, J. (2004). From sports fans to nurturers: An early Head Start program's evolution toward father involvement. *Fathering, 2*(1), 31–59. https://www.thefreelibrary.com/From+sports+fans+to+nurturers%3a+an+Early+Head+Start+program%27s...-a0116670277

McBride, B. A., Rane, T. R., & Bae, J. (2001). Intervening with teachers to encourage father/male involvement in early childhood programs. *Early Childhood Research Quarterly, 16*, 77–93. https://doi.org/10.1016/S0885-2006(01)00087-4

Perry, A. (2020, April 2). *Coronavirus stimulus package reveals America's interest in preserving patriarchy*. https://www.courier-journal.com/story/opinion/2020/04/02/coronavirus-stimulus-package-sends-poor-message-fathers-families/5109897002/.

Perry, A., Rollins, A., Sabree, R., & Grooms, W. (2016). Promoting paternal participation in maternal and child health services. *Human Service Organizations: Management, Leadership & Governance, 40*(2), 170–186. https://doi.org/10.1080/23303131.2015.1124821

Raikes, H. H., Summers, J. A., & Roggman, L. A. (2005). Father involvement in Early Head Start programs. *Fathering, 3*(1), 29–58. https://www.fatherhood.gov/research-and-resources/father-involvement-early-head-start-programs

Simon, W. H. (2020). Legality, bureaucracy, and class in the welfare system. In P. Robson (Ed.), *Welfare Law* (pp. 323–394). Routledge. https://digitalcommons.law.yale.edu/cgi/viewcontent.cgi?article=6810&context=ylj

Vann, N. (2021). Responsible Fatherhood Toolkit: Resources From the Field (2nd ed.). National Responsible Fatherhood Clearinghouse. https://www.fatherhood.gov/research-and-resources/responsible-fatherhood-toolkit-resources-field-2021

White, J. M., Brotherson, S. E., Galovan, A. M., Holmes, E. K., & Kampmann, J. A. (2011). The Dakota father friendly assessment: Measuring father friendliness in Head Start and similar settings. *Fathering, 9*(1), 22–43. https://www.fatherhood.gov/sites/default/files/resource_files/e000002290_0.pdf

Zaveri, H., Baumgartner, S., Dion, R., & Clary, L. (2015). *Parents and children together: Design and implementation of responsible fatherhood programs*. OPRE Report Number 2015-76. Washington, DC: Office of Planning, Research and Evaluation; Administration for Children and Families; U.S. Department of Health and Human Services. https://www.fatherhood.gov/sites/default/files/resource_files/e000003374.pdf

Part III
Intervention

Chapter 8
Framing Interventions with Fathers

Qiana R. Cryer-Coupet and McKenzie N. Green

Introduction

This chapter will focus on intervention strategies for engaging fathers across a variety of social service settings and on engagement strategies that may improve social work practice with fathers. It also examines the roles of social service providers in delivering *father-focused, father-inclusive,* or *father-friendly* interventions. Although these terms are widely used, they are not often explicitly defined. In this chapter, father-focused interventions are defined as interventions developed with the goal of attending to the unique needs and experiences of fathers within the target population. Father-inclusive or father-friendly interventions are family-based interventions that seek to include and prioritize fathers in the delivery of services as usual by capitalizing on the father's assets within the family system. These can include interventions that were developed for mothers or other caregivers but have been modified to address the needs of fathers. This chapter concludes with recommendations on preparing for social work practice with fathers through collaborative interventions and inclusive practices that positively impact the family system and its individual members.

Q. R. Cryer-Coupet (✉)
School of Social Work, Georgia State University, Atlanta, GA, USA
e-mail: qcryercoupet@gsu.edu

M. N. Green
School of Social Work, Virginia Commonwealth University, Richmond, VA, USA
e-mail: stokesmn@vcu.edu

J. L. Bellamy et al. (eds.), *Social Work Practice with Fathers*,
https://doi.org/10.1007/978-3-031-13686-3_8

Background and Context

Social workers across a variety of practice settings are often tasked with implementing interventions with individuals and families with the goal of enhancing wellbeing. In so doing, social workers may target a variety of outcomes, some narrow and others broad. Though not exclusive, these outcomes may include those related to social, economic, or educational well-being. In 1971, Briar and Miller defined interventions in the context of social work as "an attempt to induce change" (p. 173). As such, scholars of social work intervention have noted that "the profession of social work is distinguished from anthropology, psychology, sociology, and other disciplines by its focus on induced change" (Fraser, 2004, p. 210). Further distinguishing the field of social work, this change is often approached from a social justice perspective and with the goal of understanding individuals and families within the context of their environments.

For those practicing in settings with fathers and families, social work interventions are sometimes preventative. In such cases, programs are developed to assist and educate fathers who may be parenting for the first time, taking on fathering responsibilities in a new context, or are seeking support to improve their parenting practices with children who may be at risk (Barr et al., 2014; Caldwell et al., 2014; Rayburn & Coatsworth, 2021). In other instances, social work intervention with fathers occurs following a family-trauma related to substance misuse, the experience of homelessness, parental incarceration, a mental health crisis, or family separation due to abuse or neglect. Although social work education at the bachelor's (BSW) and master's (MSW) levels is designed to position graduates to competently engage in work related to prevention and intervention, a recent study of preparedness related to clinical competencies among MSW graduates found that nearly a quarter of respondents did not feel competent to deliver interventions related to processing trauma. Furthermore, the study found that less than half of recent graduates felt prepared to facilitate family interventions (Turner et al., 2019).

Working with families is complex and takes specialized training. Acknowledgment of these complexities is important when working with fathers, as their engagement likely has implications for child and family outcomes (Sicouri et al., 2018). Given the impact of father engagement and the historically low levels in parenting interventions, it is important to understand the factors that drive father engagement. Emerging research suggests that practitioners' attitudes about men and fatherhood influence their efforts to engage them in services (Baum, 2017). More specifically, practitioners who adopt favorable views of fathers report greater levels of paternal involvement in their cases than practitioners who hold negative attitudes about fathers (O'Donnell et al., 2005). O'Donnell and colleagues (2005) also found that providers who perceived fathers negatively were less committed to engaging them and typically "adopted a wait and see posture toward the vast majority of fathers who could not be found or who did not respond quickly and positively to an initial caseworker contact" (p. 407).

Fortunately, there is promising evidence to suggest that negative attitudes about fathers are malleable (Scourfield et al., 2012) and often result from a lack of training and organizational support (Baum, 2017; Martin, 2006). As such, practitioners who receive training related to father engagement hold more positive attitudes about them and report better engagement outcomes than practitioners who have not received training (Arroyo & Peek, 2015). Of concern, however, is that pre-service social workers rarely receive specialized training about fathers and the best practices for working with them (Alio, 2017; Burgess, 2009; Huebner et al., 2008). For example, a review of over 200 vignettes that are used to train students in schools of social work in the United States found that over half of the materials portrayed fathers as threatening, irrelevant, and absent, while depicting mothers as the primary clients (Brewsaugh & Strozier, 2016). As a result, many professionals begin their careers with a biased perception of fathers and are underprepared to serve them. Increased focus on intervention training coupled with shifts in attitudes may help practitioners demonstrate more compassion and respect, which increases the likelihood that fathers will remain involved in intervention services (Coakley, 2013; Coakley et al., 2018).

In addition to understanding the attitudes and preparedness of social work practitioners, it is important to investigate fathers' perceptions of social work interventions. In 2018, Sicouri and colleagues interviewed a group of fathers to learn more about what factors might drive the historically low levels of father engagement in parenting and father-focused interventions. Fathers in this study identified the following as barriers: (1) interventions appear to be mother-focused, (2) fathers' beliefs about gender roles and help seeking, (3) lack of awareness of interventions, and (4) lack of relevance of existing interventions (Sicouri et al., 2018). As such, fathers may feel forgotten or unimportant if the intervention design appears to prioritize the role and needs of mothers instead of taking a balanced approach to parent engagement. Additionally, the father's participation levels may be negatively impacted if the content of the intervention does not address issues that may be unique to father-child interactions. Attention to these details is important when recruiting fathers, as they are less likely to enroll in programs if the content does not appear to be relevant (Doyle et al., 2022) and does not offer opportunities to address issues related to their ability to parent, such as employment training or opportunities (Stahlschmidt et al., 2013). While Sicouri and colleagues noted the above findings in the US context, Hansen et al. (2022) found similar results when consulting a group of Australian fathers regarding the low uptake of online mental health parenting groups. In their work, they found that fathers were limited in engagement due to: (1) lack of awareness of online parenting programs, (2) perceptions and stereotypes that impacted motivation to engage, (3) uncertainty regarding fathers' role in addressing adolescent mental health, and (4) issues related to program design, such as feeling overwhelmed by the amount of content and time needed to fully engage the training. In efforts to overcome some of the stated barriers, scholars have noted the importance of making sure fathers have a seat at the table when assessing the need for interventions as well as in the design, implementation, and evaluation stages (Julion et al., 2012).

Social work interventions take on a variety of forms and are implemented in person, virtually, and in hybrid formats. To accommodate varying schedules and needs, father-focused supportive and psychoeducational interventions have even been delivered via text (Fletcher et al., 2019; Hayward et al., 2021) and online platforms such as Facebook (McLeod, 2020). A review of father-focused interventions suggests that these programs have been designed to include a variety of different subgroups of fathers, including biological and adoptive fathers, and father figures such as grandfathers, stepfathers, uncles, and other kin (Fagan & Iglesias, 1999). Programs and interventions have been developed to address the needs of fathers of children who have developmental disabilities (May et al., 2021), fathers who are co-parenting from afar (Gewirtz et al., 2019), fathers who are preparing to reenter the community post-incarceration (Calvert et al., 2020), and those who are in treatment for substance use disorders (Stover et al., 2019). Father-inclusive interventions have also worked to improve engagement early in children's lives by intentionally engaging fathers in perinatal home visiting programs (Bellamy et al., 2021). Innovative father-focused programs have been developed to engage fathers based on their specific needs. For example, Wiseman et al. (2021) implemented a family literacy program for fathers at a residential substance use treatment facility. This trauma-informed intervention facilitated discussions about substance use, co-parenting, child development, and hopes for future parenting among fathers in treatment and their families. Scholars have also begun to examine ways in which human-centered design approaches can be used to decrease parenting stress among single fathers (Burgdorf & Prabhakar, 2021).

While there have been innovations in approaches to engaging fathers and families, gaps still exist. For example, few interventions exist to address the needs of fathers from the LGBTQIA PLUS_SPI community (Bauer & Giles, 2020). Additionally, limited research and intervention development have focused on the needs and experiences of fathers who are parenting multiracial children (Stokes et al., 2021) or are co-parenting with relatives such as their mother, sister, or fictive kin (Gibson et al., 2020). Taking a life course perspective, scholars have also called for the development of fathering interventions that will support college recruitment and retention among historically marginalized students (Garcia & Mireles-Rios, 2020). Overall, these deficits highlight the fact that there is no one-size-fits-all fathering intervention. As such, the need remains for the differential development of interventions for fathers across varying contexts, with different needs, and with a focus on fathers' strengths (Higgs et al., 2018).

Conceptual Framing: Family-Centered Practice and Collaborative Competencies

The family-centered practice (FCP) approach has been championed by practitioners, researchers, and policymakers in many helping professions, including social work (Allen & Petr, 1998), as one that helps to highlight the importance of engaging fathers in family-focused interventions. In 2018, the Administration on Children and Families (ACF) released an information memorandum focused on the integration of father-friendly service approaches across the agency, including within child welfare and family support programs (U.S. Department of Health and Human Services, ACF, 2018). Recommendations for creating a father-friendly family service approach focused on examining the relationship between fathers and social service professionals. As such, agencies and practitioners were tasked with documenting and addressing policies and practices that might hinder successful father engagement. In agreement with ACF's guidance, we contend that engaging the tenets of the FCP approach will help to support the successful development and implementation of father-focused and father-inclusive interventions in social work practice.

The FCP approach includes five key tenets:

1. Family as the unit of attention—notes that social workers cannot meet the needs of a child without considering the needs of the family unit, including fathers and father figures. As such, all identified family members are included in the assessment and intervention process.
2. Family choice—highlights the importance of hearing and including the wishes of the family in the planning and intervention process.
3. Family strengths—prioritizes the assessment of strengths within the family system. These characteristics are then incorporated into the intervention planning and implementation processes.
4. Family-professional relationship—frames the relationship between families and social workers as a collaborative one. As such, all parties bring expertise to the relationship to support the implementation and success of the intervention.
5. Individualized family services—supports the provision of services that align with the unique needs of each father and family.

In 2021, the first author and colleagues investigated practitioners' perceptions of their preparation to engage nonresident fathers (e.g., those who do not live in the same home as their children) in FCP. In this study, they conducted qualitative interviews with 20 social service practitioners (Cryer-Coupet et al., 2021). The development of the interview guide was informed by the *family-professional relationship* tenet of the FCP framework. The authors argued that providers must demonstrate competency in building collaborative relationships (see Lopez et al., 1998) to facilitate the process of engaging nonresident fathers as partners in the family-professional relationship. Understanding practitioners' conceptualization of collaborative worker-client relationships is important for improving social work practice with fathers. Cryer-Coupet and colleagues' findings (2021) highlight the following competencies as those that impact partnerships between social service providers and fathers. Even though this research was developed with nonresident fathers, the competencies also apply for work with all fathers:

1. Intrapersonal competence—the process of identifying and assessing one's personal beliefs, values, and thoughts regarding fathers and engaging fathers as partners.
2. Interpersonal competence—the process of developing, maintaining, and nurturing partnerships with fathers.
3. Professional competence—the process of identifying and assessing sociocultural factors that may impact the father-practitioner relationship (i.e., power imbalances created by an individual or organizational/institutional factors).

Recommended Strategies for Engaging Fathers in Social Work Interventions

The following recommendations regarding collaborative competencies for engaging fathers in social work interventions were derived from the reflections of social work practitioners (Cryer-Coupet et al., 2021).

Intrapersonal Competence

It is important for practitioners to assess the ways in which personal life experiences have shaped their views of fathers and fatherhood. A similar examination is warranted in relation to professional experiences that may have also impacted their outlooks. Given the range of emotions that can be created by personal and professional commitments to father-focused and father-inclusive practice, providers must be reflexive when working with fathers to effectively engage and facilitate impactful partnerships.

Personal Experiences

Several practitioners mentioned that their approach to engaging and interacting with fathers was based on their personal life experiences, particularly positive relationships with their own fathers, both resident and nonresident. The following quotes provide examples of how these life experiences relate to their work with nonresident fathers:

> My dad was my first formal training, not knowing it was my formal training.
> Having a little bit of personal story. I grew up in a household with my father and my mom. My dad was a very major influence in my life and so living in a household with my dad and the things that he taught me and the trouble that he kept me out of, things that I probably would have done had he not been there, and after, you know, being on my own and then I was married for 15 years and then I became a single father and my kids were 11, 9 and 7 at

> that time. So, then raising them to adulthood, getting another perspective on the importance of fathers in a household.

Alternatively, some practitioners noted that negative personal experiences with their own father or fathers in their network also impacted the ways they approach father engagement:

> I've seen the results of adults who ... their father was not there ... and I saw the devastation that that had on their life and then I became a single father myself. And so I understand the role of fathers and how they need to be there, not just to help with their kids, as well as being there to help co-parent their child.

Among male practitioners, attitudes and beliefs about engaging nonresident fathers were also widely predicated on shared personal experiences as men. This included feeling comfortable with being vulnerable with a male practitioner because their shared gender added a layer of relatability. Below are some quotes that exemplify their perspectives:

> I think that's just the—comfort level, a comfort level, a common interest or understanding of one another, just the means of communication. I think most men are apt to communicate more so with another man. I guess we can somewhat relate to a similar mindset, even though it may not be the same mindset, but we can comprehend with that mindset maybe of a single father trying to re-engage with their families.

Female practitioners also reflected on the ways in which gender shaped their perspectives regarding father engagement. One respondent noted how the lack of gender diversity in her office negatively impacted father engagement efforts and potentially biased engagement protocols, stating:

> What's our representation on our staff of the communities that we work with in the field?... to be honest, if I'm honest right now, I think all of our staff are women. So, even from that standpoint, that's still one perspective type.

Professional Experiences

Multiple practitioners also noted that their professional experience working with fathers and families is what equipped them with the desire and skills to engage fathers. For example, one respondent said, "Yeah, I feel like most of what I've learned has come through the work experience and less through the training." Another one shared, "There is no college, no university that can help you or prepare you to deal with the dads that we encounter."

Passion

For several practitioners in the study, the idea that practitioners must be passionate about fatherhood for engagement efforts to be most effective lies at the intersection of personal and professional experiences. This was particularly the case given the complex emotions often at play when a father and family are seeking help or are referred for assistance. Some male practitioners felt that their passion for this challenging work was fueled by their shared gender identities.

> I mean it's kind of hard—I mean, formal education, you know what I'm saying, we can do the human services, social work, psychology. But you just have got to have that passion. Because you're dealing with so many different emotions. I'll tell anybody, if you're going to work in a fatherhood program, you've got to be a special kind of guy. And one of the main things that you have to have, you have to be passionate. If you don't have any passion, it's going to be extremely rough to do it because if you come and just look at it as a job, it's not going to be fun.

In addition, a few practitioners shared the importance of putting their passion to work. As such, they developed best-practices over time as they worked and learned from both their personal and professional experiences. One respondent noted that this approach was important, given the complexities presented by some cases:

> Fatherhood is hands on. I mean, there's books. I mean, don't get me wrong. There's books and there's literature and there's a whole lot of other things, there are professionals out there that can tell you about fatherhood. But the basis of my success comes from personal experiences or hands on because the demographics of fathers that we encounter is so different that there's no book. Being a male myself, and having a passion for fatherhood, and wanting to see other fathers succeed in life, I think it's twofold; I think it's professional as well as personal.

Interpersonal Competence

To develop, maintain, and nurture collaborative relationships with fathers, practitioners should consider interpersonal factors that support and inhibit successful father engagement. In social work practice, this process is often referred to as "building rapport." Rapport is defined by interpersonal connections to clients that increase the likelihood that they will remain enrolled in services (Sharf et al., 2010). Practitioners shared that establishing trust and rapport with nonresident fathers was invaluable to the work that they do:

> If people can't connect with you, they're going to shut down early … And, it's very hard to get them to open back up. So, once you get them to open back up, you've got to capitalize on that by any means necessary, you know, within reason.

The practitioners relied on multiple techniques to help build rapport with fathers, including self-disclosure, treating fathers with respect, and engaging in shared decision-making practices.

Self-Disclosure

Several practitioners felt that the fathers they worked with responded positively when they shared personal information about their own lives. This was a particularly effective technique for the practitioners who were also fathers because it helped their clients trust that the practitioner's knowledge was valid:

> I let them look at my personal life. I raised my children outside the home. But you know, I made sure I was there for everything. I had joint custody so I had access. So, I guess it's not like he's just the married guy, living on top of the hill looking down at us. No, I experienced some things. You know, I been through these headaches, as we call them.
>
> Sharing information about myself, sharing experiences that I've had as a father, connecting with the commonality with the fathers that I'm working with, letting them know that, you know, being a father is a 24/7 job, that you're always learning new information, that, you know, it's not going to be easy but it's going to be rewarding and worthwhile to be in your child's life.

A practitioner who was not a father was still able to utilize the technique to connect with his low-income clients by sharing his childhood experiences of living in public housing as a child. He shared that his clients are more accepting of him after he discloses that information:

> You get a whole bunch of kids come to you and they think that because you are on that side of the desk that, you know, you're kind of, not stuffy, but 'you don't know what I know.' So, that allows me to kind of break the ice, you know, we can have some dialogue and they can be like, oh this guy's been around the block once or twice.

Respect

The providers consistently reiterated the importance of making sure that fathers felt respected within their organizations. One father engagement specialist noted that respect was especially important coming from male practitioners:

> A man speaking to another man in a respectful way really adds a lot of energy to the work that we're doing. When a dad feels like he's respected, he's more likely to engage. He's more likely to adhere to his plans, and then there's—what am I looking for? There's something in every man that has to be challenged and when you can learn how to tap into challenging a man, I think that it really quite lends to him being motivated to want to complete his plan. Once he feels motivated, he's more likely to do it.

Practitioners believed that respect could be communicated by validating the role that fathers play in the lives of their children. For example, a male practitioner explained:

> So that's one of my challenges, how do I make them feel important? And so I found different ways to do that and that's what we try to do in each meeting that we have and each activity that we have. We stress just how important they are.

Another social worker echoed this statement and shared that normalizing the potential anxiety and the benefits of participation in programs may be particularly affirming for fathers. An example of this approach included sharing with fathers that they did not need to know everything and that it was always okay to have and ask questions:

> Letting them know that you know it's okay to have questions about everything, about things, you don't have to know everything about being a father, because you're forever learning, just like your child is, you know, but through these experiences, and through the support groups, and through the parenting classes that we offer that we direct them to, hopefully they can

> increase their skill set and increase their understanding of being a father so they can share that information and that guidance with their children.

Similarly, a male practitioner working with nonresident fathers who were court-ordered to service noted:

> Once you walk in with fathers … you can't come in and appear that you are higher than thou or greater than that. You have to acknowledge what a person has…to work with. Let them know that you see them … and reinforce it to keep them focused.

Shared Decision-Making

Multiple providers felt that valuing fathers' agency to make decisions about what to focus on during service was an important aspect of the father-practitioner relationship. A practitioner who worked as a father success coach for a private agency shared:

> I often ask my dads, what do you want out of this? Before we go and build this house—you might not want a house. You might want an apartment. But I can answer, hey man, we're going to build this house and the whole time you never say anything, you never said…I just want to live in an apartment.

A practitioner who works for a public agency as a family navigator also employed this technique. She further explained that allowing fathers to make decisions about their service plans and being transparent about the provider's or program's expectations of them can help build rapport. This approach was particularly effective when the practitioner asked fathers to center their children when considering their desires for case planning and outcomes:

> Just to talk about kind of how they see things. What do they think that they can bring to the table to help nurture their child and what do they want to see with their child and what kind of vision do they have for their child? Encourage them to tell us things that they know about their child, things that they feel are important—to their child. Then plan your—make your service plan centered around some of that … Then strategize together, make them feel a part of their plan, because it is their plan.

In some instances, the value of shared decision-making went beyond the individual father-practitioner relationship and extended to agency culture. One practitioner described how he encourages participation with a policy council that empowers nonresident fathers to participate in the governance processes of the program:

> I try to set up where the fathers could actually be engaged and they have an opportunity to share their feelings and any concerns they may have dealing with the [Redacted] program... We have to give them [nonresident fathers] the opportunity to have a shared experience with the [Redacted] program by allowing them to serve on their policy council... They are part of the program governing and decision making. They are actually just below our board of directors. So they work in conjunction with the board of directors.

Professional Competence

Professional competence is defined by factors that enable practitioners to identify and assess sociocultural dynamics that may impact the father-practitioner relationship in the context of service delivery. Participants shared several factors they believed constrained their professional practice and discussed how they were able to counteract those constraints through formal and self-initiated training.

Formal Training

Most practitioners in the sample noted that they did not receive formal training through their undergraduate or graduate programs, nor did they receive workplace orientation about fathers and how to engage them in services. However, some participants did note that they were able to apply certain skills from their formal training programs to help learn more about fathers and techniques to engage these men in the field:

> My Master of Social Work experience, I think that helped me a lot in understanding the individual, meeting families where they're at … those closest to the problem are closest to the solution and we never want to come at these different scenarios telling them what to do. But more so listen, and that in itself is the social work theory. So making sure that all of that is kind of ingrained in who I am … remembering that this individual … has human dignity that we have to respect.
>
> I mean, emotionally dealing with these types of situations, and trying to figure out what's best for a family, I would say that's probably more life experience … my undergraduate degree was in psychology, so I think that has helped a lot in terms of kind of understanding where people are coming from.

Those participants who did recall receiving formal training on father engagement found the training useful in the field. For example, one practitioner discussed the impact of a personal bias training that required reflection on fatherhood in her family over time:

> So, one of the things that I received in training … a self-reflection workshop … I carry some of my personal bias into working with them [fathers] and the training actually helped me. Formal education, formal training helped me dissolve some of those things and realize that that's how my father was brought up, that's how I was brought up.

Another practitioner noted the utility of the research skills gained during social work training, which have been helpful in locating resources for fathers; however, he wished there had been more overall emphasis on fathers in the training:

> I think most of the information that I find I have to sometimes go on the Internet and do research and find out what is available. And, fortunately, my social work training allows me to do that. You know, how to do research … but I don't think there was enough emphasis put on just dads and fathers.

There were also some who noted that they received formal father engagement training but felt it was lacking in some areas: "Formal training, workplace training did prepare me, but it hasn't prepared me for everything."

Self-Initiated Training

In efforts to fill gaps in preparation, some practitioners described the self-initiated strategies they use to obtain additional knowledge. For some, this included engaging in continuing education outside of the workplace to supplement gaps in formal training and stay abreast of changes related to their specific areas of practice: "We're required to take continuing … education, 12 hours a year, and I do try to take a lot in family law … so that I can stay up on what the new laws are regarding this area."

Conclusion

As evidenced by the strategies noted above, engaging fathers in social work intervention requires competence across several domains. Many of the engagement strategies are reflective of "good social work" and include techniques that social workers have used to engage clients with a multitude of needs. As a social work professional, it is important to be intentional and consistent when preparing to engage clients. As noted in the NASW Code of Ethics 1.05.c, this includes engaging in critical self-reflection (NASW, 2021). Therefore, examining the personal and professional biases that may lead to limited engagement of fathers in practice. Fathers are not a monolithic population. As such, the development and implementation of father-focused and father-inclusive interventions must be informed by fathers and the unique needs of their family's presenting concerns. This includes developing and implementing interventions that target different types of fathers (i.e., resident fathers, nonresident fathers, older fathers, social fathers, custodial grandfathers, and fathers from varying socioeconomic backgrounds). Additionally, successful engagement of fathers in social work practice will require the integration of father-focused content in social work education, job training, and continuing education.

Resources

Books

- Black, T., & Keyes, S. (2020). *It's a setup: Fathering from the social and economic margins*. Oxford University Press.
- Fagan, J., & Pearson, J. (Eds.) (2021). *New research on parenting programs for low-income fathers*. Routledge.
- Mazza, C., & Perry, A. R. (2017). *Fatherhood in America: Social work perspectives on a changing society*. Charles C. Thomas Publisher.

Articles

- Henry, J. B., Julion, W. A., Bounds, D. T., & Sumo, J. N. (2020). Fatherhood matters: An integrative review of fatherhood intervention research. *The Journal of School Nursing*, *36*(1), 19–32. https://doi.org/10.1177/1059840519873380
- Holmes, E. K., Egginton, B. R., Hawkins, A. J., Robbins, N. L., & Shafer, K. (2020). Do responsible fatherhood programs work? A comprehensive meta-analytic study. *Family Relations*, *69*(5), 967–982. https://doi.org/10.1111/fare.12435
- Johnson Jr, W. E., & Briggs, H. E. (2021). Interventions with fathers: Effective social work practice for enhancing individual and family well-being. *Research on Social Work Practice*, *31*(8), 791–796. https://doi.org/10.1177/10497315211047187
- Panter-Brick, C., Burgess, A., Eggerman, M., McAllister, F., Pruett, K., & Leckman, J. F. (2014). Practitioner review: Engaging fathers – recommendations for a game change in parenting interventions based on a systematic review of the global evidence. *Journal of Child Psychology and Psychiatry*, *55*(11), 1187–1212. https://doi.org/10.1111/jcpp.12280

Websites

- Institute for Research on Poverty – Strategies for Engaging Fathers in Services: https://www.irp.wisc.edu/resource/strategies-for-engaging-fathers-in-family-services/
- Fatherhood Resource Hub: https://www.fatherhoodresourcehub.org
- Birth to Five Father Engagement Guide: https://eclkc.ohs.acf.hhs.gov/family-engagement/article/engaging-fathers

Discussion Questions

1. How have your personal experiences with fathers in your life impacted your approach to engagement with fathers in social work practice?
2. What do you see as the pros and cons of using self-disclosure in social work practice with fathers?
3. Consider an agency that provides family-focused intervention services. Find their website. From the perspective of a consumer, assess whether or not their intervention services appear to be father-inclusive.
4. How has your formal social work training prepared you to engage in father-focused social work interventions?

5. What types of additional father-focused training do you feel would make you more prepared to work with fathers in your practice?

References

Allen, R. I., & Petr, C. G. (1998). Rethinking family-centered practice. *American Journal of Orthopsychiatry, 68*(1), 4–15.

Alio, A. (2017). *Rationale and strategies for engaging fathers in maternal and infant health programs: A summary of promising practices*. University of Rochester Medical Center, NYS Maternal & Infant Health Center of Excellence.

Arroyo, J., & Peek, C. W. (2015). Child welfare caseworkers' characteristics and their attitudes toward non-custodial fathers. *Child Abuse & Neglect, 47*, 140–152. https://doi.org/10.1016/j.chiabu.2015.06.007

Barr, R., Morin, M., Brito, N., Richeda, B., Rodriguez, J., & Shauffer, C. (2014). Delivering services to incarcerated teen fathers: A pilot intervention to increase the quality of father–infant interactions during visitation. *Psychological Services, 11*(1), 10. https://doi.org/10.1037/a0034877

Bauer, M. E., & Giles, A. R. (2020). Where are all the gay fathers? Reflections on recruiting gay fathers as participants in leisure research. *Leisure Studies, 39*(3), 454–462. https://doi.org/10.1080/02614367.2019.1684979

Baum, N. (2017). Gender-sensitive intervention to improve work with fathers in child welfare services. *Child & Family Social Work, 22*(1), 419–427. https://doi.org/10.1111/cfs.12259https://doi.org/10.1111/cfs.12259

Bellamy, J. L., Harty, J. S., Banman, A., & Guterman, N. B. (2021). Engaging fathers in perinatal home visiting: Early lessons from a randomized controlled study of Dads Matter-HV. In *New research on parenting programs for low-income fathers* (pp. 58–73). Routledge.

Brewsaugh, K., & Strozier, A. (2016). Fathers in child welfare: What do social work textbooks teach our students? *Children and Youth Services Review, 60*, 34–41. https://doi.org/10.1016/j.childyouth.2015.11.015

Briar, S., & Miller, H. (1971). *Problems and issues in social casework*. Columbia University Press.

Burgdorf, A. S., & Prabhakar, A. S. (2021, Oct). Designing technology for single fathers using human-centered design approach. In *Proceedings of the 22nd annual conference on information technology education* (pp. 69–70).

Burgess, A. (2009). *Fathers and parenting interventions: What works?* Fatherhood Institute.

Caldwell, C. H., Antonakos, C. L., Assari, S., Kruger, D., De Loney, E. H., & Njai, R. (2014). Pathways to prevention: Improving nonresident African American fathers' parenting skills and behaviors to reduce sons' aggression. *Child Development, 85*(1), 308–325. https://doi.org/10.1111/cdev.12127

Calvert, J. M., Winston, E., Seaver, R., & Webster, J. M. (2020). *Impact evaluation of responsible fatherhood opportunities for Reentry & Mobility (ReFORM) in Appalachian Kentucky*. Administration for Children and Families (ACF).

Coakley, T. M. (2013). A qualitative appraisal of fathers' perspectives on fatherhood and barriers to their child welfare involvement. *Journal of Human Behavior in the Social Environment, 23*(5), 627–639. https://doi.org/10.1080/10911359.2013.775935

Coakley, T. M., Washington, T., & Gruber, K. (2018). Assessing child welfare agency practices and attitudes that affect father engagement. *Journal of Social Service Research, 44*(3), 365–374. https://doi.org/10.1080/01488376.2018.1476286

Cryer-Coupet, Q. R., Stokes, M. N., Lemmons, B. P., & Dorsey, M. (2021). Engaging nonresident fathers: Exploring collaborative competencies in support of family-centered practice. *Research on Social Work Practice, 31*(8), 880–892. https://doi.org/10.1177/10497315211022830

Doyle, O., Cryer-Coupet, Q. R., & McLeod, B. A. (2022). "All About How You Couch It:" African American fathers' visions of interventions for their sons. *Journal of Child and Family Studies.* https://doi.org/10.1007/s10826-022-02346-6

Fagan, J., & Iglesias, A. (1999). Father involvement program effects on fathers, father figures, and their Head Start children: A quasi-experimental study. *Early Childhood Research Quarterly, 14*(2), 243–269.

Fletcher, R., Knight, T., Macdonald, J. A., & St. George, J. (2019). Process evaluation of text-based support for fathers during the transition to fatherhood (SMS4dads): Mechanisms of impact. *BMC Psychology, 7*(1), 1–11. https://doi.org/10.1186/s40359-019-0338-4

Fraser, M. W. (2004). Intervention research in social work: Recent advances and continuing challenges. *Research on Social Work Practice, 14*(3), 210–222. https://doi.org/10.1177/1049731503262150

Garcia, N. M., & Mireles-Rios, R. (2020). "You were going to go to college": The role of Chicano fathers' involvement in Chicana daughters' college choice. *American Educational Research Journal, 57*(5), 2059–2088. https://doi.org/10.3102/0002831219892004

Gewirtz, A. H., Snyder, J., Zamir, O., Zhang, J., & Zhang, N. (2019). Effects of the after deployment: Adaptive Parenting Tools (ADAPT) intervention on fathers and their children: A moderated mediation model. *Development and Psychopathology, 31*(5), 1837–1849. https://doi.org/10.1017/s0954579419001238

Gibson, S. M., Cryer-Coupet, Q. R., Knox, J. L., & Field, K. (2020). Father involvement in kinship care: A risk and resilience perspective. *Children and Youth Services Review, 119*, 105354. https://doi.org/10.1016/j.childyouth.2020.105354

Hansen, A., Wade, C., & Yap, M. B. (2022). Fathers' perspectives on engaging with web-based parenting programs for adolescent mental health: A qualitative study. *Mental Health & Prevention*, 200232. https://doi.org/10.1016/j.mhp.2022.200232

Hayward, R. A., McKillop, A. J., Lee, S. J., Hammock, A. C., Hong, H., & Hou, W. (2021). A text messaging intervention to increase engagement and retention of men in a community-based father involvement program. *Journal of Technology in Human Services, 39*(2), 144–162. https://doi.org/10.1080/15228835.2020.1841070

Higgs, E., Gomez-Vidal, C., & Austin, M. J. (2018). Low-income nonresident fatherhood: A literature review with implications for practice and research. *Families in Society, 99*(2), 110–120. https://doi.org/10.1177/1044389418767826

Huebner, R. A., Werner, M., Hartwig, S., White, S., & Shewa, D. (2008). Engaging fathers: Needs and satisfaction in child protective services. *Administration in Social Work, 32*(2), 87–103. https://doi.org/10.1300/J147v32n02_06

Julion, W. A., Breitenstein, S. M., & Waddell, D. (2012). Fatherhood intervention development in collaboration with African American non-resident fathers. *Research in Nursing & Health, 35*(5), 490–506. https://doi.org/10.1002/nur.21492

Lopez, S. A., Torres, A., & Norwood, P. (1998). Building partnerships: A successful collaborative experience between social work and education. *Children & Schools, 20*(3), 165–176. https://doi.org/10.1093/cs/20.3.165

Martin, P. Y. (2006). Practising gender at work: Further thoughts on reflexivity. *Gender, Work and Organization, 13*(3), 254–276. https://doi.org/10.1177/1053815109354698

May, C. D., St George, J. M., & Lane, S. (2021). From presence to participation: Engagement with an SMS program for fathers of children on the autism spectrum. *Journal of Child and Family Studies, 30*(1), 29–37. https://doi.org/10.1007/s10826-020-01845-8

McLeod, B. A. (2020). "Hello group, I need advice": A textual analysis of Black fathers' help-seeking posts on Facebook. *Family Relations, 69*(5), 944–955. https://doi.org/10.1111/fare.12500

National Association of Social Workers. (2021). NASW code of ethics.

O'Donnell, J. M., Johnson, W. E., Jr., D'Aunno, L. E., & Thornton, H. L. (2005). Fathers in child welfare: Caseworkers' perspectives. *Child Welfare, 84*(3), 387.

Rayburn, S. R., & Coatsworth, J. D. (2021). Becoming fathers: Initial exploration of a support program for new fathers. *The Journal of Perinatal Education, 30*(2), 78–88. https://doi.org/10.1891/j-pe-d-20-00015

Sharf, J., Primavera, L. H., & Diener, M. J. (2010). Dropout and therapeutic alliance: A meta-analysis of adult individual psychotherapy. *Psychotherapy: Theory, Research, Practice, Training, 47*(4), 637–645. https://doi.org/10.1037/a0021175

Sicouri, G., Tully, L., Collins, D., Burn, M., Sargeant, K., Frick, P., Anderson, V., Hawes, D., Kimonis, E., Moul, C., Lenroot, R., & Dadds, M. (2018). Toward father-friendly parenting interventions: A qualitative study. *Australian and New Zealand Journal of Family Therapy, 39*(2), 218–231. https://doi.org/10.1002/anzf.1307

Scourfield, J., Tolman, R., Maxwell, N., Holland, S., Bullock, A., & Sloan, L. (2012). Results of a training course for social workers on engaging fathers in child protection. *Children and Youth Services Review, 34*(8), 1425–1432. https://doi.org/10.1016/j.childyouth.2012.03.022

Stahlschmidt, M. J., Threlfall, J., Seay, K. D., Lewis, E. M., & Kohl, P. L. (2013). Recruiting fathers to parenting programs: Advice from dads and fatherhood program providers. *Children and Youth Services Review, 35*(10), 1734–1741. https://doi.org/10.1016/j.childyouth.2013.07.004

Stokes, M. N., Charity-Parker, B. M., & Hope, E. C. (2021). What does it mean to be Black and White? A meta-ethnographic review of racial socialization in multiracial families. *Journal of Family Theory & Review, 13*(2), 181–201. https://doi.org/10.1111/jftr.12413

Stover, C. S., McMahon, T. J., & Moore, K. (2019). A randomized pilot trial of two parenting interventions for fathers in residential substance use disorder treatment. *Journal of Substance Abuse Treatment, 104*, 116–127. https://doi.org/10.1016/j.jsat.2019.07.003

Turner, S. G., Strand, V., Bliss, S., & Sacristan, D. (2019). How well-prepared are graduating MSW students in clinical competencies? *Clinical Social Work Journal, 47*(1), 113–123. https://doi.org/10.1007/s10615-018-0695-0

U.S. Department of Health and Human Services. (2018). *Integrating approaches that prioritize and enhance father engagement.* https://www.acf.hhs.gov/sites/default/files/assets/acffatherhoodim_final.pdf

Wiseman, A. M., Atkinson, A. A., & Cryer-Coupet, Q. R. (2021). "As we talk about this more, a box opens up": Family literacy programs for fathers in treatment for substance use disorder. *Journal of Adolescent & Adult Literacy, 64*(4), 441–448. https://doi.org/10.1002/jaal.1115

Chapter 9
Expanding Our Understanding of Public Policies to Support Father Involvement

Lenna Nepomnyaschy and Daniel P. Miller

Introduction

Fathers are integral to family processes and children's well-being, and many fathers have increased their involvement with children over the last 40 years. However, social and economic changes over the last several decades have created socioeconomic and racial disparities in the ability and capacity of fathers to be involved with their children. Social policies are effective mechanisms for promoting and ensuring the well-being of fathers, but fathers are rarely the explicit target of policy efforts.

In this chapter, we first describe the social and economic changes in the United States over the last several decades that have led to disparities in fathers' ability to be involved with their children. Next, we discuss the child support enforcement system, which is the sole national policy targeting men in their roles as fathers but which also produces a heavily racialized and inequitable system that disproportionately subjects low-SES fathers and fathers of color to a series of punitive enforcement mechanisms. Based on our review of the system, we make a number of recommendations for reform of child support enforcement before turning our attention briefly to other policies that—while not specifically targeted at fathers—may promote fathers' involvement with children. We conclude by identifying and describing ideas for policy reforms that social workers can engage with and advocate for that should enhance fathers' well-being and their involvement with children, improve child well-being, and promote economic, social, and racial justice for families in the United States.

L. Nepomnyaschy (✉)
Rutgers University School of Social Work, New Brunswick, NJ, USA
e-mail: lennan@ssw.rutgers.edu

D. P. Miller
Boston University School of Social Work, Boston, MA, USA
e-mail: dpmiller@bu.edu

J. L. Bellamy et al. (eds.), *Social Work Practice with Fathers*,
https://doi.org/10.1007/978-3-031-13686-3_9

Background and Context

Fathers are key contributors to children's physical, emotional, and social development across the life course (Lamb, 2010), and many fathers cherish their parenting roles and have increased the time spent with children over the last 40 years (Livingston & Parker, 2019). However, major social and economic changes in the United States over the last several decades have had profound impacts on the economic and social well-being of men of lower socioeconomic status (SES) and men of color, specifically Black, Latino, and Indigenous men. These changes, which include deindustrialization, loss of manufacturing jobs, declines in union density, and tremendous increases in incarceration rates (Cherlin, 2014; Mincy, 2006; Sum et al., 2011; Western & Rosenfeld, 2011; Western & Wildeman, 2009; Wilson, 2011), have had dramatic consequences for lower-educated men's labor market outcomes, such as labor force participation and wages (Binder & Bound, 2019). In turn, these changes have created extensive differences in the ability and capacity of fathers to be involved with children across socioeconomic strata, racial and ethnic backgrounds, and living arrangements (Livingston & Parker, 2011).

For example, in 1965, the difference in labor force participation between men with advanced degrees and those with no high school diploma was 3.2 percentage points, but by 2015, that difference had grown to 17.6 percentage points (Binder & Bound, 2019). Related disparities are shown in Fig. 9.1, where we observe that among college-educated men, earnings grew by nearly 20% between 1979 and 2018, while the earnings of men with only a high school degree declined by 18%, and those of men with no high school diploma declined by 25% (Bureau of Labor Statistics, 2019).

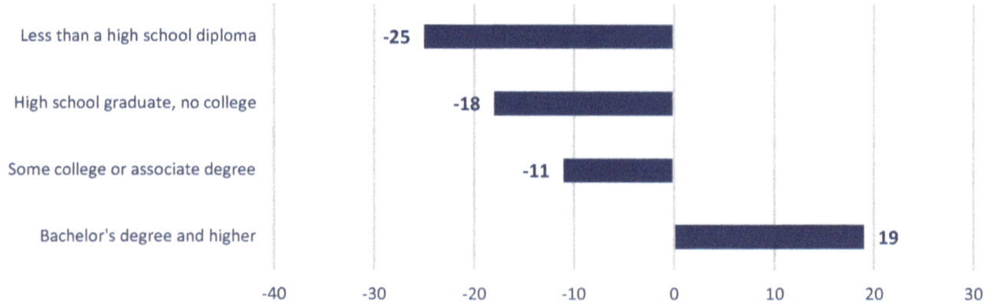

Source: Figure created by authors based on data from the US Bureau of Labor Statistics, 2019. Highlights of women's earnings in 2018. BLS Reports. Chart 4. Percentage change in inflation-adjusted median usual weekly earnings of men and women, by education attainment 1979- 2018 https://www.bls.gov/opub/reports/womens-earnings/2018/home.htm

Fig. 9.1 Percentage change in men's inflation-adjusted median usual weekly earnings, by educational attainment, 1979–2018. (Source: Figure created by authors based on data from the US Bureau of Labor Statistics, 2019. Highlights of women's earnings in 2018. BLS Reports. Chart 4. Percentage change in inflation-adjusted median usual weekly earnings of men and women, by educational attainment 1979–2018 https://www.bls.gov/opub/reports/womens-earnings/2018/home.htm)

Similarly, incarceration rates for men without a high school diploma are about four times higher than for men with at least a high school education (Pew Charitable Trusts, 2010), and incarceration rates for Black and Latino men are six and three times higher, respectively, than for White men (Sentencing Project, n.d.). Even more startling is the way that education differences compound racial disparities in incarceration risk and how these disparities have changed over time. Compared to White men, the risk of lifetime incarceration by age 30–34 was 8 points higher for Black men born in 1945–1949, growing to a 17-percentage point disparity for Black and White men born in 1975–1979. But among Black men without a high school diploma born in 1975–1979, this cumulative risk of incarceration is an astounding 70%, compared to 15% for White men (Kearney et al., 2014).[1]

This dramatic deterioration in the economic prospects of all lower-SES men, and particularly Black men, has been linked with declines in marriage and increases in divorce and nonmarital childbearing over the last four decades (Author et al., 2019; Cherlin, 2014; Lundberg et al., 2016; Smock & Schwartz, 2020; Western & Wildeman, 2009). As shown in Fig. 9.2, compared to 1970, when marriage rates among the highest and lowest educated women (ages 35–45) were more similar

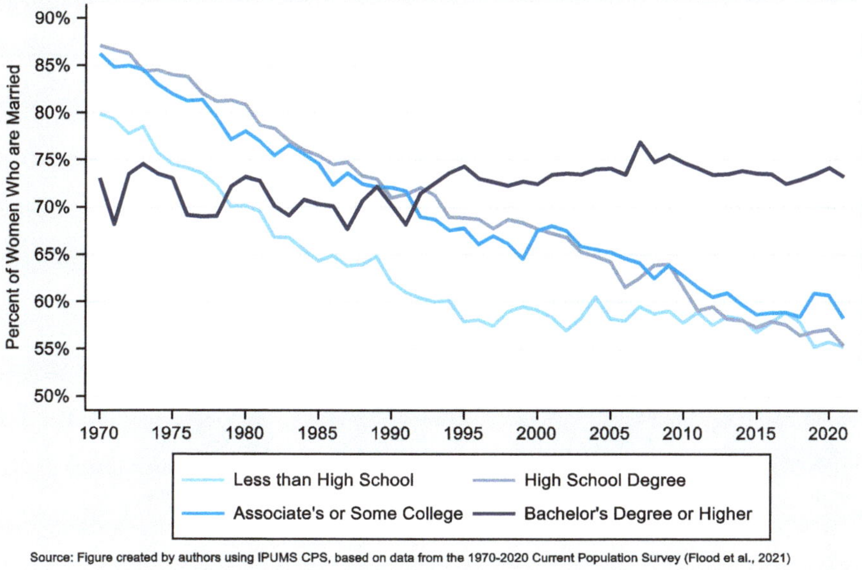

Fig. 9.2 Marriage rates for women 35–45 by educational attainment. (Source: Figure created by authors using IPUMS CPS, based on data from the 1970–2020 current population survey (Flood et al., 2020))

[1] Incarceration rates have started to decline over the last decade for all groups. However, disparities by race and ethnicity remain unchanged (Carson, 2021).

(approximately 75% vs. 80%), today, only 55% of women without a high school degree are married compared to 75% of women with a college degree or higher (Reeves et al., 2016). Similarly, the nonmarital birth rate among women without a high school degree is over 60%, compared to about 13% for women with a college degree or higher (Fig. 9.3).

Not surprisingly, these economic, social, and demographic changes have had serious implications for children's living arrangements. One-quarter of all children in the United States today live apart from one of their biological parents, most often their father, which is the highest rate among 130 countries across the world (Kramer, 2019). And given the dynamic nature of family processes, over half of children in the United States will spend some part of their childhood living apart from their biological fathers (McLanahan & Jencks, 2015). Children's living arrangements also vary widely by parents' education and racial and ethnic background. Figure 9.4 highlights these disparities. Among children of White parents, 17% live in a mother-headed household, while this number is 55% for children of Black parents, 31% for children of Latino parents, and 38% for children of American Indian/Alaska Native parents. Disparities are even larger by the highest level of education achieved by either parent. Only 15% of children whose parent had a college degree or higher lived with a single parent, compared with 80% of children whose parents did not complete high school.

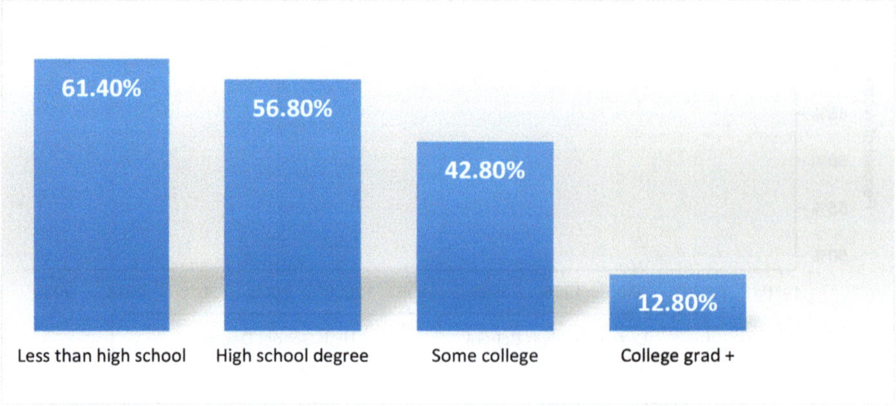

Source: Figure created by authors using IPUMS USA, based on data from the 2015-2019 American Community Survey (Ruggles, 2021).

Fig. 9.3 Percent of new mothers who are unmarried by educational attainment. (Source: Figure created by authors using IPUMS USA, based on data from the 2015–2019 American Community Survey (Ruggles et al., 2021))

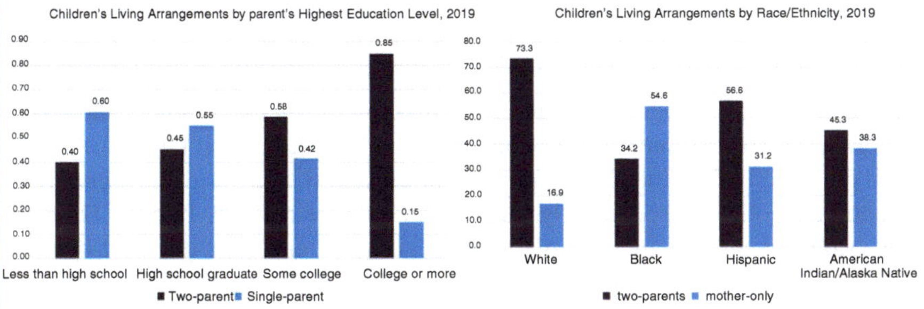

Source: Figure created by authors based on tables compiled by the National Center for Education Statistics based on data from the American Community Survey, 2019

Fig. 9.4 Children's living arrangements: variation by parental education and race/ethnicity. (Source: Figure created by authors based on tables compiled by the National Center for Education Statistics based on data from the American Community Survey, 2019)

Policies and the Well-Being of Fathers: Theoretical Foundations

While the overwhelming majority of fathers are highly committed to being involved with their children (Brigham Young University, 2018), a decades-long deterioration in the economic and social standing of lower-SES fathers and fathers of color has created a climate that is particularly detrimental for many fathers' ability to share a household with, provide for, and be highly involved with their children (Jones & Mosher, 2013). With this insight in place, we argue that only large-scale interventions of the sort represented by state and federal policy can be effective in ensuring conditions that are adequate to facilitate fathers' consistent and beneficial impacts on their children's lives. The basis for this argument derives from recent theoretical developments from the scientific literature on father involvement. Though much of the earlier theoretical work on fathers focused on conceptualizing father involvement and its impact on children (Lamb, 2010; Pleck, 2007), more recent theoretical developments have drawn attention to the factors that impact fathers' ability to remain involved with their children and the circumstances under which involvement might optimally occur. Drawing on ecological perspectives, these theories (e.g., Cabrera et al., 2007, 2014) are noteworthy for their attention to more distal factors like public policies that, while not explicitly focused on fathers, nonetheless have profound impact on their economic and social well-being, and especially for those of lower SES. For example, in their expanded model for father involvement, Cabrera et al. (2014) describe how macro-level factors like social, cultural, political, and economic conditions (within which policies are situated) shape the family resources and systems that are more proximal determinants of fathers' parenting behaviors.

Current Policies: Child Support Enforcement

Unfortunately, despite at least general theoretical support for the notion that policies could be used to effectively promote the well-being of low-SES fathers and fathers of color, fathers have typically not been considered as the explicit targets of state or federal policies. In fact, the child support enforcement (CSE) system is arguably the sole national policy to specifically target men in their roles as fathers. However, when evaluated against the complementary goals of ensuring the well-being of fathers and their children, two chief problems with the CSE system emerge: (1) CSE is not designed to support the economic or social welfare of fathers, and relatedly, (2) CSE is heavily racialized in that fathers and families of color are overrepresented and thus subject to the frequently punitive practices, policies, and requirements that characterize the system (Battle, 2018; Pratt, 2016).

The federal CSE system was established in 1975 to help recover costs to state and federal governments who were providing welfare payments to families with children when one parent—most often a father—was absent (Tollestrup, 2021).[2] In brief, families enter the CSE system in one of two ways. First, custodial parent families receiving Temporary Assistance for Needy Families (TANF) benefits or who participate in the Medicaid program must cooperate with CSE (Selekman & Holcomb, 2018; Tollestrup, 2021); in addition, as of 2018, 23 states required the cooperation of families receiving Child Care Development Fund subsidies (designed to defray child care costs for working parents), and seven states required cooperation from families receiving benefits from the Supplemental Nutrition Assistance Program (SNAP; Selekman & Holcomb, 2018). A key point here is that cooperation with CSE entails identifying the biological father and his whereabouts to the CSE system, and for mothers receiving public assistance, giving up the right to any child support collected. Only half of the states pass through any of the support paid on behalf of children on public assistance, and among those that do, most only pass through the first $50 per month (NCSL, 2020b). A much smaller proportion of families not receiving public benefits enters the system by voluntarily enlisting help from the CSE system.

Once paternity has been established (in the case of a nonmarital birth), a child support order is set that dictates the terms of the father's financial obligations. States exercise discretion in how orders are set based on different formulas and considerations. For example, some states charge retroactive support dating as far back as the child's birth, and some states add birthing costs if the birth was covered by Medicaid (Sorensen et al., 2007). Both practices result in fathers beginning their child support obligations with a sizable debt through no fault of their own. In addition, though recent federal legislation from 2016 placed restrictions on the practice, states often

[2] Though the CSE system serves both nonresident fathers and mothers, given the focus of this chapter (and that the overwhelming majority (85%) of nonresident parents are fathers), we refer exclusively to fathers, except when reporting data that refers to all custodial or noncustodial parents.

assume (or "impute") fathers' earnings if they fail to appear in court when an order is established, lack necessary documentation of their current or past earnings, or are assumed to be voluntarily unemployed or underemployed (Turetsky, 2019). Because imputed incomes in the majority of cases overestimate the ability of low-income men to pay (Plotnick & Kennedy, 2018), low-income fathers often have child support orders that—relative to their incomes—are much higher than for higher-income men and are often impossible to pay (Turetsky, 2019). Last, though most states maintain child support guidelines that include a "self-support reserve" (NCSL, 2020a), a level of income fathers need to support themselves, these reserves are not always disregarded when a child support order is created.

The next step of the enforcement system is to collect the support owed by fathers. This is most often accomplished through automatic wage withholding whereby child support is automatically withheld from fathers' paychecks. However, only 32% of custodial mothers receive any child support, and of those due support, fewer than half (46.4%) receive all that is due to them (Grall, 2020). In fact, as shown in Fig. 9.5, the proportion of all custodial mothers who report receiving any support has decreased over the past 25 years, whereas the proportion receiving all support due to them has remained mostly steady.

Why are child support payment rates so low? As noted above, social, economic, and demographic trends coupled with the scourge of mass incarceration have steadily deteriorated the economic prospects of many low-SES men (Berger et al., 2021). Despite this, the CSE system and its constituent enforcement mechanisms are based on the presumption that fathers' *willingness to pay* is the major determinant of compliance with a child support order. In turn, the system levies a series of punitive penalties that are intended to deter noncompliance (Mincy & Sorensen, 1998). Fathers who fall behind in their child support order begin to accumulate child

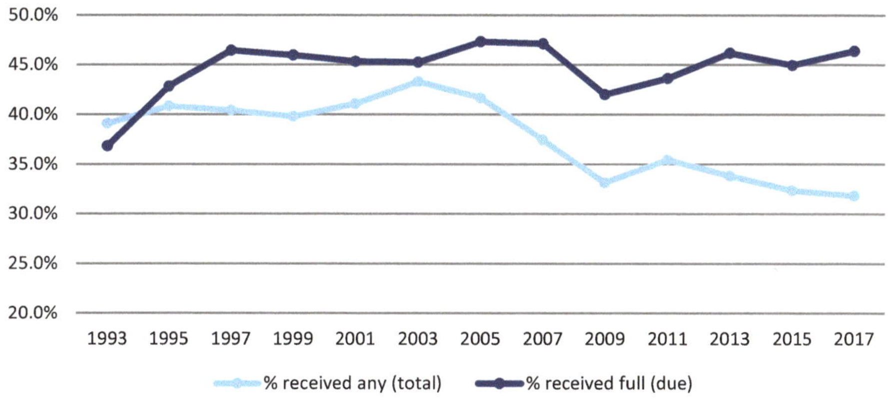

Fig. 9.5 Custodial mothers' receipt of child support. (Source: Figure created by authors based on data from the Current Population Survey Child Support Supplement (CPS-CSS), 2019 (Grall, 2020))

support debt (*arrears*), and among other sanctions, child support agencies can intercept tax refunds and unemployment benefits to pay arrears. In some instances, failure to pay sufficient support can lead courts to reduce fathers' *parenting time* with children (NCSL, 2021), meaning that children lose out on both financial support and the potential benefits that come from consistent father engagement. Notably, states may withhold up to 65% of income for fathers who are in arrears (OCSE, 2017). In addition, nonpayment or underpayment of child support may result in the suspension of fathers' drivers' and professional licenses, interception of tax returns, liens placed on assets, and in many cases, particularly for the lowest-income men, felony charges and incarceration (Tollestrup, 2021).

By focusing almost exclusively on willingness to pay, the CSE system ignores an important determinant of child support compliance, namely, fathers' *ability to pay*. This despite a substantial body of research that finds that limited resources and overly burdensome child support orders reduce fathers' child support payments and their time spent with children (Berger et al., 2021; Hodges et al., 2020; Mincy & Sorensen, 1998; Sinkewicz & Garfinkel, 2009; Waller & Plotnick, 2001). Limited ability to pay is especially salient for low-income fathers. One analysis found that those in child support arrears had median debt levels of $3750 but median annual incomes of only $8191, with more than a quarter reporting no income at all (Sorensen et al., 2007). More recent data indicate that 22% of all child support arrears are owed by a very small group of noncustodial parents (3% of the arrears caseload), of whom three-quarters report no income (Arthur, 2018). Previous analyses and common sense suggest that these arrears are uncollectible (Sorensen et al., 2007). Despite this, 35 states also levy interest charges on arrears, some at a rate of as high as 12% per year (NCSL, 2019), a practice that further decreases the likelihood of repayment and which has further contributed to the accumulation of arrears in the CSE system (Sorensen et al., 2007).

Evaluating Child Support Enforcement

While a narrow evaluation of the CSE system based solely on cost efficiency paints a picture of a highly effective system that collects $5.14 in child support for every dollar spent (OCSE, 2021), our brief summary identifies three major problems with the system: (1) Many mothers who are on public assistance receive little to no support paid by fathers, (2) it collects support for only a third of all custodial parents (Grall, 2020), and (3) that it subjects nonresident fathers—many with a limited ability to pay—to a series of punitive enforcement measures. Critically, and because of the mechanisms linking receipt of public assistance to participation in the CSE system, families of color and low-SES families are disproportionately represented.[3] In

[3] A key point here is that only poor and low-income families who receive public assistance are thus penalized. Benefits provided to families at the top of the income distribution through the tax system, including tax expenditures such as the mortgage interest deduction, employer-provided health insurance, and retirement investments, dwarf those provided to those at the bottom, but these families are never targeted for cost recovery (Abramovitz, 2001; Faricy, 2016).

2015, more than half (51%) of custodial parents in the system were either Hispanic (24%) or non-Hispanic Black (27%). Nearly two-thirds (65%) of families served by the child support system had incomes below 200% of the federal poverty line (FPL), one-third (34%) with incomes below 100%, and 17% with incomes below 50% of the FPL, referred to as "deep" poverty. A quarter of the families served by the child support program had either no income (6%) or income below $10,000 per year (18%; Sorensen et al., 2016).

Thus, it is primarily low-SES fathers and fathers of color who bear the burden of punitive CSE mechanisms. The accumulation of arrears can be especially damaging because it can not only subject fathers to higher rates of wage withholding as noted above but also affect their other benefits. For example, Congress did not exempt stimulus payments from the 2020 Coronavirus Aid, Relief, and Economic Security (CARES) Act from being intercepted. Thus, fathers who owed child support lost some or all of this important source of economic relief. Indeed, recent analyses from the federal Office of Child Support Enforcement indicate that intercepted stimulus payments were responsible for an unanticipated drop of $4 billion in the total amount of arrears in the child support program, the largest such decline in 20 years (Sorensen, 2021). Intercepting these payments likely had cascading effects as many nonresident fathers also live with new families and children (Edin & Nelson, 2013; Guzzo, 2014) who were subsequently deprived of pandemic relief through the government's seizure of this key benefit.

Moreover, a growing body of research points to the damaging effects of arrears for both nonresident fathers and their children. Arrears can lead to lower labor force participation, less involvement with children, lower child support payments, more material hardship, and increased depression and substance use among nonresident fathers (Cancian et al., 2013; Miller & Mincy, 2012; Robbins et al., 2022; Turner & Waller, 2016; Um, 2019). Unlike other forms of debt such as student loans or credit card debt, which can be beneficial to families in some circumstances, child support arrears have no such benefit, and a recent study finds that child support arrears are unique among other types of parental debt for their sizable negative effects on children's socio-emotional well-being (Nepomnyaschy et al., 2021).

Reforming Child Support Enforcement

Given its many problems and the fact that it is the sole national policy to target men in their capacity as fathers, we make recommendations for commonsense reform of the CSE system. While a full summary of potential reforms is beyond the scope of this chapter, we focus briefly on reforms that might lessen the burden of participation in the child support program, which falls heavily on low-income fathers and fathers of color, while still ensuring that these men provide financial support to their children when possible. Many of these recommendations mirror similar findings from recent reviews of the CSE system (NCSL, 2021; Pratt, 2016; Turetsky, 2019; Turetsky & Waller, 2020).

We basically recommend a wholesale reorientation of the system to one that acknowledges the practical limits on many fathers' ability to pay support. As fathers enter the CSE system, we recommend that state child support guidelines be modified to explicitly disallow earnings imputation in all cases and that orders be established with explicit evidence of fathers' earnings. In cases where they have limited (or no) ability to pay, fathers should not face sanctions that limit opportunities to spend time with their children, and, indeed, a meaningful shift would be to establish orders that credit fathers for their time spent with children or their provision of food, clothing, or other kinds of "in-kind" support. In a similar move to assure fathers' continued financial stability, all states should mandate the use of a generous and realistic self-support reserve in the initial creation of orders.

After an order has been established, we urge a shift away from enforcement measures aimed at penalizing fathers for nonpayment. Revoking professional and drivers' licenses and jailing fathers for nonpayment of support are punitive tactics that harm fathers' accumulation of economic, social, and human capital and limit their ability to remain consistently involved in their children's lives (Cancian et al., 2013). For fathers in arrears, the potential to have up to 65% of wages withheld can serve as a powerful disincentive for participation in the formal labor force (Miller & Mincy, 2012). Instead, states should mandate cooperative approaches with fathers that help them to navigate the CSE system, support them in finding gainful employment, connect them with important community resources, and facilitate their involvement and engagement with their children (NCSL, 2021; Turetsky, 2019).[4] Finally, states should consider programs that reduce or forgive child support arrears for fathers who are able to make some payments, building on encouraging evidence regarding the effectiveness of such programs (Hahn et al., 2019; Heinrich et al., 2011). Such forgiveness policies could help ensure that fathers remain financially and socially involved with their children while preventing the accumulation of unpayable debt.

[4] Over the last 20 years, a number of responsible fatherhood programs have been established across states and localities. Several rigorous studies have been funded to evaluate the effectiveness of these programs across sites and have found no evidence that these programs improve lower-income fathers' employment outcomes and child support provision or improve relationships with mothers and some weak evidence of increased engagement or time spent with children but not both (Avellar et al., 2018; Cancian et al., 2019; Pearson & Fagan, 2019). Most of these programs have been funded through state TANF funds as strengthening two-parent families was one of the explicit goals of the TANF program. In addition to the questionable effectiveness of responsible father programs, recent research points to highly racialized patterns of state use of TANF funding for purposes outside of cash assistance. Specifically, states that have higher proportions of Black residents are less likely to use TANF for cash assistance and are more likely to use funds for programs that aim to promote marriage and responsible fatherhood and reduce single parenthood, and these differences in resource allocation have increased Black-White poverty gaps among children (Parolin, 2021).

Other Policy Domains That Can Impact Father Involvement

As demonstrated, CSE practices are not particularly effective for promoting fathers' economic support of their children. In many instances, these practices can harm fathers' ability to be involved and increase the racial and ethnic disparities in children's economic precarity and well-being. Though the reforms we recommend would represent meaningful improvements, the CSE system targets only nonresident fathers. Thus, in this section, we discuss other social policies that, while not specifically targeted at fathers, have either been shown to increase or have the potential to increase fathers' ability to be involved with their children and improve fathers' well-being. In doing so, we focus on universal or near-universal policies that are likely to have the broadest impact. These universal-leaning approaches would have the greatest impact on lower-SES fathers and families and the fathers of color who are overrepresented among nonresident fathers. These policies come from a variety of social policy domains, including criminal justice, employment and wage, health care, and child-focused policies, that are currently in place.

Criminal Justice Policies

We begin with the obvious and immediate need to advocate for reforms to criminal justice policies that are key to increasing fathers' involvement with children. There is a large and compelling body of research documenting the detrimental effects of paternal incarceration for fathers', mothers', and children's well-being and fathers' ability to live with, be involved with, and contribute to their children (Dwyer Emory et al., 2020b; Geller et al., 2011, 2012; Geller, 2013; McLeod & Gottlieb, 2018; Miller, 2020; Turney & Wildeman, 2013; Wakefield & Wildeman, 2014; Washington et al., 2018; Western & Smith, 2018; Wildeman, 2010). Policies that reduce penalties for low-level offenses, decriminalize marijuana possession, and reduce police surveillance of families in lower-income neighborhoods will unambiguously reduce the exposure of lower-income fathers and fathers of color to the criminal justice system and all of the widely documented collateral consequences of criminal justice system involvement for fathers, their families, and their communities (Dwyer Emory, 2021; Miller, 2020; Pager, 2003; Uggen & McElrath, 2014; Western & Wildeman, 2009). In addition to policies that reduce incarceration and individuals' contact with the criminal justice system, policies that reduce the barriers to reentry after incarceration are also very important to consider. Such policies include lifting unnecessary prohibitions on the types of occupations and occupational licenses that individuals with incarceration histories can hold, removing bans on individuals living with their families in public housing, removing bans on receiving public assistance and higher education grants, limiting public access to criminal justice records, removing prohibitions on individuals' abilities to participate in civic and social life, and restoring voting rights, among others (Vallas & Dietrich, 2014). Removing such barriers can lead to better economic and psychosocial outcomes for fathers, which improves their ability to be involved with and provide for their children (Charles et al., 2019). A recent study examining the effect of limiting public access to criminal justice records found greater provision of support for children among previously incarcerated fathers (Dwyer Emory et al., 2020b).

Wages and Employment Policies

Another important set of policies to consider are those that increase fathers' wages and earnings from employment. First, increasing federal, state, and local minimum wages is a key policy reform to consider for increasing fathers' economic security and ability to be involved with their children. The evidence is clear that a higher minimum wage increases wages not just for workers currently working at the minimum wage but also across the wage scale as all workers gain earning power (Zipperer, 2015). Recent evidence suggests that a higher minimum wage is associated with a higher likelihood that fathers live with their children (Dwyer Emory et al., 2020a).

Another important policy reform is expansion of the Earned Income Tax Credit (EITC), a refundable tax credit for low-income workers, which functions as a wage subsidy, increasing wages by over 40% (or nearly $6000) for those receiving the maximum benefit (Tax Policy Center, 2021). Because the EITC is targeted primarily at lower-income working families with children, it is currently the most effective child poverty reduction program in the United States, reducing child poverty by 25% (CBPP, 2019). However, the benefit for childless workers is minimal even though a very large proportion of these "childless" workers are men who actually have children but either do not live with them or (more likely) live with children but do not claim them as dependents on their income taxes (Thompson et al., 2020). In addition to the federal EITC, 21 states have their own refundable EITC that delivers an additional benefit on top of the federal EITC, ranging from 3% of the federal benefit in Montana to 85% in California (Urban Institute, 2021). Research suggests that more generous EITC benefits improve fathers' ability to contribute to their children (Haralampoudis et al., 2020). Even more importantly, expansion of the EITC to substantially increase the benefit for childless workers, particularly if specifically targeted at nonresident fathers, has been shown to substantially increase fathers' employment, income, and ability to contribute to and spend time with their children (Maag et al., 2019; Miller et al., 2018; Nichols et al., 2012; Wheaton & Sorensen, 2010).

Health-Care Policies

Being uninsured or underinsured (having a plan with very meager benefits) is associated with poor physical and mental health, lower life expectancy, and medical debt (Institute of Medicine, 2002). All of these factors play a role in fathers' ability to provide for and be involved with their children. The 2012 Supreme Court ruling on

National Federation of Independent Business v. Sebelius made state expansions of Medicaid under the Affordable Care Act optional, creating stark disparities across states in coverage rates for low-income persons who would not otherwise be covered and who are overwhelmingly lower-income men and men of color (Tolbert et al., 2020). Not surprisingly, Medicaid expansion has tremendously increased coverage rates and improved the quality of care and overall health of those living in expansion states (Allen & Sommers, 2019; Bui & Sanger-Katz, 2015). In addition, recent research finds that Medicaid expansion and participation are associated with greater provision of child support for children with nonresident parents (Bullinger, 2021; Bullinger & Tello-Trillo, 2021).

Family- and Child-Focused Policies

A large body of research across many countries finds that fathers who take time off at the birth of their child are more involved with their children over the course of childhood (Huerta et al., 2014; Nepomnyaschy & Waldfogel, 2007; Petts, Knoester, & Waldfogel, 2020b). Unfortunately, because the United States is one of the only countries in the world that does not provide paid maternity or paternity leave, only a small proportion of fathers have access to paid leave through their employers, and thus leave-taking is concentrated among higher-educated and higher-income fathers (Donovan, 2019). Additionally, because paternity leave is not the norm in the United States, rates and length of leave-taking are much lower than in other countries even among American men who have access to paid leave (Petts, Knoester, & Li, 2020a). Evidence from European countries suggests that creating and enhancing parental leave policies, especially when they are gender-neutral (Patnaik, 2019), substantially increases men's leave-taking and increases fathers' involvement with children across the life course. In the absence of a federal movement to enact paid parental leave in the United States, six states have enacted their own paid parental leave policies, but thus far, only three of these extend benefits to fathers (Bipartisan Policy Center, 2021).

Another important child-focused policy whose impact on fathers is rarely considered is Head Start, a comprehensive early childhood education program serving low-income children in the United States. Head Start serves over one million children annually and over one-third of all poor children aged 3 to 5 in the United States (Office of Head Start, 2020). A unique aspect of the Head Start program is that one of its explicit goals is to increase the involvement of both mothers and fathers in children's lives (Office of Head Start, 2018). Prior work confirms that children's Head Start participation is associated with increased frequency and quality of resident father involvement (Raikes & Bellotti, 2006). More recent research extends this work to nonresident fathers and finds that children's participation in the Head Start program is associated with increased involvement (Gelber & Isen, 2013; Haralampoudis et al., 2021) and noncash contributions to children (Haralampoudis et al., 2021).

Conclusion

Despite widespread recognition of the importance of fathers to the health and well-being of children, social, economic, and demographic shifts over the past few decades have eroded the ability of many fathers to be involved with and support their children. Furthermore, the only large-scale policy to deal with men in their roles as fathers is child support enforcement, a system that assures support for only a minority of custodial mothers and children while subjecting nonresident fathers (the majority of whom are low-SES men or men of color) to punitive enforcement mechanisms that ignore a limited ability to pay as a primary driver of underpayment or nonpayment of support. These enforcement mechanisms can lead to the accumulation of back child support (arrears), an especially damaging type of debt that is unpayable for many men. Though commonsense reforms to the CSE system would help to promote the well-being of fathers and their continued support of their children, the system targets only nonresident parents so—given the complex array of social circumstances underlying father involvement—additional policy reforms are necessary to support fathers. Such efforts are necessary to ensure the economic and social standing of fathers and thus support their continued engagement with their children.

Social workers are uniquely positioned, trained, and called upon to engage with these issues and advocate for policy reforms that will improve the well-being of fathers and their families. Our mission and code of ethics call upon us to "pursue social change to promote social justice, focusing on issues of poverty, unemployment, discrimination, and other forms of social injustice" (NASW, 2021). We challenge social workers to advocate and fight for (1) comprehensive reforms to and reimagining of the criminal justice system, (2) substantial increases to the minimum wage to the creation of a living wage, (3) expansion of the EITC to create a minimum income for all workers, (4) expansion of Medicaid combined with a move to a single-payer health-care plan to provide quality care for all Americans, (5) expansion of Head Start and creation of a universal early childhood education system, and (6) the enactment of paid and protected family leave policies, particularly those that are gender-neutral. These types of policies will certainly improve the well-being of all families but particularly those that are of lower-SES and families of color, addressing and enhancing economic, social, and racial justice in the United States.

Resources

- *USDHHS, ASPE, Linking Low-Income Men to Medicaid and Health Insurance Marketplace Project*
- Issue briefs on increasing access to health care for low-income men and low-income fathers: *Why Health Matters for Low-Income Fathers*?
- https://aspe.hhs.gov/reports/why-health-matters-low-income-fathers

- *Health Care Coverage and Care for Reentering Men: What Difference Can It Make?*
- https://nicic.gov/linking-low-income-men-medicaid-and-health-insurance-marketplace-2016
- *MDRC, Focus Area: Fathers*
- MDRC has developed and tested programs to boost the earnings of low-income noncustodial fathers, augment their capacity to provide child support, and increase their involvement with their children. In addition, MDRC has been a leader in the development and evaluation of strategies to improve the relationships of fathers with the mothers of their children—whether they are married to them or not.
- https://www.mdrc.org/population/focus/fathers
- *CLASP: Center for Law and Social Policy*
- Income and Work Supports
- https://www.clasp.org/issues/income-and-work-supports
- *The Sentencing Project*
- Collateral Consequences
- https://www.sentencingproject.org/issues/collateral-consequences/
- *Prison Policy Initiative*
- Collateral Consequences
- https://www.prisonpolicy.org/collateral.html
- *Fatherhood Research and Practice Network*
- Fatherhood policy
- https://www.frpn.org/fatherhood-policy
- *Head Start: Early Childhood Learning and Knowledge Center*
- Family Engagement: Engaging Fathers
- https://eclkc.ohs.acf.hhs.gov/family-engagement/article/engaging-fathers
- *Urban Institute*
- Taxes and Budget
- https://www.urban.org/urban-wire/expanding-earned-income-tax-credit-could-provide-financial-security-millions-workers-without-children

Discussion Questions

1. How can a policy that is race-neutral on its face, like child support enforcement, have disparate impacts by race?
2. Many argue that fathers are morally obligated to support their biological children. In this light, what further reforms might be possible to the CSE system that would assure fathers' continued economic support without subjecting men to punitive enforcement mechanisms?

3. In addition to the policies identified above, what other reforms to existing policies might be effective at facilitating fathers' involvement in their children's lives? What new policies might you recommend to meet this goal?
4. How does our language around policies and those whom policies target create and reify stereotypes and negative portrayals of certain groups?
5. Expansions of social and economic policies may be necessary to assure fathers' ability to remain involved in their children's lives. However, these reforms may face political opposition because of potential cost and varied views on the appropriate role of government in family life. What arguments should social workers make in favor of expansions to policy, and how can social workers be involved in advocating for these sorts of policy changes?

References

Abramovitz, M. (2001). Everyone is still on welfare: The role of redistribution in social policy. *Social Work, 46*(4), 297–308. https://doi.org/10.1093/sw/46.4.297

Allen, H., & Sommers, B. D. (2019). Medicaid expansion and health: Assessing the evidence after 5 years. *JAMA, 322*(13), 1253–1254. https://doi.org/10.1001/jama.2019.12345

Arthur, J. (2018). *Do parents who owe the most child support debt have reported income?* Administration for Children and Families, Office of Child Support Enforcement. https://www.acf.hhs.gov/css/ocsedatablog/2018/07/do-parents-who-owe-the-most-child-support-debt-have-reported-income

Autor, D., Dorn, D., & Hanson, G. (2019). When work disappears: Manufacturing decline and the falling marriage market value of young men. *American Economic Review: Insights, 1*(2), 161–178. https://doi.org/10.1257/aeri.20180010

Avellar, S., Covington, R., & Moore, Q. (2018). *Parents and children together: Effects of four responsible fatherhood programs for low-income fathers* (OPRE Report Number 2018-50). Office of Planning, Research, and Evaluation, Administration for Children and Families US Dept. of Health and Human Services. https://www.mathematica.org/publications/parents-and-children-together-effects-of-four-responsible-fatherhood-programs-for-low-income-fathers

Battle, B. P. (2018). Deservingness, deadbeat dads, and responsible fatherhood: Child support policy and rhetorical conceptualizations of poverty, welfare, and the family. *Symbolic Interaction, 41*(4), 443–464. https://doi.org/10.1002/symb.359

Berger, L. M., Cancian, M., Guarin, A., Hodges, L., & Meyer, D. R. (2021). Barriers to formal child support payment. *Social Service Review, 95*(2), 312–357. https://doi.org/10.1086/714370

Binder, A. J., & Bound, J. (2019). The declining labor market prospects of less-educated men. *Journal of Economic Perspectives, 33*(2), 163–190. https://doi.org/10.1257/jep.33.2.163

Bipartisan Policy Center. (2021). *State paid family leave laws across the U.S. | Bipartisan Policy Center*. Bipartisan Policy Center. https://bipartisanpolicy.org/explainer/state-paid-family-leave-laws-across-the-u-s/

Brigham Young University. (2018). Today's dads are engaging more with their kids: Fatherhood norms shifting alongside masculinity. *ScienceDaily*. https://www.sciencedaily.com/releases/2018/06/180612185124.htm

Bui, Q., & Sanger-Katz, M. (2015). We mapped the uninsured. You'll notice a pattern. *The New York Times*. https://www.nytimes.com/interactive/2015/10/31/upshot/who-still-doesnt-have-health-insurance-obamacare.html.

Bullinger, L. R. (2021). Child support and the affordable care act's Medicaid expansions. *Journal of Policy Analysis and Management, 40*(1), 42–77. https://doi.org/10.1002/pam.22238

Bullinger, L. R., & Tello-Trillo, S. (2021). Connecting Medicaid and child support: Evidence from the TennCare disenrollment. *Review of Economics of the Household.* https://doi.org/10.1007/s11150-021-09547-w

Bureau of Labor Statistics. (2019). *Highlights of women's earnings in 2018: BLS Reports: U.S. Bureau of Labor Statistics*. Bureau of Labor Statistics. https://www.bls.gov/opub/reports/womens-earnings/2018/home.htm

Cabrera, N., Fitzgerald, H. E., Bradley, R. H., & Roggman, L. (2007). Modeling the dynamics of paternal influences on children over the life course. *Applied Development Science, 11*(4), 185–189.

Cabrera, N., Fitzgerald, H. E., Bradley, R. H., & Roggman, L. (2014). The ecology of father-child relationships: An expanded model. *Journal of Family Theory & Review, 6*(4), 336–354. https://doi.org/10.1111/jftr.12054

Cancian, M., Heinrich, C. J., & Chung, Y. (2013). Discouraging disadvantaged fathers' employment: An unintended consequence of policies designed to support families. *Journal of Policy Analysis and Management, 32*(4), 758–784. https://doi.org/10.1002/pam.21707

Cancian, M., Meyer, D. R., & Wood, R. (2019). Final impact findings from the child support noncustodial parent employment demonstration (CSPED). In *Mathematica Policy Research Reports* (93c8996bb09444a292e2598d2d315aa3; Mathematica Policy Research Reports). Mathematica Policy Research. https://ideas.repec.org/p/mpr/mprres/93c8996bb09444a292e2598d2d315aa3.html.

Carson, A. (2021). *Prisoners in 2020—Statistical tables*. US Department of Justice, Bureau of Justice Statistics. https://bjs.ojp.gov/content/pub/pdf/p20st.pdf

CBPP. (2019). *Policy basics: The earned income tax credit* | Center on Budget and Policy Priorities. Center for Budget and Policy Priorities. https://www.cbpp.org/research/federal-tax/the-earned-income-tax-credit

Charles, P., Muentner, L., & Kjellstrand, J. (2019). Parenting and incarceration: Perspectives on father-child involvement during reentry from prison. *Social Service Review, 93*(2), 218–261. https://doi.org/10.1086/703446

Cherlin, A. J. (2014). *Labor's love lost: The rise and fall of the working-class family in America*. Russell Sage Foundation.

Donovan, S. A. (2019). *Paid family leave in the United States* (No. RR44835; p. 19). Congressional Research Service.

Dwyer Emory, A. (2021). Protective state policies and the employment of fathers with criminal records. *Social Problems, spab069*. https://doi.org/10.1093/socpro/spab069

Dwyer Emory, A., Miller, D. P., Nepomnyaschy, L., Waller, M. R., & Haralampoudis, A. (2020a). The minimum wage and fathers' residence with children. *Journal of Family and Economic Issues. 41,* 472–491.

Dwyer Emory, A., Nepomnyaschy, L., Waller, M. R., Miller, D. P., & Haralampoudis, A. (2020b). Providing after prison: Nonresident fathers' formal and informal contributions to children. *RSF: The Russell Sage Foundation Journal of the Social Sciences, 6*(1), 84–112. https://doi.org/10.7758/RSF.2020.6.1.04

Edin, K., & Nelson, T. J. (2013). *Doing the best I can: Fatherhood in the Inner City*. University of California Press.

Faricy, C. G. (2016). Welfare for the wealthy. In *Cambridge Books*. Cambridge University Press. https://ideas.repec.org/b/cup/cbooks/9781107498402.html

Flood, S., King, M., Rodgers, R., Ruggles, S., & Warren, J. R. (2020). *Integrated Public Use Microdata Series* (IPUMS CPS: Version 8.0). Current Population Survey: Version 8.0. https://www.ipums.org/projects/ipums-cps/d030.v8.0

Gelber, A., & Isen, A. (2013). Children's schooling and parents' behavior: Evidence from the Head Start Impact Study. *Journal of Public Economics, 101*, 25–38. https://doi.org/10.1016/j.jpubeco.2013.02.005

Geller, A. (2013). Paternal incarceration and father-child contact in fragile families. *Journal of Marriage and Family; Minneapolis, 75*(5), 1288–1303. http://www.jstor.org/stable/24583372

Geller, A., Cooper, C. E., Garfinkel, I., Schwartz-Soicher, O., & Mincy, R. B. (2012). Beyond absenteeism: Father incarceration and child development. *Demography, 49*(1), 49–76.
Geller, A., Garfinkel, I., & Western, B. (2011). Paternal incarceration and support for children in fragile families. *Demography, 48*(1), 25–47. https://doi.org/10.1007/s13524-010-0009-9
Grall, T. (2020). *Custodial mothers and fathers and their child support: 2017* (No. P60-269). US Census Bureau. https://www.census.gov/library/publications/2020/demo/p60-269.html
Guzzo, K. B. (2014). New partners, more kids: Multiple-partner fertility in the United States. *The Annals of the American Academy of Political and Social Science, 654*(1), 66–86. https://doi.org/10.1177/0002716214525571
Hahn, H., Kuehn, D., Hassani, H., & Edin, K. (2019). *Relief from government-owed child support debt and its effects on parents and children*. Urban Institute. https://www.urban.org/research/publication/relief-government-owed-child-support-debt-and-its-effects-parents-and-children
Haralampoudis, A., Nepomnyaschy, L., & Donnelly, L. (2021). Head Start and nonresident fathers' involvement with children. *Journal of Marriage and Family, 83*(3), 699–716. https://doi.org/10.1111/jomf.12756
Haralampoudis, A., Nepomnyaschy, L., Miller, D. P., & Waller, M. R. (2020). *State earned income tax credits and nonresident fathers' material contributions to their children*. Society for Social Work and Research. https://sswr.confex.com/sswr/2020/webprogram/Paper39422.html
Heinrich, C. J., Burkhardt, B. C., & Shager, H. M. (2011). Reducing child support debt and its consequences: Can forgiveness benefit all? *Journal of Policy Analysis and Management, 30*(4), 755–774. https://doi.org/10.1002/pam.20599
Hodges, L., Meyer, D. R., & Cancian, M. (2020). What happens when the amount of child support due is a burden? Revisiting the relationship between child support orders and child support payments. *Social Service Review, 94*(2), 238–284. https://doi.org/10.1086/709279
Huerta, M. C., Adema, W., Baxter, J., Han, W.-J., Lausten, M., Lee, R., & Waldfogel, J. (2014). Fathers' leave and fathers' involvement: Evidence from four OECD countries. *European Journal of Social Security, 16*(4), 308–346. https://doi.org/10.1177/138826271401600403
Institute of Medicine. (2002). Effects of health insurance on health. In *Care without coverage: Too little, too late*. National Academies Press (US). https://www.ncbi.nlm.nih.gov/books/NBK220636/
Jones, J., & Mosher, W. (2013). Fathers' involvement with their children: United States, 2006–2010. *National Health Statistics Reports, 71*, 1–21.
Kearney, M., Harris, B. H., Jacome, E., & Parker, L. (2014). *Ten economic facts about crime and incarceration in the United States*. The Hamilton Project, Brookings. https://www.hamiltonproject.org/papers/ten_economic_facts_about_crime_and_incarceration_in_the_united_states.
Kramer, S. (2019). *U.S. has world's highest rate of children living in single-parent households*. Pew Research Center. https://www.pewresearch.org/fact-tank/2019/12/12/u-s-children-more-likely-than-children-in-other-countries-to-live-with-just-one-parent/
Lamb, M. (2010). *The role of the father in child development*. Wiley.
Livingston, G., & Parker, K. (2011). *A tale of two fathers: More are active, but more are absent*. Pew Research Center's Social & Demographic Trends Project. https://www.pewresearch.org/social-trends/2011/06/15/a-tale-of-two-fathers/.
Livingston, G., & Parker, K. (2019). *8 facts about American dads*. Pew Research Center. https://www.pewresearch.org/fact-tank/2019/06/12/fathers-day-facts/.
Lundberg, S., Pollak, R. A., & Stearns, J. (2016). Family inequality: Diverging patterns in marriage, cohabitation, and childbearing. *Journal of Economic Perspectives, 30*(2), 79–102. https://doi.org/10.1257/jep.30.2.79
Maag, E., Werner, K., & Wheaton, L. (2019). *Expanding the EITC for workers without resident children* (p. 22). Urban Institute.
McLanahan, S., & Jencks, C. (2015). Was Moynihan right? What happens to children of unmarried mothers. *Education Next, 15*(2), 14–21.

McLeod, B. A., & Gottlieb, A. (2018). Examining the relationship between incarceration and child support arrears among low-income fathers. *Children and Youth Services Review, 94*, 1–9. https://doi.org/10.1016/j.childyouth.2018.09.022

Miller, C., Katz, L., Azurdia, G., Isen, A., Schultz, C., & Aloise, K. (2018). *Boosting the earned income tax credit for singles* [Text]. MDRC. https://www.mdrc.org/publication/boosting-earned-income-tax-credit-singles

Miller, D. P., & Mincy, R. B. (2012). Falling further behind? Child support arrears and fathers' labor force participation. *Social Service Review, 86*(4), 604–635.

Miller, R. J. (2020). *Halfway home: Race, punishment, and the afterlife of mass incarceration.* Little, Brown and Company. https://www.littlebrown.com/titles/reuben-jonathan-miller/halfway-home/9781549173332/

Mincy, R. B. (Ed.). (2006). *Black males left behind.* Urban Institute Press.

Mincy, R. B., & Sorensen, E. (1998). Deadbeats and Turnips in child support reform. *Journal of Policy Analysis and Management, 17*(1), 44–51.

NASW. (2021). *NASW code of ethics.* NASW – National Association of Social Workers. https://www.socialworkers.org

NCSL. (2019). *Interest on child support arrears.* National Conference of State Legislatures. https://www.ncsl.org/research/human-services/interest-on-child-support-arrears.aspx

NCSL. (2020a). *Child support guideline models.* National Conference of State Legislatures. https://www.ncsl.org/research/human-services/guideline-models-by-state.aspx

NCSL. (2020b). *Child support pass-through and disregard policies for public assistance recipients.* National Conference of State Legislatures. http://www.ncsl.org/research/human-services/state-policy-pass-through-disregard-child-support.aspx#50-State%20Chart

NCSL. (2021). *Child support policies: Implications for low-income fathers and their children.* National Conference of State Legislatures. https://www.ncsl.org/research/human-services/how-child-support-affects-low-income-fathers.aspx/

Nepomnyaschy, L., Emory, A. D., Eickmeyer, K. J., Waller, M. R., & Miller, D. P. (2021). Parental debt and child well-being: What type of debt matters for child outcomes? *RSF: The Russell Sage Foundation Journal of the Social Sciences, 7*(3), 122–151. https://doi.org/10.7758/RSF.2021.7.3.06

Nepomnyaschy, L., & Waldfogel, J. (2007). Paternity leave and fathers' involvement with their young children: Evidence from the American ECLS–B. *Community, Work and Family, 10*(4), 427–453.

Nichols, A., Sorensen, E., & Lippold, K. (2012). *The New York noncustodial parent EITC: Its impact on child support payments and employment* (p. 36). Urban Institute. https://ywcss.com/sites/default/files/u258/the_new_york_noncustodial_parent_eitc-its_impact_on_child_support_payments_and_employment.pdf

OCSE. (2017). *Processing an income withholding order or notice.* Office of Child Support Enforcement. https://www.acf.hhs.gov/css/outreach-material/processing-income-withholding-order-or-notice

OCSE. (2021). *FY 2018 Annual report to congress.* Office of Child Support Enforcement. https://www.acf.hhs.gov/css/report/fy-2018-annual-report-congress

Office of Head Start. (2018). *Head Start Parent, family, and community engagement framework | ECLKC.* https://eclkc.ohs.acf.hhs.gov/school-readiness/article/head-start-parent-family-community-engagement-framework

Office of Head Start. (2020). *Head Start Services.* https://www.acf.hhs.gov/ohs/about/head-start.

Pager, D. (2003). The mark of a criminal record. *The American Journal of Sociology, 108*(5), 937.

Parolin, Z. (2021). Temporary assistance for needy families and the Black–White child poverty gap in the United States. *Socio-Economic Review, 19*(3), 1005–1035. https://doi.org/10.1093/ser/mwz025

Patnaik, A. (2019). Reserving time for daddy: The consequences of fathers' quotas. *Journal of Labor Economics, 37*(4), 1009–1059. https://doi.org/10.1086/703115

Pearson, J., & Fagan, J. (2019). State efforts to support the engagement of nonresident fathers in the lives of their children. *Families in Society, 100*(4), 392–408. https://doi.org/10.1177/1044389419874172

Petts, R. J., Knoester, C., & Li, Q. (2020a). Paid paternity leave-taking in the United States. *Community, Work & Family, 23*(2), 162–183. https://doi.org/10.1080/13668803.2018.1471589

Petts, R. J., Knoester, C., & Waldfogel, J. (2020b). Fathers' paternity leave-taking and children's perceptions of father-child relationships in the United States. *Sex Roles, 82*(3), 173–188. https://doi.org/10.1007/s11199-019-01050-y

Pew Charitable Trusts. (2010). *Collateral costs: Incarceration's effect on economic mobility*. The Pew Charitable Trusts. https://www.pewtrusts.org/~/media/legacy/uploadedfiles/pcs_assets/2010/collateralcosts1pdf.pdf

Pleck, J. (2007). Why could father involvement benefit children? Theoretical perspectives. *Applied Developmental Science, 11*(4), 196–202. https://doi.org/10.1080/10888690701762068

Plotnick, R. D., & Kennedy, A. I. (2018). How accurate are imputed child support orders? *Children and Youth Services Review, 88*, 490–496. https://doi.org/10.1016/j.childyouth.2018.03.049

Pratt, E. (2016, June 16). Child support enforcement can hurt black, low-income, non-custodial fathers and their kids. Urban Institute. https://www.urban.org/urban-wire/child-support-enforcement-can-hurt-black-low-income-noncustodial-fathers-and-their-kids

Raikes, H. H., & Bellotti, J. (2006). Two studies of father involvement in Early Head Start Programs: A national survey and a demonstration program evaluation. In *Parenting: Science and practice*. Routledge.

Reeves, R., Sawhill, I. V., & Krause, E. (2016). *The most educated women are the most likely to be married*. Social Mobility Memos; Brookings. https://www.brookings.edu/blog/social-mobility-memos/2016/08/19/the-most-educated-women-are-the-most-likely-to-be-married/

Robbins, N., Waller, M. R., Nepomnyaschy, L., & Miller, D. P. (2022). Child support debt, economic hardship, and the well-being of disadvantaged fathers. *Journal of Marriage and Family, Online First*.

Ruggles, S., Flood, S., Goeken, R., Pacas, J., Schouweiler, M., & Sobek, M. (2021). *IPUMS USA: Version 11.0*. IPUMS. https://doi.org/10.18128/D010.V11.0

Selekman, R., & Holcomb, P. (2018). Child support cooperation requirements in child care subsidy programs and SNAP: Key policy considerations. *Mathematica*. https://www.mathematica.org/publications/child-support-cooperation-requirements-in-child-care-subsidy-programs-and-snap-key-policy

Sentencing Project. (n.d.). *Criminal justice facts*. The Sentencing Project. Retrieved May 24, 2021, from https://www.sentencingproject.org/criminal-justice-facts/

Sinkewicz, M., & Garfinkel, I. (2009). Unwed fathers' ability to pay child support: New estimates accounting for multiple-partner fertility. *Demography, 46*(2), 247–263.

Smock, P. J., & Schwartz, C. R. (2020). The demography of families: A review of patterns and change. *Journal of Marriage and Family, 82*(1), 9–34. https://doi.org/10.1111/jomf.12612

Sorensen, E. (2021). *Certified child support arrears show sharp decline. The Administration for Children and Families*. Office of Child Support Enforcement. https://www.acf.hhs.gov/css/ocsedatablog/2021/05/certified-child-support-arrears-shows-sharp-decline

Sorensen, E., Pashi, A., & Morales, M. (2016). *Characteristics of Families Served by the Child Support (IV-D) Program: 2016 U.S. Census Survey Results*. 68.

Sorensen, E., Sousa, L., & Schaner, S. (2007). *Assessing child support arrears in nine large states and the nation*. Department of Health and Human Services and Office of Child Support Enforcement.

Sum, A., Khatiwada, I., McLaughlin, J., & Palma, S. (2011). No country for young men: Deteriorating labor market prospects for low-skilled men in the United States. *The Annals of the American Academy of Political and Social Science, 635*(1), 24–55.

Tax Policy Center. (2021). *What is the earned income tax credit?* Tax Policy Center. https://www.taxpolicycenter.org/briefing-book/what-earned-income-tax-credit

Thompson, D., Bunts, W., & Burnside, A. (2020). *EITC for childless workers: What's at stake for young workers*. CLASP. https://www.clasp.org/publications/report/brief/eitc-childless-workers-2020

Tolbert, J., Orgera, K., & Damico, A. (2020). *Key facts about the uninsured population*. Kaiser Family Foundation. https://www.kff.org/uninsured/issue-brief/key-facts-about-the-uninsured-population/

Tollestrup, J. (2021). *Child Support Enforcement: Program Basics* (No. RS22380; p. 16). Congressional Research Service. https://crsreports.congress.gov/product/pdf/RS/RS22380/39

Turetsky, V. (2019). Reforming child support to improve outcomes for children and families. *The Abell Report, 32*(5). Abell Foundation. https://eric.ed.gov/?id=ED596117

Turetsky, V., & Waller, M. R. (2020). Piling on debt: The intersections between child support arrears and legal financial obligations. *UCLA Criminal Justice Law Journal, 4(1)*, 117–141.

Turner, K. J., & Waller, M. (2016). Indebted relationships: Child support arrears and nonresident fathers' involvement with children. *Journal of Marriage and Family. 79*(1), 24–43

Turney, K., & Wildeman, C. (2013). Redefining relationships: Explaining the countervailing consequences of paternal incarceration for parenting. *American Sociological Review, 78*(6), 949–979. https://doi.org/10.1177/0003122413505589

Uggen, C., & McElrath, S. (2014). Parental incarceration: What we know and where we need to go. *The Journal of Criminal Law and Criminology (1973–), 104*(3), 597–604.

Um, H. (2019). *The role of child support debt on the development of mental health problems among nonresident fathers*.

Urban Institute. (2021). *State earned income tax credits*. Urban Institute. https://www.urban.org/policy-centers/cross-center-initiatives/state-and-local-finance-initiative/state-and-local-backgrounders/state-earned-income-tax-credits

Vallas, R., & Dietrich, S. (2014). *One strike and you're out*. Center for American Progress. https://www.americanprogress.org/issues/poverty/reports/2014/12/02/102308/one-strike-and-youre-out/

Wakefield, S., & Wildeman, C. (2014). *Children of the Prison Boom: Mass incarceration and the future of American inequality*. Oxford University Press.

Waller, M., & Plotnick, R. (2001). Effective child support policy for low-income families: Evidence from street level research. *Journal of Policy Analysis and Management, 20*(1), 89–110.

Washington, H. M., Juan, S.-C., & Haskins, A. R. (2018). Incapacitated involvement: Incarceration and fatherhood in fragile families at age 9. *Journal of Family Issues, 39*(13), 3463–3486. https://doi.org/10.1177/0192513X18783225

Western, B., & Rosenfeld, J. (2011). Unions, norms, and the rise in US wage inequality. *American Sociological Review, 76*(4), 513–537.

Western, B., & Smith, N. (2018). Formerly incarcerated parents and their children. *Demography, 55*(3), 823–847. https://doi.org/10.1007/s13524-018-0677-4

Western, B., & Wildeman, C. (2009). The black family and mass incarceration. *The Annals of the American Academy of Political and Social Science, 621*(1), 221–242.

Wheaton, L., & Sorensen, E. (2010). Extending the EITC to noncustodial parents: Potential impacts and design considerations. *Journal of Policy Analysis and Management, 29*(4), 749–768. https://doi.org/10.1002/pam.20533

Wildeman, C. (2010). Paternal incarceration and children's physically aggressive behaviors: Evidence from the Fragile Families and Child Wellbeing Study. *Social Forces, 89*(1), 285–309. https://doi.org/10.1353/sof.2010.0055

Wilson, W. J. (2011). *When work disappears: The world of the new urban poor*. Random House LLC.

Zipperer, B. (2015). *How raising the minimum wage ripples through the workforce* (p. 6). Washington Center for Equitable Growth. https://live-equitablegrowth.pantheonsite.io/wp-content/uploads/2015/04/27152126/042815-minwage-spillover.pdf

Chapter 10
Group Work with Fathers in Federal Pretrial Detention and a Community-Based Residential Setting: Reflections on Practice and Policies Across Contexts

Branden A. McLeod and Geoffrey L. Greif

Introduction

When fathers are incarcerated, their families and support networks also experience confinement (Arditti & McGregor, 2019). In these instances, families are what Martin (2017) referred to as the "hidden victims" of the *criminal legal system*.[1] Therefore, it is essential to expand awareness of how arrest, sentencing, and detention impact incarcerated fathers and their families (Arditti & McGregor, 2019) as well as the knowledge-base about interventions that can assist detained fathers maintain and reinforce their fatherhood identity.

[1] The "criminal legal system" versus the "criminal justice system": Erica Bryant, from the Vera Institute of Justice (2021), differentiates the two phrases, stating that using "'criminal justice system' is a misnomer. Throughout history and across the world, false language has facilitated the systemic, inhumane treatment of groups of people. This is certainly the case for people impacted by the U.S. criminal legal system.'" Bryant (2021) also writes, "Lawmakers and media often speak of the 'criminal justice system' or of 'criminal justice reform.' But more and more people and organizations are using the term 'criminal legal system' to describe policing, prosecution, courts, and corrections in the United States." Source: https://www.vera.org/blog/why-we-say-criminal-legal-system-not-criminal-justice-system

B. A. McLeod (✉)
Jane Addams College of Social Work, University of Illinois Chicago, Chicago, IL, USA
e-mail: bmcleod7@uic.edu

G. L. Greif
University of Maryland School of Social Work, Baltimore, MD, USA
e-mail: GGREIF@ssw.umaryland.edu

J. L. Bellamy et al. (eds.), *Social Work Practice with Fathers*,
https://doi.org/10.1007/978-3-031-13686-3_10

This chapter illuminates the experiences of fathers and father figures who participated in two separate social-educational groups, one in a prison and one in a residential employment center for men who had been incarcerated, homeless, or in drug treatment. While their contexts are not the same, a similar approach to understanding fathering was used for both groups. Interventions geared toward how men are socialized, their role as fathers, and their reentry into their families and communities are examined. This chapter also explores policy and program approaches that might facilitate family contact and strengthen families when fathers are actively involved in the criminal legal system.

Background and Context

Fathers are integral to their children's lives. Studies demonstrate positive associations between father involvement and infant cognitive outcomes, school readiness, socio-emotional health, and academic functioning in children (Bronte-Tinkew et al., 2008; Howard et al., 2006; Martin et al., 2010). Further, when fathers are positively involved, children are more likely to have better educational outcomes, psychological well-being, and pro-social behavior (Howard et al., 2006; Rosenberg & Wilcox, 2006). However, the overreliance on imprisonment in the United States contributes to family dissolution as well as stagnant human and financial capital for many economically vulnerable families and communities (Oliver, 2001; Western & Wildeman, 2009).

National statistics highlight how family systems are separated, leaving complex living arrangements in their wake, due to parental incarceration. Current estimates suggest that more than 5 million children in the United States under the age of 14 have an incarcerated parent (Murphey & Cooper, 2015). These estimates may be conservative given the complexities of parsing how many people involved in the criminal legal system identify as parents. Paternal incarceration in particular can be traumatic for children (Morgan-Mullane, 2018) and may be experienced differently for daughters and sons. Research suggests that girls are more likely to internalize the trauma while boys are more likely to display externalizing behaviors (Cummings et al., 2000; Newell, 2012). Paternal incarceration is often associated with increased aggression, anxiety, attention challenges, depression, and delinquency among male children (Haskins, 2016). For children of both sexes, adverse outcomes can last throughout their lifetime (Geller et al., 2011; Haskins 2014, 2015; Murray et al., 2012; Roettger & Swisher, 2011; Wilbur et al., 2007). For instance, research has found that children who experience parental incarceration are six times more likely to become incarcerated themselves (Cox, 2009).

In turn, reinforcing positive fathering identities by maintaining relationships with their children can help fathers reduce their criminal behavior (Crandell-Williams & McEvoy, 2017). Sustaining a positive parent-child relationship can be daunting, however, as families face financial barriers associated with incarceration such as costly phone calls, sending mail, and traveling to correctional facilities

(Christian, 2005; Clark & Duwe, 2017; Cochran et al., 2016). Thus, retaining family roles, paternal identity, and involvement become a challenge when such barriers exist.

Conceptual Framework

Life-course perspective and *identity theories* are helpful frameworks in understanding how societal expectations (McLaughlin & Muldoon, 2014) and social structures (Bengtson & Allen, 1993; Roy, 2006) shape fathers' identity formation and their involvement with their children and families. Fatherhood evolves over the life course as fathers, partners, and children experience life transitions. Moreover, changing social contexts shape how fathers socially construct their identities (Roy, 2006). Fathers place multiple identities (e.g., father, employee, son, and co-parent/husband) into a hierarchy based upon perceived saliency (e.g., frequency/how often occurs) and centrality (e.g., location/self-importance).

However, the identity confirmation process is interrupted during instances of incarceration, and this obscures fathers' identities, sense of purpose, and role expectations (e.g., provider and caregiver). Both physical and social contexts are essential; otherwise, fathers grow confused and boundaries become ambiguous (Roy & Dyson, 2005). Lewis and Hong (2020) found that prison settings strip away previous identities, roles, and responsibilities and provoke hypermasculine behavior (e.g., aggression and apathy).

Consequently, this environment impairs their ability to maintain pro-social roles such as fathering and co-parenting (Lewis & Hong, 2020; Tripp, 2009). Lewis and Hong (2020) suggest that the significant disruption of fatherhood identities and roles while incarcerated causes acute harm to their identity as fathers during imprisonment and ongoing harm post-release. Social interactions and identities become transitory and fluctuate (Marsiglio et al., 2005; Roy & Dyson, 2005), which impacts fathers' communication with their children's mother or caregivers (Roy & Dyson, 2005). Despite the ambiguity due to physical separation, fathers may attempt to be emotionally present through writing letters, making phone calls, and engaging in contact visits while incarcerated (Greif, 2014; McLeod, 2021). Even when fathers reenter communities after periods of imprisonment, their role expectations (e.g., provider and caregiver) and boundaries may become ambiguous (Roy & Dyson, 2005).

Discourse within the social environment shapes paternal identities (Höfner et al., 2011), so social identity and *mutual aid* groups could be leveraged as fundamental tools in reinforcing fatherhood roles (Ammari et al., 2017; Greif, 2014; McLeod, 2020). Fatherhood groups provide a setting where feelings, challenges, and aspirations are normalized (Greif, 2014), and fathers can learn to communicate and maintain healthy bonds with their children and their children's caretakers and co-parents (Loper & Tuerk, 2006). Therefore, this chapter highlights group-based interventions among incarcerated and otherwise separated fathers that can positively affect their identity and build constructive relationships.

Recommended Intervention Approaches

The Context for the Groups

Both authors co-led the group described in this chapter at the first setting (Group A). The second author co-led the group with other facilitators at the second setting (Group B). The groups for fathers operated between 2011 and 2021, with a 20-month interruption for COVID before restarting the face-to-face format. The leadership for the majority of the group meetings was biracial. The group membership was usually predominantly Black though cohorts in both settings often comprised significant numbers of Latinos, Whites, and biracial people.

Group A was conducted in a federal detention facility in an urban, east coast city (e.g., Greif, 2014, 2017). The federal judge overseeing the detention center approached one of the authors about providing such a service as she was simultaneously seeking to increase services around drug rehabilitation and other support services. The group participants, some of whom had been detained for up to 18 months, were awaiting trial or sentencing for federal charges that ranged from drug dealing, armed robbery, manslaughter, money laundering, and murder. The maximum security facility had no large cafeteria or meeting area, so the meetings were held in a room that could comfortably hold up to 15 people, with a typical group comprising 10–12 detainees.

The fathering group was advertised for fathers who wished to learn more about the fathering role. When it was first advertised, 150 detainees requested admission into the 4-week, 1-hour group. At the time of the initial group, visitation between a father and his children only occurred with a plastic or Plexiglass barrier between them, and no physical contact was permitted. After the second series of group meetings, and as requested by group members, the warden instituted a significant change in policy. From that point forward, members who completed the group were able to have a 1-hour visit with physical contact with their child(ren). This policy change increased the number of people requesting the group, which meant, with membership limited because of the size of the meeting room and with each group meeting for 4 weeks before the next group started, that some detainees were not able to participate. The authors (who provided pro bono service for the groups) and the case manager (who had added the group to his caseload at the warden's request) were not able to offer the group more frequently.

With the father-child visitation, some group members were meeting their child for the first time as they had been detained before their child's birth; others had children from different mothers with whom they were in contact and had to decide if all their children or some should attend the visit. Some fathers had been actively co-parenting with their wife or were the sole parent if the mother was unable to parent due to challenges with addiction or incarceration. A few members had children who lived at a great geographic distance and had to arrange their visits weeks or months later when travel was possible. Some had children who refused to see them or whose mother or caretaker refused to let them come to a detention center to see their father. Some of these children may have been told their father was away at work or in school in a different state, and so seeing him in a detention setting would have been very upsetting for them. A few fathers did not invite their child for the same reason. The upper age limit for child visitation was 18, so group members with adult children were not able to avail themselves of this visitation benefit.

Group B was held at an urban, east coast city residential employment program for men who had been incarcerated, were in drug rehabilitation, or were homeless. This 6-month, highly structured program was intended to provide job training with the purpose of getting the men into the workforce. Their first weeks in the program included classes that taught health and self-care, how to make a positive impression, and anger management. The men were not allowed contact with their family during the first few weeks of their residence. The fathering group was a new addition to their curriculum. Attendance at all classes was mandatory for each cohort of men, usually numbering around 10. The group members, like those in Group A, ranged in age from their 20s to their 60s. New cohorts began every 6 to 8 weeks.

Sometimes, a few participants in the group were not fathers but had to attend the group given the mandatory nature of the curriculum. Some of these men, by their own description, had played a fathering role as a brother, friend, or uncle to another person's child. The frequency of father-child contact differed between the groups. Group A members had no physical access to their children at the time of the group except for the one meeting. However, Group B included men with varying contact with their children from frequent—on the weekend when they could leave the facility—to the nonexistent because they had grown apart, were being prevented from seeing them, or had never established a relationship. The purpose of this fathering group was to help the men be the best fathers they could be given their context. While each man's fathering situation was different, the discussion often centered on the broader social context that shaped the father's identity (Roy, 2006) and the shifting expectations around fatherhood (McLaughlin & Muldoon, 2014). Men who were not fathers were invited to reflect on how they might father in the future and how they felt about the way they were fathered.

Format of the Group

Group A's 4-week format began with each member being asked why they wanted to join the fathering group, their parenting situation, and their level of contact with their children. Following the fathers' opening statements, they were asked what common themes they heard in the descriptions of the parenting situations. This was an attempt to focus on commonalities, to build group cohesion, and for the leaders to get a sense of the strengths of the members and their commitment to their fathering role. At the end of the session, members were asked to think about the topic for week two, family history.

In week two, the group focused on how they were raised and what positive messages they could pass down to their children from their upbringing. As many fathers had had traumatic childhoods, including absent fathers or mothers, criminal activity, substance use, school failure, and residential instability, it was believed that focusing on positive messages would provide a different tenor to the hour-long discussion. The messages mentioned most frequently were positive messages to teach their children, such as the importance of family togetherness, education, work, and spirituality.

Week three centered on the role of women in their lives. While the mothers of their children were the primary topic, discussion often widened to include their own mother, grandmothers, and sisters. Co-parenting, the difficulty in communicating with the caregiver about the child while incarcerated, and the traditional roles of breadwinner for the father and nurturer for the mother frequently arose. Time was also spent preparing the men for their first contact visit with their child and their expectations of their child and themselves during that visit. Such visits can help reassure a child about their parent's well-being while incarcerated (Fortune & Salmon, 2019). Such preparation included, with younger children, providing games and reading materials around which the father and child could interact and, with older children, coaching the father on how to talk and listen to the child. Time was also spent lowering expectations; fathers were encouraged to not try and cram too much interaction into the visit.

In the fourth and final meeting, members were asked for their definitions of man, father, woman, and mother, which the leaders wrote on a whiteboard. They were then asked to think about the assumptions behind those definitions. Usually, men and fathers were defined as breadwinners or providers while women were defined as nurturers. Fathers who had completed an in-person visit with their children were asked to share their experiences and give advice to the other men. This was also a time for specific parenting concerns to be addressed.

Group B followed a similar format with one exception. Providing definitions of gender roles was the topic of the first week, not the fourth. As the men had not opted to take this mandatory group and had often not known what to expect, this cognitive approach appeared to be a better way of easing the members into the topic before they were asked to talk about their own experiences.

Common Themes in the Two Fathering Groups

Children Do Not Know Their Father's History

A typical concern for fathers is what to tell their children about why they are in prison or in a residential employment center. Fathers often feel uncomfortable about different aspects of their past—from criminal and substance use histories to educational and work gaps. They are unsure if sharing their history will be taken as an excuse for their children to distance themselves emotionally from them or as a cautionary tale of what to avoid. Uncertainty could pervade the relationship going forward and stymie effective parenting.

In the residential center, Group B fathers were initially restricted from family access. Here, too, the question arose as to what to tell their children about their circumstances. While the period of physical separation was shorter for these fathers, the distance still raised the questions about their whereabouts and their past behavior.

For the fathers in both groups who shared their history with their children, their intent was usually to encourage their children not to do as they had done. Rather, it was to learn from the father's mistakes. The fathers in Group B also used their story as one of redemption in the form of "I have made mistakes, but I am taking care of myself now and am being rehabilitated." Discussion in both settings often focused on being honest with their children. Older fathers, with older children, cautioned the younger fathers with younger children to be transparent without being overly specific. Further, if fathers got out in front of the information, they could shape the narrative and thus establish more open lines of communication.

Role of Older Fathers in the Group

Older fathers in both settings often played the role of mentor to younger fathers, offering sound advice around parenting, relationships, and navigating the "system." In regard to parenting, they also offered some hope that those fathers who were out of touch with their children might renew contact when the children were over the age of 18 and no longer under the control of another family member. When interacting with women, one man in his 60s talked openly about a diminished sex drive and how, as a result, he and his child's mother, with whom he was not living before going into the residential center, were able to interact with less tension. The older men also offered advice about the legal system and connecting with institutional sources of support.

Not every group in these settings honored their older members. If there were a large number of 20-somethings in the group and only one or two older fathers, the older cohort might be ignored, and a less serious tone might be struck in general.

Feeling Incompetent as a Father and Inadequate as a Man

A few younger members verbalized not knowing how to be a father as they reported not having a father in their life. Others felt unsure about how to deal with daughters and often turned over issues that arose with their daughters to the women in the family. Fathers who had less contact with their children reported not feeling comfortable with how to engage their children.

Connected to these feelings of inadequacy was the belief, strongly reinforced by societal tropes, that a father's main contribution to the family is as a breadwinner.

For these fathers, financially contributing was often a struggle as they were cut off from the work world. If the father had children from more than one mother, supporting the mothers equally became difficult. For fathers who had children with different mothers, one child and mother were often favored, further complicating whatever financial support was possible and fueling additional emotional separation while reinforcing the trope that a father was only as good as his financial contributions.

Difficulty Parenting From Afar

Without consistent contact or with contact happening under the cloud of the father's history, parenting from afar was challenging. The father's detention meant significant life events —basketball games and graduations—were missed. Such events often build family cohesion, and when they cannot be shared, an opportunity for a positive interaction is lost.

Many fathers had significant involvement in their children's lives before detention, some were the primary caregivers, and a few were arrested in front of their children. With the loss of daily face-to-face contact, a significant rift occurred. Other adults became involved in child-rearing who, to various degrees, might try hard to sustain the father-child relationship or take steps to replace it with nurturing from other adults (perhaps sparked by their unhappiness with the father-child relationship). When parenting contact had been sporadic pre-detention or pre-residential matriculation, establishing it from afar was even more difficult.

Fathers were sometimes called upon to discipline their children over the telephone. If the caregivers perceived the father as having an influence over the child, they might ask the father to straighten out the child or offer a warning. Other times, young children were put on the phone with the father and would quickly lose interest and want to return to what they were doing before the phone call. Fathers often saw this as a rejection rather than a typical young child's behavior.

Dealing with Their Own History

For many fathers, talking about how they were raised was uncomfortable. Occasionally, tears were shed when they shared what they missed in relation to being parented. Sharing such experiences were almost always met with support from others in the group. Fathers would refer to "breaking the cycle" of abandonment that they had experienced in their own lives and said that they had promised themselves that they would be there for their children in a way that no one was there for them. Some fathers felt they fulfilled that promise, while others lamented they were unable to because they were detained.

Interacting with the Mother of Their Child

The relationships with the mother(s) of their child(ren) existed along a continuum. Some, as mentioned, were married to the mother while others were in close contact with her though not living with her, in sporadic contact, or had no contact. Access to younger children may have been encouraged or impeded by the mother depending on the parents' relationship; older children (teens and adults) usually made their own decisions about contact. Regardless of the child's age, the mother was often seen as the conduit to the child.

Fathers discussed the necessity of maintaining a good relationship with the mother in order to have access to their child. They described not wanting to anger her or challenge her about child-rearing and talked about "pretending" to be nice to her to have access.

Who Is Raising Their Child in Their Absence?

Some groups were able to openly talk about whether they had been replaced by another man as a father figure and, potentially, as a sexual partner during their absence. Because this topic is sensitive on multiple levels, not every group was able or interested in discussing it. Members might raise it derivatively but then shy away from it. Some fathers strongly resented being replaced, with specific complaints about who had replaced them; others described being happy that their children had a positive male influence in their life. In some cases, fathers described having played a similar role for other children in the absence of their biological father.

A few fathers acknowledged that they could not meet the sexual needs of their partner while they were out of the picture. Others talked about their satisfaction or dissatisfaction with the person (man or woman) who had replaced them in bed.

Positive Messages About Mothers and Grandmothers with Less Being Said About Fathers

When the fathers in both groups were asked about their upbringing and what positives they wanted to pass on to their children, their mothers and grandmothers were frequently cited in matricentric homes. The women were described as hardworking, loving, and strict. Fathers were less likely to be present in the group members' upbringing. If fathers were present, their characterizations ranged from the hardworking and engaged father to the shadowy figure who came in and out of their lives. Women were almost never characterized in that manner.

Beliefs About Men's and Women's Roles in the Family

The group members' experiences with their parents, partners, children, and society shaped how they viewed the roles of men and women and of fathers and mothers. As a group exercise, when asked for adjectives that described these various roles, it was typical to have the fathers connect adjectives related to nurturing within the women's and mothers' domains and adjectives connected to breadwinning within the men's and fathers' domains. The discussion also included how these messages were reinforced by society and that everyone is subjected to these messages.

The Fathers' Visits with Their Children

For fathers with limited contact with their children, like those in Group A, a visit can be the high point of their year but also, given its infrequency, anxiety-provoking. The fathers may not have seen their children for months, and the children may never have seen their father in a prison outfit. The fathers often wanted to make the visit perfect, which added a sense of intensity to the limited time the family members had together. Fathers in Group B were subject to the same trepidations if contact had been infrequent. Fathers whose visits occurred before the end of the group sessions reported back to the group what a wonderful experience (e.g., holding one's child for the first time; having a heart-to-heart talk with a teenager) the visit had been and offered advice to those whose visits were yet to come.

Intervening with the Fathers

These two groups were comprised of fathers who were detained against their will (Group A) and fathers who chose to be "detained" by entering a residential setting with initial restrictions on their ability to come and go (Group B). Group interventions must be offered with a keen appreciation of the context of the setting and with a solid grasp of group leadership skills and knowledge of family therapy models. The leaders were clear not to tell the fathers in either group what they should do to address the various issues that arose. We were acutely aware of our privileged positions as men with many years of education, as fathers with easy access to our children, and, in the second author's case, of race in the broader society. This privilege sensitized us to *transference* and *countertransference* issues that might arise. At the same time, as our experience of running groups for fathers increased (by the end, we had collectively led groups with over 500 fathers), we felt more comfortable sharing those experiences derivatively during discussions. For example, we would share what we had heard worked for other fathers in previous groups and would wonder if that might work for anyone in the current group.

One example was around privacy and to what extent past illegal or compromising behaviors were shared with the fathers' children. When should a full explanation be given as to why a father was in a residential center or in a federal holding facility? The group leaders shared that they have done things they did not want their own children to know. When is it appropriate for a father to tell a child their father has acted in a way he might regret?

The age of the father's child(ren) was a key variable in the discussions about what the father was willing to share. With children up to the age of three or four, and depending on the child, fathers believed little explanation was needed. The older the children, the greater the chance they would figure it out on their own or be able to navigate the Internet and get information about federal charges. The older the child, the more likely it was that the father had told them, given the difficulty of concealing information in family discussions. For the fathers in Group B, less information was usually available about them on the Internet, and the time of physical separation was shorter. While raising privacy as a parenting issue does not tell the father what to do, it normalizes what the father might be thinking, gets the topic on his radar, and reframes privacy as an ever-present parenting issue.

Member-to-member communication was encouraged. When the older fathers were mentoring the younger fathers, we felt comfortable that a level of cohesion had been built in the group, a sign of group efficacy. Group leaders want to be able to remove themselves metaphorically from the center so members can interact with each other and not funnel all communication through the leader, especially when the communication reinforces positive norms and is consistent with the purpose of the group.

Feeling unsure or incompetent about how to parent was reframed as a typical stage of parenting. Specifically, fathers who linked their insecurity around fathering with not having a father present in their own lives were asked to consider how they were "parented" by women or male teachers or coaches and if being a father has to be tied to societal tropes about gender.

Parenting from afar can be difficult if the father is cast in the role of disciplinarian. It would reduce the child's desire to talk with the father. Rather than having him cast in only one role, that of disciplinarian, one suggestion was to have the father's role be more multifaceted by having the caregiver report the good things the child was doing too. Fathers in Group A sometimes had difficulty connecting with their child over the phone. Younger children can be easily distracted, and teenagers can be recalcitrant. Fathers were asked to view the behavior in a developmental context.

For fathers who regretted actions they had taken in the past, asking them to focus on the future and how they want to behave going forward was one way to reframe their experiences. The notion of forgiveness, of self and others, was also introduced as a useful concept.

The relationship with the mother was often the most delicate topic. Discussion centered around both parents remaining parents and working as a team even if they were no longer romantically involved. This approach helped to recenter the fathers on the purpose of the group and their lifelong commitment to fathering. Fathers who may have been in a position of greater power in the community and in their partner relationship in the past now found themselves more reliant on their partner than before incarceration. Coaching around what to expect during a phone call or visit with the mother helped fathers anticipate the communication pattern and how they wanted the communication to go. This level of strategizing was helpful for some fathers and gave them a greater sense of control.

With visits (and phone calls), more nurturing roles could be reinforced as the fathers were coached about listening to their children rather than talking *at* them. While visits for fathers in Group A were an important opportunity to have a face-to-face conversation with a child, they are never perfect. Lowering expectations about them was a useful antidote to trying to cram a year of absence into a 1-hour visit.

Finally, asking the fathers in both groups to consider what the gender roles were in their family growing up and whether those gender roles still worked for them was a lead-in to reframing the father's role as both a breadwinner and a nurturer. Fathers talked about wanting time with their own fathers rather than material things. This reflection allowed them to see what role they could continue to play with their own children, even when separated.

These interventions are most effective when there is group cohesion based on a level of trust between members and between members and leaders. Understanding the stages of group development and the leaders not asking for too much information or too many revelations from the fathers too soon was one way to build cohesion. Group leaders must always respect where the group members are coming from when they enter a fathering group.

Policy Considerations and Conclusion

This chapter illustrates the need for policy to support interventions and practices that facilitate family contact and strengthen families when parents are involved in the criminal legal system. Research suggests that corrections-based fathering programs improve fathers' skills and enhance father-child contact (Hansen, 2018). However, unstable funding trends for these programs can limit their availability and effectiveness (Purvis, 2013). A 2008 study on correctional system-based fathering programs revealed a 72% decrease in the number of programs across several years (Eddy et al., 2008). More recently, many prisons, jails, community agencies, and community members have responded to the need to offer parenting programs (Eddy et al., 2019; Loper et al., 2019); however, only a small segment of incarcerated parents are enrolled in these programs (Loper et al., 2019). Fortunately, more local and state governments are enacting justice-reinvestment initiatives (JRI) to reduce incarceration rates (Austin et al., 2016; McLeod, 2021). JRI is a system-wide collaborative approach that transfers public finances from correctional institutions to community-based rehabilitation programs and supportive services (Austin et al., 2016). Families play an essential support role when individuals leave prison and reenter society (Mowen et al., 2019). For this reason, policymakers and other decision-makers should consider allocating funding to support family-strengthening programs and services that facilitate family contact and connections and improve parenting skills.

Resources

- Children of Incarcerated Parents National Conference (held annually in AZ) https://childwellbeing.asu.edu/content/national-children-incarcerated-parents-conference
- The Fatherhood Research and Practice Network provides technical assistance to practitioners and researchers, including one-on-one consulting services, mentoring, and peer support as well as Web-based communication platforms and resources. Website: https://www.frpn.org/training-assistance/frpn-technical-assistance.
- Handbook on Children with Incarcerated Parents (downloadable version available for free) https://link.springer.com/book/10.1007/978-3-030-16707-3
- Model Practices for Parents in Prisons and Jails https://s3.amazonaws.com/static.nicic.gov/Library/033094.pdf
- The National Fatherhood Initiative offers curricula to support fathers in their parenting role inside correctional facilities and within communities. Website: https://www.fatherhood.org/free-resources/topic/insideout-dad
- The Parenting Inside Out® program is an evidence-based parenting skills training program developed for mothers and fathers who are involved in the criminal legal system (i.e., in prisons and on parole and probation). Website: http://www.parentinginsideout.org/

Discussion Questions

1. How can the criminal legal system better support fathers and families?
2. In what ways can human service agencies better support fathers and families the criminal legal system has impacted?
3. What local, state, and national policies (e.g., statutes, regulations, executive orders, and government funding) support fatherhood initiatives? How can these existing policies be strengthened to support fathers who are involved in the criminal legal system?
4. Conduct an Internet search to identify local resources and programs that support fathers. What services do they provide? How can your organization form an alliance to support these programs?
5. Interview three fathers. These three fathers can be someone you know personally or work with at your agency. Ask the dads: (a) What does fatherhood mean to you? (b) What does father involvement look like? Next, reflect on their responses. What were the similarities and differences in their responses? How do their fatherhood and father involvement definitions reflect or diverge from traditional societal perceptions about masculinity?

References

Ammari, T., Schoenebeck, S., & Lindtner, S. (2017). The crafting of DIY fatherhood. In *Proceedings of the 2017 ACM conference on computer supported cooperative work and social computing* (pp. 1109–1122) https://dl.acm.org/doi/10.1145/2998181.2998270

Arditti, J. A., & McGregor, C. M. (2019). A family perspective: Caregiving and family contexts of children with an incarcerated parent. In J. M. Eddy & J. Poehlmann-Tynan (Eds.), *Handbook on children with incarcerated parents* (pp. 117–130). Springer. https://doi.org/10.1007/978-3-030-16707-3_9

Austin, J., Clear, T., & Coventry, G. (2016). Reinvigorating justice reinvestment. *Federal Sentencing Reporter, 29*(1), 6–14. https://doi.org/10.1525/fsr.2016.29.1.6

Bengtson, V., & Allen, K. (1993). The life course perspective applied to families over time. In P. Boss, W. Doherty, R. LaRossa, W. Schumm, & S. Steinmetz (Eds.), *Sourcebook of family theories and methods: A contextual approach* (pp. 469–499). Plenum. https://doi.org/10.1007/978-0-387-85764-0_19

Bronte-Tinkew, J., Carrano, J., Horowitz, A., & Kinukawa, A. (2008). Involvement among resident fathers and links to infant cognitive outcomes. *Journal of Family Issues, 29*, 1211–1244. https://doi.org/10.1177/0192513X08318145

Bryant, E. (2021, Dec 1). *Why we say "criminal legal system," not "criminal justice system."* Vera Institute of Justice. https://www.vera.org/blog/why-we-say-criminal-legal-system-not-criminal-justice-system

Christian, J. (2005). Riding the bus barriers to prison visitation and family management strategies. *Journal of Contemporary Criminal Justice, 21*(1), 31–48. https://doi.org/10.1177/1043986204271618

Clark, V. A., & Duwe, G. (2017). Distance matters: Examining the factors that impact prisoner visitation in Minnesota. *Criminal Justice and Behavior, 44*(2), 184204. https://doi.org/10.1177/0093854816667416

Cochran, J. C., Mears, D. P., Bales, W. D., & Stewart, E. A. (2016). Spatial distance, community disadvantage, and racial and ethnic variation in prison inmate access to social ties. *Journal of Research in Crime and Delinquency, 53*(2), 220–254. https://doi.org/10.1177/0022427815592675

Cox, M. (2009). *The relationships between episodes of parental incarceration and students' psycho-social and educational outcomes: An analysis of risk factors*. Temple University.

Crandell-Williams, A., & McEvoy, A. (2017). Fathers on parole: Narratives from the margin. *The Journal of Men's Studies, 25*(3), 262–277. https://doi.org/10.1177/1060826516676840

Cummings, E. M., Davies, P. T., & Campbell, S. B. (2000). *Developmental psychopathology and family process: Theory, research, and clinical implications*. Guilford Press.

Eddy, J. M., Kjellstrand, J. M., Martinez, C. R., Newton, R., Herrera, D., Wheeler, A., Shortt, J. W., Schumer, J. E., Burraston, B. O., & Lorber, M. F. (2019). Theory-based multimodal parenting intervention for incarcerated parents and their children. In J. M. Eddy & J. Poehlmann-Tynan (Eds.), *Handbook on children with incarcerated parents* (pp. 219–235). Springer. https://doi.org/10.1007/978-3-030-16707-3_9

Eddy, J. M., Martinez, C. R., Schiffmann, T., Newton, R., Olin, L., Leve, L., Foney, D. M., & Shortt, J. W. (2008). Development of a multisystemic parent management training intervention for incarcerated parents, their children and families. *Clinical Psychologist, 12*(3), 86–98. https://doi.org/10.1080/13284200802495461

Fortune, C.-A., & Salmon, K. (2019). Families, parenting, and visits in prison. In D. L. L. Polaschek, A. Day, & C. R. Hollin (Eds.), *The Wiley International handbook of correctional psychology* (pp. 169–182). Wiley. https://doi.org/10.1002/9781119139980.ch1

Geller, A., Garfinkel, I., & Western, B. (2011). Paternal incarceration and support for children in fragile families. *Demography, 48*(1), 25–47. https://link.springer.com/content/pdf/10.1007/s13524-010-0009-9.pdf

Greif, G. L. (2014). The voices of fathers in prison: Implications for family practice. *Journal of Family Social Work, 17*, 68–80. https://doi.org/10.1080/10522158.2013.865284

Greif, G. L. (2017). Group work with fathers who are incarcerated. In G. L. Greif & C. Knight (Eds.), *Group work with populations at risk* (4th ed., pp. 433–450). Oxford University Press.
Hansen, G. V. (2018). Does fatherhood training in prison improve fathering skills and reduce family challenges? *Child Care in Practice, 24*(2), 198–211. https://doi.org/10.1080/13575279.2017.1420036
Haskins, A. R. (2016). Beyond boys' bad behavior: Paternal incarceration and cognitive development in middle childhood. *Social Forces, 95*(2), 861–892. https://doi.org/10.1093/sf/sow066
Haskins, A. R. (2015). Paternal incarceration and child-reported behavioral functioning at age 9. *Social Science Research, 52*, 18–33. https://doi.org/10.1016/j.ssresearch.2015.01.001
Haskins, A. R. (2014). Unintended consequences: Effects of paternal incarceration on child school readiness and later special education placement. *Sociological Science, 1*, 141–158. https://doi.org/10.15195/v1.a11
Höfner, C., Schadler, C., & Richter, R. (2011). When men become fathers: Men's identity at the transition to parenthood. *Journal of Comparative Family Studies, 42*(5), 669–686. https://doi.org/10.3138/jcfs.42.5.669
Howard, K. S., Burke Lefever, J. E., Borkowski, J. G., & Whitman, T. L. (2006). Fathers' influence in the lives of children with adolescent mothers. *Journal of Family Psychology, 20*, 468–476. https://doi.org/10.1037/0893-3200.20.3.468
Lewis, D., & Hong, P. Y. P. (2020). Incapacitated fatherhood: The impact of mass incarceration on Black father identity. *Journal of Qualitative Criminal Justice & Criminology*. https://doi.org/10.21428/88de04a1.09b4b7aa
Loper, A. B., Clarke, C. N., & Dallaire, D. H. (2019). Parenting programs for incarcerated fathers and mothers: Current research and new directions. In J. M. Eddy & J. Poehlmann-Tynan (Eds.), *Handbook on children with incarcerated parents* (pp. 183–203). Springer. https://doi.org/10.1007/978-3-030-16707-3_9
Loper, A. B., & Tuerk, E. H. (2006). Parenting programs for incarcerated parents: Current research and future directions. *Criminal Justice Policy Review, 17*, 407–427. https://doi.org/10.1177/0887403406292692
Marsiglio, W., Roy, K., & Fox, G. L. (2005). *Situated fathering: A focus on physical and social spaces*. Rowman & Littlefield Publishers.
Martin, A., Ryan, M. R., & Brooks-Gunn, J. (2010). When fathers' supportiveness matters most: Maternal and paternal parenting and children's school readiness. *Journal of Family Psychology, 24*, 145–155. https://doi.org/10.1037/a0018073
Martin, E. (2017). Hidden consequences: The impact of incarceration on dependent children. *National Institute of Justice, 278*, 2–7. https://www.ojp.gov/pdffiles1/nij/250349.pdf
McLaughlin, K., & Muldoon, O. (2014). Father identity, involvement and work–family balance: An in-depth interview study. *Journal of Community & Applied Social Psychology, 24*(5), 439–452. https://doi.org/10.1002/casp.2183
McLeod, B. A. (2020). "Hello group, I need advice": A textual analysis of Black fathers' help-seeking posts on Facebook. *Family Relations, 69*(5), 944–955. https://doi.org/10.1111/fare.12500
McLeod, B. A. (2021). The effect of multiple forms of father-child contact during imprisonment on fathers' reports of relationship quality. *Corrections*, 1–19. https://doi.org/10.1080/23774657.2021.1874846
Morgan-Mullane, A. (2018). Trauma focused cognitive behavioral therapy with children of incarcerated parents. *Clinical Social Work Journal, 46*(3), 200–209. https://doi.org/10.1007/s10615-017-0642-5
Mowen, T. J., Stansfield, R., & Boman, J. H. (2019). Family matters: Moving beyond "if" family support matters to "why" family support matters during reentry from prison. *Journal of Research in Crime and Delinquency, 56*(4), 483–523. https://doi.org/10.1177/0022427818820902
Murphey, D., & Cooper, P. M. (2015). Parents behind bars: What happens to their children? *Child Trends.*. https://www.childtrends.org/wp-content/uploads/2015/10/2015-42ParentsBehindBars.pdf

Murray, J., Loeber, R., & Pardini, D. (2012). Parental involvement in the criminal justice system and the development of youth theft, marijuana use, depression, and poor academic performance. *Criminology, 50*(1), 255–302. https://doi.org/10.1111/j.1745-9125.2011.00257.x

Newell, D. A. A. (2012). Risk and protective factors for secondary girls of incarcerated parents. *Family Court Review, 50*(1), 106–112. https://doi.org/10.1111/j.1744-1617.2011.01432.x

Oliver, P. E. (2001). *Racial disparities in imprisonment: Some basic information*. Retrieved from http://www.ssc.wisc.edu/~oliver/RACIAL/Oliver%20Focus%202001.pdf.

Purvis, M. (2013). Paternal incarceration and parenting programs in prison: A review paper. *Psychiatry, Psychology and Law, 20*(1), 9–28. https://doi.org/10.1080/13218719.2011.615822

Roettger, M. E., & Swisher, R. R. (2011). Associations of fathers' history of incarceration with sons' delinquency and arrest among black, white, and Hispanic males in the United States. *Criminology, 49*(4), 1109–1147. https://doi.org/10.1111/j.1745-9125.2011.00253.x

Rosenberg, J., & Wilcox, W. B. (2006). *The importance of fathers in the healthy development of children*. Office on Child Abuse and Neglect, U.S. Children's Bureau.

Roy, K. M. (2006). Father stories: A life course examination of paternal identity among low-income African American men. *Journal of Family Issues, 27*(1), 31–54. https://doi.org/10.1177/0192513X05275432

Roy, K. M., & Dyson, O. L. (2005). Gatekeeping in context: Babymama drama and the involvement of incarcerated fathers. *Fathering: A Journal of Theory, Research & Practice about Men as Fathers, 3*(3), 289–310.

Tripp, B. (2009). Fathers in jail: Managing dual identities. *Applied Psychology in Criminal in Criminal Justice, 5*(1), 26–56.

Western, B., & Wildeman, C. (2009). The black family and mass incarceration. *The Annals of the American Academy of Political and Social Science, 621*(1), 221–242. https://doi.org/10.1177/0002716208324850

Wilbur, M. B., Marani, J. E., Appugliese, D., Woods, R., Siegel, J. A., Cabral, H. J., & Frank, D. A. (2007). Socioemotional effects of fathers' incarceration on low-income, urban, school-aged children. *Pediatrics, 120*(3), 678–685. https://doi.org/10.1542/peds.2006-2166

Chapter 11
Engaging Fathers in Child Welfare and Foster Care Settings: Promoting Paternal Contributions to the Safety, Permanency, and Well-being of Children and Families

Justin S. Harty and Aaron Banman

Introduction

Father involvement has positive benefits for children's social, emotional, and behavioral outcomes as well as overall family well-being and safety (Jeynes, 2017; Sarkadi et al., 2008; Yoon et al., 2018). Additionally, father involvement reduces the risk of child maltreatment, domestic violence, and family separation in child welfare (Bellamy, 2009; Berger, 2004, 2006; Berger et al., 2009). However, despite evidence that father involvement is a critical component of child well-being and an integral part of a family system, the child welfare system has historically ignored, undervalued, and failed to fully engage fathers as agents of change toward efforts to prevent or respond to maltreatment (Jaffe, 1983; Zanoni et al., 2013, 2014). Engaging fathers, especially Black fathers, with children in the child welfare system has the potential to keep children safely in the home, reduce the time children spend in foster care if they are removed, increase the chances children return home upon leaving foster care, and improve the likelihood that children live in the home of relatives if they cannot safely return home (Pate, 2005).

This chapter contains important information for social workers working with fathers in child welfare settings. It details how social workers can engage fathers in maltreatment prevention services, involve fathers in case planning, improve

J. S. Harty (✉)
School of Social Work, Watts College of Public Service and Community Solutions, Arizona State University, Phoenix, AZ, USA
e-mail: justinharty@asu.edu

A. Banman
Grace Abbott School of Social Work, University of Nebraska at Omaha, Omaha, NE, USA
e-mail: abanman@unomaha.edu

J. L. Bellamy et al. (eds.), *Social Work Practice with Fathers*,
https://doi.org/10.1007/978-3-031-13686-3_11

parental skills of fathers, and strengthen the father-child relationship. This chapter also discusses how social workers can engage an often-overlooked group of fathers in the child welfare system: young fathers in foster care. In the sections that follow, father engagement across key child welfare domains is discussed, along with practice guidance and intervention strategies targeting father engagement in the child welfare system and related services, beginning with an overview of father engagement in the child welfare system.

Background and Context

This section covers research on father engagement in the child welfare system, associations with child welfare outcomes, and barriers to father engagement in child welfare.

Father Engagement in the Child Welfare System

Several studies have revealed that father engagement in child welfare services (e.g., case planning) is associated with positive child permanency outcomes. For example, studies on nonresident father engagement in child welfare have found that simply identifying fathers (compared to not identifying them) was associated with the increased likelihood of children being reunified with one or both parents (Burrus et al., 2012), and contacting fathers (compared to just identifying them) was associated with children spending less time in care (Malm & Zielewski, 2009). In addition, Coakley (2013a) found that father engagement in case planning and case compliance was associated with children spending less time in care and a greater likelihood that the children would be reunified with parents or relatives upon exit from foster care.

Efforts to engage fathers are not well tracked in child welfare (Coakley, 2013a), oftentimes because administrative data systems are not generally set up to capture data about child welfare services for fathers. For studies that were able to obtain information on father engagement, most conceptualized it as a dichotomous outcome based on whether fathers were engaged or not engaged. Few studies have captured father engagement as a scale outcome based on the amount of engagement (e.g., not engaged, engaged, or highly engaged). One exception is a study conducted by Malm and Zielewski (2009), which found that increased nonresident father engagement in case planning was associated with an increased likelihood of reunification, and children with highly engaged nonresident fathers were more likely to spend less time in foster care. Other studies examining the quality of father engagement have found that higher quality father engagement was associated with better placement stability and permanency outcomes for their children (Shadik, 2020; Trahan et al., 2020; Yampolskaya et al., 2017). While these studies demonstrate the benefits of father engagement in child welfare services generally, fathers are often unable to participate in these services.

Barriers to Father Engagement in the Child Welfare System

Father participation in child welfare services is generally lower than mother participation (Campbell et al., 2015; Gordon et al., 2012; O'Donnell, 1999). The conditions for engagement are particularly difficult for racially and ethnically marginalized fathers, which contributes to an increased risk for child maltreatment among their children and their children being disproportionately represented in the child welfare system; it also decreases the likelihood that their children will be placed into or returned to their care. Studies point to a number of father engagement barriers associated with racism and discrimination, particularly among Black fathers in contact with the child welfare system (Icard et al., 2017). For example, studies have attributed low father engagement among Black fathers to racialized perceptions and racial bias among White child welfare caseworkers, attorneys, and judges (Arroyo et al., 2019; Harris & Hackett, 2008). For example, White workers may believe that Black fathers are uninvolved in or harmful to their families and thus are less likely to identify, locate, contact, or engage fathers who can make meaningful contributions to their families. White workers are at times apprehensive about engaging Black fathers whose participation in services may be affected by larger social forces but are resilient fathers. This is important given that other barriers to father engagement in the child welfare system likely stem from racism and oppression (Johnson, 2004). Studies on father engagement have highlighted the ways in which Black fathers are more vulnerable to poverty, unstable housing, inadequate education, high unemployment, and mass incarceration that are oftentimes consequences of racism and discrimination (Coakley, 2013a, 2013b; Coakley et al., 2014; Hill, 2004; Hindt et al., 2020; Kobulsky et al., 2021; Lee et al., 2018).

Another explanation for the low rate of father participation in child welfare services is caseworker gender bias. Some caseworkers view father engagement as not beneficial to child welfare planning, not as necessary as mother engagement, and even harmful to families (Baum, 2017; Bellamy, 2009; Brewsaugh et al., 2018; Brown et al., 2009; Coakley, 2013b; Dominelli et al., 2011; Lundahl et al., 2020; Scourfield, 2001). Other, related, explanations for lower father participation in child welfare services is that many caseworkers believe they are supposed to engage mothers more frequently than fathers, they find it easier to do so, fathers are engaged later in the case than mothers, less information is collected about father engagement than mother engagement, and maternal gatekeeping (Bellamy, 2009; Campbell et al., 2015; Coady et al., 2013; Gibson et al., 2020; O'Donnell, 1999; O'Donnell et al., 2005; Tully et al., 2018). An overview of the child welfare system is needed to better understand how these barriers affect father engagement and what child welfare workers can do to break them down. In the following section, important child welfare terms, processes, and legislation relating to fathers in contact with the child welfare system are shared.

Conceptual Framing

Child welfare in the United States has historically involved three interrelated goals: (1) protecting children from actual or potential harm; (2) preserving the family unit, including birth family and relatives; and (3) promoting child well-being, including independence for older children (Maluccio, 2006). These three goals—safety, permanency, and well-being—serve as the organizing conceptual framework for this chapter. Specifically, this chapter details how the child welfare system engages fathers in, and how fathers contribute to, the safety, permanency, and well-being of children. To best understand father engagement in the child welfare system, this section provides an overview of the child welfare system, relevant processes, and key father-related terms.

The Child Welfare System and Father Engagement

The child welfare system is designed to ensure that children are safe from maltreatment, able to achieve permanency, obtain stable placement, and strengthen their family to prevent future maltreatment through services such as maltreatment prevention, family preservation, and permanency planning (Child Welfare Information Gateway, 2020).

This process often begins when the child protection court makes a legal determination that a report of child maltreatment, made by a mandated reporter or concerned individual, has not occurred or has occurred or there is imminent risk that it will likely occur soon. If a child is removed from the home, then an emergency placement is sought until the child can safely return home or an out-of-home placement is found. During this time, the child welfare system will make concurrent plans to help children obtain permanency through reunification, adoption, guardianship, or, for older children preparing to age out of foster care, another permanent living arrangement (Child Welfare Information Gateway, 2018a, 2020).

Child welfare caseworkers engage fathers to participate in the services outlined in their case plans. Monitoring of father engagement was written into the *Child Welfare Act of 1980,* which mandates states monitor the child welfare court oversight of, and child welfare agency attempts to, engage both parents (Cohen & Sandt, 2009). The focus on father engagement is largely supported by the *Adoption and Safe Families Act of 1997* (ASFA), which granted child welfare agencies the right to use the Federal Parent Locator Service employed by child support enforcement programs to locate fathers and paternal relatives and mandated that child welfare agencies expedite and identify timely permanency placements, which includes the prompt identification of and placement determination with fathers and paternal relatives (Malm et al., 2006).

Definitions of Fathers in the Child Welfare System

In the child welfare system, there are a number of father-related terms that are used interchangeably but have distinct meanings. As displayed in Table 11.1, these terms are based on fathers' activities (e.g., involvement, contact, engagement, and participation) and status (e.g., residency, custodial, and paternity). These definitions are important when engaging fathers across the child welfare system, as will be discussed in the upcoming section.

Recommended Intervention Approaches

Many studies have acknowledged the barriers and challenges to father engagement and have attempted to change the child welfare system to be more inclusive and engaging of fathers. While some areas are more often studied, efforts have been or are currently being made to address some of the system challenges across six key domains: (1) child maltreatment prevention, (2) paternity establishment, (3) intensive family preservation, (4) permanency planning, (5) young fathers in foster care, and (6) father engagement. Descriptions, assessment data, practice guidance, and recommended intervention strategies are described in the following section and summarized in Table 11.2.

Child Maltreatment Prevention

One key goal of the child welfare system is to prevent child maltreatment from occurring, and child welfare services are increasingly emphasizing prevention efforts. Prevention among fathers means addressing the risk factors that they will maltreat their children. For example, studies have found that absence, low employment, economic hardship, age (being a young father), mental health problems, substance use, and father-mother conflict are associated with increased odds of fathers maltreating their children (Casey Family Programs, 2019; Guterman et al., 2009; Guterman & Lee, 2005; Lee et al., 2009). Unfortunately, fathers are often left out of interventions targeting maltreatment prevention, especially fathers of color who are at a greater risk of being exposed to factors associated with child maltreatment (Lee et al., 2009). Researchers recommend child welfare agencies focus on engaging fathers in prevention services (Kobulsky et al., 2021; Lee et al., 2009), such as those addressing employment, education, mental health, and substance use issues, to mitigate the maltreatment risk they pose.

Evidence-supported interventions targeting child maltreatment prevention are becoming increasingly available, and more are expanding to consider specific father-focused strategies. Early home visitation is one popular method for

Table 11.1 Key father terms used in the child welfare system

Term	Definition
Activity[a]	
Father involvement	Fathers' contributions to children, including Lamb and colleagues' (1987) conceptualizations of engagement, accessibility, and responsibility and Palkovitz's (1997) conceptualizations capturing behavioral, cognitive, and affective dimensions
Father contact	Fathers' direct in-person contact or remote/virtual contact with child, including in-person visitations, phone calls, text messages, and virtual meetings
Father engagement	Caseworkers' attempts to engage fathers in or fathers' engagement with activities outlined in case plans, such as father identification, father-child visitation, supportive services, case planning, and court attendance throughout the life of the child's case
Father participation	Fathers' compliance with case plan goals and court orders. This term is commonly used in the child welfare system to report fathers' engagement in child welfare services.
Residency status	
(Non)resident father	A father who lives with their child (resident father) or a father who does not live with their child (nonresident father)
Custodial status	
(Non)custodial father	A father who has legal custody over their child (custodial father) or a father who does not have legal custody over their child (noncustodial father)
Paternity status[a]	
Putative father	A man who is the alleged biological father of a child but whose paternity has not been legally established
Alleged father	A man who alleges himself to be, or is alleged to be, the genetic father or a possible genetic father of a child but whose paternity has not been determined
Acknowledged father	A man who has established a father-child relationship by signing an acknowledgment of paternity
Presumed father	A man who is recognized as the father of a child until that status is rebutted or confirmed in a judicial proceeding.
Adjudicated father	A man who has been adjudicated by a court of competent jurisdiction to be the father of a child
Social/fictive father	A man who serves a fatherhood role but is not the biological father or stepfather of a child

[a]Paternity status definitions drawn from the Child Welfare Information Gateway (2018b)

prevention services, and efforts are being made to target fathers within that service structure. For example, SafeCare, an evidence-based parent training curriculum targeting at-risk or identified families (Gershater-Molko et al., 2003), has a father-focused adaptation that has shown early potential for engaging fathers called Dad2K (Self-Brown et al., 2017; Whitaker et al., 2020). Other home visitation programs are in the process of adapting or focusing on fathers, while some refinements (e.g., Dads Matter-HV; Bellamy et al., 2020) are being made to broadly enhance any variation of the evidence-based home visiting model (Guterman et al., 2018).

Table 11.2 Guidance and strategies for serving fathers in child welfare

Engagement domain	Engagement guidance and strategies
Child maltreatment prevention	Engage fathers early in prevention services to address risk factors and mitigate risk of child maltreatment.
Paternity establishment	Identify and contact fathers early, make diligent efforts to locate and engage in paternity establishment.
Intensive family preservation	Engage in immediate and short-term support for and monitoring of fathers of children at imminent risk of harm.
Permanency planning	Promptly and continuously engage fathers in case planning and case compliance throughout life of case.
Young fathers in foster care	Augment existing transitional services with services targeting young fatherhood and child safety.
Improving father engagement	Improve engagement with diverse and marginalized fathers by using innovative and inclusive methods.

Parent training is another common prevention service approach, which is also used for families with open child welfare cases, particularly when child behavior is problematic. Research suggests that fathers who participate in parent training programs benefit far less than mothers. For example, small to no intervention effects were found for fathers undertaking Triple-P (Positive Parenting Program; Fletcher et al., 2011) although, because of Triple-P's focus on fathers, they exhibited more engagement and better child outcomes than fathers in the control group who did not receive the intervention (Chacko et al., 2018). Other parent training models (e.g., Parent Management Training and The Incredible Years) have also shown improved parent and child outcomes and some modest efficacy with fathers (Fabiano et al., 2012; Magill-Evans et al., 2007).

Paternity Establishment

Identifying, contacting, and locating fathers is a vital process of father engagement. At case opening, child welfare workers must make reasonable efforts to conduct a diligent search to identify, locate, and notify fathers of their children's child welfare involvement. This is a crucial first step for child welfare to ensure children's safety and permanence and allow fathers to make progress toward reunification or permanency (Campbell et al., 2015; Coakley, 2014; Malm & Zielewski, 2009). Under ASFA, the purpose for notifying fathers promptly at case opening is to engage them in early case planning, provide services so their children may be placed in their care, and identify paternal relatives if children cannot return home (Campbell et al., 2015; Coakley, 2014; Malm et al., 2006).

Putative or alleged fathers may acknowledge paternity, or the possibility of paternity, of a child by submitting information to a state's *putative father registry*. When a father cannot be initially identified or located, workers can engage with the child's mother, maternal relatives, paternal relatives, children, siblings, or friends to locate the father. Additionally, caseworkers can leverage resources such as online social media searches, federal and state parent locators, state departments of revenue, state child support enforcement agencies, putative father registries, and other state public records (American Humane Association, 2011). Helping fathers establish paternity is important as it ensures that they have legal rights within the child welfare system. While these rights may vary by state and are extended to fathers in various stages of paternity establishment, they generally include a set of the basic rights described in Table 11.3.

Paternity establishment and the resulting parental rights are often associated with fathers who were married to the child's mother when the child was born. However, the child welfare system has other ways to establish paternity and ensure fathers are entitled to their parental rights within the child welfare system. For example, paternity may be established if an alleged father completes a paternity test indicating that he is the father, acknowledges his paternity in writing, is obligated to pay child support, or a court establishes paternity using alternative legal methods. However, in some cases, paternity establishment within the child welfare system has not been clearly defined. For example, there have been difficulties and legal challenges to nonmartial paternity establishment for fathers of Native American children under the *Indian Child Welfare Act of 1978* (ICWA). Since there is no current standard of acknowledging or establishing paternity under ICWA, unwed Native American fathers who have not acknowledged or established paternity are unable to assert their rights to their biological children or must rely on varied interpretations of ICWA paternity establishment in state courts. However, efforts are currently underway to establish legal procedures for unwed Native American paternity establishment that are both constitutionally protectable and in accordance with tribal laws and customs (Dow, 2019; Heiner, 2017; Smith, 2018).

Child welfare agencies must record and assess their engagement methods and attempts to identify fathers, establish paternity, and locate nonresident fathers and report these efforts to the Children's Bureau in their annual Child and Family Services Review (American Humane Association, 2011). In terms of interventions for establishing paternity, the *Omnibus Budget Reconciliation Act of 1993* established in-hospital paternity establishing systems around the country, and legislation

Table 11.3 Fatherhood rights in the child welfare system

Basic legal rights for fathers in the child welfare system[a]	
1.	Seek physical custody of their children or have them returned to their care
2.	Be offered child welfare services and time to complete them
3.	Be provided, be informed of, and collaborate on child case planning
4.	Have father-child visitation and contact with children placed in out-of-home care
5.	Be provided court-appointed counsel or legal representation in the child welfare courts
6.	Receive notice of court proceedings and petitions for adoption
7.	Receive notifications of efforts made to terminate parental rights

[a]Adapted from American Humane Association (2011); Cohen & Sandt (2009); Malm et al. (2006)

attached to the Personal Responsibility and Work Opportunity Act of 1996 raised paternity establishment goals and expanded that documentation to unwed fathers via a voluntary paternity affidavit (Mincy et al., 2005). This early paternity establishment intervention was successful at increasing the rates of paternity documentation. Nearly six of seven births had their paternity established, yet challenges remain (Mincy et al., 2005). Some state-level VPA (volunteer paternity affidavit) programs still note significant rates of rejections of the voluntary forms, including errors in information or administrative errors when completing the forms (Weems et al., 2020). Out-of-hospital paternity establishment is often more challenging, but interventions such as the FATHER project use methods such as teaching the value of and providing individualized support to establish paternity (Wilder Research, 2010). Some child welfare jurisdictions are also testing interventions whereby mobile paternity testing services are offered alongside other services such as help with employment or housing (e.g., Fung et al., 2021).

Intensive Family Preservation Services

Intensive family preservation services (IFPS) provide immediate short-term support to families referred to the child welfare system for a maltreatment investigation and whose children are at imminent risk of placement into foster care; rapid intervention with IFPS could reduce the children's risk of future harm and allow the children to remain in the home and the family to remain intact. Engaging both resident and nonresident fathers in IFPS is needed to ensure the safety and stability of their children. For example, IFPS are family-centered and delivered in-home and provide crisis intervention, therapeutic counseling, parent training, day-care services, cash assistance, and linkages to other needed services in the community. However, nonresident fathers may also be engaged to support the children and children's mother as an alternative temporary or permanent non-foster care placement option, a source of childcare, and a provider of other co-parenting supports to supplement IFPS and assist their nonresident children in remaining safe and in the home.

Child welfare agencies can assess agency efforts to engage fathers in IFPS, fathers' participation in IFSP, and the effects of father engagement in IFPS on case outcomes. Efforts to engage fathers in IFPS can be tracked using standard child welfare reporting techniques (e.g., entered into electronic case reporting databases and agency case note narratives). Studies find mixed results of IFPS effectiveness, and it is not often recognized as an evidence-based intervention (Schweitzer et al., 2015). The Children's Bureau noted that models for IFPS offer few specifics in the literature with regard to father-specific intervention targeting maltreatment. However, IFPS interventions may still be beneficial for preventing maltreatment in child welfare-involved families. For example, Pruett et al. (2019) tested a couples-focused co-parenting intervention with child welfare-referred families. It reduced conflict in the co-parent relationship and harsh parenting and improved child outcomes. These positive outcomes were equally effective for families with or without current involvement within the child welfare system. Additionally, Nievar et al. (2020) studied a father group model called FOCUS (Families Offering Children Unfailing Support) for nonresident fathers referred by child protection services. Their studies showed the potential for improved father-child relationships and increased child support.

Permanency Planning

Fathers have an important role to play in permanency planning and should be engaged early, often, and at every point in the life of the case. Furthermore, fathers' unique insights and contributions should be leveraged as important information needed to make fully informed placement and permanency decisions. As summarized in the beginning of this chapter, father engagement in permanency planning has the potential to increase rates of reunification, decrease stays in foster care, and lead to better placement stability and permanency outcomes for children. Engaging fathers in permanency planning can occur through three case-related activities: case planning for reunification, concurrent case planning, and activities to strengthen father-child bonds.

Case plans must be developed to address the reasons the child entered foster care and stipulate goals the father must accomplish to mitigate future risk of child maltreatment so the child can be returned to or placed in his care in a timely manner and in accordance with federal and state child welfare laws. Case plan goals often include services aimed to improve the father's parenting skills, mental health problems, substance use issues, employment status, housing stability, or any needed service that will help him keep his child safe from maltreatment. They also include case-related goals such as attending and participating in child welfare agency case planning meetings, child and family team meetings, court hearings, father-child visitations, and other activities designed around case planning for the child to return home to his care (Coakley, 2008; Coakley et al., 2018; Malm et al., 2006; Yampolskaya et al., 2017).

Child welfare workers must promptly and actively engage fathers in case planning and compliance to ensure that case plans meet the safety needs of the family and fathers are able to realistically complete their case plan goals in the time allowed and to facilitate consistent father-child visitation and bonding time. If the permanency goal for a child changes to guardianship, adoption, or another living arrangement, workers should still engage fathers in seeking paternal placement options, case planning, and case compliance, for example, by partnering with them to find placement options with paternal relatives, providing child-related information (e.g., educational progress, mental health status, medical needs) to help make fully informed case management decisions, and developing visitation plans to ensure frequent father-child visitation and strong father-child bonds.

Permanency planning is a multifaceted and complicated process, and some researchers have targeted specific barriers as intervention points. For example,

Enano et al. (2017) evaluated a parent mentor intervention targeting reducing barriers to the permanency process while attempting to increase reunifications. Parent mentor programs pair parents new to the child welfare system with parents who have successfully navigated the system and have reunified with their children. The evaluation showed the parent mentor program had a higher likelihood of father participation compared to services as usual, and parents participating in the program were more likely to reunify with their child. While not directly targeting fathers, Kim et al. (2019) were able to show that innovations in family planning meetings could positively impact teamwork and permanency, particularly when fathers were more engaged. Additionally, interventions around responsible fatherhood programs may indirectly improve father engagement in permanency planning by improving outcomes such as employment, education, and economic hardships.

Young Fathers in Foster Care

While the vast majority of research and practice guidance on engaging fathers in the child welfare system has focused on fathers with children under the care of the child welfare system, young fathers who are themselves in foster care are often overlooked in father engagement efforts (Connolly et al., 2012; Eastman et al., 2019; Svoboda et al., 2012). This is especially troublesome given that fathers in foster care are approaching three difficult transitions. First, these young fathers must soon exit the foster care system and will lose the support provided while in care; second, they must prepare for transition into adulthood at an early age and without the preparedness and support often available to their non-foster care peers; and third, they have the added stress of being a young parent, often without the support, preparation, and resources to be the kind of parent they would like to be given their developmental stage (Courtney et al., 2012, 2018).

Despite the lack of research and knowledge about young fathers in care, there are still ways that caseworkers can engage them to participate in services designed to increase parenting skills, knowledge, and resources. Additionally, caseworkers can connect young fathers in foster care to financial, emotional, mental health, and social support services that will help improve parent- and child-related outcomes. Furthermore, caseworkers can consider how the needs of fathers in care differ from mothers in care and tailor services for fathers appropriately (Harty, 2021; Harty & Ethier, 2022). For example, around the birth of a child, mothers' needs may center on pregnancy and childbirth (e.g., education around pre-or postnatal care, birthing support, and breastfeeding guidance) while fathers' needs may focus on child and mother relationships (e.g., attending prenatal visits, strengthening father-child involvement, managing the co-parental relationship). Caseworker assessments of fathers in care can easily be incorporated into existing transitional living and independence reporting requirements.

There are two types of interventions that can help engage fathers in care. First, the *Federal Fostering Connections to Success and Increasing Adoptions Act of 2008* gave states the option to extend foster care past age 18, up to age 21. Employment, education, and social support services offered through extended foster care offer additional opportunities to engage in the services, including parental services, needed to prepare for early fatherhood and adulthood (Putnam-Hornstein et al., 2016). Second, the *Family First Prevention Services Act of 2018* provides funding for mental health, substance abuse, and in-home parent skill-based programs to ensure the children of expectant or parenting fathers in care are safe from maltreatment and do not enter foster care (Children's Defense Fund, 2020).

Improving Father Engagement and Intervention in the Child Welfare System

Improving father engagement and intervention in the child welfare system begins with better data collection and tracking of caseworkers' efforts to engage fathers. Assessing father engagement is challenging due to a historical lack of measurement tools and father-inclusive administrative data systems; however, recent research has helped to fill this void. There is now a growing variety of tools with which to assess quantities and qualities of father engagement, co-parenting, risk factors, and prevention service engagement (Chacko et al., 2018; Fagan & Palkovitz, 2019; Pfitzner et al., 2017). Stronger measures, and the more frequent utilization of those measures, allow for statistical methods to be more readily used. For example, father engagement and child welfare data can be linked to assess the risk factors of maltreatment, determine conditions in which child maltreatment is more likely to occur, and target prevention services accordingly (Crawford & Bradley, 2016).

One mechanism to assess father engagement in permanency planning is through child welfare administrative data. However, while federal law mandates that states and tribes use child welfare information data systems, such as the Statewide Automated Child Welfare Information System (SACWIS) and the Comprehensive Child Welfare Information System (CCWIS), to record and monitor child welfare data, these data are limited in their capacity to capture father engagement. To correctly assess father engagement in permanency planning, child welfare workers must ensure that data related to a worker's engagement efforts (e.g., diligence in locating fathers, maintaining communication with fathers) and father's case plan compliance (e.g., participation in meetings, completion of services, visitation attendance, father-child interactions) are consistently and accurately recorded in child welfare information data systems, child welfare assessments, agency documents, and court records. Other mechanisms can come from informational data obtained during case planning meetings (e.g., child and family team meetings, administrative case reviews), assessments (e.g., Child and Adolescent Needs and Strengths, Integrated Assessment Program), and agency continuous quality improvement systems (e.g., father reports of engagement and satisfaction with services). These sources also present challenges if data, case notes, or assessments do not require workers to record information about fathers or are not regularly completed.

System-specific interventions may also help improve father engagement. For example, Campbell et al. (2015) identified four ways to improve father engagement in child welfare: (1) addressing caseworker bias, (2) improving child welfare documentation, (3) reducing mother's influence on the father engagement, and (4) addressing stigma associated with fathers' prior incarceration. The innovative Fathers and Continuous Learning in Child Welfare (FCL) project takes a new approach to improving father engagement in child welfare services (Fung et al., 2021). Using the Breakthrough Series Collaborative methodology, FCL targets historical child welfare barriers to father engagement by strengthening the engagement of fathers and paternal relatives, collaborating with child welfare staff and community partners, and providing father-focused resources and support. The results from FCL's pilot study demonstrate that FCL improved team members' engagement of fathers and paternal relatives (Fung et al., 2021). Other studies note improvements might be made by addressing father-specific needs and engaging fathers early when they are most likely to participate (Pate, 2005). Studies also highlight the need to specifically target Black father engagement, improve engagement with paternal relatives as placement options, promote a positive worker-father relationship, and train caseworkers (Coakley, 2014; Coakley et al., 2018; Fung et al., 2021; Johnson Jr., 2004; Maxwell et al., 2012a, 2012b; O'Donnell, 1999; Scourfield, 2001, 2006, 2014; Scourfield et al., 2012). Making adaptive changes may be helpful as well (Kim et al., 2019; Mallette et al., 2017). For example, caseworkers can better engage fathers in child welfare services by making arrangements with criminal justice systems for incarcerated fathers, using interstate compacts for out-of-state fathers, observing provisions for Native American fathers, using interpreters for non-English speaking fathers, providing mobility support for fathers with impaired movement, supplying co-parenting services for fathers with children in different households, and providing developmentally appropriate support for young fathers in foster care.

While interventions are being developed to increase father involvement in social services, few have been replicated. Some attempts are being made to address father engagement on larger agency or system levels. For example, English et al. (2009) piloted an intervention designed to increase training and examine agency practice related to father engagement, which had modest success in moving agency practices toward more father-focused engagement. Scourfield et al.'s (2012) implementation of training directed at social workers in child protection showed the potential to change worker attitudes and address biases related to specific types of fathers. Other evidence-based interventions such as Family Assessment Response (Loman & Siegel, 2005) and Preliminary Protective Hearing Benchcard (Russell & Summers, 2013) seek to reduce racial disparity and disproportionality in the child welfare system by adding cultural competence components to child welfare decision-making processes, particularly targeting racism, institutional bias, and factors associated with families of color that may predispose them to higher risks of child maltreatment such as poverty and economic hardships.

Conclusion

Engaging and intervening with fathers in child welfare services leverages the positive benefits of father involvement in child outcomes and family well-being. Furthermore, engaging fathers in child welfare services is a key step to ensuring children have the best chance of avoiding foster care placement or returning home if family separation is necessary. It is important for social workers to understand that the child welfare system has historically struggled to engage fathers in the domains of child maltreatment prevention, paternity establishment, intensive family preservation services, permanency planning, and services for young fathers in foster care. With this knowledge, social workers may adapt practices and tailor services to strengthen father engagement and meet the unique needs of fathers across these domains. Changes to child welfare practice and services targeting father engagement can help social workers ensure that fathers are able to exercise their paternal rights and participate in services that will reunify them with their children. While this may seem like a difficult task, there are many strategies that social workers can use to strengthen father engagement. For example, Harty and Walsh (2021) suggest that social workers:

- Engage fathers as early and as equally as mothers.
- If fathers present a risk to children or mothers, continually assess if, when, and how fathers may be safely engaged in the future.
- Engage fathers in case-related decisions and tasks, even when fathers have not engaged in the past.
- View every case decision point, event, and exchange as an opportunity for father engagement.
- Use a father-focused, strengths-based approach that emphasizes fathers' self-determination and strengths.
- Address obstacles or barriers preventing fathers from engaging in services.
- Explore paternal family members as placement options and resources for support in permanency planning.
- Improve father engagement data recording, tracking, and analysis in child welfare data systems.

Resources

- The Child Welfare Information Gateway (childwelfare.gov) contains many reports, guides, toolkits, and trainings on engaging diverse fathers in child welfare and supporting young fathers in foster care.
- The American Bar Association (americanbar.org) provides publications and memos on how attorneys, court-appointed special advocates, guardian ad litems, and judges can better engage fathers in child welfare legal cases.

- Interventions on or related to father engagement in child welfare are available from the California Evidence-Based Clearinghouse for Child Welfare (cebc4cw.org).
- Additional resources on engaging fathers in the child welfare system are available from the National Center for Child Welfare Excellence (nccwe.org).

Discussion Questions

1. Why is it important for caseworkers to engage fathers in the child welfare system?
2. What benefits do fathers provide their children when they are engaged in child welfare case planning and child welfare services?
3. What obstacles do caseworkers face when trying to engage fathers in the child welfare system and how can caseworkers overcome these obstacles?
4. What barriers do fathers encounter when attempting to engage with, or participate in, child welfare services and how can caseworkers address these barriers?
5. How can the child welfare system and child welfare agencies improve father engagement, especially for racially/ethnically diverse fathers and fathers with unique needs?

References

Adoption and Safe Families Act of 1997, P.L. 105-89. http://www.govtrack.us/congress/bill.xpd?bill=h105-867

American Humane Association. (2011). Bringing back the dads: Changing practices in child welfare systems. *Protecting Children, 26*(1), 1–102.

Arroyo, J., Zsembik, B., & Peek, C. W. (2019). Ain't nobody got time for dad? Racial-ethnic disproportionalities in child welfare casework practice with nonresident fathers. *Child Abuse & Neglect, 93*, 182–196. https://doi.org/10.1016/j.chiabu.2019.03.014

Baum, N. (2017). Gender-sensitive intervention to improve work with fathers in child welfare services. *Child & Family Social Work, 22*(1), 419–427. https://doi.org/10.1111/cfs.12259

Bellamy, J. L. (2009). A national study of male involvement among families in contact with the child welfare system. *Child Maltreatment, 14*(3), 255–262. https://doi.org/10.1177/1077559508326288

Bellamy, J. L., Harty, J. S., Guterman, N. B., Morales-Mirque, S., Banman, A., & Combs, K. M. (2020). *The engagement of fathers in home visiting services: Learning from the Dads Matter–HV Study* (pp. 1–23). Fatherhood Research & Practice Network.

Berger, L. M. (2004). Income, family structure, and child maltreatment risk. *Children and Youth Services Review, 26*(8), 725–748. https://doi.org/10.1016/j.childyouth.2004.02.017

Berger, L. M. (2006). Children living out-of-home: Effects of family and environmental characteristics. *Children and Youth Services Review, 28*(2), 158–179. https://doi.org/10.1016/j.childyouth.2005.02.006

Berger, L. M., Paxson, C., & Waldfogel, J. (2009). Mothers, men, and child protective services involvement. *Child Maltreatment, 14*(3), 263–276. https://doi.org/10.1177/1077559509337255

Brewsaugh, K., Masyn, K. E., & Salloum, A. (2018). Child welfare workers' sexism and beliefs about father involvement. *Children and Youth Services Review, 89*, 132–144. https://doi.org/10.1016/j.childyouth.2018.04.029

Brown, L., Callahan, M., Strega, S., Walmsley, C., & Dominelli, L. (2009). Manufacturing ghost fathers: The paradox of father presence and absence in child welfare. *Child & Family Social Work, 14*(1), 25–34. https://doi.org/10.1111/j.1365-2206.2008.00578.x

Burrus, S. W. M., Green, B. L., Worcel, S., Finigan, M., & Furrer, C. (2012). Do dads matter? Child welfare outcomes for father-identified families. *Journal of Child Custody, 9*(3), 201–216. https://doi.org/10.1080/15379418.2012.715550

Campbell, C. A., Howard, D., Rayford, B. S., & Gordon, D. M. (2015). Fathers matter: Involving and engaging fathers in the child welfare system process. *Children and Youth Services Review, 53*, 84–91. https://doi.org/10.1016/j.childyouth.2015.03.020

Casey Family Programs. (2019). *How can we better engage fathers in prevention?* (Strong Families Issue Brief). Casey Family Programs. https://caseyfamilypro-wpengine.netdna-ssl.com/media/SF_Engaging-Fathers-Prevention.pdf.

Chacko, A., Fabiano, G. A., Doctoroff, G. L., & Fortson, B. (2018). Engaging fathers in effective parenting for preschool children using shared book reading: A randomized controlled trial. *Journal of Clinical Child & Adolescent Psychology, 47*(1), 79–93. https://doi.org/10.1080/15374416.2016.1266648

Child Welfare Act of 1980, P.L. 96-272. https://www.govtrack.us/congress/bills/96/hr3434

Child Welfare Information Gateway. (2018a). *Concurrent planning for timely permanence* (pp. 1–11). U.S. Department of Health and Human Services, Children's Bureau. https://www.childwelfare.gov/pubPDFs/concurrent_planning.pdf

Child Welfare Information Gateway. (2018b). *The rights of unmarried fathers* (pp. 1–91). U.S. Department of Health and Human Services, Children's Bureau. https://www.childwelfare.gov/pubPDFs/putative.pdf

Child Welfare Information Gateway. (2020). *How the child welfare system works* (pp. 1–8). U.S. Department of Health and Human Services, Children's Bureau. https://www.childwelfare.gov/pubPDFs/cpswork.pdf

Children's Defense Fund. (2020). *Implementing the Family First Prevention Services Act: A technical guide for agencies, policymakers and other stakeholders*. Children's Defense Fund, American Academy of Pediatrics, ChildFocus, FosterClub, Generations United, Juvenile Law Center, and National Indian Child Welfare Association. https://www.childrensdefense.org/wp-content/uploads/2020/07/FFPSA-Guide.pdf

Coady, N., Hoy, S. L., & Cameron, G. (2013). Fathers' experiences with child welfare services. *Child & Family Social Work, 18*(3), 275–284. https://doi.org/10.1111/j.1365-2206.2012.00842.x

Coakley, T. M. (2008). Examining African American fathers' involvement in permanency planning: An effort to reduce racial disproportionality in the child welfare system. *Children and Youth Services Review, 30*(4), 407–417. https://doi.org/10.1016/j.childyouth.2007.10.015

Coakley, T. M. (2013a). The influence of father involvement on child welfare permanency outcomes: A secondary data analysis. *Children and Youth Services Review, 35*(1), 174–182. https://doi.org/10.1016/j.childyouth.2012.09.023

Coakley, T. M. (2013b). An appraisal of fathers' perspectives on fatherhood and barriers to their child welfare involvement. *Journal of Human Behavior in the Social Environment, 23*(5), 627–639. https://doi.org/10.1080/10911359.2013.775935

Coakley, T. M. (2014). Fatherhood. In G. P. Mallon & P. M. Hess (Eds.), *Child welfare for the twenty-first century: A handbook of practices, policies, & programs* (2nd ed., pp. 694–709). Columbia University Press.

Coakley, T. M., Shears, J. K., & Randolph, S. D. (2014). Understanding key barriers to fathers' involvement in their children's lives. *Child & Youth Services, 35*(4), 343–364. https://doi.org/10.1080/0145935X.2014.972550

Coakley, T. M., Washington, T., & Gruber, K. (2018). Assessing child welfare agency practices and attitudes that affect father engagement. *Journal of Social Service Research, 44*(3), 365–374. https://doi.org/10.1080/01488376.2018.1476286

Cohen, A. L., & Sandt, C. (Eds.). (2009). *Advocating for nonresident fathers in child welfare court cases*. American Bar Association.

Connolly, J., Heifetz, M., & Bohr, Y. (2012). Pregnancy and motherhood among adolescent girls in child protective services: A meta-synthesis of qualitative research. *Journal of Public Child Welfare, 6*(5), 614–635. https://doi.org/10.1080/15548732.2012.723970

Courtney, M. E., Hook, J. L., & Lee, J. S. (2012). Distinct subgroups of former foster youth during young adulthood: Implications for policy and practice. *Child Care in Practice, 18*(4), 409–418. https://doi.org/10.1080/13575279.2012.718196

Courtney, M. E., Okpych, N. J., & Park, S. (2018). *Report from CalYOUTH: Findings on the relationship between extended foster care and youth's outcomes at age 21*. Chapin Hall at the University of Chicago. https://www.chapinhall.org/wp-content/uploads/PDF/Impacts-of-extended-care-age-21.pdf

Crawford, B., & Bradley, M. S. (2016). Parent gender and child removal in physical abuse and neglect cases. *Children and Youth Services Review, 65*, 224–230. https://doi.org/10.1016/j.childyouth.2016.04.013

Dominelli, L., Strega, S., Walmsley, C., Callahan, M., & Brown, L. (2011). 'Here's my story': Fathers of 'looked after' children recount their experiences in the Canadian child welfare system. *The British Journal of Social Work, 41*(2), 351–367. https://doi.org/10.1093/bjsw/bcq099

Dow, T. (2019). ICWA and the unwed father: A constitutional corrective. *University of Pennsylvania Law Review, 167*(6), 1513–1562. https://heinonline.org/HOL/P?h=hein.journals/pnlr167&i=1539

Eastman, A. L., Palmer, L., & Ahn, E. (2019). Pregnant and parenting youth in care and their children: A literature review. *Child and Adolescent Social Work Journal, 36*(6), 571–581. https://doi.org/10.1007/s10560-019-00598-8

Enano, S., Freisthler, B., Perez-Johnson, D., & Lovato-Hermann, K. (2017). Evaluating parents in partnership: A preliminary study of a child welfare intervention designed to increase reunification. *Journal of Social Service Research, 43*(2), 236–245. https://doi.org/10.1080/01488376.2016.1253634

English, D. J., Brummel, S., & Martens, P. (2009). Fatherhood in the child welfare system: Evaluation of a pilot project to improve father involvement. *Journal of Public Child Welfare, 3*(3), 213–234. https://doi.org/10.1080/15548730903129764

Fabiano, G. A., Pelham, W. E., Cunningham, C. E., Yu, J., Gangloff, B., Buck, M., Linke, S., Gormley, M., & Gera, S. (2012). A waitlist-controlled trial of behavioral parent training for fathers of children with ADHD. *Journal of Clinical Child & Adolescent Psychology, 41*(3), 337–345. https://doi.org/10.1080/15374416.2012.654464

Fagan, J., & Palkovitz, R. (2019). Coparenting and father engagement among low-income parents: Actor–partner interdependence model. *Journal of Family Psychology, 33*(8), 894–904. https://doi.org/10.1037/fam0000563

Federal Fostering Connections to Success and Increasing Adoptions Act of 2008, P.L. 110-351. https://www.govtrack.us/congress/bills/110/hr6893

Fletcher, R., Freeman, E., & Matthey, S. (2011). The impact of behavioural parent training on fathers' parenting: A meta-analysis of the triple P-positive parenting program. *Fathering: A Journal of Theory, Research, and Practice about Men as Fathers, 9*(3), 291–312. https://doi.org/10.3149/fth.0903.291

Fung, N., Bellamy, J., Abendroth, E., Mittone, D., Bess, R., & Stagner, M. (2021). *A seat at the table: Piloting continuous learning to engage fathers and parental relatives in child welfare* (OPRE Report # 2021-62; pp. 1–151). Office of Planning, Research, and Evaluation, Administration for Children and Families, U.S. Department of Health and Human Services. https://www.acf.hhs.gov/sites/default/files/documents/opre/FCL_Pilot_Study_Report.pdf

Gershater-Molko, R. M., Lutzker, J. R., & Wesch, D. (2003). Project SafeCare: Improving health, safety, and parenting skills in families reported for, and at-risk for child maltreatment. *Journal of Family Violence, 18*(6), 377–386. https://doi.org/10.1023/A:1026219920902

Gibson, S. M., Cryer-Coupet, Q. R., Knox, J. L., & Field, K. (2020). Father involvement in kinship care: A risk and resilience perspective. *Children and Youth Services Review, 119*. https://doi.org/10.1016/j.childyouth.2020.105354

Gordon, D. M., Oliveros, A., Hawes, S. W., Iwamoto, D. K., & Rayford, B. S. (2012). Engaging fathers in child protection services: A review of factors and strategies across ecological systems. *Children and Youth Services Review, 34*(8), 1399–1417. https://doi.org/10.1016/j.childyouth.2012.03.021

Guterman, N. B., Bellamy, J. L., & Banman, A. (2018). Promoting father involvement in early home visiting services for vulnerable families: Findings from a pilot study of "Dads matter". *Child Abuse & Neglect, 76*, 261–272. https://doi.org/10.1016/j.chiabu.2017.10.017

Guterman, N. B., & Lee, Y. (2005). The role of fathers in risk for physical child abuse and neglect: Possible pathways and unanswered questions. *Child Maltreatment, 10*(2), 136–149. https://doi.org/10.1177/1077559505274623

Guterman, N. B., Lee, Y., Lee, S. J., Waldfogel, J., & Rathouz, P. J. (2009). Fathers and maternal risk for physical child abuse. *Child Maltreatment, 14*(3), 277–290. https://doi.org/10.1177/1077559509337893

Harris, M. S., & Hackett, W. (2008). Decision points in child welfare: An action research model to address disproportionality. *Children and Youth Services Review, 30*(2), 199–215. https://doi.org/10.1016/j.childyouth.2007.09.006

Harty, J. S. (2021). Pregnant and parenting foster youth [Book chapter section]. In J. M. Geiger & L. A. Schelbe (Eds.), *Handbook on child welfare practice*. Springer. https://www.springer.com/gp/book/9783030739119

Harty, J. S., & Ethier, K. L. (2022). Fatherhood in Foster Care: A Scoping Review Spanning 30 Years of Research on Expectant and Parenting Fathers in State Care. *Child and Adolescent Social Work Journal, 1–18*. https://doi.org/10.1007/s10560-022-00848-2

Harty, J. S., & Walsh, T. B. (2021). Engaging fathers in child welfare practice [Book chapter section]. In J. M. Geiger & L. A. Schelbe (Eds.), *Handbook on child welfare practice*. Springer. https://www.springer.com/gp/book/9783030739119

Heiner, K. (2017). Are you my father?: Adopting a federal standard for acknowledging or establishing paternity in state court ICWA proceedings. *Columbia Law Review, 117*(8), 2151–2184. https://heinonline.org/HOL/P?h=hein.journals/clr117&i=2247

Hill, R. B. (2004). Institutional racism in child welfare. *Race and Society, 7*(1), 17–33. https://doi.org/10.1016/j.racsoc.2004.11.004

Hindt, L. A., Leon, S. C., & Lurigio, A. J. (2020). Visits with fathers involved in the criminal justice system and behavioral outcomes among children in foster care. *Children and Youth Services Review, 118*, 105371. https://doi.org/10.1016/j.childyouth.2020.105371

Icard, L. D., Fagan, J., Lee, Y., & Rutledge, S. E. (2017). Father's involvement in the lives of children in foster care. *Child & Family Social Work, 22*(1), 57–66. https://doi.org/10.1111/cfs.12196

Indian Child Welfare Act of 1978, P.L. 95–608. https://www.govtrack.us/congress/bills/95/s1214/text

Jaffe, E. D. (1983). Fathers and child welfare services: The forgotten client. In M. E. Lamb & A. Sagi (Eds.), *Fatherhood and family policy* (pp. 129–137). Routledge.

Jeynes, W. H. (2017). A meta-analysis: The relationship between parental involvement and Latino student outcomes. *Education and Urban Society, 49*(1), 4–28. https://doi.org/10.1177/0013124516630596

Johnson, W. E., Jr. (2004). Unwed african american fathers' participation in child welfare permanency planning. In V. D. Bryant, J. Everett, S. S. Chipungu, S. P. Chipungu, & B. R. Leashore (Eds.), *Child welfare revisited: An Africentric perspective* (p. 169). Rutgers University Press.

Kim, J., Trahan, M., Bellamy, J., & Hall, J. A. (2019). Advancing the innovation of family meeting models: The role of teamwork and parent engagement in improving permanency. *Children and Youth Services Review, 100*, 147–155. https://doi.org/10.1016/j.childyouth.2019.02.039

Kobulsky, J. M., Wildfeuer, R., Yoon, S., & Cage, J. (2021). Distinguishing characteristics and disparities in child protective services-investigated maltreatment by fathers. *Child Maltreatment, 26*(2), 182–194. https://doi.org/10.1177/1077559520950828

Lamb, M. E., Pleck, J. H., Charnov, E. L., & Levine, J. A. (1987). A biosocial perspective on paternal behavior and involvement. In J. B. Lancaster, J. Altmann, A. S. Rossi, & L. R. Sherrod (Eds.), *Parenting across the life span: Biosocial dimensions (pp. 111–142). Aldine Publishing Co.*

Lee, S. J., Bellamy, J. L., & Guterman, N. B. (2009). Fathers, physical child abuse, and neglect: Advancing the knowledge base. *Child Maltreatment, 14*(3), 227–231. https://doi.org/10.1177/1077559509339388

Lee, Y., Fagan, J. S., & Icard, L. D. (2018). Nonresidential fathers with children in foster care: A descriptive study in the United States. *Child & Family Social Work, 23*(2), 146–154. https://doi.org/10.1111/cfs.12393

Loman, A., & Siegel, G. L. (2005). Alternative response in Minnesota: Findings of the program evaluation. *Protecting Children, 20*(2/3), 78–92. https://citeseerx.ist.psu.edu/viewdoc/download?doi=10.1.1.577.5639&rep=rep1&type=pdf

Lundahl, B., McDonald, C., & Vanderloo, M. (2020). Service users' perspectives of child welfare services: A systematic review using the practice model as a guide. *Journal of Public Child Welfare, 14*(2), 174–191. https://doi.org/10.1080/15548732.2018.1548406

Magill-Evans, J., Harrison, M., Benzies, K., Gierl, M., & Kimak, C. (2007). Effects of parenting education on first-time fathers' skills in interactions with their infants. *Fathering: A Journal of Theory, Research, and Practice about Men as Fathers, 5*(1), 42–57. https://doi.org/10.3149/fth.0501.42

Mallette, J. K., Futris, T. G., & Schramm, D. G. (2017). Fostering a culture of family-centred care: Child welfare professionals' beliefs about fathers, family instability, and the value of relationship education. *Child & Family Social Work.* https://doi.org/10.1111/cfs.12422

Malm, K. E., Murray, J., & Geen, R. (2006). *What about the dads? Child welfare agencies' efforts to identify, locate and involve nonresident fathers*. The U.S. Department of Health and Human Services, Office of the Assistant Secretary for Planning and Evaluation, Urban Institute.

Malm, K. E., & Zielewski, E. H. (2009). Nonresident father support and reunification outcomes for children in foster care. *Children and Youth Services Review, 31*(9), 1010–1018. https://doi.org/10.1016/j.childyouth.2009.04.016

Maluccio, A. N. (2006). The nature and scope of the problem. In N. B. Webb (Ed.), *Working with traumatized youth in child welfare* (pp. 3–12). Guilford Press.

Maxwell, N., Scourfield, J., Featherstone, B., Holland, S., & Tolman, R. (2012a). Engaging fathers in child welfare services: A narrative review of recent research evidence. *Child & Family Social Work, 17*(2), 160–169. https://doi.org/10.1111/j.1365-2206.2012.00827.x

Maxwell, N., Scourfield, J., Holland, S., Featherstone, B., & Lee, J. (2012b). The benefits and challenges of training child protection social workers in father engagement. *Child Abuse Review, 21*(4), 299–310. https://doi.org/10.1002/car.2218

Mincy, R., Garfinkel, I., & Nepomnyaschy, L. (2005). In-hospital paternity establishment and father involvement in fragile families. *Journal of Marriage and Family, 67*(3), 611–626. https://doi.org/10.1111/j.1741-3737.2005.00157.x

Nievar, M. A., Ramisetty-Mikler, S., Saleh, M. F., & Cabrera, N. (2020). Families offering children unfailing support (FOCUS) fatherhood program: Changing child welfare through child support and parenting skills. *Children and Youth Services Review, 118*, 105321. https://doi.org/10.1016/j.childyouth.2020.105321

O'Donnell, J. M. (1999). Involvement of African American fathers in kinship foster care services. *Social Work, 44*(5), 428–441. https://doi.org/10.1093/sw/44.5.428

O'Donnell, J. M., Johnson, W. E., D'Aunno, L. E., & Thornton, H. L. (2005). Fathers in child welfare: Caseworkers' perspectives. *Child Welfare, 84*(3), 387–414.
Omnibus Budget Reconciliation Act of 1993, P.L. 103-66. https://www.govtrack.us/congress/bills/103/hr2264
Palkovitz, R. (1997). Reconstructing "involvement": Expanding conceptualizations of men's caring in contemporary families. In A. J. Hawkins & D. C. Dollahite (Eds.), *Generative fathering: Beyond deficit perspectives (pp. 200–216). SAGE Publications.*
Pate, D. (2005). African American fathers and their involvement in the child welfare system. In G. P. Mallon & P. M. Hess (Eds.), *Child welfare for the twenty-first century: A handbook of practices, policies, & programs* (pp. 635–654). Columbia University Press.
Personal Responsibility and Work Opportunity Act of 1996, P.L. 104–193. https://www.govtrack.us/congress/bills/104/hr3734
Pfitzner, N., Humphreys, C., & Hegarty, K. (2017). Research review: Engaging men: A multi-level model to support father engagement: A multi-level model of father engagement. *Child & Family Social Work, 22*(1), 537–547. https://doi.org/10.1111/cfs.12250
Pruett, M. K., Cowan, P. A., Cowan, C. P., Gillette, P., & Pruett, K. D. (2019). Supporting father involvement: An intervention with community and child welfare-referred couples. *Family Relations, 68*(1), 51–67. https://doi.org/10.1111/fare.12352
Putnam-Hornstein, E., Hammond, I., Eastman, A. L., McCroskey, J., & Webster, D. (2016). Extended foster care for transition-age youth: An opportunity for pregnancy prevention and parenting support. *Journal of Adolescent Health, 58*(4), 485–487. https://doi.org/10.1016/j.jadohealth.2015.11.015
Russell, J., & Summers, A. (2013). An overview of the courts catalyzing change preliminary protective hearing benchcard study: Benchcard study. *Juvenile and Family Court Journal, 64*(2), 1–16. https://doi.org/10.1111/jfcj.12003
Sarkadi, A., Kristiansson, R., Oberklaid, F., & Bremberg, S. (2008). Fathers' involvement and children's developmental outcomes: A systematic review of longitudinal studies. *Acta Paediatrica, 97*(2), 153–158. https://doi.org/10.1111/j.1651-2227.2007.00572.x
Schweitzer, D. D., Pecora, P. J., Nelson, K., Walters, B., & Blythe, B. J. (2015). Building the evidence base for intensive family preservation services. *Journal of Public Child Welfare, 9*(5), 423–443. https://doi.org/10.1080/15548732.2015.1090363
Scourfield, J. (2001). Constructing men in child protection work. *Men and Masculinities, 4*(1), 70–89. https://doi.org/10.1177/1097184X01004001004
Scourfield, J. (2006). The challenge of engaging fathers in the child protection process. *Critical Social Policy, 26*(2), 440–449. https://doi.org/10.1177/0261018306062594
Scourfield, J. (2014). Improving work with fathers to prevent child maltreatment. *Child Abuse & Neglect, 38*(6), 974–981. https://doi.org/10.1016/j.chiabu.2014.05.002
Scourfield, J., Tolman, R., Maxwell, N., Holland, S., Bullock, A., & Sloan, L. (2012). Results of a training course for social workers on engaging fathers in child protection. *Children and Youth Services Review, 34*(8), 1425–1432. https://doi.org/10.1016/j.childyouth.2012.03.022
Self-Brown, S., Osborne, M. C., Lai, B. S., De Veauuse Brown, N., Glasheen, T. L., & Adams, M. C. (2017). Initial findings from a feasibility trial examining the SafeCare Dad to Kids Program with marginalized fathers. *Journal of Family Violence, 32*(8), 751–766. https://doi.org/10.1007/s10896-017-9940-5
Shadik, J. A. (2020). Fathering and child maltreatment: Understanding the impact of fluidity in fathers' lives. *Journal of Family Social Work, 23*(3), 257–276. https://doi.org/10.1080/10522158.2020.1725794
Smith, C. (2018). Establishing paternity under the Indian Child Welfare Act. *Brigham Young University Law Review, 2018*(6), 1451–1490. https://heinonline.org/HOL/P?h=hein.journals/byulr2018&i=1501
Svoboda, D. V., Shaw, T. V., Barth, R. P., & Bright, C. L. (2012). Pregnancy and parenting among youth in foster care: A review. *Children and Youth Services Review, 34*(5), 867–875. https://doi.org/10.1016/j.childyouth.2012.01.023

Trahan, M., Kim, J., Bellamy, J., & Hall, J. (2020). Parenting engagement in foster care placement stability and permanency. *Journal of the Society for Social Work and Research, 11*(2), 211–236. https://doi.org/10.1086/709536

Tully, L. A., Collins, D. A. J., Piotrowska, P. J., Mairet, K. S., Hawes, D. J., Moul, C., Lenroot, R. K., Frick, P. J., Anderson, V. A., Kimonis, E. R., & Dadds, M. R. (2018). Examining practitioner competencies, organizational support and barriers to engaging fathers in parenting interventions. *Child Psychiatry & Human Development, 49*(1), 109–122. https://doi.org/10.1007/s10578-017-0733-0

Weems, C. F., Rouse, H. L., Melby, J. N., Jeon, S., Goudy, K., McCurdy, B. H., & Stanek, A. R. (2020). A partnership approach to paternity establishment: Child welfare research and training project ecological model and preliminary data. *Families in Society: The Journal of Contemporary Social Services, 101*(2), 180–189. https://doi.org/10.1177/1044389419892273

Whitaker, D. J., Self-Brown, S., Hayat, M. J., Osborne, M. C., Weeks, E. A., Reidy, D. E., & Lyons, M. (2020). Effect of the SafeCare intervention on parenting outcomes among parents in child welfare systems: A cluster randomized trial. *Preventive Medicine, 138*, 106167. https://doi.org/10.1016/j.ypmed.2020.106167

Wilder Research. (2010). *Return on investment to the FATHER Project* (pp. 1–34). Goodwill, Easter Seals Minnesota. https://www.wilder.org/sites/default/files/imports/Goodwill_FatherProject_ROI_10-10.pdf

Yampolskaya, S., Armstrong, M. I., Strozier, A., & Swanke, J. (2017). Can the actions of child welfare case managers predict case outcomes? *Child Abuse & Neglect, 64*, 61–70. https://doi.org/10.1016/j.chiabu.2016.12.007

Yoon, S., Bellamy, J. L., Kim, W., & Yoon, D. (2018). Father involvement and behavior problems among preadolescents at risk of maltreatment. *Journal of Child and Family Studies, 27*(2), 494–504. https://doi.org/10.1007/s10826-017-0890-6

Zanoni, L., Warburton, W., Bussey, K., & McMaugh, A. (2013). Fathers as 'core business' in child welfare practice and research: An interdisciplinary review. *Children and Youth Services Review, 35*(7), 1055–1070. https://doi.org/10.1016/j.childyouth.2013.04.018

Zanoni, L., Warburton, W., Bussey, K., & McMaugh, A. (2014). Are all fathers in child protection families uncommitted, uninvolved and unable to change? *Children and Youth Services Review, 41*, 83–94. https://doi.org/10.1016/j.childyouth.2014.03.014

Chapter 12
Father-Friendly School Interventions: Helping Schools Create Engagement Opportunities

Terrance Ruth

Introduction

Fathers are underutilized assets within the education system. As a result, schools are attempting to find the best ways to support positive father engagement. There are many factors that contribute to the varying levels of father engagement, such as school demographics, household income, and family size, among others (Gershy & Omer, 2017). This chapter explores the concept of father engagement within school systems and the ways in which schools can better understand the barriers and opportunities to engage fathers.

There are clear benefits to creating father engagement, a partnership between fathers and schools, to produce positive student outcomes. Partnerships can increase the proximity between fathers and educators and reduce any inaccurate assumptions there may be, potentially empowering fathers' voices in important domains and increasing their direct impact on learning outcomes (Park & Holloway, 2018). Engaged fathers can be key partners with education and support professionals, bring skills and expertise to the enterprise, offer different perspectives on issues, increase available resources, serve as sources of support in difficult times, and help achieve mutual goals. Students certainly benefit from father engagement, but it is important to highlight that schools benefit as well. While educators may have expertise in content and pedagogy, fathers' knowledge of their own children can be extremely helpful to teachers as they try to meet their students' needs. Fathers can also help educators view their schools from a distinctive father perspective. When fathers view the school in a positive way, they are more likely to provide the necessary time, engagement, and support for quality education.

T. Ruth (✉)
North Carolina State University, Raleigh, NC, USA
e-mail: trruth@ncsu.edu

J. L. Bellamy et al. (eds.), *Social Work Practice with Fathers*,
https://doi.org/10.1007/978-3-031-13686-3_12

Father engagement in schooling is an important and meaningful, albeit partial, predictor of educational success and well-being. In general, research suggests that it has positive effects on academic achievement and educational attainment in addition to reducing the likelihood of dropout and behavioral problems for children at various stages of their life course (Child Trends, 2013; Higgins & Katsipataki, 2015; Jeynes, 2011; Kim & Hill, 2015). An important challenge for education practitioners is designing a father-friendly school environment that promotes father engagement as a way to optimize the benefits of parenting interventions for children's well-being.

Background and Context

Fathers' engagement with their children's schooling increases children's academic achievement (Fan & Chen, 2001; Jeynes, 2005; Keith et al., 1998; Sui-Chu & Willms, 1996; Yan & Lin, 2005), particularly in primary school and among younger children. Boosting fathers' involvement may thus contribute to the reduction of negative student outcomes, in general, and ethnic educational inequality, specifically (Lee & Bowen, 2006; Turney & Kao, 2009).

The literature on parental involvement with their children's schooling agrees that father engagement is a multidimensional construct (e.g., Fan & Chen, 2001; Garcia Coll et al., 2002; Keith et al., 1998; Sui-Chu & Willms, 1996). Many different definitions and operationalizations of father engagement have been used. The widely cited model of Hoover-Dempsey and Sandler (1995, 1997; Hoover-Dempsey et al. 2005, see also Green et al., 2007) emphasizes the importance of distinguishing between home- and school-based forms of engagement (see also Sui-Chu & Willms, 1996). The first includes activities such as reading to the child and monitoring their homework, whereas the latter refers to activities such as contact with teachers and volunteering for school-based activities. According to the typology of parental involvement developed by Epstein (1986), school-based engagement is sometimes further divided into parent-teacher contact (e.g., talking to the child's teacher or attending a Parent Teacher Association (PTA) conference) and engagement in school activities (e.g., volunteering or accompanying a school trip). In their comparison of Latino, Black, and White parents in the United States, Lee and Bowen (2006) pointed out that distinguishing between different dimensions of father engagement is important as ethnic differences can be more significant on some dimensions than on others. The differences may reflect possible cultural variations in how fathers conceive positive involvement with their children in school settings. For instance, they found that Latino and Black fathers had lower levels of school-based but not home-based engagement than White parents.

Education psychologists emphasize the role of motivation for fathers' involvement with their children's schooling (Hoover-Dempsey et al., 2005). In this model, the motivation to become involved includes constructing an active role for oneself and perceiving self-efficacy ("I can contribute to the schooling of my child"), life circumstances that hamper or facilitate involvement, and the perception that the school appreciates parental involvement (Hoover-Dempsey et al., 2005). The most important psychological antecedents of this motivation thus relate to parents' construction of the parental role and their perceived efficacy in contributing to their children's schooling. Parenting roles refer to parents' ideas of their own engagement and the school's responsibility for their child's educational outcomes. Parents can construct their role as active and cooperative, perceiving their child's schooling as a responsibility shared between themselves and the school, or as passive, ceding responsibility and authority for their child's education to the school. In addition, parents are less likely to be involved if they feel they lack the skills to help their children with their schoolwork. This perceived efficacy is a specific form of general self-efficacy that reflects the individual's belief in their ability to affect or change their life outcomes (Bandura, 2010). Empirical research has found that parental involvement is greater among parents who construct their parental role as more active (Green et al., 2007) and report greater self-efficacy regarding their child's schooling (Green et al., 2007; Waanders et al., 2007). Therefore, self-efficacy and parenting goals are typically associated with father involvement. Also, it is assumed that there is a positive association between general self-efficacy and father involvement.

Furthermore, fathers who value obedience in their children are likely to expect their children to obey teachers as well. They are more likely to be more susceptible to authority and therefore to cede responsibility for their children's education to the school, resulting in lower levels of father involvement. In contrast, the more fathers strive for autonomy in their children, the more they are expected to be involved to facilitate their children's flourishing in cooperation with their teachers. Father involvement is believed to be positively related to the parenting goal of autonomy and negatively to obedience.

Despite the central importance of the psychological antecedents of motivation for father involvement, fathers additionally need skills and knowledge to engage with their children's education (Green et al., 2007). In the case of immigrant fathers, proficiency in the school language is a crucial resource, the lack of which may pose a severe barrier to parental engagement (Garcia Coll et al., 2002; Turney & Kao, 2009). For example, immigrant fathers with low levels of language proficiency are less likely to maintain contact with the school and engage in school activities, and they are also less well equipped to help their children with their schoolwork. In addition to language proficiency, education level is the most widely used indicator for parental skills and knowledge and has been found to be related to father engagement (e.g., Kohl et al., 2000; but for divergent findings relating to socioeconomic status, see Sui-Chu & Willms, 1996). Schools equate fathers' knowledge and skills with the highest level of education they have achieved and their proficiency in the English language, and the expectations are that both indicators positively relate to father engagement.

The motivation for father engagement may be restricted by the time and energy available to fathers. Single-father status is known to be a risk factor for lower father engagement (Kohl et al., 2000; Waanders et al., 2007) as single fathers are unable to share the need to attend to work, household chores, and their children's education with a partner. Similarly, following the resource dilution theory (Downey, 2001), it is suggested that the more children in the household, the less likely fathers are to be involved in the schooling of a specific child in the traditional understanding of parental involvement. Long work hours may also limit a father's involvement with their child's schooling, so both the presence of a partner and the number of children in the household provide context to father engagement.

Conceptual Framework

For theoretical considerations relevant to improving father engagement, *contact theory* (Allport, 1954) is a useful framework for understanding fathers' goals for parental school engagement. Although Allport constructed this theoretical framework around racism and racial conflict, it provides a unique lens for addressing the differences between groups. Contact theory hypothesizes that increases in positive attitudes about father engagement require learning environments that allow for contact between members of *in-groups* (e.g., teachers, principals, etc.) and *out-groups* (e.g., fathers, underrepresented groups, ethnic minorities, families with low socioeconomic status (SES)). The in-group is usually associated with the members who have access, influence, or leverage in a particular circumstance. In education, such power, access, and influence have traditionally resided with the professionals within the school buildings. The out-group is usually associated with the members who have reduced access, reduced representation, and reduced influence. In recent education history, fathers have become representatives of the individuals who have reduced representation and reduced engagement in learning communities. The assumption in this framework is that an increase in direct or indirect contact between the in-group and out-group will impact the existing intergroup perceptions and relationships.

According to Allport's contact theory, for intergroup contact to result in increased father access or increased engagement, groups must be of equal status and participate in cooperative rather than competitive tasks focused on achieving mutual goals, and intergroup interactions must be supported by decision-making individuals or structures (e.g., administrators, teachers, etc.). The legacy of the long-standing reduced representation of fathers in learning environments is not only seen as evidence of an imbalance but also in that the in-group benefits from a socially uneven education system that shifts more power for education professionals than it allows for fathers, especially of other racial minority groups (out-groups). Any effective father-friendly promotion strategy should therefore pay close attention to a systemic unrepresented father environment and the social structures inevitably present in all facets of non-father-friendly education communities and avoid inadvertently replicating those dynamics in the intervention strategy. In extending the work of Allport, authors Brewer and Miller (1988) found that there is a need to personalize the contact between the in-group (school professionals) and the out-group (fathers) such that persons from both groups can evaluate their relative similarities and differences as individuals and not merely as representative members of a group. For example, Katz and Zalk (1978) found that teaching children to individualize the faces of underrepresented group members was associated with a reduction in prejudice in high-prejudice children. Pettigrew (1998) supported the notion that the reduction of negative perceptions depends on the contact being personally meaningful and the extent to which the newly learned information can be generalized to new out-group members, new situations, and, finally, new out-groups.

Critics of contact theory, however, charge that changes in attitudes do not automatically result in behavioral changes as Allport (1954) originally proposed (Emerson et al., 2002). Dixon et al. (2005) found that reduced negative perceptions toward one member of an out-group did not automatically generalize toward other members of the out-group. We can extend that reasoning to hypothesize that reducing negative perceptions toward one out-group may not generalize into reduced negative perceptions toward other out-groups. Pettigrew (1998) noted that the original conditions of equal status, cooperation, and working toward a common goal do not adequately address the process by which prejudgments of fathers would be reduced. However, improved perceptions may be one step toward an increased perceived value of their potential contribution to the school environment and, ultimately, well-being for all students.

Barriers to Father Engagement in Schools

A substantial portion of the early research on father engagement was limited to White middle-class men who resided with their children (Marsiglio et al., 2000). Schools will need to embrace a more inclusive and less rigid perspective of positive father engagement that excludes both cultural deficit frameworks and nonresident parenting. Potential barriers concerning father engagement center a deficit narrative around the lack of engagement of fathers, with an emphasis on minoritized fathers. Research suggests that a lack of achievement motivation is unlikely to be the primary cause of minoritized fathers' lower levels of engagement (Fleischmann & Kristen, 2016). Other possible explanations for ethnic differences in father engagement may be connected to level of education and language proficiency as indicators of knowledge and skills (Fleischmann & Kristen, 2016). It is important to evaluate household resources, namely, the presence of a partner, the number of children in the household, and working hours, as indicators of the time and energy available for father engagement as these factors are known to differ across ethnic groups and SES.

The last critical variable that may impact engagement levels is the direct negative experiences of sons, fathers, and grandfathers while in the role of student or teacher in K-12 education. For example, a father who experienced negative racially motivated incidents while a student will more than likely share his stories with his children. That father may also disengage from education professionals and school activities. On the other hand, fathers who were celebrated while a student would more than likely have positive stories to share with their children. Generational experiences will influence how fathers embrace schools' efforts to create father-friendly environments that promote school-wide father engagement. The harmful generational experiences of fathers often include segregation and isolation based on racial demographics.

Historians have well documented the long and difficult journey of Native, Latinx, and African American students and teachers. Since the inception of formal education institutions, many non-White fathers have experienced negative generational segregation or isolation within schools. The effects of segregating generations of Native, Latinx, and African American students and teachers must be considered a possible negative influence on the current engagement efforts of fathers. In the nineteenth century, there was a deliberate crusade to fundamentally alter the Native American way of life, utilizing instruction as a means of installing new values and behavior on a scale not exercised with other groups (Rury, 2016). As historian David Wallace Adams poignantly observed, it was "education for extinction" (Adams, 1995). Similar threads of isolation and segregation by formal education institutions occurred for African Americans.

Education has long been a major theme in African American culture. Dating from the early nineteenth century, Black leaders emphasized the significance of schools as instruments of social uplift (Bond, 1966). Historically, all Blacks recognized that a lack of education was a mark of inferiority, one that seemed to legitimate their servile status and insure their political impotence (Bullock, 1967). When slavery was formally abolished, African Americans rushed to educate their children as schooling was seen as the road out of servitude. Themes of resistance and redemption predominate in the history of Black education in the United States (Blassingame, 1972). Formal education was typically denied to slaves, except for the training afforded by masters interested in owning skilled workers or lessons learned in church (Mintz, 2004).

After the Civil War ended in 1865, the federal government created the Freedman's Bureau, an organization charged with supervising the transition of former slaves to their new status as free citizens (Webber, 1978). A major aspect of the new agency's task was to provide schools for the freedmen, to give them critical literacy skills and citizenship education (Curry, 1981). Local African American communities donated hard-earned cash and labor to establish more schools and expand upon the government contributions (Dubois, 1935), proof of their motivation, and confidence in education. At the time, the culture focused on men and boys as the recipients of education and citizenship, who would then lead a liberalized community (Dubois, 1935; Foner, 1988; Franklin, 1961).

Unfortunately, by the late 1870s, there were abundant signs that the federal protection of Black Americans was declining, which marked an end to the expansion of the Black schooling experience (Foner & Mahoney, 1995). Southern Whites, in particular, were never enamored of Black education, and even if they did not dismantle the schools established for Blacks in the United States, they were not willing to provide them with anything more than the most basic resources. There was a belief that the cultivated White students deserved the bulk of the school resources (VanOverbeke, 2008). Several historians have documented that the decades following Reconstruction marked a time of widening disparities in Black and White education, and that trend continues in states across the country. For example, in North Carolina, more than two decades ago, five school districts in the state filed a lawsuit, *Leandro v. the State of North Carolina*. In a landmark decision in 1997, the Supreme Court of North Carolina unanimously affirmed that the state has a constitutional responsibility to provide every student—including those who are at risk, or from rural or underserved communities—with an equal opportunity for a sound, basic education (Townsend et al., 2019), Yet, 20 years later, it was documented that the state of North Carolina had not yet met its obligation to provide education that meets this constitutional standard (4). The Leandro report was released in response to the case, and it documented the racial disparities across four areas: access to effective educators, access to effective school leaders, adequate and equitable school funding and other resources, and adequate accountability and assessment systems (Willis et al., 2019). As school leaders evaluate father engagement, it is important to distinguish between levels of school engagement and levels of home engagement. As mentioned earlier, researchers found that Latino and Black American parents had lower levels of school-based but not of home-based engagement than White American parents. It is important to remember that the experiences of non-White fathers during their own childhood, the K-12 years of learning, may contribute to racial disparities in school-based engagement for their children, not to mention other potential engagement barriers. Schools can benefit from a range of interventions and recommendations that include culturally sensitive strategies to improve father engagement for all fathers.

Father Engagement Interventions

Recommendations for systemic father-friendly interventions in schools need to point toward the development of effective intervention strategies based on prevention science (e.g., Hage et al., 2007; Reese & Vera, 2007) and contact theory.

Interaction

Provide opportunities for personally meaningful, intensive, cooperative, and repetitive interactions among members of different groups (Allport, 1954; Pettigrew, 1998). Effective programs have been shown to be "intensive, multicomponent, and multilevel" (Durlak, 1995, p. 84). Schools can look at opportunities to provide meaningful, intensive, cooperative, and repetitive interactions with fathers for the purpose of encouraging increased engagement with students.

Intervention

Engage intervention school staff, helping professionals, fathers, and community leaders in modeling positive father-friendly relationships for the broader community (Allport, 1954; Bandura, 2010). Involve education professionals, vendors, and district staff, and provide additional support for prevention strategies (e.g., Shepard & Carlson, 2003).

Training

Include trainings with concrete information about specific cultural and ethnic groups (e.g., history and customs; Pettigrew, 1998) as well as development of general reasoning skills to apply to new situations and new group differences (e.g., questioning racial stereotypes as they pertain to fathering, understanding oppression and how it is perpetuated in today's society; London et al., 2002). Education practitioners can aid this process by facilitating small group discussions in which participants can discuss stereotypes, prejudice, cultural assumptions, and access and how those social indicators affect the engagement of certain fathers (Dixon et al., 2005).

Discussion

Create safe environments for honest discussions about father engagement. Discussing father-friendly learning communities can evoke difficult emotions that may hinder the promotion of positive father-school relationships (Stephan & Stephen, 1992). Facing the root cause of reduced father engagement often elicits apathy, anxiety, anger, and withdrawal in families (D'Andrea, 2005). The education professionals leading the systemic father-friendly intervention strategies will need to be skilled in managing difficult emotions and creating an atmosphere in which individuals can discuss negative reactions such as anxiety, confusion, shame, and even anger and learn how to cope with them in order to facilitate positive outcomes of intergroup contact at all levels of leadership within the field of education.

Facilitating

Facilitating age-appropriate discussions about common human experiences, cultural differences, and cultural stigmas that promote intergroup dislike of fathers may assist education practitioners in developing sophisticated cognitive skills necessary to build a more inclusive father-friendly learning community. Learning facts about fathers (including negative community impact evaluations, negative stereotypes, and perceptions about different father ethnic groups), creating emotional connections with fathers (e.g., increasing empathy, perspective-taking ability, and forming close partnerships with communities with underrepresented fathers), and, finally, revising previously held beliefs about fathers would increase the likelihood of reducing negative perceptions.

School volunteer policy interventions are examples of environment-centered prevention. From an ecological perspective (Bronfenbrenner, 1979), school policy advocacy is designed to affect the individual's macro-systems, which will eventually trickle down to affect change at the meso- and microsystems. Using Jones's (1997) typology framework, environment-centered prevention is aimed at eliminating institutional and cultural perceptions of fathers. One focus for environment-centered prevention approaches involves intervention to impact those decision makers who shape the microsystem.

Fathers as Partners

There are clear benefits to creating an effective partnership between fathers and schools. Partnerships can increase the proximity between fathers and educators and reduce any inaccurate assumptions about fathers. Also, the increase in proximity is supported by the theoretical framework of contact theory. To increase father engagement, the school must empower fathers' voices outside of schools and increase father representation inside the school, as partners. A partner can bring specific skills and expertise to the enterprise, offer a different perspective on issues, increase available resources, serve as a source of support in difficult times, and help to achieve mutual goals.

Furthermore, fathers who are positive about a school can serve as advocates for its recruitment of more fathers and contribute to its overall improvement of father engagement efforts. As Patrick Dolan (1994) writes, "If (fathers) are with you, they will bring the community with them. If they are not, they will stop you ... You need their protection when hostile winds begin to blow" (p. 157). Fathers are often called to address discipline issues or incidents that are corrective in nature. However, schools can benefit by establishing a positive relationship with fathers and engaging them on the strengths of their children. The first contact with fathers should support the positive image of their child. Finally, while there may be differences of opinion, fathers and educators share the same goal—the eventual success of the child. Thus, fathers represent a potentially powerful ally in the effort to create a school that functions as a professional learning community.

Father Engagement Strategies

The National Parent Teacher Association (PTA) has an excellent framework to adopt for the use of customizing strategies to improve father engagement. The PTA framework was developed by the Center on School, Family, and Community Partnerships to identify national standards for parental involvement. These standards have been endorsed by many professional organizations, including the American Federation of Teachers, the National Education Association, the National Association of Secondary School Principals, the National Middle School Association, and the National School Board Association. The standards fall into six categories described in Table 12.1.

Category 1 Communication

Communication between fathers and the school should be regular, two-way, and meaningful. Frequent two-way communication is critical to any partnership. Partners require communication that allows for a sharing of ideas and concerns, the establishment of mutual goals, clarification of expectations, and regular follow-up (Table 12.2).

Research indicates that when fathers receive frequent, positive, and effective communication from their children's school, their involvement increases, their overall evaluation of educators is more favorable, and their attitudes toward the school and its programs improve. Therefore, schools should strive to improve the rate and effectiveness of their communication with fathers, mindful of the fact that fathers want to be a part of their child's success.

Table 12.1 Father engagement categories: understanding father-friendly schools

Standard	Description
Category 1 *Communication*	Communication between the father and school is regular, two-way, and meaningful.
Category 2 *Fatherhood*	Fathering skills are promoted and supported.
Category 3 *Student learning*	Fathers play an integral role in assisting student learning.
Category 4 *Volunteer*	Fathers are welcome in the school, and their support and assistance are sought.
Category 5 *Decision-making*	Fathers are full partners in the decisions that affect their children.
Category 6 *Collaboration*	Community resources are used to strengthen schools, families, and students.

Table 12.2 Father engagement strategies: creating father-friendly schools

Strategy	Description
Clarity	Provide fathers with clear information regarding course expectations and offerings, student placement, school activities, student services, and optional programs.
Convenience	Establish times for conferences that are convenient for working fathers.
Routine	Develop routine procedures to allow fathers to review the work of their children on a regular basis with their input.
Expectations	Clarify what fathers can expect from the school, what the school asks of them, and how they can raise any concerns or questions.
Technology	Use the technological communication tool that is most ideal for the father rather than defaulting to the comfort of the education professional. Also, consider language barriers in selecting the technology of choice.
Feedback	Schools need to constantly seek fathers' opinions on the operation of the school through annual surveys or class assignments that ask students to survey fathers about the school and areas needing improvement.
Forums	Create a variety of forums for parents to discuss their ideas and concerns with educators. These might include such activities as parent breakfasts or luncheons located in a community setting that is most comfortable for fathers.
News	Phone a randomly selected sampling of fathers and ask them to provide the best platform for the school to share news and updates about future activities.

Category 2 Fatherhood

Fathering skills are promoted and supported. Fathers offer educators valuable information and insights about their children, but they can also benefit from the expertise of educators who are likely to be more familiar with the general characteristics of children at different ages. A father may be an expert on his daughter but may not be an expert on what his daughter is going through during the middle school years (Table 12.3).

Almost every father has occasionally felt overwhelmed and outmatched while raising a child. Most will welcome culturally informed research-based information on fathering, and schools are within a network that could provide them with that information.

Category 3 Student Learning

Fathers can play an important role in assisting student learning by helping at home. However, most fathers need guidance on how they can be most helpful. Everyone benefits when schools explain to fathers the skills their children are to learn and provide specific strategies they can use to participate in their child's development of those skills. Fathers can be more engaged if schools:

Table 12.3 Tools for schools to engage fathers

Tools	Description
Resources	Support fathers with training, resources, and other services.
Programs	Provide workshops or programs that help fathers with parenting issues such as communication, discipline, peer pressure, study habits, drug and alcohol abuse, single parenting, etc.
Support	Provide transportation and childcare services to encourage fathers to attend these workshops and programs.
Expectations	Offer fathers suggestions for establishing expectations and routines with their children. For example, student achievement is correlated with three factors that parents can control: preventing student absenteeism, having reading materials in the home, and limiting noneducational screen viewing.
Networks	Link fathers to programs and resources within the community that provide support services to families.

- Inform fathers of the specific learning expectations for students in each subject at each grade level.
- Provide fathers of elementary and middle school children with school-developed curriculum guides and learning packets for each course or grade level that suggest how fathers can foster learning of concepts at home.
- Develop procedures that enable fathers to monitor homework, provide appropriate assistance, and give feedback to teachers.
- Provide a multi-virtual platform homework hotline that offers fathers reminders of the homework that has been assigned and suggestions for helping students complete homework.
- Assign interactive homework that will require students to discuss and interact with their fathers about what they are learning in class.
- Involve fathers in setting student goals each year and in planning for postsecondary education and careers.
- Ask fathers to take an active role in reviewing student portfolios according to standards articulated in a scoring rubric.
- Suggest recommended books that fathers might read aloud to their children or encourage their children to read for themselves.

Fathers represent the unutilized labor force of schooling (Grestner & O'Day, 1994). They could reinforce what students are learning if schools would simply provide them with the information, materials, and guidance that will enable them to function, with autonomy, as teacher aides in their own homes.

Category 4 Volunteering

Fathers are welcome in schools and their support and assistance are sought. Both the financial and human resources of most schools are already overburdened as educators struggle to achieve their goals and meet the needs of each student. Father volunteers represent an asset in that struggle. Furthermore, father volunteers are more likely to express confidence in the school and serve as its advocates and engage in fundraising projects for sports equipment, new computers, playground equipment, and sport uniforms, for example. The most effective step a school can take is to create a position for a father coordinator. The impact of using funds to provide a stipend for an individual who will recruit and coordinate father volunteer services to the school and coach fathers on how to engage their children would be worth every penny. If teachers and administrators are creative in how they are used, father volunteers can contribute a great deal to the overall student well-being. Furthermore, this increased father contact can provide moments for improved father engagement.

Category 5 Making Decisions

Fathers should be fully engaged and empowered to participate in the decisions that affect their children. Engagement of fathers works best when there is a mutual respect between the school and fathers around the decision-making process. When schools view fathers as empowered partners and engage them in decision-making processes, they realize higher levels of student achievement and greater public support. The involvement of fathers, as individuals or as representatives of others, is beneficial in collaborative decision-making processes on issues ranging from course selection and discipline policies to school-wide improvement initiatives. Fathers can be more productive if they are engaged as empowered decision makers (Table 12.4).

As shared in the testimonials described in Table 12.5, fathers are more likely to feel ownership in a school and its programs when they have a voice in key decisions. This is especially true for fathers who historically felt ignored by learning communities. Schools must use decision-making processes that solicit fathers' input and provide fathers with the information they need to make informed decisions.

Category 6 Collaboration

Community resources are used to strengthen schools, fathers, and student learning. If a father-school partnership relies exclusively on the talents and assets of its partners, it will severely limit what it might accomplish. Father-school partnerships need to establish networks with people of similar interests as well as with specialists who offer unique expertise or resources that are beneficial to the partnership. While fathers and schools should form an active partnership, they should not overlook or exclude other individuals or agencies in the community that have an interest in fathers and might contribute significantly to the attainment of educational goals. If schools collaborate with the wider community, they can help fathers connect to area resources, link educational programs with the realities of the workplace, create community service opportunities for students, respond to the needs of adult

Table 12.4 Father engagement through decision-making

Strategy	Description
Inclusion	Include father representatives in the process of identifying the mission, vision, values, and goals of the schools.
Processes	Develop and use processes to solicit more broad-based diverse father input on missions, visions, values, and goals.
Decision-making	Include fathers on decision-making and advisory task forces and committees and provide them with the necessary information and training to make informed decisions.
Solicit	Facilitate active father engagement in the decisions that affect their children, such as student placement, course selection, and individualized educational plans.
Data	Work with fathers to identify the student and school performance data that fathers find most relevant and then provide them with the data on a regular basis.
Evaluation	Solicit father input in the evaluation of the programs, policies, and procedures of the school.
Advise	Advise fathers of changes in programs, policies, and procedures that have been made because of their input or engagement.

Table 12.5 Testimonials: male educators as proponents of father-friendly schools

Father-friendly advocate	Testimony
Antwaun Arnold, high school principal	"My school is designed to support students who are long-term suspended. Unfortunately, my student population is primarily Black boys. Unfortunately, most of my students are without a positive father figure. Therefore, our school has hired primarily Black males and Black fathers to help inform the daily programming and operations. This has proved to be successful for our school."
Dr. Edward Bell, education consultant	"The absence of fathers in family units have implications on father engagement in school settings. Education leaders must take advantage of opportunities to infuse father-friendly activities, planning, and programs into the school setting."
Brandon Moyer, school social worker	"Oftentimes fathers are turned away at the parent orientation and that opportunity is forever lost. So we engage and solicit the participation of fathers before the start of school. We realized how important the engagement of fathers is on our student outcomes."
Philip Lyde, middle school teacher	"I realized that my job helps me redefine the type of relationships kids can have with their fathers. I value that aspect of my job, and I lead with that during my curriculum interpretation, my pedagogy, and my class environment."

learners, and make a more effective contribution to the community. The school-father partnership will be more productive if schools embrace learning as an experience that expands beyond the building and is immersed in the direct needs of fathers.

Schools are typically viewed as institutions that provide educational services to the youth of the community, Monday through Friday. Instead, schools should be regarded as valuable resources that can make a significant contribution to the entire community, especially fathers. Schools can develop agreements that enable it to serve as a satellite campus for the community college, state university, private college, and multi-university programs that offer everything from associate to graduate degrees. Schools can provide leisure, recreational, and non-credential education programs for fathers seeking to engage in education or career advancement pathways. The additional education opportunities for fathers have the potential to indirectly increase the engagement of fathers.

While there is an abundance of research that suggests father engagement in the education of their children is highly desirable, fathers and educators continue to struggle in their efforts to define exactly what that role, of an engaged parent, should be. The best model for the relationship between the school and father is the model of a productive business partnership that allows for fathers to engage directly with their children, a relationship in which each party is expected to bring specific skills and expertise to the enterprise, to offer a different perspective on issues and support in difficult times, and to contribute on issues and toward the achievement of the mutual goal of improving the well-being of students. Schools need to use this framework to strengthen the relationships between fathers, students, and the community. Schools that function as effective learning communities will recognize the power of an active partnership with fathers and will develop specific strategies to create high levels of father engagement for the well-being of all children.

Discussion Questions

1. Interview a local school leader and ask them to identify their father-specific recruitment goals within the school's HR practices, PTA, volunteer base, and community engagement. How will these goals influence school decisions?
2. What are the potential barriers in a school's (or district's) history that may help identify the root causes for the decline or absence of father engagement?
3. In what ways can the community drive ideas for a school (or district) to develop father-friendly learning communities?
4. In five sentences (or less), state your vision or dream for a father-friendly learning community.

Resources

- My Brother's Keeper: Home – My Brother's Keeper (mybrotherskeeper.org)
- Fatherhood Tools: Fatherhood Resources – Child Welfare Information Gateway
- Father Engagement Strategies: Engaging Fathers | ECLKC (hhs.gov)

References

Adams, D. W. (1995). *Education for extinction: American Indians and the boarding school experience, 1875–1928*. University Press of Kansas.
Allport, G. W. (1954). *The nature of prejudice*. Addison Wesley.
Bandura, A. (2010). Self-efficacy. In *The Corsini encyclopedia of psychology* (pp. 1–3). Wiley. https://doi.org/10.1002/9780470479216.corpsy0836
Blassingame, J. W. (1972). *The slave community: Plantation life in the ante-bellum South*. Oxford University Press.
Brewer, M. B., & Miller, N. (1988). Contact and cooperation: When do they work? In P. Katz & D. Taylor (Eds.), *Eliminating racism: Means and controversies* (pp. 315–326). Plenum.
Bronfenbrenner, U. (1979). *The ecology of human development: Experiments by nature and design*. Harvard University Press.
Bond, H. M. (1966). *The education of the Negro in the American social order*. Octagon Books.
Bullock, H. A. (1967). *A history of Negro education in the South: From 1619 to the present*. Harvard University Press.
Trends, C. (2013). *Parental involvement in schools*. Child Trends.
Curry, L. P. (1981). *The free Black in urban America, 1800–1850: The shadow of the dream*. University of Chicago Press.
Dixon, J., Durrheim, K., & Tredoux, C. (2005). Beyond the optimal contact strategy: A reality check for the contact hypothesis. *American Psychologist, 60*(7), 697–711. https://doi.org/10.1037/0003-066x.60.7.697
Dolan, W. P. (1994). *Restructuring our schools*. Systems & Organizations.
Downey, D. B. (2001). Number of siblings and intellectual development: The resource dilution explanation. *American Psychologist, 56*, 497–504. https://doi.org/10.1037/0003-066x.56.6-7.497
Dubois, W. E. B. (1935). *Black Reconstruction: An essay toward a history of the part which black folk played in the attempt to reconstruct democracy in America, 1860–1880*. Harcourt, Brace and Company.
Durlak, J. A. (1995). *School-based prevention programs for children and adolescents* (Vol. 34). Sage.
Emerson, E., Alborz, A., Reeves, D., Mason, H., Swarbrick, R., Kiernan, C., & Mason, L. (2002). The HARC challenging behavior project. In *Report 2: The prevalence of challenging behavior*. Manchester.
Epstein, J. L. (1986). Parents' reactions to teacher practices of parent involvement. *The Elementary School Journal, 56*, 271–294. https://doi.org/10.1086/461449
Fan, X., & Chen, M. (2001). Parental involvement and students' academic achievement: A meta-analysis. *Educational Psychology Review, 13*, 1–22. https://doi.org/10.1023/A:1009048817385
Fleischmann, F., & Kristen, C. (2016). Gender inequalities in the education of the second generation in western countries. *Sociology of Education, 87*, 143–170. https://doi.org/10.1177/0038040714537836
Foner, E. (1988). *Reconstruction: America's unfinished revolution, 1863–1877*. Harper & Row.
Foner, E., & Mahoney, O. (1995). *America's reconstruction: People and politics after the Civil War*. HarperCollins.
Franklin, J. H. (1961). *Reconstruction: After the Civil War*. University of Chicago Press.
Garcia Coll, C., Akiba, D., Palacios, N., Bailey, B., Silver, R., DiMartino, L., & Chin, C. (2002). Parental involvement in children's education: Lessons from three immigrant groups. *Parenting, 2*, 303–324. https://doi.org/10.1207/S15327922PAR0203_05
Gershy, N., & Omer, H. (2017). Engaging fathers in parent training: A qualitative study. *Journal of Family Psychotherapy, 28*(1), 38–58. https://doi.org/10.1080/08975353.2017.1283143
Green, C. L., Walker, J. M. T., Hoover-Dempsey, K. V., & Sandler, H. M. (2007). Parents' motivations for involvement in children's education: An empirical test of a theoretical model of parental involvement. *Journal of Educational Psychology, 99*, 532–544. https://doi.org/10.1037/0022-0663.99.3.532

Grestner, C., & O'Day, D. (1994). Cross-cultural comparison of leadership prototypes. *The Leadership Quarterly, 5*(2), 121–134. https://doi.org/10.1016/1048-9843(94)90024-8
Hage, S. M., Romano, J. L., Conyne, R. K., Kenny, M., Matthews, C., Schwartz, J. P., & Waldo, M. (2007). Best practice guidelines on prevention practice, research, training, and social advocacy for psychologists. *The Counseling Psychologist, 35*(4), 493–566. https://doi.org/10.1177/0011000006291411
Higgins, S., & Katsipataki, M. (2015). Evidence from meta-analysis about parental involvement in education which supports their children's learning. *Journal of Children's Services, 10*(3), 28. https://doi.org/10.1108/jcs-02-2015-0009
Hoover-Dempsey, K. V., & Sandler, H. M. (1995). Parental involvement in children's education: Why does it make a difference? *Teachers College Record, 97*, 310–331. https://doi.org/10.1177/016146819509700202
Hoover-Dempsey, K. V., & Sandler, H. M. (1997). Why do parents become involved in their children's education? *Review of Educational Research, 67*, 3–42. https://doi.org/10.3102/00346543067001003
Hoover-Dempsey, K. V., Walker, J. M. T., Sandler, H. M., Whetsel, D., Green, C. L., Wilkins, A. S., & Closson, K. (2005). Why do parents become involved? Research findings and implications. *The Elementary School Journal, 106*, 105–130. https://doi.org/10.1086/499194
Jeynes, W. H. (2005). A meta-analysis of the relation of parental involvement to urban elementary school student academic achievement. *Urban Education, 40*, 237–269. https://doi.org/10.1177/0042085905274540
Jeynes, W. H. (2011). *Parental involvement and academic success*. Routledge.
Jones, J. M. (1997). *Prejudice and racism* (2nd ed.). McGraw-Hill.
Katz, P. A., & Zalk, S. R. (1978). Modification of children's racial attitudes. *Developmental Psychology, 14*(5), 447–461. https://doi.org/10.1037/0012-1649.14.5.447
Keith, T. Z., Keith, P. B., Quirk, K. J., Sperduto, J., Santillo, S., & Killings, S. (1998). Longitudinal effects of parent involvement on high school grades: Similarities and differences across gender and ethnic groups. *Journal of School Psychology, 36*, 335–363. https://doi.org/10.1016/S0022-4405(98)00008-9
Kim, S. W., & Hill, N. E. (2015). Including fathers in the picture: A meta-analysis of parental involvement and students' academic achievement. *Journal of Educational Psychology, 107*(4), 919–934. https://doi.org/10.1037/edu0000023
Kohl, G. O., Lengua, L. J., & McMahon, R. J. (2000). Parent involvement in school conceptualizing multiple dimensions and their relations with family and demographic risk factors. *Journal of School Psychology, 38*, 501–523. https://doi.org/10.1016/S0022-4405(00)00050-9
Lee, J.-S., & Bowen, N. K. (2006). Parent involvement, cultural capital, and the achievement gap among elementary school children. *American Educational Research Journal, 43*, 193–218. https://doi.org/10.3102/00028312043002193
London, L. H., Tierney, G., Buhin, L., Greco, D. M., & Cooper, C. J. (2002). Kids' College: Enhancing children's appreciation and acceptance of cultural diversity. *Journal of Prevention & Intervention in the Community, 24*, 63–78. https://doi.org/10.1300/J005v24n02_06
Marsiglio, W., Amato, P., Day, R. D., & Lamb, M. E. (2000). Scholarship on fatherhood in the 1990s and beyond. *Journal of Marriage and Family, 62*, 1173–1191. https://doi.org/10.1111/j.1741-3737.2000.01173
Mintz, S. (2004). *Huck's raft: A history of American childhood*. Harvard University Press.
Park, S., & Holloway, S. (2018). Parental involvement in adolescents' education: An examination of the interplay among school factors, parental role construction, and family income. *School Community Journal, 28*(1), 9–36.
Pettigrew, T. F. (1998). Intergroup contact theory. *Annual Review of Psychology, 49*, 65–85. https://doi.org/10.1146/annurev.psych.49.1.65
Reese, L. E., & Vera, E. M. (2007). Culturally relevant prevention: The scientific and practical considerations of community-based programs. *The Counseling Psychologist, 35*, 763–778. https://doi.org/10.1177/0011000007304588

Rury, J. L. (2016). *Education and social change: Contours in the history of American schooling* (5th ed.). Routledge.

Shepard, J., & Carlson, J. S. (2003). An empirical evaluation of school-based prevention programs that involve parents. *Psychology in the Schools, 40*, 641–656. https://doi.org/10.1002/pits.10126

Stephan, C. W., & Stephen, W. G. (1992). Reducing intercultural anxiety through intercultural contact. *International Journal of Intercultural Relations, 16*, 89–106. https://doi.org/10.1016/0147-1767(92)90007-H

Sui-Chu, E. H., & Willms, J. D. (1996). Effects of parental involvement on eighth-grade achievement. *Sociology of Education, 69*, 126–141. https://doi.org/10.2307/2112802

Townsend, L., Mullennix, A., Tyrone, B., & Samberg, M. (2019). *Leandro Action Plan: Ensuring a sound basic education for all North Carolina students' success factors study*. William and Ida Friday Institute for Innovation at North Carolina State University.

Turney, K., & Kao, G. (2009). Barriers to school involvement: Are immigrant parents disadvantaged? *The Journal of Educational Research, 102*, 257–271. https://doi.org/10.3200/JOER.102.4.257-271

VanOverbeke, M. (2008). *The standardization of American schooling: Linking secondary and higher education*. Palgrave Macmillan.

Waanders, C., Mendez, J. L., & Downer, J. T. (2007). Parent characteristics, economic stress and neighborhood context as predictors of parent involvement in preschool children's education. *Journal of School Psychology, 45*, 619–636. https://doi.org/10.1016/j.jsp.2007.07.003

Webber, T. L. (1978). *Deep like the rivers: Education in the slave quarter community, 1831–1865*. Norton.

Willis, J., Krausen, K., Berg-Jacobson, A., Taylor, L., Caparas, R., Lewis, R., & Jaquet, K. (2019). *A study of cost adequacy, distribution, and alignment of funding for North Carolina's K–12 public education system*. WestEd.

Yan, W., & Lin, Q. (2005). Parent involvement and mathematics achievement: Contrast across racial and ethnic groups. *The Journal of Educational Research, 99*, 116–127. https://doi.org/10.3200/JOER.99.2.116

Chapter 13
Fathers' Participation in Early Childhood Programs

Yu Chen, Natasha J. Cabrera, Angelica Alonso, Rachel Ghosh, and S. Alexa McDorman

Introduction

Over the past few decades, the structure and composition of families in the United States have undergone substantial changes, especially in relation to fathers. Several trends are notable. First, fathers' residency status has changed significantly. In 2020, 70% of children under 18 lived with both parents compared to 85% in 1968 (Hemez & Washington, 2021). Second, there has been a large increase in the number of single-father-led households. Between 1968 and 2020, the percentage of children across racial and ethnic groups living only with their fathers quadrupled from 1.1% to 4.5%. Third, contemporary fathers provide more hands-on parenting than in previous decades. The majority of fathers in resident households reported being moderately involved (e.g., once a week) with their children in activities such as playing and reading (Astone et al., 2016). This trend is also observed among nonresident fathers. Although the percentage of children under 18, mostly from African American households, living in single mother households has doubled since 1968 (from 10.7% to 21%), most of them see their fathers regularly to play games or read (Astone et al., 2016). Overall, these trends point to the conclusion that fathers' commitment to their children is changing for the better, and residency status does not necessarily define their involvement in their children's lives.

Research on the importance of fathers for child development has consistently shown that fathers contribute uniquely to children's development, including cognitive, language, and social-emotional skills, over and above the contribution of mothers (e.g., Cabrera et al., 2020; Cabrera et al., 2007; Gerhardt et al., 2020; LaBounty et al., 2008). Across ethnically and economically diverse families, children whose

Y. Chen (✉) · N. J. Cabrera · A. Alonso · R. Ghosh · S. A. McDorman
University of Maryland, College Park, College Park, MD, USA
e-mail: ychen189@umd.edu; ncabrera@umd.edu; aalonso1@umd.edu; ghoshra@terpmail.umd.edu; samcdor@umd.edu

J. L. Bellamy et al. (eds.), *Social Work Practice with Fathers*,
https://doi.org/10.1007/978-3-031-13686-3_13

fathers are supportive (e.g., providing emotional support, being responsive) and provide cognitive stimulation (e.g., teaching or scaffolding the child's current abilities) when interacting with them have better cognitive and executive function skills at age 3 than children whose fathers are less sensitive and stimulating (Cabrera et al., 2007; Towe-Goodman et al., 2014). There is also evidence of unique effects of fathers' literacy practices, including reading, storytelling, and singing songs, on children's language skills (Cabrera et al., 2020). Although fathers read less often to their children than mothers, they may be "better readers" because they tend to use more *wh*-questions and metalingual talk (e.g., prompting the child to produce language, labeling, and recasting the child's language), which promote children's language skills (Duursma, 2016; Malin et al., 2014; Rowe et al., 2004).

As has been demonstrated with mothers, the quality of fathers' interaction with their children (e.g., discussing emotions, being responsive to the child) is robustly related to children's social-emotional development. Fathers who talk more about emotions and desires with their 3-year-olds have children with stronger theory-of-mind skills (i.e., the ability to take another's perspective and to understand beliefs and thoughts different from one's own) and more positive emotional expressions than children with fathers who talk less about these topics (Gerhardt et al., 2020; LaBounty et al., 2008). In a study of predominantly White mothers, fathers, and their firstborn child, Jeon and Neppl (2019) found that when fathers used more positive parenting practices (e.g., response to child's verbalizations) on their 3- and 4-year-old children, those children at age five had a higher social competence (e.g., "helps with everyday tasks"), controlling for family income and maternal and paternal education. These findings point to an enormous opportunity—policymakers and practitioners interested in closing the achievement gap should tap father involvement to promote child well-being and design services that also target fathers, not just mothers. Given their unique contribution, including fathers in early childhood programs, would validate fathers' role in children's learning and successfully strengthen the goals of the programs to improve children's experiences at home and, in turn, developmental outcomes.

In this chapter, our goal is to selectively review the literature on early childhood programs and offer recommendations for program designers and social workers to effectively engage fathers into programs and services. We begin with a brief overview of early childhood programs and present a conceptual framework to illustrate potential points of intervention and engagement strategies for father-inclusive programs. We then synthesize some exemplary programs that have engaged fathers and conclude with a list of evidence-based approaches that foster fathers' participation in programs.

Background and Context

An Overview of Early Childhood Programs

Early childhood (EC) programs are typically delivered through childcare centers, home visits, or a combination of both settings (e.g., Campbell et al., 2002; Love et al., 2013). EC programs often target children from economically vulnerable backgrounds, with an intention to buffer or reverse the negative influence of adverse childhood experiences and better prepare those children for academic success (Cabrera et al., 2009). However, most EC programs include mothers as the primary caregiver, and few engage fathers or both parents (Panter-Brick et al., 2014). In this section, we highlight EC programs that have been extensively examined and shown significant improvement in child outcomes: the Abecedarian Project, the Infant Health and Development Project, Early Head Start, and Head Start (see Anderson et al., 2003 for review on other EC programs).

The Abecedarian Project and the Infant Health and Development Project

One of the best-known early childhood programs is the Abecedarian Project (ABC), which provides empirical evidence on the positive and long-term effects of high-quality early childcare on children's health, cognitive skills, academic achievement, and risk behaviors (Campbell et al., 2002, 2014; Sparling et al., 2021). The ABC project included infants ($N = 111$) born between 1972 and 1977, most of whom were from low-income African American families. Infants were randomly assigned to an intervention group that received full-time high-quality childcare from birth to 5 years or to a control group that participated in other programs or stayed at home (Campbell et al., 2014; Sparling et al., 2021). A number of follow-up studies documented both the short- and long-term impacts of the ABC project across various developmental domains, including cognitive and social development, physical and mental health, problem behaviors, and academic success (see Sparling et al., 2021). The interpretation that the ABC project is beneficial for *all children at risk* has been challenged on grounds that although it targeted at-risk children and race was not an enrollment criterion, most of children enrolled in the program were African American (Bruno & Iruka, 2022).

The Infant Health and Developmental Project (IHDP) is a multisite randomized control trial (RCT) intervention that included a large sample of preterm and low birthweight children and followed them from birth to 3 years (Brooks-Gunn et al., 1993). The goal of IHDP was to improve child outcomes through mother-child interactions at home during the first 3 years and through full-day center-based education during the second and third year (McCormick, 2006). Mothers in the intervention group received training on parenting practices and had access to social support (Brooks-Gunn et al., 1993). Both intervention and control children had regular pediatric visits throughout the project (Martin et al., 2008). Studies on the effects of IHDP found that children in the intervention group showed better cognitive skills, which remained till age 5 but only for heavier low birthweight (2000–2500 g) children (Martin et al., 2008).

Head Start and Early Head Start

Head Start (HS) is one of the only lasting programs from the 1960's war on poverty and is considered to be the most cost-effective federal program to promote development (see Zigler & Bishop-Josef, 2006; Zigler & Muenchow, 1992; Zigler & Styfco, 2010; Zigler & Valentine, 1979). In a nutshell, HS is a two-generation, community-based program designed to enhance parenting and child development through center- or home-based services or both (e.g., full- or part-time childcare, weekly home visits; Cabrera et al., 2009; Zigler, 1978). Services for children in HS focus on education and health, and for parents include parental involvement, mental health, and referrals to social services (Cabrera et al., 2009).

Launched in 2002, the Head Start Impact Study followed two cohorts of 5000 children (3- and 4-year-olds) to third grade, who were randomly assigned to HS or a control group (Administration for Children and Families, 2010). Findings showed that children who had access to HS had better outcomes in language and literacy (e.g., vocabulary skills, letter-word identification, etc.), math (e.g., applied problems), behavior problems (e.g., withdrawn behaviors), and health status at the end of HS compared to the control group. Parental effects included less spanking and more frequent book reading (Administration for Children and Families, 2010). However, these positive effects, which were relatively small, were more evident for the 3-year-old cohort compared to the 4-year-old cohort (Administration for Children and Families, 2010; Puma et al., 2012).

In contrast, Early Head Start (EHS) offers child development and family support services to low-income pregnant mothers and children from birth to 3 years (Cabrera et al., 2009). The Early Head Start Research and Evaluation Project was launched in 1994 as a national evaluation study to provide empirical evidence regarding the benefits of EHS for children and their families (Boller et al., 2006; Love et al., 2013; Raikes et al., 2013). Although most EHS families (91%) showed minimal program participation, with the average length of participation being 21 months (Love et al., 2002), EHS has shown positive short- and long-term effects for children and for parents (Vogel et al., 2010, 2015).

In summary, these early childhood programs have reliably demonstrated that intervening early (i.e., infancy), providing high-quality childcare through home visits or childcare centers or both that address a multitude of children's needs, and offering services to both parents (i.e., two-generation programs) can make short- and long-term differences in the well-being of children facing multiple risks (Boller et al., 2006; Campbell et al., 2014; Raikes et al., 2013; Sparling et al., 2021).

However, these landmark programs did not include fathers; the focus was exclusively on mothers. Such omission is consequential because strong empirical evidence shows that father involvement is beneficial for children's development over and above the influence of mothers (e.g., Cabrera et al., 2020; Malin et al., 2014). To this end, this chapter will shed light on the conceptual framework and the best practices for including fathers in early childhood programs.

Conceptual Framing

Early childhood programs serving fathers are often guided by theories on parenting and child development in general, and few conceptualize the unique contribution of fathers (Karberg et al., 2017). This lack of focus on theories specific for father involvement may hinder researchers and practitioners from designing and implementing interventions that are successful at engaging fathers and changing their behavior. Theories and conceptual models are crucial because they delineate the direct and indirect pathways through which fathers influence children and the various contextual factors that shape father involvement. Here, we discuss the *Ecology of father-child relationships: An expanded model* as a conceptual framework for designing father-inclusive programs that aim to promote child outcomes during the early years (Cabrera et al., 2014; see Fig. 13.1).

This model draws from bioecological systems theory (Bronfenbrenner & Morris, 2006) and Belsky's (1984) parenting process model, highlighting the ways that contextual factors, including environmental and psychological contexts, impact fathers' caregiving and children's development. By centering fathering within an ecological context, this model theorizes the reciprocal influences between fathers and their children that are often neglected in general parenting models. Specifically, it emphasizes the dynamic and bidirectional relations between components within the family system and the interconnection between various family members; for example, fathers' parenting behaviors are affected directly by the characteristics of other members (e.g., mother, child) and family relationships (e.g., mother-father and father-child relationships) and indirectly by member characteristics through family relationships. At the same time, fathers' parenting behaviors also loop back to family relationships and to the characteristics of other family members through those relationships, hence the bidirectional relations within the family system. This model also accounts for factors external to the family system, including both proximal (e.g., father's work, family socioeconomic status (SES), parenting history) and distal (e.g., cultural and societal values, public policy) contexts. These intertwined connections internal and external to the family system function together in the broader social context to shape child development (Cabrera et al., 2014).

This model alludes to important considerations for early childhood programs that are intended to engage fathers as a means to enhance child well-being: (1) fathers should not be placed in a vacuum, and it is beneficial to include mothers (and other members) in the program at the same time; (2) in addition to directly changing

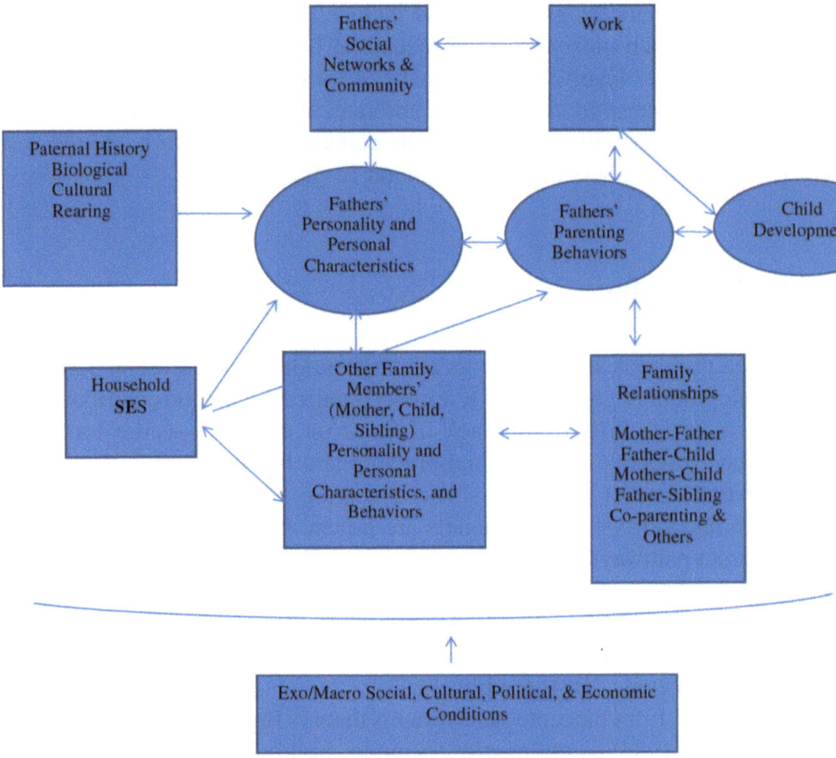

Fig. 13.1 The ecology of father-child relationships: An expanded model

fathers' parenting behaviors, programs should also consider changing the immediate factors that affect these behaviors, such as couple and co-parenting relationships and the characteristics and behaviors of other members (e.g., mother's parenting behaviors and mental health); and (3) programs need to be malleable to the specific contexts where fathers and their families reside and provide appropriate services that accommodate fathers' individual needs and ability to access resources.

Early Childhood Programs That Engage Fathers

Over the past few decades, substantial federal funding has been allocated to programs that support men's role as fathers (Cabrera, 2010). The Responsible Fatherhood (RF) programs initiated through the Deficit Reduction Act of 2005 and the Claims Resolution Act of 2010 target a multitude of factors (e.g., mother-father and father-child relationships) to (1) improve fathers' parenting skills and involvement with children, (2) ameliorate fathers' relationships with their children's mothers, and (3) support fathers' economic self-efficacy (Cabrera et al., 2015; Karberg et al., 2017; for more on the history of RF programs, please see Chap. 2). Although many programs lack rigorous evaluation, in general, they have improved father involvement, co-parenting relationships, and child outcomes (Karberg et al., 2017). In this section, we categorize EC programs with fathers into those that are focused primarily on fathers' financial contributions and others that are primarily focused on father involvement (i.e., the frequency and quality of fathers' parenting behaviors).

Programs Focused on Fathers' Financial Contributions

Fathers Offering Children Unfailing Support (FOCUS) focuses on increasing non-resident fathers' financial contributions to their children of all ages, and it does so more effectively than traditional enforcement methods (Garasky et al., 2010; Nievar et al., 2020). Designed by Texas nonprofit NewDay Services, FOCUS serves fathers who are referred by Child Protective Services, the Attorney General's Office, and many other agencies and organizations (Nievar et al., 2020). Fathers sign up for the FOCUS program for various reasons, including Child Protective Services involvement, overdue child support, or as part of addiction rehabilitation. The FOCUS program consists of 10 weeks of 2-hour group classes where fathers discuss topics such as child development, managing emotions and expectations, positive communication with their children, co-parenting, control-seeking behaviors, understanding their own father's influence, and defining paternal roles (Nievar et al., 2020). Nievar et al. (2020) recruited 250 fathers who were court-ordered to participate in FOCUS due to nonpayment of child support and found that fathers who took part in FOCUS increased their child support payments by nearly 100% in the year after program completion.

Despite the promise of court-ordered programs such as FOCUS, the state child support systems in which these programs are embedded are flawed. Child support agencies can be highly punitive to fathers who, for a variety of reasons, are not able to fulfill their court-ordered child support obligations. States charge exorbitant rates on arrears, and neither unemployment nor incarceration automatically lowers mandated payments (Cancian et al., 2013). A large child support debt can have a negative influence on fathers' employment prospects and earnings (Cancian et al., 2013; Miller & Mincy, 2012).

Fathers' inability to pay regular child support can lead to worse relationships with their partners (Cabrera, 2010; Osborne, 2020). Critics have also noted that by focusing solely on formal court-ordered child support payments, states overlook the importance of informal payments made outside of the system (Nepomnyaschy, 2007). Informal payments, which are often preferred by families because they rely on goodwill between parents, have been found to have a stronger association with fathers' frequency of contact with their child than formal support payment (Nepomnyaschy, 2007; please see Chap. 14 for more details on serving fathers in the child support system).

Programs Focused on Fathers' Involvement

Programs targeting fathers *and* mothers in interventions are still scarce, but there are a few that offer very promising results and appear to be cost-effective. In this section, we highlight a few of these interventions to illustrate the type and scope of these programs.

The Tennessee Early Intervention System (TEIS) is a state program designed to provide family-centered services to parents of young children with special needs (Tennessee Department of Education, 2021). The program connects families to available services within their community using a family-centered approach that encourages professionals to work with parents through flexible or home-based appointments rather than disrupting daily routines. Using identity theory, Fox et al. (2015) examined the impact of TEIS on fathers' parenting self-efficacy (e.g., how confident fathers were in caring for their child), identity (i.e., salience, satisfaction, and appraisal of father role), and involvement with their young children. Researchers included a sample of predominantly White fathers and their young children who had been diagnosed with disabilities or developmental delays. Results showed that fathers who self-reported higher levels of parenting self-efficacy also reported higher levels of involvement (e.g., more time spent in activities and instrumental care with child). As expected, father identity partially mediated the association between parenting self-efficacy and father involvement (Fox et al., 2015). Therefore, using a family-centered service delivery model to enhance fathers' parenting self-efficacy and identity may be an effective way to increase their involvement with children who have disabilities.

The Oregon Model of Parent Management Training (PMTO) focuses on parenting behaviors (e.g., monitoring, noncoercive discipline) and is guided by the social interaction learning model, which postulates that children's conduct problems are reinforced by parents' coercive parenting (DeGarmo & Forgatch, 2007; Forgatch & Domenech Rodríguez, 2016). A small-scale RCT of PMTO included a socioeconomically diverse sample of newly formed stepfamilies (i.e., married within the last 2 years) with young school-aged children who showed moderate levels of problem behaviors (e.g., 4 out of 35; DeGarmo & Forgatch, 2007). Stepfathers in the intervention group showed greater improvement in observed effective fathering (e.g., effective interpersonal problem-solving and monitoring, low levels of coercive discipline) at the 6- and 12-month follow-up compared to stepfathers in the control group (DeGarmo & Forgatch, 2007). Greater improvement in effective fathering over the first 6 months was also associated with greater decreases in child-reported depression and observed noncompliance at the 24-month follow-up (DeGarmo & Forgatch, 2007).

Fathers Supporting Success in Preschoolers (FSSP) focuses on promoting father-child interactions in the context of family routines, such as reading. It is a group-based parent education program that incorporates behavioral parent training into shared book reading interactions (Chacko et al., 2018). Guided by **social learning theory**, the intervention aims to influence fathers' behaviors by presenting them with videotaped models of high-quality father-child reading interactions (e.g., following the child's lead) in 90-minute weekly sessions for 8 weeks. A small-scale RCT examining the effectiveness of FSSP found that FSSP fathers exhibited improvement in their self-reported discipline and observed positive (e.g., use of praise) and negative (e.g., use of critical statements) parenting and that preschoolers showed increased observed expressive and receptive language skills (Chacko et al., 2018).

The Supporting Father Involvement (SFI) program for mothers and fathers was designed to improve father involvement (i.e., fathers' share of instrumental caregiving relative to mothers'; Pruett et al., 2017). One iteration of SFI served predominantly low-income White and Mexican American families in California (Cowan et al., 2014). Researchers recruited parents from the community (e.g., soccer games, malls) and family resource centers, where they decorated and advertised with pictures of fathers to create a welcoming environment for them. Parents in intervention groups (couple and father-only groups) participated in a 32-hour curriculum that included discussions of co-parenting and fathers' parental roles and a father-child play session (Pruett et al., 2017). Mothers and fathers across groups had high attendance rates and were well compensated for completing each assessment (Cowan et al., 2014). Analyses showed that families who stayed in the program reported more father involvement in caregiving and less harsh parenting. In contrast, families who dropped out endorsed harsher parenting statements (e.g., using scolding and punishment) and reported lower levels of household income (Cowan et al., 2014). In another SFI evaluation that included a control, a couple-only, and a father-only group, fathers in the control group reported more behavior problems in their children and lower couple satisfaction 3 years later. Fathers in the fathers-only group reported no increase in children's behavior problems, increased father involvement, and decreased couple satisfaction. Fathers and mothers in the couple-only intervention group reported increased father involvement, reduced parenting stress, and no decrease in couple satisfaction (Cowan et al., 2014). Furthermore, both intervention designs (i.e., fathers-only and couple-only groups) were equally effective across ethnic and racial groups, with above average effects compared to other interventions with low-income families (Cohen's d from 0.20s to mid-0.40s; Pruett et al., 2017). In a more recent study, Pruett et al. (2019) found that SFI reduced couple conflict for all participants, which then reduced anxious and harsh parenting behaviors and, in turn, led to fewer child behavior problems (Pruett et al., 2019).

Using a sample of 1354 African American children from the HS Impact Study (described above), a recent study examined whether the association between participating in HS and fathers' school-based involvement (e.g., attending school events) differed for resident versus nonresident fathers (Lee & Rispoli, 2019). There was a significant association between participating in HS and fathers' school involvement, but only for nonresident fathers. Specifically, nonresident fathers enrolled in HS engaged in more school involvement (as reported by mothers) compared to nonresident fathers in the control group. However, participation in HS was not associated with greater school-based involvement among resident fathers (Lee & Rispoli, 2019). Thus, HS seems to have some benefits for fathers and children depending on fathers' resident status.

Baby Books 2 (BB2) is an ongoing parenting intervention designed for low-income first-time mothers and fathers recruited from local clinics, day-care centers, and farmers' markets to increase parenting knowledge of child development and, in turn, improve parenting and child outcomes (Cabrera et al., 2021; McKee et al., 2021). BB2 is an RCT (i.e., mother only, father only, both parents, and control) that collects observational and interview data at 9, 12, 15, 18, 24, 30, and 37–47 months of age. Parents in the intervention group receive a baby's book specifically designed to incorporate anticipatory guidance messages that provide parents with information about children's socioemotional, cognitive, language, math, and physical development and safety and health. Parents in the control group receive an educational book. Parents in BB2 (N = 420) are primarily Latino and African American and have a lower household income but vary across educational levels (McKee et al., 2021). Thus far, findings revealed that on average, fathers read less often to a child (i.e., 2.4 times per week) than mothers. Although the majority of mothers and fathers reported enjoying the book, more mothers than fathers did so. A strong predictor of fathers' engagement was mothers' engagement in the intervention (McKee et al., 2021).

Overall, the early childhood programs reviewed in this section (see Table 13.1 for a summary) demonstrate promising results. It is worth noting that the effects were observed among low-income and ethnically and racially diverse families. Evidence on child support suggests that programs for children with nonresident or noncustodial fathers should pay more attention to fathers' relationship with their child rather than universally enforcing their financial contributions and also provide more resources (e.g., health care, parenting education, housing vouchers) to support father involvement (Osborne, 2020). Additionally, programs that include both mothers and fathers are more likely to be successful. However, fathers' participation in early childhood programs is generally low (Burwick et al., 2004; McKee et al., 2021). Moving forward, we need research that is theoretically grounded to enable researchers and practitioners to identify potential points of intervention and capitalize on the multiple factors that affect child outcomes through fathers (Cabrera et al., 2014).

Recommended Intervention Approaches

One of the most significant findings of intervention research is that engagement in the intervention is relatively low (Fagan & Pearson, 2020; McKee et al., 2021; Panter-Brick et al., 2014). Researchers and practitioners have written extensively about the multiple barriers to engaging fathers (and mothers) in early childhood programs and intervention services (Fagan & Pearson, 2020; Pearson & Fagan, 2019; see Fatherhood Research and Practice Network, n.d.). The most significant barriers include fathers' inflexible and long work schedules, fathers' nonresidence status, providers' traditional beliefs about gender roles, and providers' lack of ability to adapt the services to fathers' needs (Cabrera, 2010; McBride et al., 2017;

Table 13.1 Summary of early childhood programs that engage fathers

Program name	Target population	Service provided	Outcomes
Fathers Offering Children Unfailing Support (FOCUS)	Fathers with children of all ages, referred by social welfare agencies	Ten weeks of 2-hour group classes on topics such as child development, managing emotions and expectations, co-parenting, and paternal roles	Drastically increased fathers' child support payments (by 100%)
Tennessee Early Intervention System (TEIS)	Tennessee parents with a child aged 3 years and under with special needs	Family-centered liaison to services available in the community	Fathers' increased parenting self-efficacy was related to higher levels of involvement, partially through strengthening their identity as fathers.
The Oregon Model Parent Management Training (PMTO)	Newly formed stepfamilies	Thirteen weekly parent training sessions that included exercises, role-playing, home practice assignments, and marital-enhancement strategies	Compared to control groups: Stepfathers showed more positive involvement, more effective interpersonal problem-solving, more monitoring, and lower levels of coercive discipline. Children had fewer depressive symptoms and engaged in less noncompliance.
Fathers Supporting Success in Preschoolers (FSSP)	Fathers and male guardians with a young child enrolled in Head Start	Group-based behavioral parent training embedded in father-child shared book-reading interactions, including videotaped vignettes, discussion, and dialogic reading	Compared to control groups: Fathers engaged in less harsh discipline, more positive parenting behaviors, and fewer negative parenting behaviors. Children had fewer behavioral problems and greater increases in language skills.
Supporting Father Involvement (SFI)	Low-income, English-/Spanish-speaking parents with a child aged 7 years or under	Sixteen weeks of customizable 2-hour group meetings covering topics around the couple relationship, parenting, and mental health	Compared to control groups: Fewer child behavior problems More father involvement Reduced parenting stress Higher couple satisfaction
Baby Books 2 (BB2)	First-time, cohabiting mothers and fathers with annual incomes $75,000 or below	Baby books with anticipatory guidance messages that provide information about child safety, health, and development at 9, 12, 18, and 24 months	Fathers were more likely to read baby books to their child when mothers did so; this intervention is ongoing and its effects on parents and children are to be evaluated.

McKee et al., 2021; Mitchell et al., 2007). In this section, we highlight the most important recommendations for including fathers in early childhood programs.

Design Interventions for Fathers and Mothers

A common finding in the literature on preventive research is that studies did not include fathers because they were not in the home when researchers visited mothers. Ancell et al. (2018) noted that most Early Childhood Special Education (ECSE) programs do not actively engage fathers. Often, this is part of the narrative by providers that fathers are ineffective or neglectful parents (Panter-Brick et al., 2014). This is a huge barrier to father engagement and may further marginalize them. Including fathers should not be an afterthought; father participation in programs is different from mothers' participation and therefore may be more resource-intense. Including both parents is understandably more expensive and challenging. Programs should allocate sufficient resources to reaching and communicating with both parents, which may require considerable persistence and time (Panter-Brick et al., 2014).

Instead of prioritizing mothers, intentionally designing programs for fathers *and* mothers will require a general overhaul of early childhood programs and a "game change in this field" (Panter-Brick et al., 2014, p. 1205). McKee et al. (2021) found that the most important predictor of mothers' and fathers' engagement in their early childhood RCT parenting intervention, BB2 (described above), was the participation of their partner. Fathers were more likely to read the books given by the intervention with their infant if their partner was also reading the books with their child. Their findings suggest that when both co-parents are explicitly targeted in an intervention, fathers are just as likely to participate as mothers, and one partner's participation may encourage or motivate their partner to participate due to a spillover effect (McKee et al., 2021).

Make Intervention Content Relevant for Fathers and Mothers

Another common problem is the use of program content that is relevant to mothers only (maternal template) for both parents. Programs need to intentionally modify the content of interventions to be culturally compelling (i.e., using male social workers, using staff from the same cultural group as fathers) and relevant and appropriate to all parents (Ancell et al., 2018; Bronte-Tinkew et al., 2012; Panter-Brick et al., 2014). Staff who are empathetic and well connected in the community and interact with fathers in one-on-one sessions for a personalized experience are important for fathers to feel welcome and included. This recommendation aligns with Cabrera et al.' (2014) conceptual model that emphasizes the contextual influences on fathers and the reciprocal relationships within the family system. Relatedly, Ancell et al. (2018) suggested that program staff should survey fathers about their needs and preferences (e.g., some fathers have asked for information about their own health) and develop father-friendly activities that would give fathers the opportunity to showcase their unique strengths with their children (e.g., sports activities, nature walks, treasure hunts).

Modify Service Delivery to Be Suitable to Fathers

Delivering content in a way that is engaging and interactive (e.g., small group discussions, role-play) is more effective than just lecturing to fathers (Panter-Brick et al., 2014). Additionally, programs should focus their curricula on a few core topics and allow fathers the opportunity to practice using newly learned skills (Bronte-Tinkew et al., 2012). Based on their review of 92 father-inclusive parenting and co-parenting programs from 20 different countries, Panter-Brick et al. (2014) argue that it is best to involve fathers by considering their unique circumstances and offering flexible hours or home visits, maintaining persistence in communicating the positive effects on child development of fathers' involvement in the program, and recruiting fathers personally to participate. Program facilitators should try to use approaches that are sensitive to fathers' individual needs (e.g., offer remote or online services for nonresident fathers who live farther away) and explicitly monitor the participation and activities of both parents (Panter-Brick et al., 2014).

Offer Proper and Meaningful Compensation

If the goal of the intervention is to recruit low-income fathers who work in the low-skill economy, researchers need to compensate them for their time. Many fathers will not participate in a study if it means not working and earning income for their family. Cash incentives need to be sufficiently meaningful to encourage fathers' and families' participation (Bronte-Tinkew et al., 2012). In the BB2 intervention, for example, fathers and mothers are offered up to $500 dollars for their participation in a 2-year study (McKee et al., 2021).

Include Fathers' Voices and Understand Their Individual Needs

An important recognition in the field of fatherhood research is that collecting information from mothers about father engagement is not collecting father engagement data; rather, it is collecting *mothers' perceptions* of father engagement. This information does not always align with fathers' own perceptions and feelings about their parenting behaviors. If programs extend to include fathers, they must also collect information directly from fathers about the way they are involved with their children, the obstacles they face, and the resources they value in their experiences as parents (Aldoney & Cabrera, 2016; Bronte-Tinkew et al., 2012; Fagan & Pearson, 2020; Panter-Brick et al., 2014). This approach will enable researchers and practitioners to understand fathers' needs and concerns and at the same time empower fathers to enhance the services that will ultimately support themselves and their families.

Today's fathers are diverse (e.g., biological, social, legal, stepfathers, grandfathers) and therefore reflect a diverse set of barriers (e.g., incarceration, military, nonresident status) to their involvement with their children and families (Walsh et al., 2020). In this vein, collecting the right type of information about fathers is critical to furthering our knowledge of the variability of father involvement and the points of intervention. In a qualitative study of seven African American and Latino fathers in the EHS fathering program, Hayes et al. (2010) reported that fathers' own family experiences, such as being reared without a father figure, lacking social support, and experiencing conflict with the child's mother, were major impediments to involvement. The theme of parental abandonment seems an important component of how fathers form positive relationships with their own children when they did not experience it themselves (Aldoney & Cabrera, 2016). The perception of not being accepted by their own fathers also colored their perception of how fathers balanced work and family (Aldoney & Cabrera, 2016).

In contrast, participating fathers noted that being in a program where they felt accepted, safe, and supported was key to expanding their understanding of fatherhood to include caregiving and educating (Hayes et al., 2010). Understanding what fathers are struggling with as well as what they appreciate allows programs and partitioners to design and deliver their services to fathers more effectively.

Use Technology to Recruit and Retain Fathers

One of the most salient challenges of including fathers in research is locating and recruiting them (Mitchell et al., 2007). Yet a very common method of allowing individuals to connect and relate to one another is through social media. Creative and technology-driven changes to traditional methods of service delivery in response to the COVID-19 public health emergency have unintentionally highlighted benefits for father engagement (Abendroth et al., 2021). Fathers participating in the *Fathers and Continuous Learning (FCL) Child Welfare Project* received a tablet and one-on-one technology support to attend virtual meetings and classes, which reduced barriers such as transportation, schedule conflicts, and childcare, and had weekly telephone calls and text messages. This resulted in higher attendance, lower cancellation rates, improved father-social worker relationships, and greater caregiver involvement in cases (Abendroth et al., 2021).

To conclude, the set of recommendations that are empirically supported to enhance fathers' participation in early childhood programs include designing programs for and *intentionally* including fathers, acknowledging their unique needs and concerns, engaging both fathers and mothers in the program, maintaining regular communication with both parents, adjusting services to accommodate fathers' work schedules, matching fathers with social workers from the same cultural group, and incorporating activities that particularly capitalize on fathers' strengths. We recognize the intensive efforts and costs required to carry out services for both parents. However, if our intent is to improve and support father engagement with their children and families, then we need to provide the resources and adopt the paradigmatic shift that parenting research and interventions include both mothers and fathers. Failure to do so will result in additional research that gives us more questions than answers and squanders an opportunity to improve the lives of children and their families.

Discussion Questions

1. What was your interaction with your father and mother when you were young? How do you think your relationship with your father and mother has shaped your development?
2. If you are asked to recruit fathers to participate in an intervention for infants and toddlers, what recruitment strategies would you use (e.g., what would you say to motivate fathers to sign up for the intervention)?
3. What key components would you include in an early childhood program to ensure optimal participation and retention of fathers?
4. If you are working as a social worker, how would you adapt programs to better serve various groups of fathers, such as nonresident fathers, social fathers, and fathers from diverse cultural backgrounds?
5. What measures can be used to evaluate the effects of the early childhood programs on fathers and on children?

Resources

- Strengthening Families, Healthy Marriage & Responsible Fatherhood: https://www.acf.hhs.gov/opre/topic/strengthening-families-healthy-marriage-responsible-fatherhood
- Supporting Father Involvement Program: http://supportingfatherinvolvementsfi.com/
- FIND-F (a video coaching program that aims to strengthen positive interactions between low-income fathers and children): https://www.thefindprogram.org

References

Abendroth, E., Bellamy, J., Mittone, D., Bess, R., & Stagner, M. (2021). *Opening up possibilities: Father engagement lessons during the COVID-19 public health emergency*. OPRE Report # 2021-82. Office of Planning, Research, and Evaluation, Administration for Children and Families, U.S. Department of Health and Human Services.

Administration for Children and Families, U.S. Department of Health and Human Services. (2010, January). *Head start impact study*. Final Report. https://www.acf.hhs.gov/opre/report/head-start-impact-study-final-report-executive-summary

Aldoney, D., & Cabrera, N. J. (2016). Raising American citizens: Socialization goals of low-income immigrant Latino mothers and fathers of young children. *Journal of Child and Family Studies, 25*(12), 3607–3618. https://doi.org/10.1007/s10826-016-0510-x

Ancell, K. S., Bruns, D. A., & Chitiyo, J. (2018). The importance of father involvement in early childhood programs. *Young Exceptional Children, 21*(1), 22–33. https://doi.org/10.1177/1096250615621355

Anderson, L. M., Shinn, C., Fullilove, M. T., Scrimshaw, S. C., Fielding, J. E., Normand, J., & Carande-Kulis, V. G. (2003). The effectiveness of early childhood development programs: A systematic review. *American Journal of Preventive Medicine, 24*(3, Supplement), 32–46. https://doi.org/10.1016/S0749-3797(02)00655-4

Astone, N. M., Karas, A., & Stolte, A. (2016, December). *Fathers' time with children: Income and residential differences*. Urban Institute. https://www.urban.org/sites/default/files/publication/86341/fathers_time_with_children_0.pdf

Belsky, J. (1984). The determinants of parenting: A process model. Child Development, *55*(1), 83–96. https://doi.org/10.2307/1129836

Boller, K., Bradley, R., Cabrera, N., Raikes, H., Pan, B., & Roggman, L. (2006). The Early Head Start father studies: Design, data collection, and summary of father presence in the lives of infants and toddlers. *Parenting: Science and Practice, 6*(2–3), 117–143. https://doi.org/10.1207/s15327922par0602&3_1

Bronfenbrenner, U., & Morris, P. A. (2006). The bioecological model of human development. In W. Damon & R. M. Lerner (Eds.), *Handbook of child psychology: Theoretical models of human development* (Vol. 12, 6th ed., pp. 793–828). Wiley. https://doi.org/10.1002/9780470147658.chpsy0114

Bronte-Tinkew, J., Burkhauser, M., & Metz, A. J. R. (2012). Elements of promising practices in fatherhood programs: Evidenced-based research findings on interventions for fathers. *Fathering: A Journal of Theory, Research, and Practice about Men as Fathers, 10*(1), 6–30. https://doi.org/10.3149/fth.1001.6

Brooks-Gunn, J., Klebanov, P. K., Liaw, F., & Spiker, D. (1993). Enhancing the development of low-birthweight, premature infants: Changes in cognition and behavior over the first three years. *Child Development, 64*(3), 736–753. https://doi.org/10.2307/1131215

Bruno, E. P., & Iruka, I. U. (2022). Reexamining the Carolina Abecedarian Project using an antiracist perspective: Implications for early care and education research. *Early Childhood Research Quarterly, 58*, 165–176. https://doi.org/10.1016/j.ecresq.2021.09.001

Burwick, A., Bellotti, J., & Nagatoshi, C. (2004). *Paths to father involvement: The Early Head Start fatherhood demonstration in its third year*. Final Report. U.S. Department of Health and Human Services, Head Start Bureau.

Cabrera, N. J. (2010). Father involvement and public policies. In M. E. Lamb (Ed.), *The role of the father in child development* (pp. 517–550). Wiley.

Cabrera, N. J., Shannon, J. D., & Tamis-LeMonda, C. (2007). Fathers' influence on their children's cognitive and emotional development: From toddlers to pre-K. *Applied Development Science, 11*(4), 208–213. https://doi.org/10.1080/10888690701762100

Cabrera, N., Shannon, J., Rodriguez, V. J., & Lubar, A. (2009). Early intervention programs: The case of Head Start for Latino children. In F. Villarruel, G. Carlo, J. Grau, M. Azmitia, N. Cabrera, & J. Chahin (Eds.), *Handbook of U.S. Latino psychology: Developmental and community-based perspectives* (pp. 251–266). Sage.

Cabrera, N. J., Fitzgerald, H. E., Bradley, R. H., & Roggman, L. (2014). The ecology of father-child relationships: An expanded model. *Journal of Family Theory & Review, 6*(4), 336–354. https://doi.org/10.1111/jftr.12054

Cabrera, N., Torres, L., Dion, R., & Baumgartner, S. (2015). *H-PACT: A descriptive study of Responsible Fatherhood programs serving Hispanic men*. OPRE Report # 2015-112. Office of Planning, Research and Evaluation, Administration for Children and Families, U.S. Department of Health and Human Services.

Cabrera, N. J., Jeong Moon, U., Fagan, J., West, J., & Aldoney, D. (2020). Cognitive stimulation at home and in child care and children's preacademic skills in two-parent families. *Child Development, 91*, 1709–1717. https://doi.org/10.1111/cdev.13380

Cabrera, N. J., Hennigar, A., Alonso, A., McDorman, S. A., & Reich, S. M. (2021). The protective effects of maternal and paternal factors on children's social development. *Adversity and Resilience Science, 2*(2), 85–98. https://doi.org/10.1007/s42844-021-00041-x

Campbell, F. A., Ramey, C. T., Pungello, E., Sparling, J., & Miller-Johnson, S. (2002). Early childhood education: Young adult outcomes from the Abecedarian Project. *Applied Developmental Science, 6*(1), 42–57. https://doi.org/10.1207/S1532480XADS0601_05

Campbell, F., Conti, G., Heckman, J. J., Moon, S. H., Pinto, R., Pungello, E., & Pan, Y. (2014). Early childhood investments substantially boost adult health. *Science, 343*(6178), 1478–1485. https://doi.org/10.1126/science.1248429

Cancian, M., Heinrich, C., & Chung, Y. (2013). Discouraging disadvantaged fathers' employment: An unintended consequence of policies designed to support families. *Journal of Policy Analysis and Management, 32*(4), 758–784. http://www.jstor.org/stable/42001562

Chacko, A., Fabiano, G. A., Doctoroff, G. L., & Fortson, B. (2018). Engaging fathers in effective parenting for preschool children using shared book reading: A randomized controlled trial. *Journal of Clinical Child & Adolescent Psychology, 47*(1), 79–93. https://doi.org/10.1080/15374416.2016.1266648

Cowan, P. A., Cowan, C. P., Pruett, M. K., Pruett, K., & Gillette, P. (2014). Evaluating a couples group to enhance father involvement in low-income families using a benchmark comparison. *Family Relations, 63*(3), 356–370. https://doi.org/10.1111/fare.12072

DeGarmo, D. S., & Forgatch, M. S. (2007). Efficacy of parent training for stepfathers: From playful spectator and polite stranger to effective stepfathering. *Parenting, 7*(4), 331–355. https://doi.org/10.1080/15295190701665631

Duursma, E. (2016). Who does the reading, who the talking? Low-income fathers and mothers in the US interacting with their young children around a picture book. *First Language, 36*(5), 465–484. https://doi.org/10.1177/0142723716648849

Fagan, J., & Pearson, J. (2020). Fathers' dosage in community-based programs for low-income fathers. *Family Process, 59*(1), 81–93. https://doi.org/10.1111/famp.12416

Fatherhood Research & Practice Network. (n.d.). https://www.frpn.org/

Forgatch, M. S., & Domenech Rodríguez, M. M. (2016). Interrupting coercion: The iterative loops among theory, science, and practice. In T. J. Dishion & J. J. Snyder (Eds.), *The Oxford handbook of coercive relationship dynamics* (pp. 194–214). Oxford University Press.

Fox, G. L., Nordquist, V. M., Billen, R. M., & Savoca, E. F. (2015). Father involvement and early intervention: Effects of empowerment and father role identity. *Family Relations, 64*(4), 461–475. https://doi.org/10.1111/fare.12156

Garasky, S., Stewart, S. D., Gundersen, C., & Lohman, B. J. (2010). Toward a fuller understanding of nonresident father involvement: An examination of child support, in-kind support, and visitation. *Population Research and Policy Review, 29*(3), 363–393. https://doi.org/10.1007/s11113-009-9148-3

Gerhardt, M., Feng, X., Wu, Q., Hooper, E. G., Ku, S., & Chan, M. H. (2020). A naturalistic study of parental emotion socialization: Unique contributions of fathers. *Journal of Family Psychology, 34*(2), 204–214. https://doi.org/10.1037/fam0000602

Hayes, D., Jones, D. A., Silverstein, L. B., & Auerbach, C. F. (2010). In their own words: Early Head Start fathers. *Psychology of Men & Masculinity, 11*(4), 241–250. https://doi.org/10.1037/a0021036

Hemez, P., & Washington, C. (2021, April 12). *Percentage and number of children living with two parents has dropped since 1968*. United States Census Bureau. https://www.census.gov/library/stories/2021/04/number-of-children-living-only-with-their-mothers-has-doubled-in-past-50-years.html

Jeon, S., & Neppl, T. K. (2019). Economic pressure, parent positivity, positive parenting, and child social competence. *Journal of Child and Family Studies, 28*(5), 1402–1412. https://doi.org/10.1007/s10826-019-01372-1

Mitchell, S. J., See, H. M., Tarkow, A. K. H., Cabrera, N., McFadden, K. E., & Shannon, J. D. (2007). Conducting studies with fathers: Challenges and opportunities. *Applied Developmental Science, 11*(4), 239–244. https://doi.org/10.1080/10888690701762159

Karberg, E., Aldoney, D., & Cabrera, N. (2017). Fatherhood in America: The context, practice, and gaps in responsible fatherhood programs. In C. Mazza & A. Perry (Eds.), *Fatherhood in America: Social work perspectives on a changing society* (pp. 302–352). Charles C. Thomas Pub. Ltd..

LaBounty, J., Wellman, H. M., Olson, S., Lagattuta, K., & Liu, D. (2008). Mothers' and fathers' use of internal state talk with their young children. *Social Development, 17*(4), 757–775. https://doi.org/10.1111/j.1467-9507.2007.00450.x

Lee, K., & Rispoli, K. (2019). Head Start impact on fathers' involvement and Black children's development. *Journal of Social Work Education, 55*(4), 777–797. https://doi.org/10.1080/10437797.2019.1567413

Love, J. M., Kisker, E. E., Ross, C. M., Schochet, P. Z., Brooks-Gunn, J., Paulsell, D., Boller, K., Constantine, J., Vogel, C., Fuligni, A. S., & Brady-Smith, C. (2002). *Making a difference in the lives of infants and toddlers and their families: The impacts of Early Head Start. Volumes I–III:* Final Technical Report. For full text: https://eric.ed.gov/?id=ED472186

Love, J. M., Chazan-Cohen, R., Raikes, H., & Brooks-Gunn, J. (2013). What makes a difference: Early Head Start evaluation findings in a developmental context. *Monographs of the Society for Research in Child Development, 78*(1), vii–viii, 1–173. https://doi.org/10.1111/j.1540-5834.2012.00699.x

Malin, J. L., Cabrera, N. J., & Rowe, M. L. (2014). Low-income minority mothers' and fathers' reading and children's interest: Longitudinal contributions to children's receptive vocabulary skills. *Early Childhood Research Quarterly, 29*(4), 425–432. https://doi.org/10.1016/j.ecresq.2014.04.010

Martin, A., Brooks-Gunn, J., Klebanov, P., Buka, S. L., & McCormick, M. C. (2008). Long-term maternal effects of early childhood intervention: Findings from the Infant Health and Development Program (IHDP). *Journal of Applied Developmental Psychology, 29*(2), 101–117. https://doi.org/10.1016/j.appdev.2007.12.007

McBride, B. A., Curtiss, S. J., Uchima, K., Laxman, D. J., Santos, R. M., Weglarz-Ward, J., Dyer, W. J., Jeans, L. M., & Kern, J. (2017). Father involvement in early intervention: Exploring the gap between service providers' perceptions and practices. *Journal of Early Intervention, 39*(2), 71–87. https://doi.org/10.1177/1053815116686118

McCormick, M. C. (2006). Early intervention in low birth weight premature infants: Results at 18 years of age for the Infant Health and Development Program. *Pediatrics, 117*(3), 771–780. https://doi.org/10.1542/peds.2005-1316

McKee, K., Cabrera, N., Alonso, A., Turcios, M., & Reich, S. (2021). Determinants of fathers' and mothers' involvement in a parenting intervention. *Psychology of Men & Masculinities, 22*(3), 521–537. https://doi.org/10.1037/men0000320

Miller, D. P., & Mincy, R. B. (2012). Falling further behind? Child support arrears and fathers' labor force participation. *The Social Service Review, 86*(4), 604–635. https://doi.org/10.1086/668761

Nepomnyaschy, L. (2007). Child support and father-child contact: Testing reciprocal pathways. *Demography, 44*(1), 93–112. http://www.jstor.org/stable/4137223

Nievar, M. A., Ramisetty-Mikler, S., Saleh, M. F., & Cabrera, N. (2020). Families Offering Children Unfailing Support (FOCUS) Fatherhood Program: Changing child welfare through child support and parenting skills. *Children and Youth Services Review, 118*. https://doi.org/10.1016/j.childyouth.2020.105321

Osborne, C. (2020). Fathers and public policy. In H. E. Fitzgerald, K. von Klitzing, N. J. Cabrera, J. Scarano de Mendonça, & T. Skjøthaug (Eds.), *Handbook of fathers and child development* (pp. 121–132). Springer. https://doi.org/10.1007/978-3-030-51027-5_8

Panter-Brick, C., Burgess, A., Eggerman, M., McAllister, F., Pruett, K., & Leckman, J. F. (2014). Practitioner Review: Engaging fathers – Recommendations for a game change in parenting interventions based on a systematic review of the global evidence. *Journal of Child Psychology and Psychiatry, 55*(11), 1187–1212. https://doi.org/10.1111/jcpp.12280

Pearson, J., & Fagan, J. (2019). State efforts to support the engagement of nonresident fathers in the lives of their children. *Families in Society, 100*(4), 392–408. https://doi.org/10.1177/1044389419874172

Pruett, M. K., Pruett, K., Cowan, C. P., & Cowan, P. A. (2017). Enhancing father involvement in low-income families: A couples group approach to preventive intervention. *Child Development, 88*(2), 398–407. https://doi.org/10.1111/cdev.12744

Pruett, M. K., Cowan, P. A., Cowan, C. P., Gillette, P., & Pruett, K. D. (2019). Supporting father involvement: An intervention with community and child welfare–referred couples. *Family Relations, 68*(1), 51–67. https://doi.org/10.1111/fare.12352

Puma, M., Bell, S., Cook, R., Heid, C., Broene, P., Jenkins, F., Mashburn, A., & Downer, J. (2012). *Third grade follow-up to the Head Start Impact Study final report, executive summary*. OPRE Report # 2012-45b. Office of Planning, Research and Evaluation, Administration for Children and Families, U.S. Department of Health and Human Services. https://www.acf.hhs.gov/opre/report/third-grade-follow-head-start-impact-study-final-report-executive-summary

Raikes, H., Brooks-Gunn, J., & Love, J. (2013). I. Background literature review pertaining to the Early Head Start study. *Monographs of the Society for Research in Child Development, 78*(1), 1–19. http://www.jstor.org/stable/23361870

Rowe, M. L., Coker, D. L., & Pan, B. A. (2004). A comparison of fathers' and mothers' talk to toddlers in low-income families. *Social Development, 13*(2), 278–291. https://doi.org/10.1111/J.1467-9507.2004.000267.X

Sparling, J., Ramey, S. L., & Ramey, C. T. (2021). Mental health and social development effects of the Abecedarian approach. *International Journal of Environmental Research and Public Health, 18*(13), 6997. https://doi.org/10.3390/ijerph18136997

Tennessee Department of Education. (2021, August 3). *Tennessee Early Intervention System*. https://www.tn.gov/didd/for-consumers/tennessee-early-intervention-system-teis.html

Towe-Goodman, N. R., Willoughby, M., Blair, C., Gustafsson, H. C., Mills-Koonce, W. R., & Cox, M. J. (2014). Fathers' sensitive parenting and the development of early executive functioning. *Journal of Family Psychology, 28*(6), 867–876. https://doi.org/10.1037/a0038128

Vogel, C. A., Xue, Y., Moiduddin, E. M., Kisker, E. E., & Carlson, B. L. (2010). *Early Head Start children in Grade 5: Long-term follow-up of the Early Head Start Research and Evaluation Study sample*. OPRE Report # 2011-8. Office of Planning, Research, and Evaluation, Administration for Children and Families, U.S. Department of Health and Human Services.

Vogel, C. A., Caronongan, P., Xue, Y., Thomas, J., Bandel, E., Aikens, N., Boller, K., & Murphy, L. (2015). *Toddlers in Early Head Start: A portrait of 3-year-olds, their families, and the programs serving them*. OPRE Report 2015–28. Office of Planning, Research and Evaluation, Administration for Children and Families, U.S. Department of Health and Human Services.

Walsh, T., Zach, L., Fendt, P., & Davidson, D. (2020). *Strategies for engaging fathers in family services*. Fast Focus No. 46. Institute for Research on Poverty, University of Wisconsin–Madison. https://www.irp.wisc.edu/resource/strategies-for-engaging-fathers-in-family-services/

Zigler, E. (1978). The effectiveness of head start: Another look. *Educational Psychologist, 13*, 71–77. https://doi.org/10.1080/00461527809529196

Zigler, E. F., & Bishop-Josef, S. J. (2006). The cognitive child versus the whole child: Lessons from 40 years of Head Start. In *Play = Learning*. Oxford University Press. https://doi.org/10.1093/acprof:oso/9780195304381.003.0002
Zigler, E. F., & Muenchow, S. (1992). *Head Start: The inside story of America's most successful educational experiment*. Basic Books.
Zigler, E. F., & Styfco, S. J. (2010). *The hidden history of Head Start* (1st ed.). Oxford University Press.
Zigler, E. F., & Valentine, J. (1979). *Project Head Start: A legacy of the war on poverty*. Free Press.

Chapter 14
Fathers and Child Support: How Money Transfers and Other Interactions Impact Family Dynamics

Jeffrey D. Ball

Introduction

This chapter delves into the issues that surround *child support*, their impact on a child's relationship with their father, and how disparate parents deal with a government system that historically was not tailored to nuanced case management depending on an individual's circumstances. Child support programs aim to economically strengthen children whose parents live apart by transferring income from the parent who does not reside a majority of the time with the children (the *noncustodial parent*) to the parent with whom the children live for the majority of the time (the *custodial parent* or a relative caretaker). Accomplishing this transfer may require coercive steps to separate the income from the paying parent, who in about 80 percent of cases is the father (Grall, 2020b).

The child support program (program) manifests elements of a collection agency, law enforcement, and social work. The first two elements set the program apart from the other social services programs and can lead to tensions between parents and between the program and the noncustodial parent.

As a program that actively intervenes in the lives of two-household adults to ensure that the children of those parents have adequate financial support in the primary household, the program's workers deal with sensitive questions such as: Who is the biological father? How much income does each parent earn? How can the use of enforcement tools work to separate money from the parent who is under a court obligation to pay support?

J. D. Ball (✉)
Former Chair of the Colorado Child Support Commission and Former Project Manager for the El Paso County CO Child Support Services program, La Mesa, CA, USA
e-mail: jeffballchildsupport@gmail.com

J. L. Bellamy et al. (eds.), *Social Work Practice with Fathers*,
https://doi.org/10.1007/978-3-031-13686-3_14

The program leaders at the state and federal levels are now examining the abilities of the parents, particularly fathers, to produce enough income to support themselves before subjecting a paying parent to the harsh collection remedies available to child support workers to enforce an order (NCSEA Policy Forum Agenda, 2021). The changes in the program may lead to new measures of program success, such as healthful family interaction and positive emotional sustainability even when parents live in separate households.

Background and Context

Until recently, the history of the child support or Title IV-D program, so named because of its place in the Social Security Act, was one of increasing types of familial situations that qualify for services and expanding enforcement remedies to improve the efficacy of collecting support. Only in the last two decades has the program looked at the lives of both parents more closely to see if there are ways it can facilitate the transfer of income between parents to pay for children's costs while considering the economic and emotional impacts that affect people's lives over time.

Local programs have, for the most part, placed a new emphasis on fatherhood to bring separate-household fathers out of the shadows of the "deadbeat dad" moniker that has followed them for two generations. For example, see the results of the federally funded eight-state demonstration grant focused on noncustodial parents (US DHHS, Office of Child Support Enforcement (OCSE), 2018). Stereotypes die hard, but gradually, the country is looking at noncustodial fathers in a more nuanced, multifaceted light. Just as with society at large, noncustodial fathers run the gamut from caring, nurturing, supporting parents to those who intentionally financially and emotionally abandon their children.

One in Four Children Lives in a Single-Parent Home

Few people's family ties and income levels follow a straight-line upward trajectory over their lifetimes. Relationships and income ebb and flow, experiencing successes and roadblocks. It is the challenge of the current child support program to better react to those changes without ultra-legalistic, antagonistic, and time-consuming court involvement. Both parents deserve support levels that reflect accurate accountings of their current situations.

Single-parent households represent about 25 percent of households with children, caring for over 18 million children (US Census Bureau, 2020). For 15 million children, fathers do not live the majority of the time with their children. Children who do not live in two-parent households on average have a higher chance of living in poverty. Two-parent households had a poverty rate of 4% in 2019, mother-headed households without a spouse had a poverty rate of 22.2%, and father-headed households without a spouse had a poverty rate of 11.5% (US Census Bureau, 2019). Some older studies found that children living in single-parent households without an actively participating father have on average lower academic achievement and a higher likelihood of juvenile delinquency and are more likely to have mental health issues than children in two-parent households (Maginnis, 1997). Newer research points to poverty as a more impactful correlation than household intactness. Family structure by itself is not necessarily a determinative variable for children's outcomes (Cross, 2019). How often a noncustodial father interacts with his children, the quality of the interaction, and the degree of engagement or involvement may have various degrees of impact on the children's mental and emotional growth (Rosenberg & Wilcox, 2017). For the purpose of this chapter, father engagement and father involvement are treated similarly as activities in which the father actively participates directly and indirectly with his children to support them educationally, emotionally, morally, and recreationally. Children who grow up with involved fathers are more likely to have more positive outcomes in academic achievement (Rosenberg & Wilcox, 2006).

For many years, some fathers (and mothers) felt alienated from their children when parents lived in separate households. One random sample poll indicated that 13.4 percent of parents felt alienated from their children, which could be due to a variety of reasons (Harman, 2016). As times change, a movement toward co-parenting and father inclusion has begun to erase decades of father alienation, with intended long-term positive benefits to children emotionally, socially, and economically (Rosenberg & Wilcox, 2006).

For many nonintact families, alienation is not the main issue as both parents cooperate to raise their children. Financial stress may cast a stressful undercurrent that is felt by children regardless of household makeup (Friedline et al., 2020), but single-parent families have higher poverty rates than intact families (Census Bureau, 2019). Furthermore, Black and Hispanic families live in poverty at a higher percentage than White families. Financial stress is real for a significant number of children and parents living in poverty. Family structures have evolved over the last two generations. A minority of children reside with two parents in a first marriage today, down from almost three-fourths of children in 1960 (Pew Research Center, 2015) (Fig. 14.1).

Economically Independent Women Becoming Increasingly the Norm After World War II

In mid-twentieth-century America, the paradigm of father as breadwinner and mother as housekeeper and sole child raiser began to change. In 1920, under 20% of women worked outside the home. By 1950, the percentage had risen to about 30%, and by 1970 about 46% (OECD, 2017). The percentage peaked at 60% in 1999 and now hovers in the mid-fifties range in the last decade. While the numbers grew for

Fig. 14.1 American family structures from 1960 to 2014

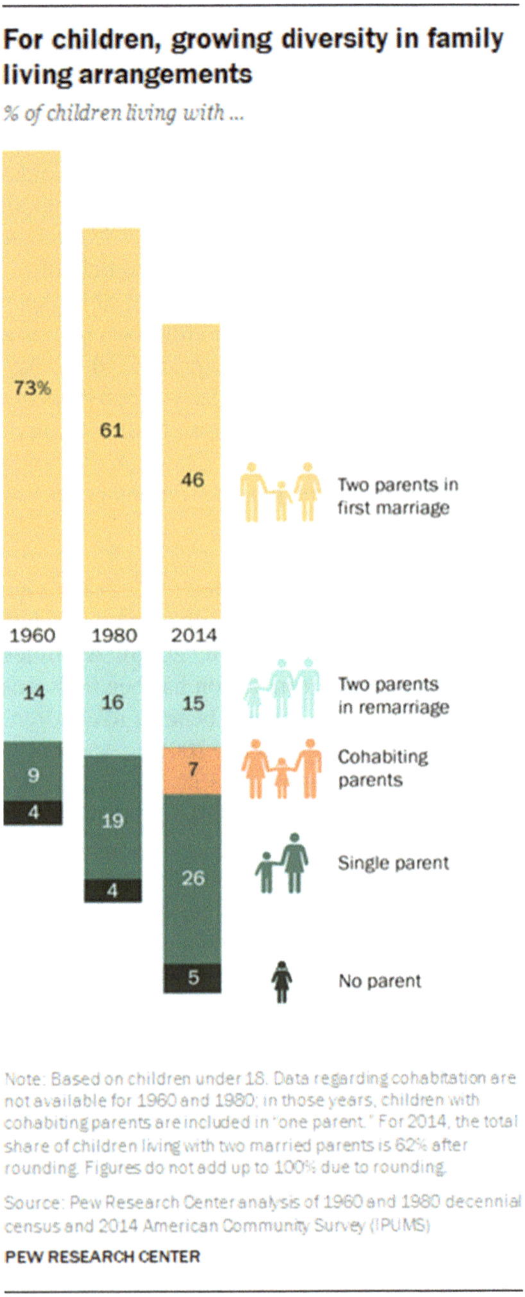

women, they fell for men, where 80% of men aged 20–64 participated in the labor market in 1970 and 69% in December 2019 (Bureau of Labor Statistics, 2021). The Federal Reserve Bank of Richmond concluded that three factors drive the downward workforce participation by males: (1) broader availability of disability benefits and other government policy changes; (2) structural changes in the workforce, in which many manufacturing jobs disappeared while job opportunities arose in other industries such as health; and (3) cultural reasons that lead to more nonwork activities (Ullrich, 2021). The biggest time use disparity between working men and non-working men is that nonworking men spend an average of 3.7 hours per day more than working men on leisure activities and sports.

More economically independent women did not have to tie their identities solely to their families. Women explored the roads men often took for granted, such as careers, sexual freedom, and stronger self-worth (Ferguson, 2019). The economic reliance on a father as sole income source that kept many an unhappy family together was replaced by economically independent women who could forge a life independent of economic reliance on men with whom they were no longer compatible.

By the 1970s and 1980s, the changed mores led to an increase in the out-of-wedlock, or nonmarital, birth rate (Census Bureau, 1999), and divorce became easier to secure when states adopted no-fault divorce laws during this time (Parkman, 2019). The number of single-parent households climbed in the 1960s and 1970s (Mather, 2010). For many Americans, the rising governmental cost of caring for single-never-married parents and their children became a trope for the downfall of the traditional family. The percentage of single-parent households rose to become higher among Black (48.8%) and Hispanic (28.7%) households than non-Hispanic White (21.1%) households (Grall, 2020a). Economically, 49.4% of poverty-level families live in a single-parent household. Welfare transmogrified from a word denoting sustenance into a canard representing the lack of self-fortitude (New York Times, 2008). A backlash formed to ensure that the "absent parent," almost always the man, be responsible for his child economically even if not living in the same household. While the courts had always included a support provision in divorces, the support was generally a menial amount prior to the child support program's national implementation.

Two households, of course, cost more to maintain than one household. If a mother worked, raised the children the majority of the time, and paid for daycare and health care, the costs were typically prohibitive without assistance from the father. The poverty rate for a mother head of household with children in 1980 was 34.6% while the poverty rate for a father head of household without children was 11.4% (Census Bureau, 1987). Irregular and non-guaranteed levels of support could no longer sustain a household with children.

Today, women earn about 85% of what men earn doing the same job with the same experience (Pew Research Center, 2019), and the historical difference in industry sector earnings between male-dominated industries and female-dominated industries has hurt. But women are making inroads into industries once the dominion of males, where many of the jobs are more lucrative. Compare what a childcare worker averages per week ($548, 5% male) to what a miner makes per week ($1596, 9% female; Bureau of Labor Statistics, 2021). Therefore, when child support guidelines use the proportionate incomes of both parents to calculate the amount of support that the noncustodial parent is to pay, it is often the case that the higher-earning father owes support to the mother, even in cases where the parenting time is close to even between parents.

The Emergence of the Deadbeat Dad Myth

Most fathers want to and do take care of the economic needs of their families, whether in the same household or not. However, a significant percentage of noncustodial fathers do not have the means to provide financial support (Cancian & Meyer, 2004), and a minority, but statistically significant percentage, of fathers with the means to pay do not pay (Sorensen & Zibman, 2001a) because they do not have visitation rights, use their earnings instead for themselves or a new family, deny paternity of a child, or to show animosity toward the other parent. This created the "deadbeat dad" myth as a universal assumption of a noncustodial father—the absent parent who abandoned his kids. Stereotypes based on race accentuated the myth as Black men in particular were castigated as absent parents, leaving the mother and children on the public dole.

In a 1976 campaign speech, presidential candidate Ronald Reagan used an example of a woman he called a "welfare queen" living large off the public dole. The astonishing story had no basis. In fact, it was later learned, but the term stuck and became a trope (Dolnick, 2019). The mythical counterpart to the welfare queen was the Black man who fathered children indiscriminately and never visited them. The truth is different. First, 86% of children are born to parents of the same race (Livingston, 2017). Examining how many children women bear by race, the average non-Hispanic Black woman between ages 40–44 has 2.5 children, Hispanic women 2.6 children, non-Hispanic White women 2.3, and Asian women 2.2 (Livingston, 2015). Only 20% of Hispanic women had four or more children, 18% of non-Hispanic Black women, 11% of non-Hispanic White women, and 10% of Asian women. Sixty-seven percent of Black men who live apart from their children see them at least once a month, compared to 59% for White men (Cadet, 2014). Most men, regardless of ethnicity, are involved in the lives of their children who reside primarily in a separate household (Maccoby et al., 1993).

History of the Child Support Program

Early History of the Child Support Program—Reimburse the Government

Only Pennsylvania, Michigan, and Ohio had robust statewide child support programs long before the federalization of the program in 1975 (Ball & Wellbank, 2017). Many states did not have a way to systematically use government resources to help establish paternity and a support order and then enforce that order for parents not living together despite federal efforts in the 1950s and 1960s to encourage states to engage in these tasks (Morgan, 2021).

An exception existed in interstate cases when parents lived in different states. Uniform interstate laws voluntarily adopted by states included the Uniform Desertion and Non-Support Act (1910) and the Uniform Reciprocal Enforcement of

Support Act (URESA, 1950, 1952, 1958, 1968 versions). Local prosecuting attorneys handled these interstate cases to ensure that children whose parents lived in different states still received child support.

In 1974, Senator Russell Long of Louisiana submitted a title in a larger bill that would require all states to have a statewide program regulated by the federal government to recoup the cost of welfare, then known as Aid to Families with Dependent Children (AFDC) or Aid to Dependent Children (ADC; Social Services Amendments, 1974). In order to recoup the cost, paternity had to be legally established for children born of unmarried parents, after which a support order would be issued by a court. State child support programs would ensure that the child support order was enforced. Contempt of court (for failing to follow a court order), and criminal prosecution were the two most common enforcement tools for the first few years of the program (Katz, 2019). Prosecutors used the threat of incarceration to secure payment whenever it was delinquent.

Over the next 21 years, Congress added more tools to collect, including income withholding; federal and state income tax refund offset; financial institution data matches; driver's, recreational, and professional license suspensions; and credit reporting to credit bureaus.

Critically, a parent receiving Aid to Families with Dependent Children/Aid to Dependent Children (AFDC/ADC) had to assign their rights to the child support so the state could pursue collections as the debt owner. These generally were non-divorce cases in which support orders were seldom entered on behalf of the non-married parents prior to the program's involvement.

The new law created Title IV-D of the Social Security Act. States had to pass legislation and rules to implement the new federal law or risk losing their Title IV-A (AFDC/ADC) funding. The newly created federal OCSE was tasked with producing uniform rules to ensure that all states and "territories" (Guam, Virgin Islands, Puerto Rico, and the District of Columbia) followed a similar set of procedures and offered similar services. In return, the states and territories received federal funding to defray most of their expenses.

States were free to set up the programs in different configurations. Most chose a statewide model with local state-operated offices and were housed in their departments of human services, but some states chose to put their programs under the state attorney general or state department of revenue. About one-third of the states, mostly the larger ones, chose to work through their local counties, using either their county legal departments (e.g., district attorneys, state attorneys, county attorneys) or their welfare departments (e.g., human services, children and family services; US DHHS, 2021a, b).

Social work concepts were not a paramount consideration in the structure created to secure and enforce child support orders. The program focused on collecting money regardless of the situation of the noncustodial parent, who was tagged the absent parent for much of the history of the program, de-emphasizing the role they played in the nurturing of the children. Today, "noncustodial parent" is still the most common term for the paying parent, although *nonresidential parent* is gaining some favor.

The universal basic child support services were (1) receive referrals from AFDC/ADC offices of persons receiving welfare and have rights to child support assigned from the welfare recipient to the state, (2) locate the whereabouts of the alleged father, (3) determine paternity if the child was born out of wedlock, (4) establish a support order for the child(ren), (5) enforce the order, and (6) collect the payments to reimburse the federal and state government for the cost of the AFDC/ADC, now called Temporary Assistance to Needy Families (TANF) (Fig. 14.2).

At first, all the collected money went to reimburse the government for the welfare expended, even if the family no longer received welfare but past-due child support was still owed. In 1981, the program expanded to include non-AFDC/ADC cases (New York Times, 2008). Anyone who lived in a different household from the other parent could apply for service regardless of income or welfare status. States received federal incentive dollars for their collections, but the non-welfare incentives were capped as a percentage of the welfare collections to keep the focus on collecting the welfare dollars. Federal tax refunds could be intercepted to pay off welfare costs, and if there were any refund dollars remaining after paying off the government cost of assistance, the remainder could be applied and paid to families still owed past-due support (Morgan, 2021).

The Child Support Enforcement Amendments of 1984 (Pub. L. 98–78) added many tools to the enforcement toolbox. The act authorized states to use continuous garnishment, also known as income withholding, against an employer to collect child support. It added liens on real and personal property, bonds, federal tax refund offset in non-welfare cases, and credit reporting as additional methods to directly or indirectly pressure the noncustodial parent to pay.

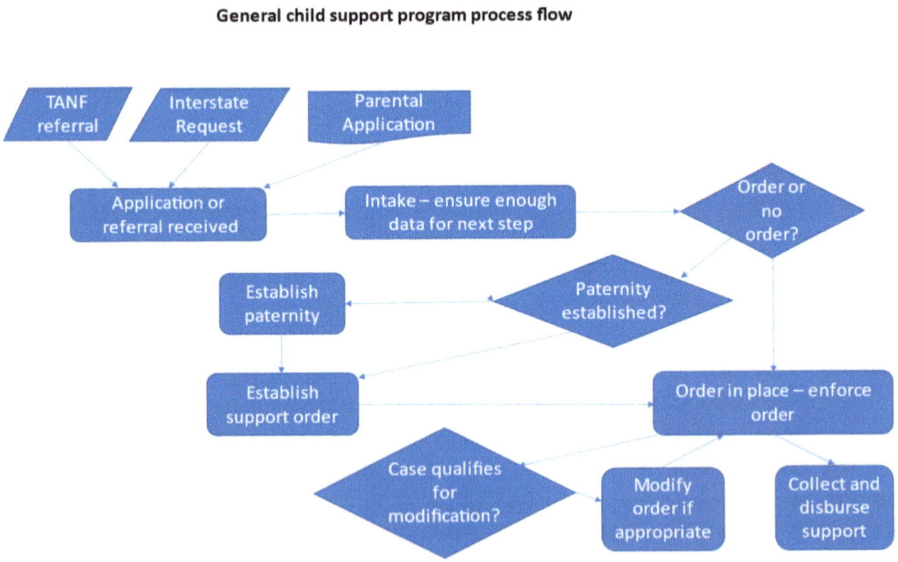

Fig. 14.2 Child support program process flow

Mid-history of the Program—Maximize Collections for Custodial Parents and Government

By the mid-1980s, the state child support programs had similar tools to enforce cases, but they were used differently by states. In many local offices, for example, the prosecuting attorney used criminal prosecution and contempt of court as the primary enforcement remedies; in others, the caseworkers went directly after income and assets through garnishment, withholding, liens, intercepts, etc. (White et al., 2016). There was no uniform way to determine how much someone should pay in child support as this was left to the court's discretion or a loose framework of principles.

In 1988, Congress passed the Family Support Act of 1988 (Pub. L. 100–485) in which income withholding was made mandatory in program cases regardless of whether the payor was past due or not (Drake, 2013). This means that any employed paying parent is subject to a continuous garnishment of their pay if the case is in the child support program. For private or pro se cases that are separate from the program, income withholding is not automatically triggered but could be sought through additional actions by the custodial parent. For the first time, states had to use presumptive guidelines to determine how much child support had to be paid, and the amount had to be a sum that did not vary as weekly paychecks fluctuated. Child support guidelines are based on the income ratio of both parents or, in a few states, based solely on the income of the noncustodial parent (NCSL, 2021). The support amount may be ratcheted up or down by factors such as the number of overnights the noncustodial parent has with the child, the cost of health insurance premiums for the child, and day-care costs. The calculated amount became the ordered support amount unless rebutted by other evidence, such as extraordinary medical expenses (U.S. Government Printing Office, 45 CFR § 303.4).

The act also requires states to have automated systems so that all state and local child support workers would use the same computer system, with the same screens and logic, to make the operations more uniform (Drake, 2013). The act created a commission that worked with the National Conference of Commissioners on Uniform State Laws to improve interstate case processing. The Uniform Interstate Family Support Act (UIFSA) (1992, 1996, 2001, 2008) eventually replaced URESA, impacting about three in ten child support cases where parents resided in different states (Government Accountability Office Report, 1990).

President Clinton worked with Congress to partially reimagine welfare as a time-limited benefit that emphasized work. In 1996, Congress passed the Personal Responsibility and Work Opportunity Reconciliation Act of 1996 (PRWORA). PRWORA's headlines focused on the new TANF program. Congress "*block-granted*" the funding to states for the program, meaning that states had a lot of flexibility to shape their TANF program with a few uniform parameters.

On the other hand, the child support section of PRWORA continued the 1980's movement toward greater specificity in that Congress required states to operate a more comprehensive child support program. Congress added additional automation requirements, a required central depository and disbursement point of child support collections, additional automated enforcement tools, mandatory state passage of the 1996 revised version of UIFSA (1992, 1996, 2001, 2008), a revised distribution of collected child support to favor family-owed child support over state-owed debt from TANF/AFDC/ADC grant episodes, and a standard approach to modification of child support orders based on a substantial and continuous change in circumstances.

Under PRWORA, tribal governments could start their own child support programs and receive enhanced federal funding. The state department could enter into bilateral agreements with other countries regarding child support. Importantly, with a small nod to noncustodial parents, PRWORA authorized grants to states to address access and visitation programs to enhance the ability of paying parents to see their children on a regular basis.

The final piece of major legislation occurred 2 years later with the passage of the Child Support Performance Incentive Act of 1998 (CSPIA). Congress gave states a pot of money as an incentive to perform well. States under CSPIA are measured by their percentage of children born of unmarried parents for whom paternity is established, percentage of cases that need child support orders having orders, percentage of current support dollars owed in a given month collected in that month, number of cases with past-due support in which an arrearage payment was made during the course of the year, and cost-effectiveness (cost to run the program compared to dollars collected). The pot is finite so it is a zero-sum competition among the states and territories to divvy up the money based on these five performance indicators and the amount collected in both TANF and non-TANF cases. The desire of states to maximize their incentives drove the program's emphasis for the next decade or two.

The wealth of legislation in the 1980s and 1990s transformed the program from a loose confederation of state programs into a tightly knit, efficient national collection program. After PRWORA and its TANF time limitations, work requirements, and allowable state restrictions, TANF rolls declined precipitously so that by the 2010s, most programs collected more dollars for cases that never had a parent receiving assistance than for parents who were currently on assistance or on assistance in the past.

The program morphed in recent years from one that focused on state debt recoupment to one that emphasized collections for the parent with primary custody, generally referred to as the custodial parent. In federal fiscal year 2020, 94% of distributed collections went to families (OCSE, 2021). In 1995, 65% of distributed collections went to families and the rest to federal, state, and local governments for welfare reimbursement (OCSE, 1996).

While the child support programs did and do not represent either party (they represent the state or the county), it was clear that the paradigm for most of the history of the program was for caseworkers to try to collect what they could regardless of the hardship on the paying parent. Many child support caseworkers did not see the father as much more than a wallet. This proved to be shortsighted not only morally but also for the program's collection goals. By exacerbating the alienation of fathers from their families through strong collection measures, the program relied less on voluntary compliance and more on involuntary compliance. It turned out that it may have been unfruitful for the program and counterproductive for the family to strong-arm noncustodial parents with the same arsenal despite differences in circumstances that led to nonpayment (NCSL, 2021; Waller & Plotnick, 2001).

Recent Child Support History—Moving from Government Reimbursement to Income Transfer Between Parents

A movement within the child support community sparked by pushback from father's rights groups grew from the early 2000s through the 2010s to correct the unbalanced treatment between parents. If child support programs do not represent either parent, are the caseworkers taking stock of the financial hardships facing paying parents? Since child support funding cannot be used for most access and visitation activities, what are workers doing to address any obstacles in the way of the father having access to his children? Since low-income parents have the largest past-due support debts overall, should we forgive more of the debt rather than bury a parent in never-ending payment obligations?

As the child support program moves away from being a cost-recovery program and instead focuses on serving the parents' needs, it is increasingly apparent that the definition of child support as financial support is too narrow. Should the program figure out ways to expand its work to include access and visitation, and if so, can this be done without expanding federal funding sources? Some states have already taken baby steps in this area. Texas has default parenting plans that allow for some optional variations. Once the parties agree to a plan, it is filed with the courts. The Texas child support program will not enforce or modify the plan on behalf of either parent but promotes the establishment of one (Texas Office of the Attorney General, Co-Parenting Guide, n.d.).

If one looks at the disparate treatment between children born to a married couple and those outside of a marriage, one sees a two-tiered approach that often hurts the children of parents who never married. Forty percent of all births are to parents who were not married to one another (US DHHS, 2019). Non-Hispanic Black children were born out of wedlock in 57% of births, Hispanic children in 58% of births, and non-Hispanic White children in 29% of births. On the basis of income and education, a higher percentage of children are born out of wedlock to lower-income parents and to those who have up to a high school degree compared to parents with a higher income and postsecondary degrees. About 64% of pregnant women who did not finish high school had a child while unmarried compared to about 7% of pregnant women with a bachelor's degree or higher (Census Bureau, 1995).

Since fathers tend to be closely aligned socioeconomically to the mothers (known as *homogamy* or *assortative mating*; Chadwick & Solon, 2002), and poverty correlates to educational attainment (UC Davis, Center for Poverty and Inequality, n.d.), a child born out of wedlock has two parents who tend to have lower incomes than children born to married couples (US Census Bureau, 2017).

This racial and economic disparity has resulted in a child support program constituted to take harsher enforcement actions against the parents of children born out of wedlock than what often occurs in divorce cases. In the divorce case, parents may seek mediation, use private attorneys to reconcile differences, and reach a non-adversarial outcome. Many never-married parents do not have similar resources and rely on the child support system to routinely use its enforcement tools or the court system to resolve issues through the highly antagonistic world of litigation.

The majority of child support debt is owed by low-income parents (Brito et al., 2020). Sorensen and Zibman (2001b) found that many poor noncustodial parents, with or without a child support order, pay no support. While most noncustodial parents pay most of the child support due or none at all, there is a group who pay intermittently due to job loss, injury, illness, or lack of modification of an order to reflect current economic realities (Hodges et al., 2019).

Over 75% of parents do not have legal representation in a divorce case (Gardner, 2016). In nonmarital cases, non-representation may be higher than 90% of the cases. Texas recorded 92.5% of paying parents and 97.2% of majority-time parents in Title IV-D cases represented themselves in 2011 (Texas Access to Justice Commission, 2012). By appearing pro se in court without a legal education, one misses opportunities to best present one's case. Formal evidentiary rules and parental testimony that is not precise and relevant may cost parents their best legal arguments in court.

While the child support agencies do not represent either parent, the evidence presented to the court is based on documentation from the majority-time custodial parent and perhaps some payment stubs and other evidence from the noncustodial parent. The adversarial system is an impediment to better justice for both parents and their children, but particularly for the noncustodial parent.

Deviations from the guidelines are the exception in most states. Federal regulations require states to consider guideline fixes that limit deviations based on gathered data when reviewing their guidelines every 4 years. In one state, about 2% in establishment of order cases and about 6% in modification of order cases deviated from the guideline calculation (Colorado Child Support Commission, 2019). A Wisconsin study showed 45.2% of divorce cases where the guideline proposed amount was known deviated upward or downward, while the paternity cases resulted in 28.4% deviations (Hodges & Cook, 2019).

Implicit and explicit bias leads to a disproportionate number of Black and Hispanic men being incarcerated, including for not paying child support (Western & Petit, 2010). Low-income paying parents represent most of the $117 billion in past-due child support that has remained unpaid (Heinrich et al., 2010), updated with OCSE's arrears balance figure for FFY2019.

The program has historically served mostly parents who are slightly below or above the poverty threshold, whether or not the children were born to a married couple (Lyon, 1999). The more affluent parents can work out their finances, including their child support issues, through private lawyers if they can avoid emotional fallout from their breakup.

The program's workers learn how to process cases by mastering the state computer system to accomplish the next step in the child support process. This has led to a strong reliance on automation, with the result of limiting individual case enforcement creativity. Most enforcement remedies today are triggered by a delinquency period or amount leading to an automated enforcement action with or without prior approval by a worker, although as the program progresses, it is expected that more self-help remedies will be available to both parents through smartphone and tablet applications. This will reduce the cost of customer service and, in turn, reduce the number of people working in the program. The increasing use of smartphone technology in the program means parents can get up-to-date information about their case and communicate directly with their caseworker. The program is evolving into less of a confrontational paradigm to one encouraging mediation and cooperation. Since *parenting plans* and child support go hand in hand—because so many states factor in the number of overnights with the noncustodial parent in the guideline calculation, and some elements of child support itself could be resolved outside of a court setting—pretrial mediation and attempts to settle before the hearing are becoming more common (Bowling et al., 2019).

The program expanded its noncore emphasis under the Obama administration to include additional managerial time and resource focus on topics such as domestic violence, work opportunities for noncustodial parents, health-care coverage for children from governmental as well as private insurance sources, involving parents during early childhood, and reducing often vast amounts of accumulated debt by low-income payors as presented by OCSE Commissioner Turetsky, 2009–2017. The federal government made grants available to states to fund program opportunities that combine traditional child support services with additional services such as visitation mediation, employment services, and fatherhood and parenting classes (Cancian & Meyer, 2019).

OCSE issued its Final Rule in 2016 to tweak various aspects of state requirements for the program (OCSE Action Transmittal 16-06, 2016). One important theme in the rule was focusing on the ability to pay. The rule nationalizes the practice to downwardly adjust a noncustodial parent's support during incarceration if the sentence is greater than 6 months. The rule requires states reviewing their guidelines to include adjustments for low-income noncustodial parents and allow for a self-reserve upon which the noncustodial parent can pay basic living expenses for themself.

The Future—Decoupling Enforcement to Focus on Thriving Dual Household Families

Better integrating child support into the safety net for families could produce a program that focuses on guaranteed child support, or forward funding, to the custodial parent, with an invoice to the paying parent that could be paid monthly or annually as a taxable event back to the government. As the program de-emphasizes coercive enforcement, it could expand to tackle co-parenting issues, with the goal of providing children a stable dual-household lifestyle with strong emotional contributions from both parents. Federal funding should not be "siloed" or limited so the program can address issues it currently does not have the funding to do, such as mediation, counseling, educational support for children, technology for distant two-household communication, etc. Noncustodial parent employment services, which can be funded by TANF currently, could be directly funded by child support funding to create a more universal service provision by program offices.

Conceptual Framing

A program that exacerbates tensions between parents by focusing almost exclusively on money transfer from the parent (mainly fathers) who has less child time than the other parent can lead to frustration. First, many custodial parents have to wait for a bureaucratic system to march through its procedures to collect the money that the court order stated was owed to them. Second, the program does not countenance the hardships experienced by many noncustodial parents, insisting on consistent payments regardless of their life situation.

Motivational interviewing could be more universally used in the program. Motivational interviewing is where a caseworker begins an intake interview with a parent by listening to the issues that the parent brings to the table rather than only asking for the personal data needed for processing. This approach emphasizes empathy and naturally makes the parent more of a partner in the child support efforts (Arneson & Keister, 2019).

As program offices focus more on reasons for nonpayment instead of just the nonpayment itself, holistic approaches may help fathers not only have sustained employment through job searches aided by child support offices but also stronger bonds with their children through parenting time and child support mediation and fatherhood programs.

Limiting contempt of court and criminal nonsupport to the most egregious cases also provides an opportunity for those who want to comply with child support orders but do not have sufficient wages that allow for compliance without undue hardship. Alternative payment plans, new job skill sets, and connecting noncustodial parents to better-paying jobs may result in better long-term compliance than incarceration.

Reducing Contempt of Court and Incarceration

A tragic situation occurred in Summerville, South Carolina, in 2015. Walter Scott, a 50-year-old Black man, ran away from a police officer after a traffic stop. The officer fatally shot him. Scott's relatives maintained that he fled out of fear of being jailed again because he was more than $18,000 behind in child support payments (CBS Interactive Online, 2015).

While disappearing from the child support enforcement program as a primary enforcement tool, many child support offices use contempt of court as a method to coerce payments, which can mean jail times that can last several months. A US Supreme Court decision, Turner v. Rogers (2011), 564 US 431, held that the contemnor had to have a present or current ability to pay in order to be jailed for contempt in civil proceedings at the time of the hearing. Otherwise, they could not pay the amount ordered as the "purge" amount to get out of jail. It is estimated that at any given time, 50,000 or so parents are serving time for nonpayment of child support due to civil contempt proceedings (Galbi, 2011). Incarcerating nonpaying parents does little to support the custodial parent's familial financial needs. Actually, a criminal record is an albatross around the neck of the noncustodial parent when they try to find a job upon their release (Visher et al., 2008). As the program moves from a government reimbursement emphasis to a focus on stability in dual household situations, a legislative reset is needed to allow funding to match the new direction.

Low-Income Parents and Inability to Consistently Comply

While the national aspersion has traditionally castigated nonpaying parents as "deadbeats," the truth is most nonpayers are dead broke. The Urban Institute studied California's child support program's statistics and found that most of the past-due child support (also called arrearages when they are not paid in the month in which they are due) were owed by low-income fathers (Sorensen et al., 2003) (Table 14.1).

States that routinely add interest to the past-due support, such as California, drive low-income parents deeper into debt. Many choose to go into the unreported, sometimes illegal underground economy to avoid garnishments that can take from 50% to 65% of their net income (Consumer Credit Protection Act, 1968); others to avoid

Table 14.1 Number and percent of debtors in 2000 by amount of recent income (California)

Income category	Number of debtors	Percent of debtors (%)
Total	834,908	100
Has recent income: Net income is:	623,597	75
$1–$10,000	300,586	36
$10,001–$20,000	169,203	20
$20,001–$30,000	93,128	11
30,001–$50,000	52,233	6
Over $50,000	8447	1
No recent income	210,310	25
Has prior income	32,101	4
No prior income	178,209	21

income withholding, which could garnish at least half of the worker's disposable income (Miller & Mincy, 2012).

A study conducted by Orange County California's child support program showed that once the amount collected exceeded 20–22% of net income, compliance with an order dropped (Takayesu, 2011). Less money was available for the payor to use for self-support. Matters were worse when a second or third family was involved that needed support as well. In a Wisconsin study, 30% of custodial mothers have children with different birth fathers and 36% with only one father, and 34% have not had paternity established for all the children to determine if there is more than one father of the children. Because of the way child support guidelines work, the yearly support due for three children with one father was $5800, and $10,200 if each of the three children had a different father. Conversely, if one father had three children with one woman, the support due was $5800, but if he fathered three children with different women, he would owe a total of $8564 under the Wisconsin child support guidelines then in effect (Meyer et al., 2005).

The amount of past-due support in this country exceeds $117 billion (OCSE, 2019 Preliminary Data Report), with the majority owed by those least equipped to pay it (Sorensen et al., 2003). Some states have extended, or have no, statute of limitations on collecting past-due child support, meaning that child support arrears may be routinely collected for 20 years or longer after the child emancipates (OCSE Intergovernmental Referral Guide, 2021). It is routine to intercept Social Security Retirement benefits to pay arrearages that accrued decades earlier.

This has sparked a movement in legislatures to enact minimum orders that reflect a self-support reserve that begins to recognize the need for paying parents to be able to have enough money to live on for themselves (Colorado Child Support Commission, 2019). The thinking is that there are social safety net programs such as TANF, SNAP, Medicaid, subsidized daycare, and Title I school lunches that help children, while few programs support single adults. Lower orders also slow down the increase in arrearages particularly for incarcerated noncustodial parents so they do not face a monumental wall of accumulated arrearages when released.

Disproportionate Impact on Minority Families

Looking at poverty rates for children who live in a female-headed households, 32% of Black children, 31% of Hispanic children, and 21% of non-Hispanic White children live in poverty (Creamer & Mohanty, 2019). While the female-headed household rate may be declining somewhat, the national average for all households is 13% (US Department of Commerce, Census Bureau, 2020).

Black fathers in particular have a higher incidence of poverty than their White counterparts. About 28% of Black male-headed households live in poverty (Black Demographics, 2020). In child support, the self-support reserve for fathers found in guidelines may be inadequate for the father to eke out a basic living standard. As the Orange County study showed, once child support orders take more than 22–25% of the income of the noncustodial parent, the harder it is for them to comply consistently with the order. This results in a disproportionate number of harsher enforcement actions taken against minority parents. Generally, income withholding and tax refund intercepts cover most of the collections in a case (US DHHS, OCSE, 2021). About $30 billion of the $37 billion collected by program offices in federal fiscal year 2020 came from those two remedies. The tougher remedies, such as bank account seizure, driver's license suspension, contempt, and criminal nonsupport, are reserved for those who fall several months behind. In general, Black males are six times more likely to be incarcerated for all crimes compared to White males (Drake, 2013). While actual statistics are not readily available, if one extrapolates that general incarceration ratio to incarceration due to child support delinquencies, a huge disproportionate number of Black men serve time for nonpayment. Some recent literature compares onerous child support orders for low-income Black men that result in delinquency and then incarceration as a modern version of slavery (see, e.g., Meyerson, 2016; Mohammed, 2012).

While many states provide Spanish versions of forms, not all local offices can provide a Spanish interpreter to answer questions or provide additional information. Some offices use translation services for phone inquiries; even so it is difficult to provide equivalent services to the non-English-speaking population. Few offices have forms or live interpreters for languages other than Spanish. In those cases, either a phone translator may assist or a bilingual friend can translate. In any event, the language and cultural barriers for persons who do not use English as their first language are significant.

Fathers' Integration into the Lives of Children

Many, if not most, payors want to contribute to their children's economic well-being and be involved in many aspects of their lives. Sometimes, the lack of money hinders that involvement (Nepomnyaschy & Garfinkel, 2011).

Emotional support, or the love and positive interaction a father provides to his children, can be as or more important than financial support. Fathers bring a gender balance to a child's upbringing that provides the richness of having mom and dad's different *weltanschuung* (worldview). This is not to say same sex couples raise children devoid of the two gender outlooks. It is more a statement that the biological or nurturing by parents greatly impact a child, and as long as the interaction is not abusive, a child greatly benefits from both parents' caring involvements. Traditionally, a feminine and masculine approach shaped children for their adult interactions. It may be that this paradigm is changing and gender differences are less important; however, having two strong parental or adult figures in a child's life still seems to be important (Annie E. Casey Foundation, 2021).

Recommended Intervention Approaches

Because a child has two households instead of one in which to live when parents separate, it is meaningful to strive to make each household a complement to the other, enriching the child with two healthful environments (Mayo Clinic, 2020). Much depends on the integration of the father into the child's daily schedule, from school to play to general interaction with others.

Social workers and well-trained child-support caseworkers could use motivational interviewing to show empathy to the difficulties fathers are going through. Referrals to programs that can assist fathers overcome the barriers in their way to giving strong financial and emotional support to their children may also provide the lift they need to reach the next level of self-worth, confidence, and understanding. These characteristics may be missing from those who do not know where to start to deal with the dilemmas they face as noncustodial fathers.

The child support system has traditionally focused on the monetary contribution by the paying parent, who often is the father, without any support for the other activities and qualities that fathers bring to child-raising. Funding for the child support program limits expansive efforts to address the nonfinancial issues. With federal and state reforms and funds, additional resources could offer fathers who want to participate in their children's lives beyond financial support:

1. Free or low-cost parenting plan mediation for parents who need to determine the extent and timing of both parent's interaction with the child(ren), plus fatherhood classes for those who are new to parenting and for those who would like to bond with fathers in similar situations.
2. Non-adversarial family law resolutions in which a skilled mediator can address all the particular issues addressing a two-household family, not only financial and parenting time issue but also schooling, religious instruction, and health issues.
3. Equality of treatment of children who are born to nonmarital parents with children born to marital parents. Throughout the country, services for marital children, such as mandatory parenting time mediation, do not exist for children whose parents were not married to each other. This adversely impacts children of color, fathers, and low-income parents in particular.
4. Recognition of fathers as co-parents who should have an equal say in their children's lives, from custody determinations and time with the children to decisions about the child's well-being.
5. Treatment of domestic violence as an issue that should be dealt with from both the victim's and perpetrator's sides, with appropriate counseling to mitigate past damage and avoid future adverse behavior so that steps can be taken to determine if constructive interaction between the perpetrator and the children is feasible without risk to the children.
6. Job counseling and employment services for unemployed or underemployed noncustodial parents so that regular employment in jobs that engage the noncustodial parent may result in more consistent child support payments and less tension between the parents, which would benefit the children.

Discussion Questions

1. Should the government be involved in the forced transfer of money from the noncustodial parent to the parent who has the child the majority of the time? Should the government establish and enforce parenting plans that detail when a child visits or stays overnight with the paying parent? Why or why not?
2. What if parents divorce, remarry, and then divorce a second time? Should the first set of children get more support than the second set of children, or should they receive the same amount? Should stepparents be required to contribute to the support of their stepchildren?
3. Is it more important that the paying parent have enough income to meet basic needs before paying more than a token amount of support or that the paying parent figure out a way to find the income needed to better support the children?
4. Do you think a child thrives better when two parents live together but bicker all the time or if the parents live apart but work together for the benefit of the child?
5. Is the traditional male role model necessary or may one substitute a second female role model and achieve similar outcomes for the child?

Resources

Government

- US Congress, Congressional Research Service, for occasional child support research. https://www.loc.gov/crsinfo/
- US Department of Commerce, Census Bureau, for historical tables, current population surveys, child support statistics, household demographics, and focused papers. https://www.commerce.gov/bureaus-and-offices/census
- US Department of Health and Human Services, Office of the Assistant Secretary for Planning and Evaluation (ASPE), for its internal and funded research papers. https://aspe.hhs.gov/
- US Department of Health and Human Services, National Vital Statistics Reports, for information regarding children born out of wedlock. https://www.cdc.gov/nchs/nvss/index.htm
- US Department of Health and Human Services, OCSE, for its annual report, intergovernmental referral guide, and funded research papers. https://www.acf.hhs.gov/css
- US Department of Labor, Bureau of Labor Statistics, for information regarding employment by race and income. https://www.bls.gov/
- US Government Accountability Office, for its congressionally requested analysis of various aspects of the child support program. https://www.gao.gov/

Other Sources

- Annie E. Casey Foundation, for data on the well-being of children, KIDS COUNT—The Annie E. Casey Foundation (aecf.org).
- Ball, J. and Wellbank, M.A., *Insiders' Guide to Child Support*, Montcolo Publishing, 2017, the only child support book in general circulation that focuses on Title IV-D services.
- Center for Policy Research, which has authored many studies and guideline analyses. https://centerforpolicyresearch.org/
- Mathematica, which has completed numerous child support studies. https://www.mathematica.org/
- Morgan, Laura W. and Family Law Consulting, for reports written by Professor Morgan that compare child support guidelines among the states and the history of child support. https://famlawconsult.com/who.html
- National Child Support Enforcement Association, for its collection of research. https://www.ncsea.org/
- National Conference of State Legislatures, for its research on state child support legislation. https://www.ncsl.org/
- National Responsible Fatherhood Clearinghouse, for its well-researched articles on fatherhood in general and fatherhood and child support, Library Search/Fatherhood.gov
- Pew Research Center, Family and Relationships/Pew Research Center https://www.pewresearch.org/topic/family-relationships/
- University of Wisconsin, Institute of Research on Poverty, for their decades-long research into child support demographics and outcomes, perhaps the best research source, https://www.irp.wisc.edu/
- Urban Institute, which has written on child support issues for many years, Child Development & Youth Research/Urban Institute https://www.urban.org/

References

Annie E. Casey Foundation. (2021). *Children in single-parent families in the United States*. Kids Count Data Center, 2021, Children in single-parent families/KIDS COUNT Data Center.

Arneson, K., & Keister, J. (2019). *Motivational interviewing round two: A deeper dive into using MI to empower parents*. NCSEA Webtalk.

Ball, J., & Wellbank, M. A. (2017). *Insiders' guide to child support*. Montcolo Publishing.

Black Demographics. (2020). *Data chart: Black families above and below poverty*. INCOME – https://blackdemographics.com

Bowling, K., Challa, J., & Graski, D. (2019). *Improving child support outcomes with online dispute resolution*. National Center For State Courts.

Brito, T. L., Pate, D. J., Jr., & Wong, J.-H. S. (2020). Negotiating race and racial inequality in family court. *IRP Focus, 36*(4). https://www.irp.wisc.edu/resource/negotiating-race-and-racial-inequality-in-family-court/

Bureau of Labor Statistics. (2021). *Women in the labor force: A databook*. BLS Report no. 1092 https://www.bls.gov/opub/reports/womens-databook/2020/home.htm

Cadet, D. Huffpost *citing* Center for Disease Control, 5 lies we should stop telling about Black fatherhood, June 13, 2014. 5 Lies We Should Stop Telling About Black Fatherhood | HuffPost Communities
Cancian, M., & Meyer, D. (2004). Fathers of children receiving welfare: Can they provide more child support? *Social Service Review, 78*(2), 179–206. https://doi.org/10.1086/382766
Cancian, M., & Meyer, D. (2019). *Impact results from the Child Support Noncustodial Parent Employment Demonstration (CSPED)*. Institute for Research on Poverty.
Census Bureau, American Housing Survey for the United States in 1987 (census.gov).
Chadwick, L., & Solon, G. (2002). Intergenerational income mobility among daughters. *American Economic Review, 92*(1), 335–344. https://doi.org/10.1257/000282802760015766
Child Support Performance Incentive Act of 1998 (Pub. Law 105–200).
Colorado Child Support Commission Final Report (2019). 2019 - Google Drive
Columbia Broadcasting System, CBS Interactive, online, updated April 11, 2015. South Carolina records reveal details about Walter Scott, man shot by cop Michael Slager – CBS News
Consumer Credit Protection Act of 1968 (Pub. L. 90-321).
Creamer, J., & Mohanty, A. (2019). *Poverty rate for female-householder families lowest on record*. U.S. Census Bureau.
Cross, C. (2019). Racial/ethnic differences in the association between family structure and children's education. *Journal of Marriage and Family, 82*(2), 691–712. https://doi.org/10.1111/jomf.12625
Dolnick, S. (2019). The life and crimes of the original welfare queen. *New York Times*, May 20, 2019.
Drake, B. (2013). Incarceration gap widens between whites and Blacks, *PEW Research Center*. Family Support Act of 1988 (Pub. L. 100-485).
Ferguson, A. (2019). *Sexual democracy: Women, oppression and revolution*.
Friedline, T., Chen, Z., & Morrow, S. P. (2020). Families' financial stress & Well-being: The importance of the economy and economic environments. *Journal of Family and Economic Issues, 42*, 34–51. https://doi.org/10.1007/s10834-020-09694-9
Galbi, D. (2011). *Persons in jail or in prison for child-support debt*. Purple Motes, incarcerating child-support debtors without the benefit of counsel – purple motes.
Gardner, N. (2016). A crisis in Colorado's civil courts. *5280 Magazine*, June 2016. Government Accountability Office Report (1990).
Grall, T. (2020a). *Custodial mothers and fathers and their child support: 2017*. Census Bureau, App. Table 1.
Grall, T. (2020b). *Support Providers: 2018, U.S. Census Bureau, Current Population Reports 2018*. Census Bureau Current Population Survey.
Government Accountability Office (GAO). (1990). *Interstate child support: Better information needed on absent parents for case pursuit. U.S. GAO.*
Harman, J. (2016). *"Parental alienation": What it means and why it matters*. Colorado State University College News.
Heinrich, C. J., Burkhardt, B. C., & Hager, H. M. (2010). *Reducing child support debt and its consequences: Can forgiveness benefit all?* University of Wisconsin–Madison.
Hodges, L., & Cook, S. (2019). *The use of child support guidelines in Wisconsin: 2010 and 2013*. Institute for Research on Poverty.
Hodges, L., Meyer, D. L., & Cancian, M. (2019). *How are child support burdens related to child support payments, compliance, and regularity?* Institute for Research on Poverty.
Katz, E. (2019). Criminal Law in a civil guise: The evolution of family courts and support laws. *University of Chicago Law Review, 86*(5).
Livingston, G. (2015). *Family size among mothers*. Pew Research Center.
Livingston, G. (2017). The rise of multiracial and multiethnic babies in the U.S., Pew Research. https://www.pewresearch.org/facttank/2017/06/06/the-rise-of-multiracial-and-multiethnic-babies-in-the-u-s/
Lyon, M. (1999). *Characteristics of families using Title IV-D Services in 1995*. U.S. Department of Health and Human Services, Office of the Assistant Secretary for Planning and Evaluation.

Maccoby, E. E., Buchanan, C. M., Mnookin, R. H., & Dornbusch, S. M. (1993). Postdivorce roles of mothers and fathers in the lives of their children. *Journal of Family Psychology, 7*(1), 24–38. https://doi.org/10.1037/0893-3200.7.1.24

Maginnis, R. L. (1997). Single-parent families cause juvenile crime. In *Juvenile Crime: Opposing Viewpoints* (pp. 62–66). A E Sadler, ed. -- See NCJ-167319) | Office of Justice Programs (ojp.gov)

Mather, M. (2010). *Data Brief.* Population Reference Bureau.

Mayo Clinic. (2020). *Children and divorce: Helping kids after a breakup.* www.mayoclinic.org

Meyer, D., Cancian, M., & Cook, S. (2005). *Multiple-partner fertility: Incidence and implication for child support policy.* Institute for Research on Poverty.

Meyerson, C. (2016). How our racist child support laws hurt poor. Black fathers the most. *Splinter* (splinternews.com).

Miller, D., & Mincy, R. (2012). Falling further behind? Child support arrears and fathers' labor force participation. *Social Service Review, 86*(4), 604–635. https://doi.org/10.1086/668761

Mohammed, N. (2012). *Child support: Enslaving Black men.* ThyBlackMan.com.

Morgan, L. (2021). *Child support enforcement in the United States and the role of the private bar.* Child Support Enforcement Council.

National Child Support Enforcement Association (NCSEA). (2021). *2021 Policy Forum Agenda | NCSEA Policy Forum.*

National Conference of State Legislatures. (2021). *Child support policies: Implications for low-income fathers and their children.* Child Support Resource Directory (ncsl.org)

Nepomnyaschy, L., & Garfinkel, I. (2011). Fathers' involvement with their nonresident children and material hardship. *Social Service Review, 85*(1), 3–38. https://doi.org/10.1086/658394

New York Times. (2008). *Why do Americans still hate welfare?* (nytimes.com Dec 10, 2008). Omnibus Budget Reconciliation Act of 1981 (Pub. L. 97–35).

OECD. (2017). *The Pursuit of Gender Equality: An Uphill Battle.* OECD Publishing, Paris, https://doi.org/10.1787/9789264281318-en.

OCSE Action Transmittal 16-06. (2016). https://www.acf.hhs.gov/css/policy-guidance/final-rule-flexibility-efficiency-and-modernization-child-support-enforcement

Parkman, A. (2019). *No fault divorce: What went wrong?* Taylor and Francis.

Personal Responsibility and Work Opportunity Reconciliation Act of 1996 (Pub. L. 104–193). Pew Research Center: Fact Tank 2019.

PEW Research Center, (2015). https://www.fact-tank/2015/12/30/its-no-longer-a-leave-it-to-beaver-worldfor-american-families-but-it-wasnt-back-then-either/

Rosenberg, J., & Wilcox, W. B. (2006). *The importance of fathers in the healthy development of children. Fatherhood.gov.*

Rosenberg, J., & Wilcox W. B. (2017). *The importance of fathers in the healthy development of children.* U. S. Department of Health and Human Services, Office on Child Abuse and Neglect, U.S. Children's Bureau, Child Welfare Information Gateway; 2006. https://www.childwelfare.gov/pubs/usermanuals/fatherhood/chaptertwo.cfm

Social Services Amendments of 1974 (Pub. L. No. 93–647).

Sorensen, E., & Zibman, C. (2001a). *Poor dads who don't pay child support: Deadbeat or disadvantaged?* Urban Institute.

Sorensen, E., & Zibman, C. (2001b). Getting to know poor fathers who do not pay child support. Social Service Review, 75(3), 420–434.

Sorensen, E., Koball, H., Pomper, K., & Zibman, C. (2003). *Examining child support arrears in California: The collectability study.* Urban Institute.

Takayesu, M. (2011). *How do child support order amounts affect payments and compliance?* Department of Child Support Services.

Texas Access to Justice Commission (2012). Pro Se Statistics.

Texas Office of the Attorney General, Co-Parenting Guide, https://texasattorneygeneral.gov/

Turner v. Rogers, 564 U.S. 431 (2011).

US DHHS, OCSE. (2016). *Final rule: Flexibility, efficiency, and modernization in child support enforcement programs. The Administration for Children and Families. hhs.gov.*

US DHHS, OCSE. (2021). *Intergovernmental reference guide (IRG). hhs.gov.*

U.S. Department of Commerce, Census Bureau. (1987). *Current Population Survey, Money, Income and Poverty Status of Families and Persons in the United States 1986.*

U.S. Department of Commerce, Census Bureau. (2017). *Current Population Survey 2017.*

U.S. Department of Commerce, Census Bureau. (2018). *Current Population Survey.* Child Support Supplement.

U.S. Department of Commerce, Census Bureau. (2019). *Family and People in Poverty by Type of Family: 2018–2019.* Table B-2.

U.S. Department of Commerce, Census Bureau, American Community Survey Briefs, 2020.

U.S. Department of Commerce, Census Bureau. (1995). *Census Bureau.* Current Population Survey 1995.

U.S. Department of Commerce. (1999). Census Bureau, Trends in Premarital Childbearing: 1930 to 1994 (census.gov).

U.S. Department of Health and Human Services. (1989). Office of Child Support Enforcement Action Transmittal 89–17.

U.S. Department of Health and Human Services. (1993). Office of Child Support Enforcement (1993). Action Transmittal 93–04.

U.S. Department of Health and Human Services. (2019). *National vital statistics reports*, Table 10.

U.S. Department of Health and Human Services. (1996). *Office of Child Support Enforcement.* Annual Report to Congress 1995.

U.S. Department of Health and Human Services. (2012). *Office of Child Support Enforcement.* Annual Report to Congress 2010, Table 1.

U.S. Department of Health and Human Services. (2021a). *Office of Child Support Enforcement.* 2019 Preliminary Data Report.

U.S. Department of Health and Human Services. (2021b). *Office of Child Support Enforcement.* Interstate Referral Guide.

U.S. Department of Labor. (2021). *Bureau of Labor Statistics.* Current Employment Statistics, 2021, Table B-3b.

U.S. Government Printing Office, 45 CFR § 303.4.

Ullrich, L. D. (2021). Male labor force participation: Patterns and trends, *Econ Focus*, 1st qtr.

Uniform Desertion and Non-Support Act, 1910.

Uniform Reciprocal Enforcement of Support Act (URESA) (1950, 1952, 1958 and 1968).

Uniform Interstate Family Support Act (UIFSA) (1992, 1996, 2001, 2008).

University of California, Davis, Center for Poverty and Inequality. (n.d.). *How does level of education relate to poverty?* Center for Poverty and Inequality Research (ucdavis.edu).

Visher, C., Debus-Sherrill, S. A., & Yahner, J. (2008). *Employment after prison: A longitudinal study in three states.* Urban Institute.

Waller, M., & Plotnick, R. (2001). Effective child support policy for low-income families: Evidence from street level research. *Journal of Policy Analysis and Management, 20*(1), 89–110. https://doi.org/10.1002/1520-6688(200124)20:1<89::AID-PAM1005>3.0.CO;2-H

Western, B., & Petit, B. (2010). Incarceration and social inequality. *Daedalus*, Summer 2010.

White, J., Bean, M., Fishman, T., & O'Leary, J. (2016). *Next gen child support: Improving outcomes for families, modernizing the federal child support program.* Deloitte Insights, Deloitte. Modernizing the federal child support program | Deloitte Insights.

Chapter 15
Engaging Fathers in Intimate Partner Violence Interventions

Miriam G. Valdovinos and Jennifer L. Bellamy

Introduction

It was a frigid winter morning in Texas. In the shelter's cafeteria, mothers and their children gathered for breakfast before starting their day. I (first author) was in my office, waiting for a call from one of my clients who was a father. He had been driving to the shelter's parking lot for 2 weeks to have breakfast and dinner with his two daughters before and after his work shift. The girls had been two of the approximately 15.5 million children living in homes with *intimate partner violence* (IPV) in the United States at the time (McDonald et al., 2006).[1] He was residing at a nearby hotel that our agency had secured with hotel vouchers because male survivors could not stay at the shelter, even if they had children with them. This morning was colder than usual, so I set aside a couple of donated jackets in case the girls needed an extra layer to stay warm. Next, I picked up three foil-covered plates with eggs, sausage, and toast. I thanked the kitchen lead for preparing a plate for the dad too. The shelter policies did not automatically include fathers in the meal count, unlike the mothers residing in the shelter.

That day was the last time I saw this client. He informed me he would be returning to his wife, the mother of their children, the person arrested for a physical altercation in which the father was injured (and the children witnessed). His wife had apologized and demonstrated remorse for the incident. He explained that living on

[1] This estimate is from one of the few nationally representative samples of married and cohabiting couples with children (ages 0–17 years) living in the household. This estimate includes IPV reports from both partners.

M. G. Valdovinos (✉) · J. L. Bellamy
University of Denver, Graduate School of Social Work, Denver, CO, USA
e-mail: Miriam.Valdovinos@du.edu; Jennifer.Bellamy@du.edu

J. L. Bellamy et al. (eds.), *Social Work Practice with Fathers*,
https://doi.org/10.1007/978-3-031-13686-3_15

his own with the children was not the long-term plan. He thanked me for my assistance, the breakfast, and the winter jackets. I wished him luck, reminded him of essential numbers and agency contacts if a future incident required him to leave home again. I waved to the kids as they drove off with their father.

Although the overlap between IPV and fathering is large, little is known about IPV interventions including issues related to fathers.[2] More than 60% of men arrested for IPV are in a fathering role (Rothman et al., 2007), and more than 60% of children continue to live with or visit their fathers regularly following an IPV incident (Israel & Stover, 2009). Though few in number, some services are emerging to serve fathers. Federal initiatives, such as *Responsible Fatherhood programs*, include programs that focus on serving men in the community who may be at an increased risk for IPV. This includes fathers who are young, disengaged with services, noncustodial, low-income, and experience challenges such as not graduating from high school, having a history of criminal justice involvement, or having mental or physical health conditions (Karberg et al., 2020). However, there are few details about the effectiveness of IPV interventions for fathers and *how* interventions might effectively address IPV with fathers. We define IPV as physical violence, sexual violence, stalking, and psychological aggression carried out by an individual's current or former intimate partner (Smith et al., 2018). Fathers can be perpetrators or victims of IPV or both. In this chapter, we provide our conceptual framing for these interventions, a background of previous research related to IPV interventions with fathers, recommendations for future intervention approaches, and a call for action for the field to address father engagement in IPV interventions.

Background and Context

Unfortunately, IPV is a widespread problem. Almost a third (29.4%) of children in two-parent homes live in a family where IPV has recently occurred (McDonald et al., 2006). IPV is a serious form of interpersonal violence that can result in negative mental and physical health consequences for the survivor and family members exposed to the violence, including children (Bair-Merritt et al., 2006; Kitzmann et al., 2003; Wathen & MacMillan, 2013). Violence in families is complex and overlaps with other stressors, risks, and family problems. For example, IPV is associated with negative parenting and child welfare involvement (Chiesa et al., 2018). Estimates of the overlap between IPV and child maltreatment vary widely, ranging from 17% to 67% (Edleson, 2001; Hamby et al., 2010; Jouriles et al., 2008). Previous research also demonstrates that men who use violence are more likely to have experienced *complex trauma* in childhood than the general population (Lee et al., 2020; Rangul Askeland et al., 2011).

[2] In this chapter, "fathers" include biological fathers, stepfathers, and father figures unless otherwise noted.

Gendered experiences of violence are debated in the IPV field, specifically regarding lifetime prevalence differences between men and women as well as gender differences in experiences of violence as perpetrators versus survivors. One source of this debate is the critique of the feminist psychoeducational program (the Duluth Model), which asserts that IPV offenders can only be men because men are socialized to be violent and to maintain patriarchy (Dutton, 2007; Dutton & Corvo, 2007). Research refutes this claim and suggests a more nuanced approach using a typology of IPV rather than understanding all IPV through a single gendered lens. For example, IPV experts have distinguished "intimate terrorism" (prolonged and severe) from "situational violence" (acute and often less severe; Johnson, 2008). This typology distinguishes violence based on the control context in which it is embedded. For example, intimate terrorism in heterosexual relationships is most often perpetrated by men. This is the type of violence that is often observed in shelter populations, hospital emergency rooms, and cases with law enforcement involvement. Situational violence, by contrast, is not about control and power differences but rather occurs from the escalation of specific conflicts (Johnson, 2008) and is perpetrated by both women and men. Even within these typologies, it is important to recognize that not all families or partners share the same power dynamics, and there are instances of IPV that are not easily categorized. It is also important to recognize that most fathers, even those in high-risk groups such as child welfare-involved families, do not perpetrate IPV (Bellamy, 2009) (Fig. 15.1).

In the United States, nationally representative survey data from the National Intimate Partner and Sexual Violence Survey (NISVS) describe rates of intimate partner victimization and sexual violence across different demographic groups (Breiding et al., 2014; Smith et al., 2018). According to the 2010 survey, 33.6% of men, or 37.3 million men, experienced sexual violence, physical violence, or stalking by an intimate partner during their lifetime, and 34.2% experienced psychological aggression (Smith et al., 2018). This is compared to 36.4% of women, or 43.6 million women, who report lifetime sexual violence, physical violence, or stalking and the 36.4% who experienced psychological aggression (Smith et al., 2018). Higher lifetime prevalence rates are observed for men who are American Indian or Alaska Native, Black, and multiracial non-Hispanic compared to White

Fig. 15.1 Racial and ethnic minority men and IPV

NEARLY HALF (45.3%) OF AMERICAN INDIAN OR ALASKA NATIVE MEN AND ALMOST FOUR OUT OF EVERY 10 BLACK AND MULTIRACIAL NON-HISPANIC MEN (38.6% & 39.3% RESPECTIVELY) HAVE EXPERIENCED IPV DURING THEIR LIFETIME.

Fig. 15.2 Men in the United States and IPV

MEN WHO WERE BORN IN THE UNITED STATES HAVE EXPERIENCED MORE IPV DURING THEIR LIFETIME (30.2%) THAN MEN BORN OUTSIDE OF THE UNITED STATES (17.0%).

non-Hispanic men (Breiding et al., 2014). Also, men who are 18–24 years old, men who experienced food insecurity in the past 12 months, and men born in the United States compared to men born outside of the country are at a higher risk of experiencing violence (Breiding et al., 2014) (Fig. 15.2).

When the respondents in the NISVS were asked about *IPV-related impacts*, including but not limited to concerns for safety or injury and needs for various services as well as effects on their work or school schedules, the gender differences become more apparent. For instance, nearly 1 in 10 (10.9% or 12.1 million) men reported some form of IPV-related impact, such as impacts on their mental health or financial well-being, based on their experiences. In contrast, about 1 in 4 women (25.1% or 30.0 million) reported some form of IPV-related impact. These gender differences are related to factors such as differences in power, systemic responses, cultural gender expectations (Malley-Morrison & Hines, 2004), and how sexism intertwines with other structural forces (Moe, 2007). In addition, men are more likely to use severe violence against their intimate partners, so women are more likely to be injured or killed by a partner who uses IPV as compared to men (Breiding et al., 2014).

Based on my practice experience, I (first author) have seen the multiple barriers faced by fathers who are survivors of IPV and living with their children. These barriers are often related to the stigma and shame about being a survivor. Oftentimes, they do not disclose their experience of violence to receive services because they perceive that IPV services are not for men (Tsui et al., 2010). Another set of barriers includes institutional policies and practices that do not make space for IPV survivors who are fathers, which is reflected in the story at the beginning of this chapter. There is limited research that focuses on male IPV survivors (e.g., Douglas & Hines, 2011; Durfee, 2011; Migliaccio, 2002; Tsui, 2014), making it even harder to identify what is needed to intervene on behalf of father IPV survivors. Despite some gender differences, a qualitative narrative analysis study with abused husbands revealed that the accounts of the relationships of IPV survivors, both men and women, follow similar patterns, including the structure of the relationships, the acceptance of the violence, and the social context of the situation (Migliaccio, 2002). However, the shortage in the number of programs that serve families affected by IPV generally (see National Network to End Domestic Violence, 2019) makes finding services for fathers specifically even more challenging. Given these factors, father IPV survivors are at risk of not being identified and not seeking needed services.

When men use violence against an intimate partner, they have historically been met with a criminal justice response. In the United States, adjudicated offenders are often mandated to complete some form of "batterer treatment." This is often in the form of batterer's intervention programs (BIPs). It is unclear how often or how well fathering is addressed as a part of those interventions. There are also questions about how fathering relates to the experiences and outcomes of those interventions (Poole & Murphy, 2019). For example, would a father's relationship with and love for his children change how he engages with IPV experiences, either as a perpetrator or a survivor? Are fathers aware of the impact IPV may have on their children who witness the violence, and could this moderate their engagement in services? How we engage fathers in these questions and conversations for meaningful change is part of our motivation to write this chapter.

Conceptual Framing

We use two conceptual frames to further structure our discussion of fathers and IPV. First, we use a *family systems framework* as fathers who are perpetrators or survivors of violence experience IPV in the context of a family. In addition, we use a *critical feminist perspective* because men and women engage in violence differently in terms of frequency and magnitude, and they experience different rates of victimization as well as differential impacts. We acknowledge that there are other frames that have been written about and researched in the literature such as social learning, person-in-environment, and a trauma focus. However, the use of family systems and critical feminist perspective coalesce the authors' expertise areas, and these combined perspectives add to the literature.

The family systems framework is useful because the behavior and experience of individuals is influenced and shaped within the system of a family. In family systems, there is an emphasis on reciprocal influences where all outcomes have multiple causes, and the outcomes both shape and are reshaped by multiple causal pathways. For example, violent behavior can be influenced by a multitude of family-related factors including the impact of families of origin, family structure, mental health, substance use, and stress. While useful in understanding how violence is situated within and influenced by current relationships as well as intergenerational influences and transmission of violence, the family systems approach to family violence interventions has been critiqued for its failure to address power differentials (Murray, 2006).

We address this gap by also using a critical feminist perspective. A critical feminist perspective includes the theoretical contributions of women of color scholars and practitioners. With this stance, we assert the importance of understanding how

IPV affects women differently than men. IPV does not impact women in the same way as men because a societal context that has included legacies of colonialism, racism, sexism, and class oppression has changed the way systems respond to IPV survivors and offenders (Crenshaw, 1994). For example, there are harsh realities faced by undocumented immigrant women if they leave a violent partner and must provide for their child or children as single parents in precarious circumstances without legal work authorization (Valdovinos et al., 2021).

The mainstream feminist movement in the United States has focused on ending violence against women and has not always considered the larger movement against violence. Bell Hooks (1984) offers an argument that acknowledges these limitations by stating, "The concentration being solely on ending male violence against women, feminist activists may overlook the severity of the problem. They may encourage women to resist male coercive domination without encouraging them to oppose all forms of coercive domination" (p. 119). This includes coercive dominance experienced by men as well. For example, structural inequalities and social power differentials influenced by racism and discrimination affect how men of color interact with systems (i.e., police, courts, and child welfare systems). Similarly, we think it is important to note that binary applications of gender leave out the power differentials and dynamics for nonbinary, a group with distinct needs and barriers to services that also deserve attention in the field of intimate partner violence.

Recommended Intervention Approaches

Information about interventions offered to fathers who have IPV experiences are predominantly related to men who have used violence against an intimate partner. This reflects that the criminal justice response and dominant narrative around men and violence often equate patriarchy with socially conditioned violent men (Dutton, 2010). Though these are limited perspectives, and certainly do not represent the needs and experiences of all fathers, interventions for IPV offenders are an important subset of services. Programs and services for IPV survivors who are fathers continue to be scarce (Douglas & Hines, 2011), so we recognize these programs are important interventions, but the research is at an earlier stage of development. In this section, we summarize research about fathering and IPV offenders that can inform interventions more broadly. Then we discuss four types of interventions focused on serving men who are offenders or at risk for using IPV. These interventions are included because they have had some form of evaluation on their effectiveness addressing issues related to fathers and IPV: BIPs, Responsible Fatherhood programs, Caring Dads (a stand-alone program), and Fathers for Change (an intervention that includes mothers and fathers).

General Approaches to Fathering and IPV

Some patterns and experiences of fathers and IPV have been identified in the literature and can be helpful in developing and delivering interventions. One example is the relationship between fathers' awareness, or lack thereof, of the effects of their IPV on their children. For example, a survey study with 464 men in a BIP group indicated 53% were worried about the long-term effects of their violent behavior on their children (Rothman et al., 2007). In this study, more than half of the biological fathers reported they would seek professional help for themselves if they felt their violence was impacting their children. Another large survey of 3824 men arrested for IPV in a court-ordered evaluation found that most fathers admitted that their children had been exposed to interparental conflicts. However, few noticed that their children had been affected by the IPV exposure (Salisbury et al., 2009). Another study focused on Latino fathers asked fathers who used IPV about their parenting stress and competence (Baker et al., 2001). Some of these fathers were aware of the effect of the IPV on their children and felt less competent as parents. Further, 70% of this sample of Latino fathers said they had no one to turn to for advice or questions related to parenting (Baker et al., 2001). These studies highlight how fathers' understanding about how IPV impacts their children could be a fruitful target of service engagement and intervention.

Additional research provides insight into the parenting context and dynamics for fathers who use IPV toward the mothers of their children. For example, Bancroft et al. (2012) delineate how IPV offenders may exercise control as fathers by undermining the mother's parenting or assaulting her due to the children's behaviors. Furthermore, this contributes to a dynamic where children are positioned against the mother, with potential for this pattern to continue throughout the IPV relationship. A study analyzing data from the National Survey of Families and Households documenting differences in parenting behavior associated with IPV found that men inclined to use aggressive behavior with an intimate partner were more likely to use hostile-coercive parenting behavior as well (Fox & Benson, 2004). These relationships make it imperative to assess safety and risk when considering father involvement with children and the impact of IPV on the whole family system.

Considering the dynamics involved in IPV experiences for fathers, Gewirtz and Menakem (2004) offer recommendations to facilitate intervention approaches with fathers. In their research, they point to the importance of effective parenting interventions (defined as those that include information about child development, effects of violence exposure on children, and the important role of fathering) for IPV offenders. These include helping fathers to (a) understand their children's expectations as this relates to child development; (b) learn how behaviors impact kids; (c) deal with family-of-origin issues, particularly with their own fathers; and (d) explore the use of non-abusive behavior for the well-being of their children.

Batterer Intervention Programs

BIPs are commonly court-mandated for men who use IPV. Most of the clients in BIPs are men and represent 90% of the court-mandated or child protective services referral requirements (Adams, 2003). BIPs generally use the Duluth Model, the feminist psychoeducational approach that focuses on group facilitators leading consciousness-raising exercises to challenge the client's perceived right to control or dominate his partner (Hamel, 2015). As a didactic group format, this model focuses on exposing the patriarchal or misogynistic attitudes of male offenders, promotes gender-egalitarian behaviors, and encourages offender accountability and responsibility (Eckhardt et al., 2014). Most BIPs focus on anger management, power and control issues, and providing alternatives to address violent behaviors. Unfortunately, little empirical evidence demonstrates that BIPs reduce the offenders' use of violence, and studies that do show positive outcomes have small overall effects (e.g., Arias et al., 2013; Babcock et al., 2004; Corvo et al., 2008; Feder & Wilson, 2005; Miller et al., 2013).

There are several gaps in the practice of and research on BIP interventions for fathers. First, it is unclear how much material is included in BIPs to address the effects of IPV exposure on children. Even though many men who are arrested for IPV are fathers, there are few nationwide mandates that require the inclusion of parenting or fathering materials in BIPs (Gewirtz & Menakem, 2004). Similarly, little research has focused on understanding the impacts of fathering on the effectiveness of BIPs. One study that analyzed ten interventions for fathers, which included four IPV and fathering curriculums that are used in BIPs (Labarre et al., 2016), found that they had either not been evaluated or the evaluation was underway at the time of the publication. Other gaps in knowledge exist for subgroups of fathers. For example, in most cases, interventions are aimed at understanding violence against mothers since IPV experiences for same-sex couples or couples with other gender identities are sparse (e.g., Langenderfer-Magruder et al., 2015, 2016). Even with the limitations of BIPs, these groups can offer opportunities to address fathering with men who have been adjudicated for IPV.

Responsible Fatherhood Programs

Another more established service area in which interventions have been developed to address fathers and IPV is the federal Responsible Fatherhood (RF) programs. Not all RF programs were created to assist men who may be at an increased risk for IPV perpetration or being IPV survivors, but some have been funded specifically to target subgroups of fathers who may have an increased risk for IPV. Some have been designed to serve incarcerated fathers and fathers reentering communities following incarceration (Responsible Fatherhood Opportunities for Reentry and Mobility [ReFORM]), while others are more broadly aimed at fathers in the community

(New Pathways for Fathers and Families [New Pathways]). Many RF programs operate in urban, low income, and communities that are predominantly racially and ethnically minoritized, so they target and serve diverse fathers. Even though most of the fathers who enroll in these programs are not involved in IPV (Karberg et al., 2020), these initiatives have the specific goal of reaching fathers who may be motivated to seek out IPV services in the bid to become better fathers. Thus, RF programs are in a unique position to address IPV among fathers, particularly as a prevention effort.

RF program services include education and training on responsible parenting, co-parenting, healthy relationships, and economic stability. Other services may be provided to meet the needs of the programs' diverse participants. The Preventing and Addressing Intimate Violence when Engaging Dads (PAIVED) project[3] examines how RF programs aim to prevent and address IPV through their fatherhood programming. The PAIVED report presents information about the approaches that RF programs take to provide IPV-related services. It also discusses the challenges inherent in providing these services and the successes, promising practices, and areas for growth. Specific programs such as Nurturing Fathers, which is adapted from the evidence-supported intervention Nurturing Parenting program (Matthew et al., 2005; Vespo et al., 2006), may be a promising approach for addressing the use of violence in families among fathers in RF programs (https://nurturingfathers.com/). Nurturing Fathers is a 13-week peer-group curriculum that supports nurturing and positive fathering and specifically addresses the use of violence in relationships with partners and children.

The PAIVED research study provides important considerations related to RF programs and how IPV-related materials are incorporated across different RF curricula. Most RF programs include some IPV education, but this varies across programs (e.g., number of sessions, types of programs offered). All the programs identified the issue of addressing IPV as essential to achieving the program objectives, but no information was included about addressing IPV when fathers are survivors. Interestingly, if IPV came up in these groups, it was hard to address because of the concern that the fathers would stop participating, especially given that recruitment and retention are major challenges for RF programs.

Other barriers to addressing IPV in RF programs described in the PAIVED study included the ongoing stigma attached to IPV, the normalization of violence for participants of these programs, and a lack of free and accessible programs that address IPV and parenting. These programs also identified strengths that helped them address some of these barriers. This included creating a safe space to share about IPV experiences without feeling shame. Like findings from other studies, facilitating discussions related to IPV grounded in understanding consequences for children proved beneficial. Since the RF programs do not serve IPV-specific populations, a collaborative approach in partnership with other IPV interventions is needed.

[3] PAIVED is funded by the Office of Family Assistance (OFA) and overseen by the Office of Planning, Research, and Evaluation (OPRE). Child Trends and their partners, Boston Medical Center and Futures Without Violence, conducted the study.

Caring Dads

Various stand-alone programs also address issues of fathering and IPV. Labarre et al. (2016) provide a detailed analysis of ten programs targeting fathers who have perpetrated IPV. We focus on Caring Dads (Scott & Crooks, 2007) as one of the programs that has undergone intensive evaluation. Caring Dads is a group intervention that began in 2001 in Canada and has been adapted in the United States, the UK, and Australia. The program includes 17 group sessions where the facilitators use motivational interviewing, cognitive behavioral therapy, and psychoeducation to work with fathers. The curriculum content aims to engage fathers who have used violence to develop skills in child-centered fathering and take responsibility for the impact of the violence on their children and their children's mother (Scott & Lishak, 2012). A philosophical tenet of this program is to value men's roles as fathers to motivate them to change their behavior and reduce the risk of further harm to their children. The three core components of the program include (1) weekly groups with fathers, (2) engagement with the mothers of their children to provide program information and also monitor risk from the father while in the program, and (3) interagency case management.

The program evaluations published for Caring Dads are mostly from Canada, Australia, and European countries. The outcomes documented in these evaluations include improvement of the fathers' co-parenting relationship with their children's mother, development of healthier parenting practices for fathers, and a decrease in fathers' over-reactivity to child misbehavior (Scott & Lishak, 2012; Scott et al., 2021). A research evaluation of three program sites in Australia also expanded on the significant changes observed in the participants of the Caring Dads program. In their evaluation, Diemer et al. (2020) indicated that most men who participated in the program were able to reflect on their harmful fathering practices; however, only a small group of the men implemented the program tools of action to interrupt the behavior and to demonstrate respect for their children's mother. These researchers found that even though most fathers moved toward improvement, the fathers who had the most significant behavioral change were those who also had other forms of support such as case management or counseling. Additional studies in the European context have also documented promising evidence of reducing IPV risk for children and families that participate in the program (McConnell et al., 2017), including increases in the fathers' awareness of children's needs and the impact of the parental relationship on children, which in turn led to positive behavior change (Bourassa, 2018).

Fathers for Change (Intervention That Includes Both Parents)

Very few IPV interventions for fathers include both parents. Father for Change (F4C) (Stover, 2013, 2015) is one of the few interventions (if not the only one) that uses a family systems approach along with cognitive behavioral techniques and attachment theories. Substance abuse reduction is also addressed in this curriculum since it was initially designed to target co-parenting and the father-child relationship in an intervention for men with co-occurring IPV and substance abuse (Stover, 2015). The curriculum also addresses the fathers' individual childhood experiences with violence and alternatives to violence. Other components focus on dyadic work with father and mother to improve their co-parenting relationship as well as dyadic work with father and child to rebuild a positive father-child relationship (Stover, 2015; Stover & Morgos, 2013). The central premise of this intervention is to focus on men as fathers and increase their feelings of competence and meaning within their parenting role while providing motivation to change the maladaptive patterns that have led to the use of aggression and substances to control negative feelings (Stover, 2013).

Participating men have mostly been referred by the courts or the Department of Children and Families (DCF) following an arrest for domestic violence or drug-related charges, or a call for an investigation to DCF due to these co-occurring issues. The defining features of F4C include the focus on (1) the fathering role as a motivator for change, (2) the integration of strategies for reducing IPV and substance abuse (SA) in each session, (3) the intergenerational transmission of IPV and SA, (4) communication skills and co-parenting, (5) the impact of IPV and SA on child development, and (6) parenting skills (Stover, 2013).

Program evaluation findings for F4C have indicated a decrease of IPV and substance abuse. The initial community pilot findings compared fathers in F4C with fathers in individual drug court programs and demonstrated an improvement in the father-child relationship and a trend toward less use of IPV over time for fathers in F4C (Stover, 2015). However, no effect was documented as it relates to the co-parenting group intervention (Stover, 2015). The evaluations conducted for this program in recent years have begun to document other changes for fathers and their children. One of these studies (Stover et al., 2019) compared fathers in residential substance use disorder treatment facilities who participated in F4C to another parenting program called Dads 'n' Kids (DNK). Both groups demonstrated significant declines in aggression, and at the end of the interventions, the IPV reported rates were low for both groups. In a recent evaluation of statewide implementation of F4C (Stover et al., 2020), 204 fathers and their co-parents reported a decrease in IPV and exposure of conflict for children as well as significant improvements in emotional regulation for fathers and their parental reflective functioning.

Future Directions

There is a great deal of work yet to do in the field of fathers and IPV. We have identified a lack of programs for father survivors of IPV, limited attention to fathering in BIPs, varied approaches and knowledge about effectiveness of addressing IPV in RF programs, the need to address same-sex partner relationships, and a lack of attention to racial and cultural differences in fathering and IPV as well as other factors that could bring more clarity to this important intersection between fathering and IPV. Another particular area for future intervention development is prevention. Perinatal and early childhood interventions such as home visiting may represent a promising platform for services. Home visiting is an effective approach for reducing child maltreatment risk and improving parenting, and some programs have been found initially effective in addressing IPV (Prosman et al., 2015). However, home visiting programs have only just begun to engage fathers (Guterman et al., 2018).

Lastly, we want to acknowledge that culturally based programs such as the National Compadres Network's La Cultura Cura are often not considered in these conversations because the programs may not have the resources for formal evaluations. These programs encompass more than IPV issues and incorporate ancestral teachings about manhood, fatherhood, and toxic masculinity. They offer options for men to address IPV and fathering through a cultural lens that honors the complexities and teachings of elders in the community, holding men accountable in a community context. Such interventions may offer a critical perspective that continues to be missing in mainstream interventions, which is particularly relevant when working with culturally diverse populations.

Based on existing knowledge, we offer the following recommendations to researchers, practitioners, and decision-makers to build father-inclusive approaches to preventing and addressing IPV.

1. Focus on the father-child relationship in the context of the IPV exposure. This requires the assessment of risks or safety concerns when fathers are involved in their children's lives and when child maltreatment is a concern. Children living in homes with IPV are at significant risk for child maltreatment. Seventy-six percent of child maltreatment is perpetrated by a biological parent, with 43% of those cases at the hands of biological fathers (Sedlak et al., 2010). Oftentimes, fathers are not aware of how the IPV is impacting their children's lives. However, some research has also found that fathers who cause harm are motivated by their love for their children to change their use of IPV.
2. Service providers, programs, and assessment practices need to provide a safe environment for the disclosure of IPV experiences and a specific plan for addressing IPV concerns when they arise. Efforts to reduce the stigma and shame associated with IPV disclosure by fathers are needed as these are clearly barriers to intervention. Furthermore, we must consider the substantial fear on the part of fathers that disclosure of IPV could lead to criminal charges or the loss of their children. This is particularly true for men of color who have historically faced racism by child protection systems. Staff who work with children and families in

a variety of social service settings need to understand the risks related to IPV, that fathers can be survivors as well as perpetrators of IPV, how to assess for IPV with mothers and fathers, and provide referral resources when needed.
3. Interagency relationships are critical to provide various supports for fathers. For example, RF programs are better at addressing IPV concerns when they have a mutual respectful relationship with IPV agencies. Social service programs such as home visiting, child support, substance abuse programs, family therapy providers, and others cannot all offer IPV interventions as well; therefore, partnership and referral resources are essential. Social workers who are engaging with fathers should also be familiar with local BIP and RF programs and their approaches to addressing parenting and IPV with fathers.

A Call to Action for Future Work

Engaging fathers in IPV interventions amplifies the need for social workers to employ creativity, advocacy, a family perspective, and a critical lens because the current systems and services in place have several gaps. Limited research evidence is available to guide our work with fathers who are perpetrators or survivors of IPV. Services and systems do not always engage a family systems approach or a critical feminist lens, barriers related to stigma and biases reduce the likelihood fathers will seek out or be retained in services, and the needs of diverse fathers, including those in same-sex partnerships and those who have a history of trauma, are not well addressed. Issues of safety and assessment of risk for children after IPV should be prioritized, but so too should space be made for a nuanced approach to the intersection of fathering and violence. All social workers should be working with fathers. There is bias against fathers in the field that must be addressed through training on father engagement and ensuring staff feel safe and value fathers in the lives of their children. Particularly, IPV programs have historically focused on mothers. Until that changes, engagement with fathers will continue to be a challenge. We conclude this chapter with a call to action for social workers to advocate for father-inclusive IPV services and increased investment in prevention, programs, and service systems that are better positioned to intervene with fathers and IPV.

Discussion Questions

1. What assessment and other considerations need to be prioritized when working with fathers who have been involved in IPV (both survivors and perpetrators)?
2. What services and policies must be extended and deepened to reach fathers involved in IPV (both survivors and perpetrators)?
3. What strategies will help to expand research on prevention efforts and interventions that focus on working with fathers involved in IPV?

4. How do we address the shame and stigma that are often connected to IPV experiences to better reach fathers with IPV experiences?
5. What other theoretical and conceptual lenses might be useful for framing approaches to fathers and IPV?

Resources

- National Responsible Fatherhood Clearinghouse https://www.fatherhood.gov/for-dads/domestic-violence
- Futures Without Violence—Fathering after Violence Framework (a national initiative that aims to end violence against women by motivating men to renounce their abuse and become better parents) https://www.futureswithoutviolence.org/engaging-men/national-institute-on-fatherhood-domestic/
- National Compadre Network https://www.nationalcompadresnetwork.org/ initiatives include the National Latino Fatherhood and Family Institute and *La Cultura Cura* to restore cultural identity.
- The National Intimate Partner and Sexual Violence Survey – 2010 Findings. (Source: Breiding et al., 2014)

References

Adams, D. (2003). *Certified batterer intervention programs: History, philosophies, techniques, collaborations, innovations and challenges*. Futures without Violence. https://www.futureswithoutviolence.org/userfiles/file/Children_and_Families/Certified%20Batterer%20Intervention%20Programs.pdf

Arias, E., Arce, R., & Vilarino, M. (2013). Batterer intervention programmes: A meta-analytic review of effectiveness. *Psychosocial Intervention, 22*, 153–160. https://doi.org/10.5093/in2013a18

Babcock, J. C., Green, C. E., & Robie, C. (2004). Does batters' treatment work? A meta-analytic view of domestic violence treatment. *Clinical Psychology Review, 23*, 1023–1053. https://doi.org/10.1016/j.cpr.2002.07.001

Bair-Merritt, M. H., Blackstone, M., & Feudtner, C. (2006). Physical health outcomes of childhood exposure to intimate partner violence: A systematic review. *Pediatrics, 117*(2), e278–e290. https://doi.org/10.1542/peds.2005-1473

Baker, C. K., Perilla, J. L., & Norris, F. H. (2001). Parenting stress and parenting competence among Latino men who batter. *Journal of Interpersonal Violence, 16*(11), 1139–1157. https://doi.org/10.1177/088626001016011003

Bancroft, L., Silverman, J. G., & Ritchie, D. (2012). *The batterer as parent: Addressing the impact of domestic violence on family dynamics* (2nd ed.). SAGE Publications. https://doi.org/10.4135/9781452240480

Bellamy, J. L. (2009). A national study of male involvement among families in contact with the child welfare system. *Child Maltreatment, 14*(3), 255–262. https://doi.org/10.1177/1077559508326288

Bourassa, C. (2018). Caring Dads intervention program's impact on fathering. *La revue internationale de l'éducation familiale, 43*, 117–141. https://doi.org/10.3917/rief.043.0117
Breiding, M. J., Chen J., & Black, M. C. (2014). *Intimate partner violence in the United States–2010.* National Center for Injury Prevention and Control, Centers for Disease Control and Prevention. https://www.cdc.gov/violenceprevention/pdf/cdc_nisvs_ipv_report_2013_v17_single_a.pdf
Chiesa, A. E., Kallechey, L., Harlaar, N., Rashaan Ford, C., Garrido, E. F., Betts, W. R., & Maguire, S. (2018). Intimate partner violence victimization and parenting: A systematic review. *Child Abuse & Neglect, 80*, 285–300. https://doi.org/10.1016/j.chiabu.2018.03.028
Corvo, K., Dutton, D., & Chen, W.-Y. (2008). Toward evidence-based practice with domestic violence perpetrators. *Journal of Aggression, Maltreatment & Trauma, 16*(2), 111–130. https://doi.org/10.1080/10926770801921246
Crenshaw, K. (1994). Mapping the margins: Intersectionality, identity politics, and violence against women of color. In M. A. Fineman & R. Mykitiuk (Eds.), *The public nature of private violence* (pp. 93–118). Routledge. https://doi.org/10.2307/1229039
Diemer, K., Humphreys, C., Fogden, L., Gallant, D., Spiteri-Staines, A., Bornemisza, A., & Vercoe, E. (2020). *Caring Dads program: Helping fathers value their children.* https://violenceagainstwomenandchildren.com/wp-content/uploads/2020/05/2020-Caring-Dads-Final-Report-23-3-2020.pdf
Douglas, E., & Hines, D. (2011). The help-seeking experiences of men who sustain intimate partner violence: An overlooked population and implications for practice. *Journal of Family Violence, 6*, 473–485. https://doi.org/10.1007/s10896-011-9382-4
Durfee, A. (2011). "I'm not a victim, she's an abuser": Masculinity, victimization, and protection orders. *Gender & Society, 25*(3), 316–334. https://doi.org/10.1177/0891243211404889
Dutton, D. G. (2007). Thinking outside the box: Gender and court-mandated therapy. In J. Hamel & T. L. Nicholls (Eds.), *Family interventions in domestic violence* (pp. 27–58). Springer.
Dutton, D. G. (2010). The gender paradigm and the architecture of antiscience. *Partner Abuse, 1*, 5–25. https://doi.org/10.1891/1946-6560.1.1.5
Dutton, D. G., & Corvo, K. (2007). The Duluth model: A data-impervious paradigm and a failed strategy. *Aggression and Violent Behavior, 12*, 658–667. https://doi.org/10.1016/j.avb.2007.03.002
Eckhardt, C. I., Murphy, C., & Sprunger, J. G. (2014). Interventions for perpetrators of intimate partner violence. *Psychiatric Times, 31*(8), 1–11. https://www.psychiatrictimes.com/view/interventions-perpetrators-intimate-partner-violence
Edleson, J. L. (2001). Studying the co-occurrence of child maltreatment and domestic violence in families. In S. A. Graham-Bermann & J. L. Edleson (Eds.), *Domestic violence in the lives of children: The future of research, intervention, and social policy* (pp. 91–110). American Psychological Association.
Feder, L., & Wilson, D. B. (2005). A meta-analytic review of court-mandated batterer intervention programs: Can courts affect abusers' behavior? *Journal of Experimental Criminology, 1*, 239–262. https://doi.org/10.1007/s11292-005-1179-0
Fox, G. L., & Benson, M. L. (2004). Violent men, bad dads? Fathering profiles of men involved in intimate partner violence. In R. D. Day & M. E. Lamb (Eds.), *Conceptualizing and measuring father involvement* (pp. 359–384). Lawrence Erlbaum Associates Publishers.
Gewirtz, A., & Menakem, R. (2004). Working with young children and their families: Recommendations for domestic violence agencies and batterer intervention programs. *Paper #5 in the series early childhood, domestic violence, and poverty: Helping young children and their families.* The University of Iowa. https://clas.uiowa.edu/sites/clas.uiowa.edu.socialwork/files/paper_1.pdf
Guterman, N. B., Bellamy, J. L., & Banman, A. (2018). Promoting father involvement in early home visiting services for vulnerable families: Findings from a pilot study of "Dads Matter". *Child Abuse & Neglect, 76*, 261–272. https://doi.org/10.1016/j.chiabu.2017.10.017

Hamby, S., Finkelhor, D., Turner, H., & Ormrod, R. (2010). The overlap of witnessing partner violence with child maltreatment and other victimizations in a nationally representative survey of youth. *Child Abuse & Neglect, 34*(10), 734–741. https://doi.org/10.1016/j.chiabu.2010.03.001

Hamel, J. (2015). *Evidence-based domestic violence perpetrator treatment.* DV Trainings. https://domesticviolencetrainings.org/evidence-based-domestic-violence-perpetrator-treatment/

Hooks, B. (1984). *Feminist theory: From margin to center.* South End. https://doi.org/10.4324/9781315743172

Israel, E., & Stover, C. S. (2009). Intimate partner violence: The role of the relationship between perpetrators and children who witness violence. *Journal of Interpersonal Violence, 24*(10), 1755–1764. https://doi.org/10.1177/0886260509334044

Johnson, M. P. (2008). *A typology of domestic violence: Intimate terrorism, violent resistance, and situational couple violence*. Northeastern University Press.

Jouriles, E. N., McDonald, R., Slep, A. M. S., Heyman, R. E., & Garrido, E. (2008). Child abuse in the context of domestic violence: Prevalence, explanations, and practice implications. *Violence and Victims, 23*(2), 221–235. https://doi.org/10.1891/0886-6708.23.2.221

Karberg, E., Parekh, J., Scott, M. E., Areán, J. C., Kim, L., Laurore, J., & Bair-Merritt, M. (2020). *Preventing and addressing intimate violence when engaging dads (PAIVED): Challenges, successes, and promising practices from responsible fatherhood programs* (Vol. 22). OPRE Report. https://www.acf.hhs.gov/sites/default/files/documents/opre/paived_challenges_successes_promising_practices_mar_2020.pdf

Kitzmann, K. M., Gaylord, N. K., Holt, A. R., & Kenny, E. D. (2003). Child witnesses to domestic violence: A meta-analytic review. *Journal of Consulting and Clinical Psychology, 71*(2), 339–352. https://doi.org/10.1037/0022-006X.71.2.339

Labarre, M., Bourassa, C., Holden, G. W., Turcotte, P., & Letourneau, N. (2016). Intervening with fathers in the context of intimate partner violence: An analysis of ten programs and suggestions for a research agenda. *Journal of Child Custody, 13*(1), 1–29. https://doi.org/10.1080/15379418.2016.1127793

Langenderfer-Magruder, L., Walls, N. E., Whitfield, D., Brown, S., & Barrett, C. (2015). Partner violence victimization among lesbian, gay, bisexual, transgender, and queer youth: Associations among risk factors. *Child & Adolescent Social Work, 33*, 55–68. https://doi.org/10.1007/s10560-015-0402-8

Langenderfer-Magruder, L. L., Whitfield, D. L., Walls, N. E., Kattari, S. K., & Ramos, D. (2016). Experiences of intimate partner violence and subsequent police reporting among lesbian, gay, bisexual, transgender and queer adults in Colorado: Comparing rates of cisgender and transgender victimization. *Journal of Interpersonal Violence, 31*, 855–871. https://doi.org/10.1177/0886260514556767

Lee, K. A., Bright, C. L., & Betz, G. (2020). Adverse childhood experiences (ACEs), alcohol use in adulthood, and intimate partner violence (IPV) perpetration by Black men: A systematic review. *Trauma, Violence, & Abuse*, 1–18. https://doi.org/10.1177/1524838020953101

Malley-Morrison, K., & Hines, D. (2004). *Family violence in a cultural perspective: Defining, understanding, and combating abuse*. SAGE Publications. https://doi.org/10.4135/9781452232577

Matthew, R. F., Wang, M. Q., Bellamy, N., & Copeland, E. (2005). Test of efficacy of model family strengthening programs. *American Journal of Health Studies, 20*(3/4), 164–170.

McConnell, N., Barnard, M., & Taylor, J. (2017). Caring Dads Safer Children: Families' perspectives on an intervention for maltreating fathers. *Psychology of Violence, 7*(3), 406–416. https://doi.org/10.1037/vio0000105

McDonald, R., Jouriles, E. N., Ramisetty-Mikler, S., Caetano, R., & Green, C. E. (2006). Estimating the number of American children living in partner-violent families. *Journal of Family Psychology, 20*(1), 137–142. https://doi.org/10.1037/0893-3200.20.1.137

Migliaccio, T. A. (2002). Abused husbands: A narrative analysis. *Journal of Family Issues, 23*(1), 26–52. https://doi.org/10.1177/0192513X02023001002

Miller, M., Drake, E., & Nafziger, M. (2013). *What works to reduce recidivism by domestic violence offenders?* Washington State Institute for Public Policy. https://s3.amazonaws.com/static.nicic.gov/Library/027743.pdf

Moe, A. M. (2007). Silenced voices and structured survival: Battered women's help seeking. *Violence Against Women, 13*, 676–699. https://doi.org/10.1177/1077801207302041

Murray, C. E. (2006). Controversy, constraints, and context: Understanding family violence through family systems theory. *The Family Journal, 14*(3), 234–239. https://doi.org/10.1177/1066480706287277

National Network to End Domestic Violence. (2019). *14th annual domestic violence counts report*. https://nnedv.org/wp-content/uploads/2020/03/Library_Census-2019_Report_web.pdf

Poole, G. M., & Murphy, C. M. (2019). Fatherhood status as a predictor of intimate partner violence (IPV) treatment engagement. *Psychology of Violence, 9*(3), 340–349. https://doi.org/10.1037/vio0000124

Prosman, G., Lo Fo Wong, S. H., van der Wouden, J. C., & Lagro-Janssen, A. L. M. (2015). Effectiveness of home visiting in reducing partner violence for families experiencing abuse: A systematic review. *Family Practice, 32*(3), 247–256. https://doi.org/10.1093/fampra/cmu091

Rangul Askeland, I., Evang, A., & Heir, T. (2011). Association of violence against partner and former victim experiences: A sample of clients voluntarily attending therapy. *Journal of Interpersonal Violence, 26*(6), 1095–1110. https://doi.org/10.1177/0886260510368152

Rothman, E., Mandel, D. G., & Silverman, J. G. (2007). Abuser's perceptions of the effect of their intimate partner violence on children. *Violence Against Women, 13*, 1179–1191. https://doi.org/10.1177/1077801207308260

Salisbury, E. J., Henning, K., & Holdford, R. (2009). Fathering by partner-abusive men: Attitudes on children's exposure to interparental conflict and risk factors for child abuse. *Child Maltreatment, 14*(3), 232–242. https://doi.org/10.1177/1077559509338407

Scott, K. L., & Crooks, C. V. (2007). Preliminary evaluation of an intervention program for maltreating fathers. *Brief Treatment and Crisis Intervention, 7*(3), 224–238. https://doi.org/10.1093/brief-treatment/mhm007

Scott, K. L., & Lishak, V. (2012). Intervention for maltreating fathers: Statistically and clinically significant change. *Child Abuse & Neglect, 36*(9), 680–684. https://doi.org/10.1016/j.chiabu.2012.06.003

Scott, K., Dubov, V., Devine, C., Colquhoun, C., Hoffelner, C., Niki, I., et al. (2021). Caring Dads intervention for fathers who have perpetrated abuse within their families: Quasi-experimental evaluation of child protection outcomes over two years. *Child Abuse & Neglect, 120*, 105–204. https://doi.org/10.1016/j.chiabu.2021.105204

Sedlak, A. J., Mettenburg, J., Basena, M., Petta, I., McPherson, K., Greene, A., & Li, S. (2010). *Fourth national incidence study of child abuse and neglect (NIS–4): Report to Congress, executive summary*. U.S. Department of Health and Human Services, Administration for Children and Families. https://www.ncwwi.org/files/Cultural_Responsiveness__Disproportionality/NIS-4_Executive_Summary.pdf

Smith, S. G., Zhang, X., Basile, K. C., Merrick, M. T., Wang, J., Kresnow, M., Chen, J. (2018). *The national intimate partner and sexual violence survey (NISVS): 2015 data brief – Updated release*. National Center for Injury Prevention and Control, Centers for Disease Control and Prevention. https://www.cdc.gov/violenceprevention/pdf/2015data-brief508.pdf

Stover, C. S. (2013). Fathers for Change: A new approach to working with fathers with histories of intimate partner violence and substance abuse. *Journal of the American Academy of Psychiatry and the Law, 41*(1), 1–9. https://www.ncbi.nlm.nih.gov/pmc/articles/PMC3641144/

Stover, C. S. (2015). Fathers for Change for intimate partner violence and substance abuse: An initial community pilot. *Family Process, 54*(4), 600–609. https://doi.org/10.1111/famp.12136

Stover, C. S., & Morgos, D. (2013). Fatherhood and intimate partner violence: Bringing the parenting role into intervention strategies. *Professional Psychology: Research and Practice, 44*(4), 247–256. https://doi.org/10.1037/a0031837

Stover, C. S., McMahon, T. J., & Moore, K. (2019). A randomized pilot trial of two parenting interventions for fathers in residential substance use disorder treatment. *Journal of Substance Abuse Treatment, 104*, 116–127. https://doi.org/10.1016/j.jsat.2019.07.003

Stover, C. S., Beebe, R. Clough, M., et al. (2020). Evaluation of a statewide implementation of Fathers for Change: A fathering intervention for families impacted by partner violence. *Journal of Family Violence.* https://doi.org/10.1007/s10896-020-00199-5

Tsui, V. (2014). Male victims of intimate partner abuse: Use and helpfulness of services. *Social Work, 59*(2), 121–130. https://doi.org/10.1093/sw/swu007

Tsui, V., Cheung, M., & Leung, P. (2010). Help-seeking among male victims of partner abuse: Men's hard times. *Journal of Community Psychology, 38*(6), 769–780. https://doi.org/10.1002/jcop.20394

Valdovinos, M. G., Nightingale, S. D., & Vasquez Reyes, M. (2021). Intimate partner violence help-seeking for Latina undocumented immigrant survivors: Feminist intersectional experiences narrated through testimonio. *Affilia, 36*(4), 533–551. https://doi.org/10.1177/0886109920985772

Vespo, J. E., Capece, D., & Behforooz, B. (2006). Effects of the nurturing curriculum on social, emotional, and academic behaviors in kindergarten classrooms. *Journal of Research in Childhood Education, 20*(4), 275–285. https://doi.org/10.1080/02568540609594567

Wathen, C. N., & MacMillan, H. L. (2013). Children's exposure to intimate partner violence: Impacts and interventions. *Pediatrics & Child Health, 18*(8), 419–422. https://doi.org/10.1093/pch/18.8.419

Part IV
Conclusion

Chapter 16
Setting the Course for Future Theory, Research, and Practice with Fathers

Brianna P. Lemmons, Jennifer L. Bellamy, Qiana R. Cryer-Coupet, and Jennifer A. Shadik

Introduction

In this chapter, we will consider important factors for moving the field of social work forward in consideration of the strengths and needs of fathers and families. We look toward the future by examining the current state of social work theory, research, education, and practice as well as the opportunities for advancing each of these areas as vectors for social change. We also connect work with fathers to the values, ethics, and initiatives of social work.

Theory

Theory plays an important role in guiding social work research and practice. Having well-developed theory supports the development of programs and opportunities for intervention. Theory also guides assessment practices and tools as well as data

B. P. Lemmons
Diana R. Garland School of Social Work, Baylor University, Waco, TX, USA
e-mail: Brianna_Lemmons@baylor.edu

J. L. Bellamy
University of Denver, Graduate School of Social work, Denver, CO, USA
e-mail: Jennifer.Bellamy@du.edu

Q. R. Cryer-Coupet (✉)
School of Social Work, Georgia State University, Atlanta, GA, USA
e-mail: qcryercoupet@gsu.edu

J. A. Shadik
Department of Social Work, Ohio University, Athens, OH, USA
e-mail: Shadik@ohio.edu

J. L. Bellamy et al. (eds.), *Social Work Practice with Fathers*,
https://doi.org/10.1007/978-3-031-13686-3_16

collection and research. Here, we use theory in its broadest sense to include grand overarching theories such as *critical race theory*, *systems theory*, *identity theory*, and *feminist theory*, as well as frameworks and perspectives such as the *strengths perspective*, *developmental perspective*, and the *family systems*. In this book, the authors have drawn on multiple theories and concepts that are important to engaging, assessing, and serving fathers across a variety of systems. Many of the same theories have been used to study both mothering and fathering. For example, *attachment theory* has often been used to understand the relationships between children and their mothers and fathers (e.g., Belsky et al., 1984; Punyanunt-Carter, 2007).

There is no predominant, comprehensive, or grand theory of fathering (Adamsons & Palkovitz, 2014; Palkovitz & Hull, 2018) and little consensus on which theories best explain varying aspects of fathering (Adamsons & Palkovitz, 2014; Cabrera et al., 2007; Palkovitz, 2007). No single theory to date has been sufficient to capture the diversity and complex dynamics of fathering (Adamsons & Palkovitz, 2014; Palkovitz, 2007). Therefore, researchers and practitioners must draw on a wide range of sociological, psychological, ecological, family, child development, and economically based theories and perspectives as lenses for exploring and explaining different aspects of fathering and providing services for fathers and their families (Adamsons & Palkovitz, 2014; Doherty et al., 1998; Palkovitz, 2007).

There has also been some development and application of father-specific theories, many of which broadly focus on father involvement or involvement among specific subgroups of fathers. Some theorists have focused on other important dimensions of fathering, including co-parenting (Feinberg, 2003). Others have shaped theories for specific racial or ethnic groups of fathers, such as Cabrera et al.'s (2007) and Planalp et al.'s (2020) work adding of the concept of acculturation and cultural concepts for Latino fathers. Other researchers have studied and challenged the *deficit theory* of fatherhood (e.g., Stone et al., 2005), seeking instead to bring a more balanced conceptualization of fathering with due attention to strengths and opportunities. One such example, Fathering in a Context of Challenge and Complexity, is a substantive theory centered on fathers who have maltreated a child; this theory focuses on understanding the strengths, challenges, and contexts of these fathers in order to improve engagement and intervention (Shadik & O'Connor, 2016). In addition to these advances, some critics have argued against the *essential father paradigm* that espouses the role of fathers as one that is essential for optimal child well-being (Silverstein & Auerbach, 1999). Below, we outline some of the father-specific theories that have been offered within the research and practice literature to date.

Father Involvement Theory

Two of the most influential theoretical contributions in the field of fatherhood have been Pleck (2010) and Lamb's (1987) work on paternal involvement and Doherty's *responsible fathering framework* (Doherty et al., 1998). Drawing from Lamb's work, Pleck proposed a revised framing of the construct of paternal involvement that includes five overarching concepts: (1) positive engagement activities, (2) warmth and responsiveness, (3) control, (4) indirect care, and (5) process responsibility. Pleck's work also connects these concepts explicitly to child development using the *parental capital model*. This model combines elements of social capital theory, parental style research, and the ecological perspective, and its conceptualization of father involvement has broadly guided many studies, measures, clinical assessment tools, and programming for fathers. It is an important theoretical foundation for those working in fatherhood. This conceptualization and the parental capital model are not without their limitations. For example, Pleck points out that most of the research upon which this work is based was drawn from married residential fathers.

Doherty and colleagues (1998) developed the responsible fathering framework within the context of the increased interest in fathering in the late nineties in the United States, concerns about father absence, and increasing cultural expectations for men's involvement in the lives of their children. They framed fathering as a social, historical, and systemic process and used the term "responsible fathering" to reflect the language used by the U.S. Department of Health and Human Services (HHS) at the time. Their framing and its implementation in programming and funding supported by HHS has had a tremendous impact on fatherhood work in the United States. Doherty and colleagues are explicit, however, about the value and moral judgments embedded in this framing, which suggest there is a responsible, or a right, way to father and, by extension, an irresponsible, or wrong, way to father. Although their intent was to apply this framing to fathers of all races, ethnicities, and socioeconomic statuses and move away from the negative, absent, or deadbeat conceptualizations of minoritized fathers, this framing is biased. For example, one of the markers of a responsible father is one who waits to have a child until he is financially able to support a child. This standard is unfair to low-income fathers living in contexts where access to education, livable wages, and other resources are not readily available.

More recently, the *resource theory of fathering* was developed by Palkovitz and Hull (2018). This theory is a midrange, comprehensive, father-centered theory that takes into consideration the diversity of fathering experiences on micro, mezzo, and macro levels as well as the cognitive, affective, and behavioral aspects of fathers' lived experiences. In addition, it highlights many of the under-researched areas in the field and situates theoretical concepts within the contexts and relationships in which fathering is embedded. This theory offers promise for advancing the field of fatherhood as well as social work research, practice, policy, and education and addresses some of the weaknesses of earlier theories of father involvement.

Father Engagement Theory

One of the gaps in theoretical work on fathers and social work is the lack of a general theory of father engagement. Some authors have started to synthesize engagement models for specific service systems and outcomes. For example, Pfitzner et al. (2017) integrated the broader literature using a narrative review of prior work on engagement and applied it to inform the development of a multilevel model of father engagement in domestic violence prevention. These authors conceptualized father engagement in services using a three-stage process of (1) getting (recruitment and initial attendance), (2) keeping (retaining attendance), and (3) engaging (active engagement in the program) fathers. Research indicates that each stage is influenced by a different collection of factors. These factors may be practical, such as accessibility issues like transportation or the marketing of a program to the community; relational, including issues such as staff attitudes and behaviors or trust; or cultural, contextual, and situational factors like life circumstances, demands, stressors, and cultural alignment. This model also includes strategic factors like incentives and structural factors like the format of services (e.g., group versus individual and duration).

Opportunities for Theory Development

There are many opportunities for future theoretical work to improve upon, or build new models and frameworks, for better understanding and guiding research and practice with fathers. The dominant models of father involvement do not address all dimensions of fathering (Pleck, 2010) and may not reflect the needs, experiences, and realities of all fathers, particularly minoritized fathers with limited income opportunities. Because fathers are highly diverse and fathering can be carried out in a variety of ways, there is also a need for group or context-specific theories of fathering. Researchers have identified the need to hear directly from fathers to acquire in-depth knowledge and better understand their perspectives and needs (Dubowitz, 2009; Guterman & Lee, 2005; Sicouri et al., 2018). The biases and limitations of widely used models of fathers and fathering also call for future theoretical work. Given the critical role of these theories in shaping social work practice and research, there is a great need to improve existing models or build new ones that reflect a holistic, just, and nuanced approach to understanding fathers.

Research

The chapters in this book have highlighted several important gaps in the literature. Broadly, these include:

1. Studies that capture the diversity among fathers and fathering. Fathers are not a monolithic group, and their needs vary by a great number of intersecting identities and experiences
2. Research that contextualizes the experience of fathering and looks at systemic influences on fathers and fathering at all ecological levels and their intersections
3. More balanced and holistic approaches to studying fathers and fathering, including attending to strengths and resources, not just deficits and fathers' needs and not just because fathers benefit children
4. Carrying out research in partnership with, or with input from, fathers in the design, conduct, interpretation, and implementation of research
5. Studies that examine the impact of fathering on male development, considering the development of fathers alongside the development of children
6. Research that is grounded in developmental theories and perspectives on fathering, taking into consideration the evolution of fathering roles and experiences across the life span
7. Studies that intentionally and meaningfully consider the impact of macro-level, structural variables (especially institutional racism and oppression) on fathering experiences, using thoughtful methodological approaches that can help uncover and uproot systemic, macro-level problems

Other efforts in the field, including the Grand Challenges (GC) for Social Work, have the potential to bring scholars together to focus on long-standing critical challenges in the field. In Appendix B of this book, we included a table of the GCs developed by the American Academy of Social Work and Social Welfare. The table highlights the GC areas that scholars have begun to investigate in relation to father and family well-being and those that need additional work. For example, the first GC calls on scholars and practitioners to ensure the healthy development of youth, a goal for which the inclusion of fathers is essential (Flouri & Buchanan, 2003; Johnson Jr et al., 2020; Cryer-Coupet et al., 2020). More recently, in relation to GC number two, scholars have begun to examine the intersections of fatherhood and health, with the goal of understanding how they each support the other (Caldwell et al., 2019; Torche & Rauf, 2021). Building healthy relationships to end violence, the aim of GC number three, has also been the focus of fatherhood scholarship and practice (Pennell et al., 2013; Stover, 2013). The GCs also point to opportunities to develop further research on fathers, such as into mechanisms for achieving equal opportunities and justice, building financial capability for all, and reducing extreme financial inequalities.

The Fatherhood Research and Practice Network (FRPN) has also played a critical role in bridging the gap between research and practice by expanding the number of researchers and practitioners collaborating to evaluate fatherhood programs, promoting rigorous evaluation of fatherhood programs, disseminating evaluation findings that lead to effective fatherhood programming and evaluation research, and advocating for father inclusion in programs and policies that serve children and families. FRPN offers a number of researcher and practitioner resources, such as a researcher/practitioner forums, measurement tools, research briefs, peer-reviewed journal articles, and more. All of these resources can be found at https://www.frpn.org/.

Education and Training

If the field is to make progress toward better engaging fathers in research and practice, social work education must attend to men and their role as parents, and there are many opportunities to do so. Social work educators need to address the biases that can be reflected in social work training. These biases include failing to include fathers specifically or including fathers as secondary or adjunctive to mothers in classes on parenting and child well-being. There is also a tendency to focus on men in social work training from a risk or deficit perspective, and this is even more pronounced for low-income and minoritized men. In some cases, social work educators may lack the expertise or training to integrate fathers and fathering in their coursework. We hope this book provides the resources to help address this need. We also encourage social work educators and programs to attend to the inclusion of fathers in coursework when they are engaging in curricular self-studies or assessments for accreditation or for the inclusion of diverse content. Social work educators and programs should review course content for when and how men are included in coursework broadly, including their role as fathers. We encourage educators to explicitly discuss the lack of positive fathering narratives in textbooks and direct students to consider ways to engage fathers and view them from a strengths-based perspective. It is important to help students consider the importance of fathers in coursework, field placements, and throughout their careers.

In Appendix C of this book, we included a table with the CSWE EPAS. In the table, we map each of the chapters in this book onto specific competencies, indicating where information related to each of the competencies can be found. We have also included additional tables with syllabus maps that provide ideas for how to integrate this content into social work curricula. This book can be used in father-focused classes as well as integrated into existing foundational coursework, such as Human Behavior and Social Environment (HBSE), and in courses related to assessment, diversity, gender, children, and families.

Field education presents another opportunity to improve training for students on engaging, assessing, and intervening with fathers. Field placements can be cultivated in fatherhood programs, and attention to fathers in the service systems that intersect with men, including those described in this book, can be discussed in field seminars or other coursework that integrates the field experience into the classroom. Similarly, continuing education opportunities can be cultivated to help train social workers postgraduation on the rapidly evolving strategies to assess, engage, and intervene with fathers.

Practice

This book is also being written at a unique time in the field of social work due to the impact of the COVID-19 pandemic and public health crisis. Though much of the discussion around the impact of the pandemic has centered on the negative effects on health and mental health, for some fathers and families, the COVID-19 pandemic presented opportunities for father-child bonding. Some fathers who spent many hours away from their children due to work and school schedules before the pandemic found that shelter-in-place orders required them to work from home while also supervising their children's virtual school activities. These arrangements may have allowed fathers to engage in aspects of their children's educational experiences that they were unable to participate in prior to the pandemic. But these shifts also caused stress for fathers and mothers who were struggling to meet their children's needs while also working. Of course, the impacts varied greatly by other socioeconomic and other factors. For example, some fathers lost their jobs as restaurants shuttered. Some were unable to work from home because their essential roles in food production, health care, or other roles required in-person work. The impact of COVID-19 on parenting and families' functioning and well-being will likely last many years into the future and will be an important area of consideration for practitioners.

The pandemic also had immediate impacts on social work service provision, which presented many barriers to serving clients, including fathers. When the crisis began, social workers had to quickly shift to rely on technology and other creative service delivery efforts to work with families. In child welfare, for example, fatherhood programming was set aside in some jurisdictions while the system was in crisis (Abendroth et al., 2021). In some cases, the response to the pandemic crowded out work with fathers, because those efforts were not viewed as critical or central to child welfare work. However, in other cases, the pandemic also opened up new possibilities for serving more fathers because technology made services either more accessible or less intimidating, and in some programs, father engagement actually increased during the pandemic (Abendroth et al., 2021). Some fathers appreciated having the opportunity to engage in services virtually, not having to drive or find childcare. In other cases, fathers and workers found virtual service delivery to be less invasive and intimidating (Abendroth et al., 2021).

COVID-19 may have amplified the use of technology in father work, but there are many examples of more opportunities to increase the use of technology both as a tool of engagement and as a way to intervene with fathers—some of which were developed prior to the pandemic. Some programs have tried developing apps to support dads, either by providing information or supporting directly or connecting them with services. For example, the mDad (Mobile Device Assisted Dad) app was developed to provide fathers with information about engaging their infants and toddlers (Lee & Walsh, 2015). Similarly, the SMS4dads intervention has demonstrated some promise in delivering parenting and mental health information to men at and around the birth of a child (Fletcher et al., 2017).

Although there is increasing research on the efficaciousness of father-inclusive and father-focused interventions, there is still a great deal of work to be done to better establish evidence-based practice and evidence-supported interventions for fathers. It can be challenging for practitioners to identify which interventions are evidence-supported and which ones have been tested with fathers. It can be further challenging to access the training and resources needed to fully implement evidence-supported interventions. Some of the efforts in this area include those being made by FRPN, which was mentioned earlier in this chapter. FRPN offers several resources for practitioners, such as learning community webinars, measurement tools, and evaluation toolkits. In addition, Pearson and Fagan (2021), co-directors of FRPN, recently published a book based on the results of FRPN-funded projects describing parenting programs for low-income fathers.

In this chapter, we considered important factors for moving the field of social work forward, such as theory, research, practice, and education, while also taking into consideration the strengths and needs of fathers and families. Just as social work research should work to include fathers in the process of research, fatherhood practice should work with fathers to improve practice. As noted by NASW (2008), one of the key values of the profession is recognizing the central importance of human relationships. In so doing, fathers must be key partners in the work of moving the field of social work forward across the domains of engagement, assessment, and intervention. Fathers can be engaged as mentors to other fathers, hired into programs, supported through leadership programs, and invited to serve on boards or advisory committees. Opening opportunities for fathers to shape and deliver services is an important strategy for improving their engagement in social work practice.

Finally, as we write this book, the critical role of social work in addressing racism has taken on a new prominence in the context of renewed calls for social justice. In May 2020, national racial unrest followed the murders of Breonna Taylor, Ahmaud Arbery, and George Floyd in quick succession, and this racial unrest put a spotlight on the inequities and disparities in social work as well (Agosti et al., 2021). Social work prides itself on serving people who are vulnerable and oppressed, and this commitment requires us to explicitly address racism as a social justice and ethical imperative. Engaging fathers in social work is a critical aspect of dismantling the racially biased policies, procedures, and programming within systems. Furthermore, the provision of services that were not designed or tested for fathers is problematic from a service and social justice standpoint. Discrimination in all forms influences perceptions of fathers' strengths and abilities, which, left unaddressed, can lead to actions and interventions that are harmful to fathers and their families. We call on the field to continuously, intentionally, and vigorously seek to address racism and social justice as we advance social work research and practice with fathers.

References

Abendroth, E., Bellamy, J., Mittone, D., Bess, R., & Stagner, M. (2021). *Opening up possibilities: Father engagement lessons during the COVID-19 public health emergency*. OPRE Report # 2021-82. Washington, DC: Office of Planning, Research, and Evaluation, Administration for Children and Families, U.S. Department of Health and Human Services. https://www.acf.hhs.gov/sites/default/files/documents/opre/FCL_COVID_Issue_Brief_508.pdf

Adamsons, K., & Palkovitz, R. (2014). Theorizing about fathering: An introduction to the special issue. *Journal of Family Theory & Review, 6*(4), 279–281. https://doi.org/10.1111/jftr.12053

Agosti, J., Bellamy, J. L., Burton, L., Graves, A. M., Lau, C., & Mahoney, J. (2021). A breakthrough series on engaging fathers and paternal relatives in child welfare: A system response to COVID-19 and racial unrest. *Journal of the Society for Social Work and Research, 12*(3), 437–444. https://doi.org/10.1086/715214

Belsky, J., Gilstrap, B., & Rovine, M. (1984). The Pennsylvania Infant and Family Development Project, I: Stability and change in mother-infant and father-infant interaction in a family setting at one, three, and nine months. *Child Development, 55*(3), 692–705.

Cabrera, N. J., Fitzgerald, H. E., Bradley, R. H., & Roggman, L. (2007). Modeling the dynamics of paternal influences on children over the life course. *Applied Developmental Science, 11*, 185–189. https://doi.org/10.1080/10888690701762027

Caldwell, C. H., Tsuchiya, K., Assari, S., & Thomas, A. (2019). Fatherhood as a social context for reducing men's health disparities: Lessons learned from the fathers and sons program. In D. M. Griffith, M. A. Bruce, & R. J. Thorpe Jr. (Eds.), *Men's health equity: A handbook* (pp. 42–56). Routledge/Taylor & Francis Group. https://doi.org/10.4324/9781315167428-4

Cryer-Coupet, Q. R., Dorsey, M. S., Lemmons, B. P., & Hope, E. C. (2020). Examining multiple dimensions of father involvement as predictors of risk-taking intentions among black adolescent females. *Children and Youth Services Review, 108*, 104604. https://doi.org/10.1016/j.childyouth.2019.104604

Doherty, W. J., Kouneski, E. F., & Erickson, M. F. (1998). Responsible fathering: An overview and conceptual framework. *Journal of Marriage and Family, 60*(2), 277–292. https://doi.org/10.2307/353848

Dubowitz, H. (2009). Commentary on fathers and children and maltreatment: Relationships matter most. *Child Maltreatment, 14*, 291–293. https://doi.org/10.1111/j.1741-3729.2011.00672.x

Feinberg, M. E. (2003). The internal structure and ecological context of coparenting: A framework for research and intervention. *Parenting: Science and Practice, 3*(2), 95–131. https://doi.org/10.1207/s15327922par0302_01

Fletcher, R., May, C., Kay Lambkin, F., Gemmill, A. W., Cann, W., Nicholson, J. M., et al. (2017). SMS4dads: Providing information and support to new fathers through mobile phones–a pilot study. *Advances in Mental Health, 15*(2), 121–131. https://doi.org/10.1080/18387357.2016.1245586

Flouri, E., & Buchanan, A. (2003). The role of father involvement and mother involvement in adolescents' psychological well-being. *British Journal of Social Work, 33*(3), 399–406. https://doi.org/10.1093/bjsw/33.3.399

Guterman, N. B., & Lee, Y. (2005). The role of fathers in risk for physical child abuse: Possible pathways and unanswered questions. *Child Maltreatment, 10*, 136–149. https://doi.org/10.1177/1077559505274623

Johnson, W. E., Jr., Dorsey, M. S., Rich, L. M., & Brooks, L. L. (2020). "Remain calm, negotiate or defer but by all means, call me": Father-son communication to keep sons safe from violence involvement and victimization. *Journal of Applied Developmental Psychology, 71*, 101213. https://doi.org/10.1016/j.appdev.2020.101213

Lamb, M. E. (1987). Introduction: The emergent American father.

Lee, S. J., & Walsh, T. B. (2015). Using technology in social work practice: The mDad (Mobile Device Assisted Dad) case study. *Advances in Social Work, 16*(1), 107–124. https://doi.org/10.18060/18134

National Association of Social Workers. (2008). *Code of Ethics of the National Association of the National Association of Social Workers*. Retrieved April 12, 2022, from https://www.socialworkers.org/About/Ethics/Code-of-Ethics/Code-of-Ethics-English

Palkovitz, R. (2007). Challenges to modeling dynamics in developing a developmental understanding of father-child relationships. *Applied Development Science, 11*(4), 190–195. https://doi.org/10.1080/10888690701762050

Palkovitz, R., & Hull, J. (2018). Toward a resource theory of fathering. *Journal of Family Theory & Review, 10*(1), 181–198. https://doi.org/10.1111/jftr.12239

Pearson, J., & Fagan, J. (Eds.). (2021). *New research on parenting programs for low-income fathers*. Routledge.

Pennell, J., Sanders, T., Rikard, R. V., Shepherd, J., & Starsoneck, L. (2013). Family violence, fathers, and restoring personhood. *Restorative Justice, 1*(2), 268–289.

Pfitzner, N., Humphreys, C., & Hegarty, K. (2017). Research review: Engaging men: A multi-level model to support father engagement. *Child & Family Social Work, 22*(1), 537–547. https://doi.org/10.1111/cfs.12250

Planalp, E. M., Frausto, A., & Braungart-Rieker, J. M. (2020). Latino resident fathers' early involvement with infants. *Psychology of Men & Masculinities, 22*(3), 466–475. https://psycnet.apa.org/doi/10.1037/men0000325

Pleck, J. H. (2010). Paternal involvement: Revised conceptualization and theoretical linkages with child outcomes. In M. E. Lamb (Ed.), *The role of the father in child development* (pp. 58–93). Wiley.

Punyanunt-Carter, N. M. (2007). Using attachment theory to study communication motives in father–daughter relationships. *Communication Research Reports, 24*(4), 311–318. https://doi.org/10.1080/08824090701624213

Shadik, J. A., & O'Connor, M. K. (2016). Fathering and child maltreatment: Building theory to enhance treatment interventions. *Social Work Research, 40*(4), 213–224. https://doi.org/10.1093/swr/svw016

Sicouri, G., Tully, L., Collins, D., Burn, M., Sargeant, K., Frick, P., Anderson, V., Hawes, D., Kimonis, E., Moul, C., Lenroot, R., & Dadds, M. (2018). Toward father-friendly parenting interventions: A qualitative study. *Australian & New Zealand Journal of Family Therapy, 39*(2), 218–231. https://doi.org/10.1002/anzf.1307

Silverstein, L. B., & Auerbach, C. F. (1999). Deconstructing the essential father. *American Psychologist, 54*(6), 397.

Stone, G., Roer-Strier, D., Strier, R., Este, D., Shimoni, R., & Clark, D. (2005). Fatherhood and immigration: Challenging the deficit theory. *Child & Family Social Work, 10*(4), 315–329. https://doi.org/10.1111/j.1365-2206.2005.00374.x

Stover, C. S. (2013). Fathers for change: A new approach to working with fathers who perpetrate intimate partner violence. *The journal of the American Academy of Psychiatry and the Law, 41*(1), 65. https://www.ncbi.nlm.nih.gov/pmc/articles/PMC3641144/pdf/nihms463571.pdf

Torche, F., & Rauf, T. (2021). The transition to fatherhood and the health of men. *Journal of Marriage and Family, 83*(2), 446–465. https://doi.org/10.1111/jomf.12732

Appendix A: Glossary

Adoption Transfer of parental rights and custody to a relative or nonrelative adult.

Arrears Child support debt accrued by noncustodial parents with formal child support orders.

Assortative mating See homogamy.

Attachment theory Theory that describes the development of long-term relationships and bonds between people that impact feelings, thoughts, and subsequent relationships.

Blended families Families in which one or both partners have children from former relationships, sometimes used to refer specifically to families where there are children from both a former relationship or relationships, and this also includes a child or children born to both parents.

Bioecological systems theory A theory of interactions between humans and their environment that extends ecological theory by incorporating the impact of an individual on their own development.

Block grant **A** fixed amount of money provided to a state or local authority to use for a program or service.

Child welfare placement Out-of-home care with relative caregivers or nonrelative foster parents.

Child welfare permanency Stable and permanent family relationships and living arrangements.

Child welfarepermanency planning Case planning, parent-child visits, court attendance, and other activities designed to facilitate permanency for children in child welfare.

Q. R. Cryer-Coupet
School of Social Work, Georgia State University, Atlanta, GA, USA
e-mail: qcryercoupet@gsu.edu

J. L. Bellamy et al. (eds.), *Social Work Practice with Fathers*,
https://doi.org/10.1007/978-3-031-13686-3

Child support (child maintenance) Ongoing, regular, financial contributions to support a child or children often determined aspart of a formal custody arrangement.

Cis-gender Identifying as the same gender as that assigned at birth.

Co-parenting (coparenting) Shared support, agreement, duties, and tasks two or more parents carry out together for one or more children.

Complex trauma Trauma resulting from repeated and often prolonged exposure to multiple traumatic events that negatively impacts development.

Concurrent plans Planning and efforts toward two separate permanency goals simultaneously in child welfare.

Contact theory Contact between two groups can promote tolerance and acceptance, but only under certain conditions, such as equal status among groups and common goals.

Countertransference A psychodynamic concept used to describe instances where a therapist or service provider projects their own feelings onto their client.

Criminal legal system Policing, prosecution, courts, and corrections.

Critical feminist perspective Theoretical contributions of women of color scholars and practitioners that account for the differential effects of societal context including legacies of colonialism, racism, sexism, and class oppression.

Critical race theory A theory that describes how race and racism is socially constructed and embedded in systems and structures that create and reinforce racial disparities and power differentials.

Custodial parent A parent who lives with and cares for a child or children all or most of the time.

Deficit perspective (deficits-based perspective or deficit theory) A reductionist and pejorative view of groups that casts them in negative, often stereotyped, terms.

Deficits-based perspective See deficit perspective.

Deficit theory See deficit perspective.

Developmental perspective A broad framework for understanding human development across a broad array of dimensions (e.g., cognitive, emotional, social) and in stages from birth until death.

Early childhood programs Interventions serving children in their first 3–5 years and their families through preschools or childcare centers.

Ecological framework A theory of development that provides a framework through which to understand human interactions with the environment.

Ecomap A diagram that shows the social and personal relationships of an individual within their environment.

Essential father paradigm A perspective that views the role of fathers as one that is essential for optimal child well-being.

Family preservation Services and interventions employed in child welfare to keep families intact to avoid foster care placement.

Family systems theory (family systems framework) A framework that applies principles of general systems theory to the study of the family as an organized system.

Father An adult who identifies as male and carries out parenting roles and responsibilities for one or more children and/or is biologically or legally related to one or more children.

Father engagement Purposeful inclusion of fathers (including biological, social, resident, social, nonresident, and stepfathers) in program services and activities, with the objective of improving outcomes for fathers, children, and families.

Father friendliness of organizations The degree to which an organization's operations encourage father engagement in the services and programs it offers.

Father-inclusive interventions (father friendly interventions) Interventions that seek to engage and prioritize fathers in the delivery of services by capitalizing on the father's assets within the family system.

Father involvement Fathers' direct and indirect participation in families and the care of children.

Father-focused interventions Interventions developed with the goal of attending to the unique needs and experiences of fathers within the target population.

Feminist theory A critical sociological theory that was originally developed to better understand and disrupt the oppression of women and has evolved to more broadly address power differentials, oppressive systems, and structures.

General systems theory A broad framework for understanding phenomena from a holistic rather than reductionistic lens that accounts for patterns and structures.

Generativity A theoretical stage of development described by Erikson as the 7th stage of psychosocial development whereby individuals strive to contribute to things (e.g., children, work) that will outlast them.

Genogram A visual representation of an individual's family relationships and history.

Guardianship Transfer of custody (not parental rights) to a relative or nonrelative guardian in child welfare.

Homogamy (assortative mating) The tendency for people with similar social, economic, or cultural backgrounds to marry.

In-group Members of a group, organization, or system who have access, influence, or leverage in a particular circumstance.

Identity theory (social identity theory) A psychological theory that describes how individuals build an understanding of themselves through relationships with others.

Intimate partner violence Physical violence, sexual violence, stalking, and psychological aggression carried out by an individual's current or former intimate partner.

Just practice framework A practice framework developed by Finn and Jacobsen designed to center social work practice on social justice.

Life course theory (life course perspective) An interdisciplinary perspective focused on important, socially constructed events and roles that unfold sequentially over the lifetime and within the lived context of individuals.

Life course perspective See life course theory.

Mandatory minimums Court sentences that automatically require a specified prison term, regardless of the circumstances of the offender or the offense.

Maternal gatekeeping Efforts by mothers or members of the mother's family to impede fathers' involvement with children.

Motivational interviewing An evidence-supported intervention, originally developed to treat alcohol misuse, that is focused on helping people increase their readiness to change a behavior.

Multiple partner fertility (multi-partner fertility) Having biological children by more than one partner.

Mutual aid The voluntary, community-based, exchange of resources, services, or supports to meet the needs of a community.

Noncustodial father See noncustodial parent.

Noncustodial parent (noncustodial father) Parents whose children do not live with them the majority of the time.

Nonresidential parent A parent who does not live with their child or children, on a full-time basis, but has some legal or financial obligation to them.

Out-group Members of a group, system, or organization who have reduced access, reduced representation, and reduced influence.

Parenting A broad collection of direct and indirect roles and responsibilities carried out by adults as a mechanism of socialization and care for children.

Parenting self-efficacy See paternal self-efficacy.

Parenting plan A court-approved document that describes how parents will share custody and responsibilities for a child or children.

Parenting time See visitation.

Parental capital model A model of fathering that combines elements of social capital theory, parental style research, and the ecological perspective.

Paternal self-efficacy (parenting self-efficacy) A psychological concept developed from social cognitive theory that describes a parents' belief in their own ability to carry out the role of parenting.

Program evaluation Research that is conducted to assess social programs.

Repartnering Establishing a relationship with a new partner after the dissolution of a romantic relationship.

Responsible fatherhood Every father taking responsibility for a child's intellectual, emotional, and financial well-being, being present in the child's life, actively contributing to a child's healthy development, sharing economic responsibilities, and cooperating with a child's mother in addressing the full range of a child's and family's needs.

Responsible fathering framework An ecological framework designed to organize influences on fathering by father, co-parental, mother, child, and contextual factors.

Reunification Returning children to the care of their families after placement in out-of-home care in the child welfare system.

Social father Men who carry out parenting roles and responsibilities, although they are not biologically or legally related to the child or children they are parenting.

Social identity theory See identity theory.

Social learning theory A psychological theory that describes how behavior is learned by observing and modeling the behaviors of others.

Sociocultural factors Factors related to roles, societal or family norms, values, and expectations that shape fathering behaviors and identity.

Strengths-based perspective An approach to understanding individuals or communities by focusing on their positive attributes or characteristics.

Strengths perspective See strengths-based perspective.

Stepfamilies Families in which one or both partners have children from former relationships.

Systems theory A framework for understanding how smaller elements of systems are interconnected and mutually influencing in complex ways.

Three-strike rules An approach to felony sentencing that requires harsher, often lifetime, sentences for repeat offenders.

Transference A psychodynamic theory concept used to describe instances where an individual client projects their feelings onto the therapist.

Truth-in-sentencing laws A collection of laws that limit the amount of time offenders can have reduced from their sentences for good behavior and participation in programming.

Visitation (parenting time) Parenting time given to noncustodial parents to visit with children on a specific schedule, often described in legal custody arrangements, or when children are placed in foster care.

Appendix B: Social Work Grand Challenges Related to Fathers and Fathering

The Grand Challenges for Social Work were initiated by the American Academy of Social Work and Social Welfare to address some of our nation's greatest social concerns. This appendix highlights the Grand Challenge areas that scholars have begun to investigate in relation to father and family well-being and those that need additional work. Visit https://grandchallengesforsocialwork.org to learn more.

J. L. Bellamy et al. (eds.), *Social Work Practice with Fathers*,
https://doi.org/10.1007/978-3-031-13686-3

Domain	Grand challenge	Description	Father-focused approach to addressing grand challenges	Examples from current literature
Individual and family well-being				
	Ensure healthy development for all youth	Each year, more than six million young people receive treatment for severe mental, emotional, or behavioral problems. Strong evidence shows us how to prevent many behavioral health problems before they emerge. By unleashing the power of prevention through widespread use of proven approaches, we can help all youth grow up to become healthy and productive adults.	Father-child communication to mitigate risk-taking Impacts of father involvement on children's physical health	Johnson Jr, W. E., Dorsey, M. S., Rich, L. M., & Brooks, L. L. (2020). "Remain calm, negotiate or defer but by all means, call me": Father-son communication to keep sons safe from violence involvement and victimization. *Journal of Applied Developmental Psychology*, *71*, 101213. Pollock, E. R., Young, M. D., Lubans, D. R., Barnes, A. T., Eather, N., Coffey, J. E., ... Morgan, P. J. (2020). Impact of a father–daughter physical activity intervention: An exploration of fathers' experiences. *Journal of Child and Family Studies*, *29*(12), 3609–3620.
	Close the health gap	More than 60 million Americans experience devastating one to two punches to their health—they have inadequate access to basic health care while also enduring the effects of discrimination, poverty, and dangerous environments that accelerate higher rates of illness. Innovative and evidence-based social strategies can improve health care and lead to broad gains in the health of our entire society.	Fatherhood as a context for understanding men's health Fatherhood and reducing health disparities	Torche, F., & Rauf, T. (2021). The transition to fatherhood and the health of men. *Journal of Marriage and Family*, *83*(2), 446–465. Caldwell, C. H., Tsuchiya, K., Assari, S., & Thomas, A. (2019). Fatherhood as a social context for reducing men's health disparities: Lessons learned from the fathers and sons program. In D. M. Griffith, M. A. Bruce, & R. J. Thorpe Jr. (Eds.), *Men's health equity: A handbook* (pp. 42–56). Routledge/Taylor & Francis Group. https://doi.org/10.4324/9781315167428-4

	Build healthy relationships to end violence	Interpersonal violence has a traumatizing impact—across the life span—on individuals, families, communities, and society. Oppression based on factors such as a person's age, race, gender, identities, abilities, or socioeconomic status alter these experiences. Healthy relationships foster emotional resilience and strength. Developing and broadly implementing interventions, both universal and targeted, with individual, relationship, community, and service delivery systems can bolster a range of interpersonal relationships, reduce violence more broadly, and strengthen our mental and physical health, our families, and our communities.	Fathers and family violence Interventions for fathers who use intimate partner violence	Pennell, J., Sanders, T., Rikard, R. V., Shepherd, J., & Starsoneck, L. (2013). Family violence, fathers, and restoring personhood. *Restorative Justice*, *1*(2), 268–289. Stover, C. S. (2013). Fathers for change: A new approach to working with fathers who perpetrate intimate partner violence. *The Journal of the American Academy of Psychiatry and the Law*, *41*(1), 65.
	Advance long and productive lives	Increased automation and longevity demand new thinking by employers and employees regarding productivity. Young people are increasingly disconnected from education or work, and the labor force faces significant retirements in the next decades. Throughout the life span, fuller engagement in education and paid and unpaid productive activities can generate a wealth of benefits, including better health and well-being, greater financial security, and a more vital society.	Fatherhood and work-life balance Student fathers	Atkinson, J. (2021). Involved fatherhood and the workplace context: A new theoretical approach. *Gender, Work & Organization*. https://doi.org/10.1111/gwao.12789 Estes, D. K. (2011). Managing the student-parent dilemma: Mothers and fathers in higher education. *Symbolic Interaction, 34*(2), 198–219.
Stronger social fabric				

(continued)

Domain	Grand challenge	Description	Father-focused approach to addressing grand challenges	Examples from current literature
	Eradicate social isolation	Social isolation is a silent killer—as dangerous to health as smoking. National and global health organizations have underscored the hidden, deadly, and pervasive hazards stemming from feeling alone and abandoned. Our challenge is to educate the public on this health hazard, encourage health and human service professionals to address social isolation, and promote effective ways to deepen social connections and community for people of all ages.	Fathers' experiences of social support Supporting fathers of children with chronic illnesses	Gill, P., Scacco, S., De Haan, S., Gent, A., Chapin, L., Ganci, M., & Morda, R. (2021). Getting into the "dad zone": How do primary caregiving fathers of young children experience social support? *Journal of Child and Family Studies*, *30*(4), 1028–1042. https://doi.org/10.1007/s10826-021-01919-1 Nicholas, D. B. (2017). Examining the roles and experiences of fathers of children with chronic kidney disease. *Global Qualitative Nursing Research*, *4*, 2333393617705035.
	End homelessness	During the course of a year, nearly 1.5 million Americans will experience homelessness for at least one night. Periods of homelessness often have serious and lasting effects on personal development, health, and well-being. Our challenge is to expand proven approaches that have worked in communities across the country, develop new service innovations and technologies, and adopt policies that promote affordable housing and basic income security.	Fathers' experiences of homelessness	Stokes, M. N., Cryer-Coupet, Q. R., & Tall, K. G. (2020). "You get more training to drive a car": Examining the parenting experiences and service needs of nonresident fathers who are experiencing homelessness. *Psychology of Men & Masculinities*, *21*(4), 558. Roche, S., Barker, J., & McArthur, M. (2018). 'Performing' fathering while homeless: Utilising a critical social work perspective. *British Journal of Social Work*, *48*(2), 283–301.

	Create social responses to a changing environment	The environmental challenges reshaping contemporary societies pose profound risks to human well-being, particularly for marginalized communities. Climate change and urban development threaten health, undermine coping, and deepen existing social and environmental inequities. A changing global environment requires transformative social responses: New partnerships, deep engagement with local communities, and innovations to strengthen individual and collective assets.	Fathers' concerns about climate change	Ekholm, S. (2020). Swedish mothers' and fathers' worries about climate change: A gendered story. *Journal of Risk Research*, *23*(3), 288–296. Pratt, M. W., Norris, J. E., Alisat, S., & Bisson, E. (2013). Earth mothers (and fathers): Examining generativity and environmental concerns in adolescents and their parents. *Journal of MoralEducation*, *42*(1), 12–27.
	Harness technology for social good	Innovative applications of new digital technology present opportunities for social and human services to reach more people with greater impact on our most vexing social problems. These new technologies can be deployed to more strategically target social spending, speed up the development of effective programs, and bring a wider array of help to more individuals and communities.	Using mobile applications to support father involvement and support	White, B., Giglia, R. C., White, J. A., Dhaliwal, S., Burns, S. K., & Scott, J. A. (2019). Gamifying breastfeeding for fathers: Process evaluation of the Milk Man mobile app. *JMIR Pediatrics andParenting*, *2*(1), e12157. Fletcher, R., May, C., Kay Lambkin, F., Gemmill, A. W., Cann, W., Nicholson, J. M., ... Skinner, G. (2017). SMS4dads: Providing information and support to new fathers through mobile phones–a pilot study. *Advances in Mental Health*, *15*(2), 121–131.
Just society				

(continued)

Domain	Grand challenge	Description	Father-focused approach to addressing grand challenges	Examples from current literature
	Eliminate racism	The United States is built on a legacy of racism and white supremacy that has consistently and significantly impacted the daily lives of millions of people. Today, racist policies, bias, and discriminatory practices continue to promote racial inequality in myriad ways. Social work has provided considerable leadership in the civil rights and race equity movements but has much more work to do, internal to the profession and for society as a whole. We propose to develop a model for eliminating racism by identifying evidence- and practice-based interventions that will end racism and ameliorate the negative outcomes of our history of racism.	Father and family discussions about race and racism Fathers' parenting strategies to address race	Eveland Jr, W. P., & Nathanson, A. I. (2020). Contexts for family talk about racism: Historical, dyadic, and geographic. *Journal of Family Communication*, *20*(4), 267–284. Cooper, S. M., Burnett, M., Johnson, M. S., Brooks, J., Shaheed, J., & McBride, M. (2020). 'That is why we raise children': African American fathers' race-related concerns for their adolescents and parenting strategies. *Journal of Adolescence*, *82*, 67–81.
	Achieve equal opportunity and justice	In the United States, some groups of people have long been consigned to society's margins. Historic and current prejudice and injustice bar access to success in education and employment. Addressing racial and social injustices, deconstructing stereotypes, dismantling inequality, exposing unfair practices, and accepting the super diversity of the population will advance this challenge. All of this work is critical to fostering a successful society.	Parenting experiences of transnational fathers Fathers' and sons' experience of racism in schools	Parke, R. D., & Cookston, J. T. (2021). Transnational fathers: New theoretical and conceptual challenges. *Journal of Family Theory & Review*, *13*(3), 266–282. Allen, Q. (2013). "They think minority means lesser than": Black middle-class sons and fathers resisting microaggressions in the school. *UrbanEducation*, *48*(2), 171–197.

	Promote smart decarceration	The United States has the world's largest proportion of people behind bars. Mass incarceration and failed rehabilitation have resulted in staggering economic and human costs. Our challenge is to develop a proactive, comprehensive, evidence-based "smart decarceration" strategy that will dramatically reduce the number of people who are imprisoned and enable the nation to embrace a more effective and just approach to public safety.	Impact of mass imprisonment across the life span	Charles, P., Wilson, A. B., McLeod, B., Gottlieb, A., & Villodas, M. (2022). Incarcerated parents and their children: Perspectives from the Smart Decarceration Social Work Grand Challenge. In *Children of incarcerated parents* (pp. 241–256). Springer. Patterson, E. J., & Wildeman, C. (2015). Mass imprisonment and the life course revisited: Cumulative years spent imprisoned and marked for working-age black and white men. *Social Science Research, 53*, 325–337. https://doi.org/10.1016/j.ssresearch.2015.06.011
	Build financial capability for all	Nearly half of all American households are financially insecure, without adequate savings to meet basic living expenses for 3 months. We can significantly reduce economic hardship and the debilitating effects of poverty by adopting social policies that bolster lifelong income generation and safe retirement accounts, expand workforce training and retraining, and provide financial literacy and access to quality affordable financial services.	Improving economic outcomes for fathers and families	Kohl, P. L., Krauss, M. J., King, C., Cheng, S. Y., Fowler, P., Goodwin, D. N., Tillis, C. D., Sullivan, H., Sorg, A., & Mueller, N. B. (2022). The impact of responsible fatherhoodprograms on parenting, psychological well-being, and financial outcomes: A randomized controlled trial. *Family Process*, 1–19. https://doi.org/10.1111/famp.12752. Epub ahead of print. PMID: 34988991. Cowan, P. A., Cowan, C. P., & Gillette, P. F. (2022). TRUE Dads: The impact of a couples-based fatherhood intervention on family relationships, child outcomes, and economic self-sufficiency. *Family Process*, 1–24. https://doi.org/10.1111/famp.12748. Online ahead of print.

(continued)

Domain	Grand challenge	Description	Father-focused approach to addressing grand challenges	Examples from current literature
	Reduce extreme financial inequality	The top 1% owns nearly half of the total wealth in the United States, while one in five children live in poverty. The consequences for health and well-being are immeasurable. We can correct the broad inequality of wealth and income through a variety of innovative means related to wages and tax benefits associated with capital gains, retirement accounts, and home ownership. Greater lifelong access to education will also provide broader economic opportunities.	Financial impacts of responsible fatherhoodprograms for fathers and families Child support policy and income inequality	Chase, R.A. (2019). *Potential monetary value of responsible fatherhoodprogramoutcomes for fathers and children: A framework for monetizing the future stream of two-generation benefits and avoided costs.* Fatherhood Research & Practice Network Grantee Report. https://www.frpn.org/file/1476/download?token=BxsXTojU Ha, Y., Cancian, M., & Meyer, D. R. (2018). Child support and income inequality. *Poverty & Public Policy*, *10*(2), 147–158.

Source: Grand Challenges for Social Work. https://grandchallengesforsocialwork.org. Used with permission of the American Academy of Social Work and Social Welfare

Appendix C: Council on Social Work Education (CSWE) Educational Policy and Accreditation Standards (EPAS) Competency Map for Book Chapters

This table is intended to provide a framework for linking each of the CSWE EPAS competencies with the relevant content in this book. *We have applied the 2015 version of the CSWEEPAS competencies as the 2022 standards had not yet been finalized upon the submission of this book for publication.*

Competency #	Competency description	Relevant book chapter (s)
Competency 1: Demonstrate Ethical and Professional Behavior	Make ethical decisions by applying the standards of the NASW Code of Ethics, relevant laws and regulations, models for ethical decision-making, ethical conduct of research, and additional codes of ethics as appropriate to the context. Demonstrate professional demeanor in behavior, appearance, and oral, written, and electronic communication. Manage personal and professional value conflicts and affective reactions. Use technology ethically and appropriately to facilitate practice outcomes. Use supervision and consultation to guide professional judgment and behavior.	Chapter 1
Competency 2: Engage Anti-racism, Diversity, Equity, and Inclusion in Practice	Demonstrate anti-racist social work practice at the individual, family, group, organizational, community, research, and policy levels, informed by the theories and voices of those who have been marginalized. Demonstrate cultural humility applying critical reflexivity, self-awareness, and self-regulation to manage the influence of bias, power, privilege, and values in working with clients and constituencies acknowledging them as experts of their own lived experiences.	Chapter 1 Chapter 16

(continued)

J. L. Bellamy et al. (eds.), *Social Work Practice with Fathers*,
https://doi.org/10.1007/978-3-031-13686-3

Competency #	Competency description	Relevant book chapter (s)
Competency 3: Advance Human Rights and Social, Racial, Economic, and Environmental Justice	Advocate for human rights at the individual and system levels. Engage in practices that advance social, racial, economic, and environmental justice for equal justice and the dismantling of structural racism and oppression.	Chapter 5 Chapter 16
Competency 4: Engage Practice-Informed Research and Research-Informed Practice	Apply research findings to inform and improve practice, policy, and programs. Identify strategies for use of quantitative and qualitative methods of research to advance the purposes of social work.	Chapter 5
Competency 5: Engage in Policy Practice	Assess how social welfare policies affect the delivery of and access to social services. Apply critical thinking to analyze, formulate, and advocate for policies that advance human rights and social, racial, economic, and environmental justice.	Chapter 9
Competency 6: Engage with Individuals, Families, Groups, Organizations, and Communities	Apply knowledge of human behavior and person-in-environment and other multidisciplinary theoretical frameworks to engage with clients and constituencies. Use empathy, reflection, and interpersonal skills to effectively engage diverse clients and constituencies.	Chapter 2 Chapter 3 Chapter 4
Competency 7: Assess Individuals, Families, Groups, Organizations, and Communities	Apply knowledge of human behavior and person-in-environment and other culturally responsive multidisciplinary theoretical frameworks when assessing clients and constituencies. Demonstrate respect for client self-determination during the assessment process collaborating with clients and constituencies in developing mutually agreed-on goals.	Chapter 6 Chapter 7
Competency 8: Intervene with Individuals, Families, Groups, Organizations, and Communities	Engage with clients and constituencies to critically choose and implement culturally responsive, evidenced-based interventions to achieve mutually agreed-on practice goals and enhance capacities of clients and constituencies. Incorporate culturally responsive methods to negotiate, mediate, and advocate, with and on behalf of clients and constituencies.	Chapter 8 Chapter 10 Chapter 11 Chapter 12 Chapter 13 Chapter 14 Chapter 15
Competency 9: Evaluate Practice with Individuals, Families, Groups, Organizations, and Communities	Select and use appropriate methods for evaluation of outcomes. Critically analyze outcomes and apply evaluation findings to improve practice effectiveness with individuals, families, groups, organizations, and communities.	Chapter 5

Source: Council on Social Work Education (CSWE) Commission on Educational Policy and CSWE Commission on Accreditation. (2015). *Educational policy and accreditation standards for Baccalaureate and Master's Social Work Programs*, pp. 79. https://cswe.org/getattachment/Accreditation/Standards-and-Policies/2015-EPAS/2015EPASandGlossary.pdf. Reprinted with permission of the Council on Social Work Education

Appendix D: Syllabi Maps

These syllabi maps provide some ideas about how to incorporate fatherhood content into social work courses. It is not intended to be prescriptive or exhaustive but to give instructors ideas for how to integrate this content into their existing courses. These maps outline competencies and link them to book chapters, course objectives, and example assignments. The courses covered include human behavior and the social environment, social work practice, research methods, and social welfare policy (Tables D.1, D.2, D.3, and D.4).

J. L. Bellamy et al. (eds.), *Social Work Practice with Fathers*,
https://doi.org/10.1007/978-3-031-13686-3

Table D.1 Sample syllabi components for human behavior and the social environment (HBSE) courses

Competency #	Competency description	Relevant book chapters	Sample course objectives(s) that can be added to existing syllabi	Sample exercise(s)/assignment(s) that can be added to existing syllabi
Competency 2: Engage diversity and difference in practice.	Apply and communicate understanding of the importance of diversity and difference in shaping life experiences in practice at the micro, mezzo, and macro levels. Present themselves as learners and engage clients and constituencies as experts of their own experiences. Apply self-awareness and self-regulation to manage the influence of personal biases and values in working with diverse clients and constituencies.	Chapter 1 Chapter 2 Chapter 3 Chapter 10 Chapter 11 Chapter 12 Chapter 13 Chapter 14 Chapter 15 Chapter 16	Demonstrate an understanding of how personal views and biases can directly impact social work practice with diverse groups of fathers. Apply the person-in-environment perspective to communicate an understanding of how diversity and difference can shape the lived experiences of fathers at micro, mezzo, and macro levels.	*Assignment example 1:* Select a group of fathers that have identities or lived experiences that are different from your own. Reflect on your own world views and personal biases (i.e., thoughts, feelings, actions) related to engaging with this group of fathers in practice. Write a 1- to 2-page reflection paper on how such views and biases may influence how you engage and work with this group of fathers in practice. In your paper, also discuss some strategies you might employ in order to regulate these biases in order to better serve fathers in your practice. *Assignment example 2:* Select a minoritized or marginalized group of fathers that are of interest to you (i.e., Black fathers, single fathers, Hispanic fathers, LGBTQ PLUS_SPI fathers, fathers who are homeless, etc.). Develop a PowerPoint presentation to share with the class that outlines the following: (1) an application of the person-in-environment perspective to their lived experiences, considering dynamics such as oppression, racism, discrimination, poverty, marginalization, alienation privilege, and power; (2) how these dynamics impact their lived experiences at micro, mezzo, and macro levels; (3) how these dynamics might influence practitioner engagement with this group of fathers; and (4) strategies for effective practitioner engagement with this group of fathers, taking these dynamics into consideration.

Competency 3: Advance human rights and social, economic, and environmental justice.	Apply their understanding of social, economic, and environmental justice to advocate for human rights at the individual and system levels. Engage in practices that advance social, economic, and environmental justice.	Chapter 1 Chapter 2 Chapter 3 Chapter 4 Chapter 7 Chapter 9 Chapter 16	Understand the mechanisms of oppression and discrimination that impact minoritized and marginalized groups of fathers. Engage in practices that advance social and economic justice for marginalized and minoritized groups of fathers.	Select a marginalized or minoritized group of fathers that you'd like to focus on (i.e., Black fathers, single fathers, Hispanic fathers, LGBTQ PLUS_SPI fathers, fathers who are homeless, etc.). Conduct a structural analysis of the oppression experienced by this group of fathers, considering the tenets of Critical Race Theory and the five forms of oppression outlined in *Sandra Hinson and Alexa Bradley's* Structural Analysis of Oppression Framework (source: https://strategicpractice.org/system/files/structural_analysis_oppression.pdf). In your analysis, discuss the following: 1. Your critical assessment of how the various forms of oppression outlined in the framework directly affect this group of fathers. In your analysis, also take into consideration the tenets of critical race theory. 2. Your understanding of the social structures that create or perpetuate oppressive conditions for this group of fathers. In your analysis, also take into consideration the tenets of critical race theory. 3. Your role as a social work practitioner in reimagining and advocating for a more just society for this group of fathers.
Competency 6: Engage with individuals, families, groups, organizations, and communities.	Apply knowledge of human behavior and person-in-environment and other multidisciplinary theoretical frameworks to engage with clients and constituencies. Use empathy, reflection, and interpersonal skills to effectively engage diverse clients and constituencies.	Chapter 1 Chapter 2 Chapter 3 Chapter 4 Chapter 16	Apply knowledge of life course theory and/or family systems theory to effectively engage individual fathers. Apply multidisciplinary theoretical frameworks to enhance practice with individual fathers.	*Assignment example 1:* Conduct an interview with a father using life course theory or family systems theory as a guiding framework. Write a 1- to 2-page summary of what you learned about how to effectively engage fathers in practice, applying the tenets of the theory you've selected. *Assignment example 2:* Select two theoretical frameworks from another discipline that are of interest to you (i.e., psychology, sociology, public health, etc.). Apply these frameworks to your work with a father that in your field placement. After applying the frameworks, write a 1- to 2-page reflection comparing the relevance and usefulness of each framework for working with and engaging the father that you've selected.

(continued)

Competency #	Competency description	Relevant book chapters	Sample course objectives(s) that can be added to existing syllabi	Sample exercise(s)/assignment(s) that can be added to existing syllabi
Competency 7: Assess individuals, families, groups, organizations, and communities.	Collect and organize data and apply critical thinking to interpret information from clients and constituencies. Apply knowledge of human behavior and the social environment, person-in-environment, and other multidisciplinary theoretical frameworks in the analysis of assessment data from clients and constituencies. Develop mutually agreed-on intervention goals and objectives based on the critical assessment of strengths, needs, and challenges within clients and constituencies. Select appropriate intervention strategies based on the assessment, research knowledge, and values and preferences of clients and constituencies.	Chapter 6 Chapter 7	Apply knowledge of recommended approaches that are most appropriate for assessing fathers in practice.	*Assignment example 1:* Select an assessment tool of your choice. Evaluate the tool in terms of its appropriateness for use with fathers. Take into consideration three elements: comprehensiveness, fluidity, and strengths-based lens (see Chap. 6). Write a 1- to 2-page summary of your critique of the tool in these three areas. *Assignment example 2:* Select a father of your choice from your field placement and do the following: (1) Develop a critical assessment plan to monitor progress on an agreed-upon treatment outcome, taking into consideration the strengths, needs, and challenges of the father you've selected, and (2) collect and organize the assessment data received from the father you've selected. Apply your knowledge of the person-in-environment perspective, as well as at least one relevant theoretical framework, to your interpretation of the father's assessment data, and (3) share the results of the assessment with the father you've selected and your field liaison/supervisor.

Table D.2 Sample syllabi components for social work practice courses

Competency #	Competency description	Relevant book chapters	Sample course objective(s) that can be added to existing syllabi	Sample exercise(s)/assignments(s) that can be added to existing syllabi
Competency 1: Demonstrate ethical and professional behavior.	Make ethical decisions by applying the standards of the NASW Code of Ethics, relevant laws and regulations, models for ethical decision-making, ethical conduct of research, and additional codes of ethics as appropriate to context. Use reflection and self-regulation to manage personal values and maintain professionalism in practice situations. Demonstrate professional demeanor in behavior, appearance, and oral, written, and electronic communication. Use technology ethically and appropriately to facilitate practice outcomes. Use supervision and consultation to guide professional judgment and behavior.	Chapter 1 Chapter 2	Identify barriers to social justice in practice with fathers or how social work practice with fathers is a social justice issue.	In a brief paper, identify how a failure to include a focus on fathers, their roles, and their inclusion in services is antithetical to the value of social justice in social work. Include content related to engagement, assessment, and intervention.
Competency 2: Engage diversity and difference in practice.	Apply and communicate understanding of the importance of diversity and difference in shaping life experiences in practice at the micro, mezzo, and macro levels. Present themselves as learners and engage clients and constituencies as experts of their own experiences. Apply self-awareness and self-regulation to manage the influence of personal biases and values when working with diverse clients and constituencies.	Chapter 1 Chapter 2 Chapter 6	Reflect on knowledge and biases related to fatherhood.	Write a brief self-reflection on fathering. What do you see as the primary roles of fathers? Are any of your expectations different from how fathers were perceived historically? What are the potential strengths and challenges of fathers? What biases might you hold about fathers and their roles?
Competency 6: Engage with individuals, families, groups, organizations, and communities.	Apply knowledge of human behavior and the social environment, person-in-environment, and other multidisciplinary theoretical frameworks to engage with clients and constituencies. Use empathy, reflection, and interpersonal skills to effectively engage diverse clients and constituencies.	Chapter 2 Chapter 3 Chapter 4	Explain how to effectively engage with fathers.	Conduct an interview with a father, demonstrating empathy and effective interpersonal skills. Ask how his experiences and the messages he has received have impacted him and his fathering.

(continued)

Competency #	Competency description	Relevant book chapters	Sample course objective(s) that can be added to existing syllabi	Sample exercise(s)/assignments(s) that can be added to existing syllabi
Competency 7: Assess individuals, families, groups, organizations, and communities.	Collect and organize data, and apply critical thinking to interpret information from clients and constituencies. Apply knowledge of human behavior and the social environment, person-in-environment, and other multidisciplinary theoretical frameworks in the analysis of assessment data from clients and constituencies. Develop mutually agreed-on intervention goals and objectives based on the critical assessment of strengths, needs, and challenges within clients and constituencies. Select appropriate intervention strategies based on the assessment, research knowledge, and values and preferences of clients and constituencies.	Chapter 6 Chapter 7	Describe elements of a comprehensive assessment with fathers.	Complete a bio-psycho-social-spiritual assessment with a father. Write out specific questions you would ask fathers in different settings to better understand their strengths and challenges: Teen father in high school Incarcerated father Father involved in child welfare system Father of three in a custody dispute Gay father in the adoption process
Competency 8: Intervene with individuals, families, groups, organizations, and communities.	Critically choose and implement interventions to achieve practice goals and enhance capacities of clients and constituencies. Apply knowledge of human behavior and the social environment, person-in-environment, and other multidisciplinary theoretical frameworks in interventions with clients and constituencies. Use interprofessional collaboration as appropriate to achieve beneficial practice outcomes. Negotiate, mediate, and advocate with and on behalf of diverse clients and constituencies. Facilitate effective transitions and endings that advance mutually agreed-on goals.	Chapter 8 Chapter 10 Chapter 11 Chapter 12 Chapter 13 Chapter 14 Chapter 15	Utilize effective intervention skills with fathers.	Identify elements of the individual practitioner and agency that may impact intervention with fathers. In a 2- to 3-page paper, identify and discuss a minimum of three factors at each level (individual, agency) that are likely to enhance intervention and three factors at each level likely to diminish intervention efforts.

Table D.3 Sample syllabi components for social work research methods courses

Competency #	Competency description	Relevant book chapters	Sample course objectives (s) that can be added to existing syllabi	Sample exercise(s)/assignment(s) that can be added to existing syllabi
Competency 1: Demonstrate ethical and professional behavior.	Make ethical decisions by applying the standards of the NASW Code of Ethics, relevant laws and regulations, models for ethical decision-making, ethical conduct of research, and additional codes of ethics as appropriate to context.	Chapter 5 Chapter 16	Articulate ethical issues and necessary procedures in the research process to ensure the ethical conduct of research with fathers.	Complete CITI Research Ethics Training: Group 2 (Social-Behavioral-Educational Researchers) Using a template from your university's IRB, develop a mock-informed consent document for a cross-sectional qualitative study with fathers of child welfare system-impacted children.
Competency 2: Engage diversity and difference in practice.	Apply and communicate understanding of the importance of diversity and difference in shaping life experiences in practice at the micro, mezzo, and macro levels.	Chapter 2 Chapter 5 Chapter 10 Chapter 11 Chapter 15	Identify the impact of research methods and findings, including relevance and generalizability, on diverse subpopulations of fathers.	Find an empirical article about father involvement and/or engagement that was recently published in a social work journal. Identify whether or not the findings are generalizable to a subpopulation of fathers. Describe how you arrived at this determination. What are the potential impacts of the research findings for the lives of this group of fathers? Who among this group of fathers is missing from the current study?

(continued)

Competency #	Competency description	Relevant book chapters	Sample course objectives (s) that can be added to existing syllabi	Sample exercise(s)/assignment(s) that can be added to existing syllabi
Competency 4: Engage in practice-informed research and research-informed practice.	Use practice experience and theory to inform scientific inquiry and research. Apply critical thinking to engage in analysis of quantitative and qualitative research methods and research findings. Use and translate research evidence to inform and improve practice, policy, and service delivery. Demonstrate knowledge of research methods and literature that provide a foundation for practice.	Chapter 4 Chapter 5 Chapter 13 Chapter 14	Develop and critique research questions appropriate to all levels of practice with fathers while attending to organizational and political constraints that influence the research process practice implications. Select appropriate quantitative and qualitative approaches to guide research with fathers, including the use of available data, experimental and quasi-experimental designs, surveys, intensive interviewing, and participant observation.	Interview a social work practitioner who serves fathers and families. Ask about their experience with research-informed practice. How do they access up-to-date evidence? Do they have relationships with researchers to facilitate the sharing of knowledge from their practice? Use the information from your interview to outline organizational constraints within the research-to-practice pipeline.
Competency 9: Evaluate practice with individuals, families, groups, organizations, and communities.	Select and use appropriate methods for evaluation of outcomes. Apply knowledge of human behavior and the social environment, person-in-environment, and other multidisciplinary theoretical frameworks in the evaluation of outcomes. Critically analyze, monitor, and evaluate intervention and program processes and outcomes. Apply evaluation findings to improve practice effectiveness at the micro, mezzo, and macro levels.	Chapter 5 Chapter 8 Chapter 10 Chapter 11 Chapter 13	Design research that is compatible with social work's aims, values, and ethics and with different worldviews that contribute to knowledge about social work with fathers.	Identify a social problem that has been experienced by fathers who have returned to their communities following incarceration. Develop a research proposal to examine this social problem. Include the following sections in your proposal: Problem statement Review of the literature Theoretical frame Research question(s) Methods Research design Sample selection Measures Human subjects protection plan

Appendix E: Policy Reflection Activity

Qiana R. Cryer-Coupet

J. L. Bellamy et al. (eds.), *Social Work Practice with Fathers*,
https://doi.org/10.1007/978-3-031-13686-3

Table D.4 Sample syllabi components for social welfare policy courses

Competency #	Competency description	Relevant book chapters	Sample course objectives(s) that can be added to existing syllabi	Sample exercise(s)/assignment(s) that can be added to existing syllabi
Competency 3: Advance human rights and social, economic, and environmental justice.	Apply their understanding of social, economic, and environmental justice to advocate for human rights at the individual and system levels. Engage in practices that advance social, economic, and environmental justice.	Chapter 1 Chapter 2 Chapter 9 Chapter 16	Integrate multiple sources of knowledge in evaluating and advocating for relevant and effective policies that impact fathers and families and their adherence to the principles of social and economic justice.	Assign each student to be a member of a team that will argue, debate style, for or against a current father-focused policy issue (i.e., an issue addressed in a key social welfare policy that impacts fathers). This exercise promotes the development of skills in defending and/or opposing current or proposed policies. Select a father-focused policy issue (i.e., an issue addressed in a key social welfare policy that impacts fathers). Examine the following list of advocacy strategies and develop an "Advocacy Strategic Plan for Fathers." Specifically, select a mix of *TWO (2)* different strategies that can be used to advocate for the rights of fathers. *Five advocacy strategies:* (1) testifying, (2) coalition building, (3) face-to-face lobbying, (4) field organizing, and (5) media campaign. Specify in your plan exactly how these strategies will be utilized and provide a rationale for why they were chosen over others.

Competency 5: Engage in policy practice.	Identify social policy at the local, state, and federal level that impacts well-being, service delivery, and access to social services. Assess how social welfare and economic policies impact the delivery of and access to social services. Apply critical thinking to analyze, formulate, and advocate for policies that advance human rights and social, economic, and environmental justice.	Chapter 4 Chapter 7 Chapter 9 Chapter 10 Chapter 12 Chapter 14	Critically analyze public discourse, legislative bills, research findings, and theoretical perspectives regarding social welfare policies that affect fathers and families.	In 5–7 pages, discuss how a failure to consider the impacts of social policy on father involvement and engagement is antithetical to the values of social and economic justice in social work. Identify an existing policy at the agency, state, or federal level. Describe how changes to this policy could positively impact social and/or economic justice for fathers. Detail an advocacy plan for implementing the suggested policy shifts. Use Congress.gov (https://www.congress.gov) to locate a bill that impacts fathers (i.e., child support policies, paternal leave policies, child welfare policies, etc.). Summarize the bill and its major provisions in your own words and consider the following questions: 1. What is being proposed in the bill? 2. What is the current status of the bill? (Which committee has jurisdiction? Have there been any hearings? A markup? Any important votes?) 3. If there are bills in both houses, how do they differ? What is the current status of each? Has this, or a similar bill, been introduced before? If so, how far did it get toward enactment? 4. How do the provisions included in the bill impact fathers?

Source: Council on Social Work Education (CSWE) Commission on Educational Policy and CSWE Commission on Accreditation. (2015). *Educational policy and accreditation standards for Baccalaureate and Master's Social Work Programs*, pp. 7–9. https://cswe.org/getattachment/Accreditation/Standards-and-Policies/2015-EPAS/2015EPASandGlossary.pdf. Reprinted with permission of the Council on Social Work Education

Efforts to support father involvement and engage fathers in services should include attention to policies that may support or hinder participation. This includes detailed policy analysis and social justice-focused advocacy. Below, we highlight a useful policy analysis framework for considering the impacts of various policies on father involvement and engagement. After reviewing the passage, visit https://www.purdue.edu/hhs/hdfs/fii/ to learn more about the family impact analysis framework. Next, identify a state-level policy that may affect father involvement or engagement. Finally, follow the steps outlined in Fig. A.1 to examine the impacts of the policy on fathers and families who may be served by your agency.

Family Impact Analysis

The family impact analysis (FIA) framework provides a comprehensive tool for the analysis of policies that affect the lives of fathers and their families. In the past, the FIA framework, developed in 1976 by a team of researchers at the Policy Institute for Family Impact Seminars, was used to analyze father-related topics such as child support enforcement policies. Ory (1980) notes that FIA grew out of concern with "the rapidly changing structure of the American family and the relationship of the family to other social institutions, policy makers, administrators and the general public" (p. 942). Ooms (1995) notes that there were several public policies and programs at the time that were impacting families in a negative way. The theoretical underpinnings of FIA are based on Bronfenbrenner's ecological model, Minuchin's family system's theory, and the sociological family-centered approach.

Issues regarding family are often emotionally charged. As such, family-centered policy analysis and research are not value-free areas of practice. Therefore, it is important to understand the power structure of organizations, political parties, and other key stakeholders as they each contribute to the intended and unintended outcomes of family-related policies (Ooms, 1995). According to Bogenschneider et al. (2012), the FIA framework should highlight family impacts related to the culture, policies, and practices of agencies. Additionally, FIA should identify the strengths and gaps in organizational support of families.

According to Gross et al. (n.d.), when conducting an FIA, the analyst should consider the eight steps outlined in Fig. A.1.

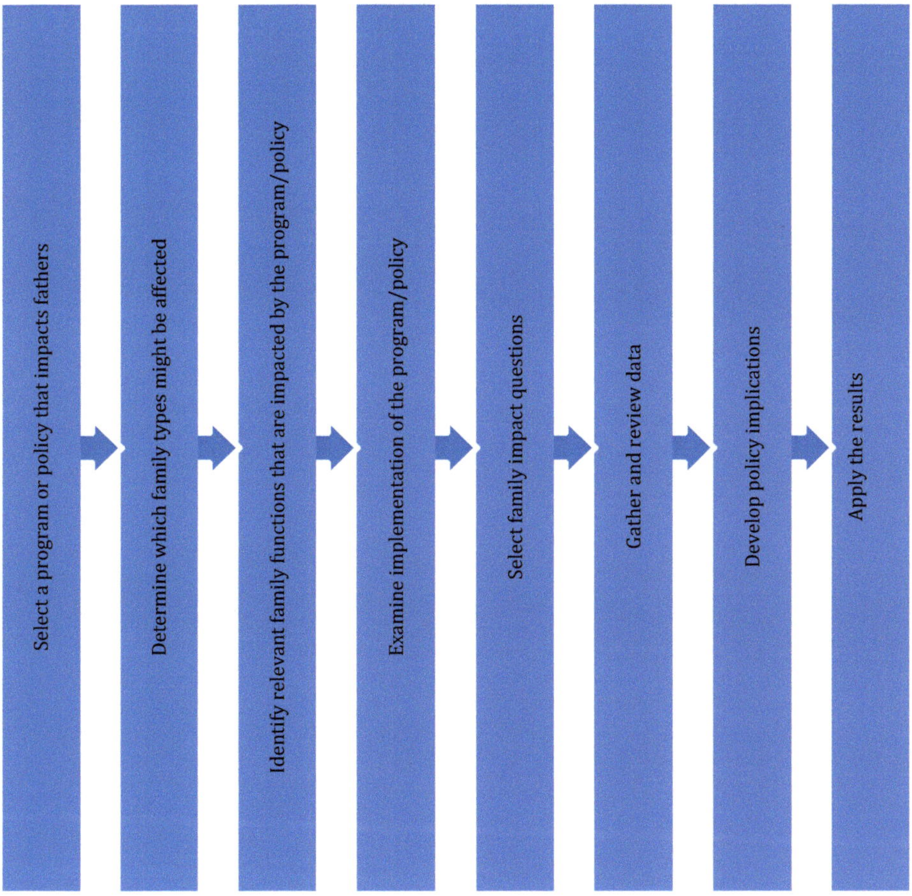

Fig. A.1 Guidance for family impact analysis

Appendix F: Practice Reflection Activity

Use the JUST Practice Framework that was introduced in Chap. 8 to reflect on the following issue brief. Using the five key tenets of the framework, identify the practice and social justice implications outlined in the brief.

Examining the Impacts of Mass Incarceration on Black Fathers

Clinton Boyd Jr

cboyd@ffhc.org

Mass Incarceration

The principal aim of the criminal justice system was, for most of the twentieth century, purportedly rehabilitation. During this period, the general public and policymakers believed criminal offenders were worthy of redemption; only irredeemable transgressors deserved to languish behind bars. Judges had the legal discretion to determine whether—and for how long—an offender would be imprisoned, a process known as indeterminate sentencing. Whenever a criminal conviction did not warrant correctional confinement, offenders were placed under community supervision and assigned a probation officer. Even more, if imprisoned, parole boards could reduce an offender's prison sentence after prudently assessing a wide array of

J. L. Bellamy et al. (eds.), *Social Work Practice with Fathers*,
https://doi.org/10.1007/978-3-031-13686-3

factors. These considerations ranged from the detainee's criminal history to the circumstances surrounding their imprisonment and their likelihood of successful rehabilitation. Despite racial imbalances in US incarceration rates between 1880 and 1950 (Muller, 2012), particularly in the South (Blackmon, 2008; Muller, 2018), incarcerations in the American penal system had yet to reach unprecedented levels. However, that would soon change.

The oft-repeated statistic that the United States constitutes 5% of the world's population but houses roughly 25% of those incarcerated throughout the globe is well known (National Research Council, 2014). More alarming is the fact that the United States has become the imprisonment capital of the world. In 2012, the United States had the highest incarceration rate of all nations, with 707 out of every 100,000 residents imprisoned. Russia placed second on the list with an incarceration rate of 474 per 100,000 residents (National Research Council, 2014). As a matter of historical significance, the US incarceration rate in 2012 surpassed the 1972 figure of 161 per 100,000 residents. Given the exponential rise in US incarceration between 1970 and 2010, one may ask why the US criminal justice system changed in such a profound manner? The answer is simple: A new ideological perspective came to define US criminal justice policy, one that favored retribution and "repudiated the philosophy of rehabilitation" (Western, 2006, p. 59).

The war waged against poverty during the Johnson administration was replaced by a crusade against crime, disorder, and lawlessness by President Nixon (Hinton, 2016). In the 1970s, the institution of mass incarceration gained political traction and effectively reincarnated racialized oppression in the post-civil rights period (Alexander, 2012). Widespread social and economic changes, punitive criminal justice policies, aggressive policing tactics in chronically disadvantaged neighborhoods, and a conservative backlash to the civil rights movement of the 1960s also contributed to the rise of mass incarceration (Travis & Western, 2017). Let us now examine the political origins of the prison boom.

Commencing in the 1960s, the Republican party devised a *Southern Strategy* to reclaim the presidency and regain their congressional power (Aistrup, 1996). Taking their cues from Barry Goldwater, a former Republican presidential nominee, the Republican party concluded that their pathway to political victory required that they vehemently oppose issues of racial justice, distance themselves from the civil rights movement, and appeal to the conservative and segregationist members of their constituency by deploying racially coded language. Adhering to their new political strategy, right-wing conservatives such as Barry Goldwater and Richard Nixon linked civil rights protests to issues of crime and racial violence (Western & Wildeman, 2009). Moreover, the Black-initiated race riots of the 1960s, which were responses to "white terror campaigns against black people" (Bentley-Edwards et al., 2018, p. 22), also played into the hands of the Republican party's newfound tough-on-crime approach. In short, the Republican party unleashed a rhetorical onslaught against crime, lawlessness, and disorder by stoking the racial anxieties of southern and ethnic-identifying Whites. The Democratic party is also complicit on this front. The Johnson administration allocated federal resources and funds to local jails, state prisons, and law enforcement institutions to quell the Black urban uprisings of the

1960s (Hinton, 2016). This was the first time the federal government involved itself in matters of crime prevention, which were traditionally handled by state and local governments.

Moving into subsequent decades, the trend of political intervention in criminal justice policy persisted. Under the guise of a "War on Drugs" campaign (Alexander, 2012), both the Republican and Democratic parties supported tough-on-crime legislation in the form of mandatory minimums, three-strike rules, and truth-in-sentencing laws. There was also a national movement to abolish and limit parole boards, which proved to be highly successful. Prison expansion and the newly enacted criminal sentencing laws were eagerly embraced by Republican governors and state legislators, particularly those in the South (Western, 2006). However, while many believe that the US jail and prison population grew the largest under Republican presidential leadership (e.g., President Ronald Regan), that is not necessarily true. The Violent Crime Control and Law Enforcement Act of 1994, signed into law by President Clinton, was the primary policy tool that caused the number of our nation's prisons and jails to grow at an exponential rate (Evans & Owens, 2007). Racial disparities exist within the US incarceration rate, with Blacks, specifically Black males, being disproportionately affected by punitive criminal sentencing policies.

Black males constitute roughly 6% of the nation's population (US Census Bureau, 2020) but nearly 40% of those incarcerated in the United States. Black males are six times more likely to be incarcerated than White males (Bronson & Carson, 2019). This is especially the case for nonviolent drug offenses (Alexander, 2012). Due to racial disparities in criminal sentencing, the lifetime risk of imprisonment is 20% for all Black men, 30% for Black men without a college education, and 60% for those pushed out of high school (Pettit & Western, 2004). Therefore, it is more likely for a Black man without a high school degree to be incarcerated than graduate from college or join the armed forces (Western, 2006). For ex-offender African American men who are fathers (Glaze & Maruschak, 2010), criminal justice system involvement can undercut their labor market outcomes.

The Collateral Consequences of Paternal Incarceration

Prime working-age Black men (25–54 years of age) with a high school degree or less and prior criminal justice system involvement are more likely to be the victims of racial discrimination in hiring practices. A landmark study by the late sociologist Devah Pager highlights this point (Pager, 2003). Pager (2009) conducted a study focused on the effect incarceration had on the employment outcomes of Black and White male job applicants. According to Pager, a Black job applicant with a criminal record was 3.4 times less likely to receive a callback for a job than a White job seeker who also had a criminal conviction. Furthermore, highlighting how race interacts with perceived criminality, Pager's findings also concluded that Blacks *without a criminal record* received less consideration for a job than Whites with a criminal background. A follow-up study by Pager et al. (2009) yielded similar results.

The labor market discrimination experienced by Black male ex-offenders has severe implications for those who are fathers. Using Panel Study of Income Dynamics data, Joseph (2010) concluded that nearly 74,000 African American fathers reentering society yearly are estimated to lose more than $600 million in annual earnings collectively. There are several explanations for this. First, as previously stated, potential employers may be reluctant to hire ex-offenders because of their criminal background. Second, punitive criminal justice policies prevent ex-offenders from securing specific public sector jobs, which severely constrains their employment options (Charles et al., 2019; Holcomb et al., 2015). Third, potential employers may be concerned that ex-offenders lack the necessary skills and labor market experience to be an asset to their company. As a result, they are less likely to receive high-wage career jobs and are more likely to be channeled into a secondary labor market where employment is insecure and pay is poor (Nagin & Waldfogel, 1998).

For example, Lewis Jr and colleagues (2007) discovered that ex-offender fathers worked fewer hours and earned considerably less money than fathers with no criminal record. Other studies support these findings. In terms of employment duration, it is estimated that a Black man with an incarceration history will spend 14 fewer weeks on the job than one with no incarceration history (Western, 2006). As it relates to total earnings, incarceration reduces the earnings of Black males by 9% (The Pew Charitable Trusts, 2010). As the previous evidence suggests, incarceration has negative consequences for the labor market outcome of Black fathers, which undermines their ability to support their children materially.

The individual downsides of mass incarceration have been well documented for ex-offender fathers. However, we must also consider the intergenerational impact of incarceration on children. Ninety-two percent (approximately 744,200) of fathers in state and federal prisons had between them 1,559,200 children under the age of 18, with more than 40% of those fathers being African American (Glaze & Maruschak, 2010). Approximately 36% of the 744,200 fathers detained in state prisons resided with their young children in the month before incarceration, and roughly 54% of these fathers provided primary financial support to their minor children (Glaze & Maruschak, 2010). These figures indicate that the punitive nature of the criminal justice system extends far past incarcerated and ex-offender fathers and affects their socioeconomically vulnerable children.

Results from a study conducted by Sykes and Pettit (2015) indicate that children who experience parental incarceration encounter severe deprivation in the form of material hardship, unmet health needs, and residential stability. The study also found that social service utilization was higher among children exposed to parental incarceration than children unexposed to parental incarceration. Specific to paternal incarceration, material hardship is much more pronounced for children whose father has an incarceration history (Schwartz-Soicher et al., 2011). As the authors suggest, the father's criminal record undercuts his economic stability, thereby reducing the financial contributions he can make to his family of procreation.

Additional research indicates that children with an incarcerated or ex-offender father are more likely to receive public assistance, have a higher risk of developmental delays and behavioral challenges, experience heightened levels of physical aggression, and are at increased risk of homelessness and food insecurity (Cox & Wallace, 2016; Perry & Bright, 2012; Wakefield & Wildeman, 2016). Ex-offender fathers are also regularly prohibited from Pell grants, excluded from housing support, banned from certain occupational endeavors, and often accrue debt for use of the judicial system (Harding et al., 2014; Western, 2018), all of which contribute to the material hardship their children experience.

For Black fathers awaiting release from prison, their time behind bars can be fraught with sleepless nights as they are often unable to establish or sustain meaningful relationships with their children. Once freed from the constraints of prison life, newly emancipated fathers set out on a road of redemption. However, their process of reacclimating to civilian life is far from rosy. Their criminal conviction frequently constrains their employment prospects, prevents them from securing stable housing, and precludes them from participating in public assistance programs (Halushka, 2020).

Recommended Strategies and Practices

Considering the interrelated challenges of Black fathers during returning, it is critical that community-based programs develop incisive fatherhood interventions to address their complex needs. As research indicates, when fatherhood interventions are thoughtfully crafted and successfully implemented for returning citizens, these programs make a positive difference in the lives of fathers, their children, their partners, and their communities. While fatherhood programs for returning citizens may differ in terms of their approach, these interventions generally help fathers socially reintegrate into society by offering them education, mental health care, substance abuse treatment, job training, counseling, and mentoring services. Below is an overview of the essential elements of most fatherhood programs:

- *Effectivefatherhood programsoffer cohort-based peer support groups to reentry fathers.* Providing cohort-based peer support groups to reentry fathers is one of the most effective ways to engage Black men in fatherhood programs. The integrated approach to service delivery is an effective way to increase program participation and ensure program retention among a subset of fathers with increasingly complex needs (Dion et al., 2018). Led by a trained peer support specialist or facilitator, these groups serve as a safe space for fathers to be emotionally vulnerable. Aside from being a venue to discuss their life triumphs and tribulations, cohort-based, peer support groups offer a platform for reentry fathers to establish social networks with other men who can provide them with emotional, financial, in-kind, and housing support and resources (D'Angelo et al., 2016).
- *Effectivefatherhood programsoffer flexible, highly personalized, case management support to reentry fathers.* Most successful fatherhood programs tailor their service delivery approach to meet the individual needs of reentry fathers. Case managers not only assess the needs of fathers but also identify their parental strengths and talents. Once positive attributes have been discerned, case manag-

ers then motivate fathers to share their paternal skills and insights with other men in the program. Case managers must also have flexible schedules as fathers typically need access to them outside traditional business hours.

- *Effectivefatherhood programsrely on a combination of traditional and innovative strategies to recruit and retain reentry fathers in programming.* Specific tactics are required to successfully recruit and retain young fathers in fatherhood programs. They include strategies such as community canvassing (i.e., street outreach), social media marketing, offering monetary and nonmonetary incentives, and continual post-program support.
- *Effectivefatherhood programshire program staff who have overcome life challenges like those encountered by reentry fathers enrolling in programming.*
- *Effectivefatherhood programsoffer workforce development and placement supports to reentry fathers.* Reentry fathers experience multiple barriers to employment, primarily because their criminal records make them unattractive to potential employers. To help reentry fathers overcome their employment barriers, fatherhood programs offer them a variety of workforce development and placement services to help them secure living-wage jobs. For instance, fatherhood organizations assist fathers by offering them economic stability workshops. These workshops help fathers to create cover letters and resumes, guide them through the online job application process, and prepare them for job interviews. Other aspects of the economic stability workshops typically cover the topics of banking, budgeting, financing, and wealth literacy. Additionally, fatherhood programs establish formal partnerships with community organizations that specialize in local workforce systems. Local workforce systems consist of organizations and activities that ensure individuals can meet the work-related demands of their jobs, assist in facilitating career advancement among workers, and guarantee that workers are properly trained to support their local industry and economy over time (Eyster et al., 2016). Local workforce systems generally serve individuals with personal challenges to work, adults in need of basic skills, and workers seeking career changes or advancement. Considering the populations that local workforce systems are intended to serve, reentry fathers are uniquely situated to benefit from these services.
- *Effectivefatherhood programscreate trauma-informed systems of care for reentry fathers.* Fatherhood organizations utilizing this approach are most successful when they (1) take a trauma-informed approach to service delivery and (2) offer trauma-specific services to reentry fathers in need of direct clinical services (Dion et al., 2019). Urban Black men experience toxic stress due to racism, discrimination, and poverty exposure. Chronic trauma exposure can take an emotional and psychological toll on Black men throughout their life course and impair their help-seeking behaviors. That said, understanding the mental health challenges of reentry men, the most successful fatherhood organizations offer these men culturally responsive trauma-specific services.

Appendix G: Case Vignettes

These case vignettes are intended to be utilized as a tool to facilitate classroom dialogue, reflect on the lived experiences of fathers, and contemplate what the most effective approaches are to tackling the challenges they face in real world contexts. The vignettes can be used in training or coursework.

Case #1

When we had a baby, it was a surprise. We weren't expecting to be parents together. I liked her, but we weren't that serious. When our little girl was born, it was stressful. I wanted to try and make it work. Sometimes, we just screamed at each other. Other times, we were fighting each other. It was bad. We probably fought four or five times. If I did something she didn't like, she'd hit me. One day, I was supposed to run errands for her. I just got off work and was tired. She told me to go pick the stuff up, and I said I just needed a little break before I went out. Before I knew it, she threw the plate she was holding at me. She hit me right in the head. That was pretty typical when she was mad at me. I didn't call the cops. I didn't want her going to jail. I stayed with my parents for a few days and then went back when she cooled down. We eventually broke up, but it was rough. We just couldn't be together.

Case #2

I've been a dad for 12 years now. When my son was first born, I was still into partying. Still into drinking. I dropped him off at the babysitter all the time. It was my time. So I kind of put that above him. I was running around with the wrong crowd.

J. L. Bellamy et al. (eds.), *Social Work Practice with Fathers*,
https://doi.org/10.1007/978-3-031-13686-3

I got in trouble. Went to prison two times. I spent 3 years locked up. The times that I went to prison, my mom helped take care of him, so he was in good hands. My son's mom, I don't want to say anything bad about her, but she's not the best parent. When I was in prison, they had this program where I met with other dads and we talked about father stuff. It was the first time I got to really think about how I wanted to be a dad, and people listened to me and understood. Now that I am out of prison and parenting, it has been amazing and completely different from before. I don't drink anymore. I haven't had a drink in over 8 years. I'm more active as a father, and my son lives with me. My son spends half his time with me and half with his mom. I have a new daughter, she's two. Taking care of her, watching her, it's amazing. There is just so much stuff that I don't remember about my son, or stuff I missed out on.

Case #3

My girlfriend got pregnant when we were 17. We were just kids. At that time, I was selling drugs and always had a gun on me. When she told me she was pregnant, I gave it all up. Just stopped. I got my GED and got a job. My dad wasn't in my life. I knew who he was, but he wasn't ever around. I knew I wanted to do better. I wanted to be there for my kids. My daughter is six now, and she's the best thing in my life. I braid her hair and fix her breakfast before school. I help her with homework and want to see her finish high school, and maybe go to college. If my girlfriend didn't get pregnant then, I think I'd be dead or in prison by now. Having my daughter changed my whole life. She saved my life.

Case #4

I tried to get custody for 5 years after CPS got called on our family. The courts kept giving her [the mother of my children] chances even when she didn't show up to court. She didn't do what she was supposed to. I had to take weekly drug tests. I had to go to classes on anger management and parenting even though I didn't do anything. I was really stressed during this time. The courts tend to back the woman. I don't think judges realize that the dad can be supportive, can take care of the kids. They forget that fathers have feelings. I shouldn't have to prove myself as a father. I am just as much a parent as my ex. My faith in the system wasn't good at all. I wish CPS got to know you, saw each parent as an individual and not just the situation, and treated dads like moms, not just the backup plan. I really wish the system knew how much I love my kids and that I am a good father. I'm not perfect, but I'm trying, and I will always be there for my kids.

Case #5

When I found out that we were pregnant, I was so excited. I wanted to go to every single appointment. I loved dreaming about our baby, what we would do together, what I would teach him. But then I went to the first prenatal appointment and I felt really frustrated. First, they wouldn't let me go into the room with my wife. They made me sit in the waiting room. I found out later from my wife it's because they wanted to ask her questions about whether or not I was abusive to her alone. Then when they finally let me in, there was nowhere to sit. Nowhere to put my coat. The only question that the nurse asked me is whether or not I had an STD. She didn't even ask my name or look me in the eye. She just called me "dad." By the time we left the appointment, I was really angry. It's clear that they didn't want me there. It kind of took the excitement out of being a new dad.

Case #6

I've been taking care of my kids on my own for a long time now. The mother of my kids has had mental problems for a long time. She was really depressed. She couldn't care for them. She couldn't work. She's still struggling. The kids still see her sometimes, and she does what she can, but she doesn't pay child support or anything, so it's all on me. When I first was doing this on my own, I looked for help, but all of the programs were for moms. I went to a parent group one time, but I was literally the only guy there. The moms just stared at me. I could tell I wasn't welcome. All the pictures on the wall were of moms and babies. All the staff were women. The intake form even had a question about my menstrual cycle. I've found that getting help as a single dad is hard. I don't even know where to look, so I just sort of figure it out on my own.

Appendix H: Resource List

Resource	
Organizations	*Link*
National Fatherhood Initiative	https://www.fatherhood.org
Fatherhood Research and Practice Network	https://www.frpn.org/
National Responsible Fatherhood Clearinghouse	https://fatherhood.gov
Head Start Early Childhood Learning and Knowledge Center: Birth to 5 Engaging Guide	https://eclkc.ohs.acf.hhs.gov
Office of the Assistant Secretary for Planning and Evaluation	https://aspe.hhs.gov
Child Welfare Information Gateway	https://www.childwelfare.gov
Ohio Commission on Fatherhood	https://fatherhood.ohio.gov
Urban Institute	https://www.urban.org
Institute for Research on Poverty	https://www.irp.wisc.edu
Fatherhood Resource Hub	https://fatherhoodresourcehub.org
Books	
Abdill, A. M. (2018). *Fathering from the margins*. Columbia University Press.	
Edin, K., & Nelson, T. J. (2013). *Doing the best I can: Fatherhood in the inner city*. University of California Press.	
Fagan, J., & Pearson, J. (Eds.). (2021). *New research onparentingprograms for low-income fathers*. Routledge.	
Fitzgerald, H. E., von Klitzing, K., Cabrera, N., Scarano de Mendonça, J., & Skjøthaug, T. (2020). *Handbook of fathers and child development: Prenatal to preschool*. Springer International Publishing.	
Johnson, W. E. (Ed.). (2010). *Social work with African American males: Health, mental health, and social policy*. OUP USA.	
Lamb, M. E. (Ed.). (2004). *The role of the father in child development*. Wiley.	
Mazza, C., & Perry, A. R. (2017). *Fatherhood in America: Social work perspectives on a changing society.* Charles C Thomas Publisher.	
Rollins, L. S. (Ed.). (2021). *Engaging and working with African American fathers: Strategies and lessons learned*. Routledge.	

J. L. Bellamy et al. (eds.), *Social Work Practice with Fathers*,
https://doi.org/10.1007/978-3-031-13686-3

References

Appendix E: Policy Reflection Activity

Bogenschneider, K., Little, O., Ooms, T., Benning, S., Cadigan, K., & Corbett, T. (2012). The family impact lens: A family-focused, evidence-informed approach to policy and practice. *Family Relations, 61*, 514–531. https://doi.org/10.1111/j.1741-3729.2012.00704.x

Gross, E., Bogenschneider, K., & Johnson, C. (n.d.). *How to conduct a family impact analysis*. Retrieved from Policy Institute for Family Impact Seminars website: http://wisfamilyimpact.org/wp-content/uploads/2014/10/fi_howtocondfia.pdf

Ooms, T. (1995). *Taking families seriously: Family impact analysis as an essential policy tool*. Retrieved from https://www.purdue.edu/hhs/hdfs/fii/wp-content/uploads/2015/06/pf_fis02supreport1.pdf

Ory, M. C. (1980). Family impact analysis: Concepts and methodologies. *Policy Studies Journal, 8*, 941–950. https://doi.org/10.1111/j.1541-0072.1980.tb01186.x

Appendix F: Practice Reflection Activity

Aistrup, J. A. (1996). *The Southern Strategy revisited: Republican top-down advancement in the South*. University Press of Kentucky.

Alexander, M. (2012). *The new Jim Crow: Mass incarceration in the age of colorblindness*. The New Press.

Bentley-Edwards, K. L., Edwards, M. C., Spence, C. N., Darity, W. A., Jr., Hamilton, D., & Perez, J. (2018). How does it feel to be a problem? The missing Kerner Commission Report. *RSF: The Russell Sage Foundation Journal of the Social Sciences, 4*(6), 20. https://doi.org/10.7758/rsf.2018.4.6.02

Blackmon, D. A. (2008). *Slavery by another name: The re-enslavement of Black Americans from the Civil War to World War II*. Anchor.

Bronson, J., & Carson, E. A. (2019). *Prisoners in 2017* (pp. 1–44). Bureau of Justice Statistics.

Charles, P., Muentner, L., & Kjellstrand, J. (2019). Parenting and incarceration: Perspectives on father-child involvement during reentry from prison. *Social Service Review, 93*(2), 218–261. https://doi.org/10.1086/703446

Cox, R., & Wallace, S. (2016). Identifying the link between food security and incarceration. *Southern Economic Journal, 82*(4), 1062–1077. https://doi.org/10.1002/soej.12080

J. L. Bellamy et al. (eds.), *Social Work Practice with Fathers*, https://doi.org/10.1007/978-3-031-13686-3

D'Angelo, A. V., Knas, E., Holcomb, P., & Edin, K. (2016). *The role of social networks among low-income fathers: Findings from the PACT evaluation* (pp. 1–16). Mathematica Policy Research.

Dion, R., Azur, M., Morzuch, M., & LaFlair, L. (2019). *Creating a trauma-informed system of care for formerly incarcerated dads* (pp. 1–22). Mathematica Policy Research.

Dion, R., Holcomb, P., Zaveri, H., D'Angelo, A. V., Clary, E., Friend, D., & Baumgartner, S. (2018). *Parents and children together: The complex needs of low-income men and how responsible fatherhood programs address them* (p. 69). Mathematica Policy Research.

Evans, W. N., & Owens, E. G. (2007). COPS and crime. *Journal of Public Economics, 91*(1–2), 181–201. https://doi.org/10.1016/j.jpubeco.2006.05.014

Eyster, L., Durham, C., Noy, M. V., & Damron, N. (2016). *Understanding local workforce systems* (pp. 1–26). Urban Institute.

Glaze, L. E., & Maruschak, L. M. (2010). *Parents in prison and their minor children* (pp. 1–25). U.S. Department of Justice.

Harding, D. J., Wyse, J. J. B., Dobson, C., & Morenoff, J. D. (2014). Making ends meet after prison. *Journal of Policy Analysis and Management [The Journal of the Association for Public Policy Analysis and Management], 33*(2), 440–470. https://doi.org/10.1002/pam.21741

Hinton, E. (2016). *From the war on poverty to the war on crime: The making of mass incarceration in America*. Harvard University Press.

Holcomb, P., Edin, K., Max, J., Young, A. A., Jr., D'Angelo, A. V., Friend, D., Clary, E., & Johnson, W. E., Jr. (2015). *In their own voices: The hopes and struggles of responsible fatherhood program participants in the parents and children together evaluation* (pp. 1–132).

Halushka, J. M. (2020). The runaround: Punishment, welfare, and poverty survival after prison. *Social Problems, 67*(2), 233–250. https://doi.org/10.1093/socpro/spz018

Joseph, M. L. (2010). Understanding the economic costs of incarceration for African American males. In W. E. Johnson Jr. (Ed.), *Social work with African American males: Health, mental health, and social policy* (pp. 311–324). Oxford University Press.

Lewis, C. E., Jr., Garfinkel, I., & Gao, Q. (2007). Incarceration and unwed fathers in fragile families. *Journal of Sociology, 34*(3), 77–94.

Muller, C. (2012). Northward migration and the rise of racial disparity in American incarceration, 1880–1950. *American Journal of Sociology, 118*(2), 281–326. https://doi.org/10.1086/666384

Muller, C. (2018). Freedom and convict leasing in the postbellum South. *American Journal of Sociology, 124*(2), 367–405. https://doi.org/10.1086/698481

Nagin, D., & Waldfogel, J. (1998). The effect of conviction on income through the life cycle. 1515. We thank Linda Babcock, Donald Fullerton, Lowell Taylor, Joe Tracy, and seminar participants at Carnegie Mellon and Yale for helpful comments. All errors, of course, remain our own. *International Review of Law and Economics, 18*(1), 25–40. https://doi.org/10.1016/S0144-8188(97)00055-0

National Research Council. (2014). *The growth of incarceration in the United States: Exploring causes and consequences* (B. Western, S. Redburn, & J. Travis, Eds.). National Academies Press. https://doi.org/10.17226/18613

Pager, D. (2003). The mark of a criminal record. *American Journal of Sociology, 108*(5), 937–975. https://doi.org/10.1086/374403

Pager, D. (2009). *Marked: Race, crime, and finding work in an era of mass incarceration* (Reprint edition). University of Chicago Press.

Pager, D., Western, B., & Bonikowski, B. (2009). Discrimination in a low-wage labor market: A field experiment. *American Sociological Review, 74*(5), 777–799. https://doi.org/10.1177/000312240907400505

Perry, A. R., & Bright, M. (2012). African American fathers and incarceration: Paternal involvement and child outcomes. *Social Work in Public Health, 27*(1–2), 187–203. https://doi.org/10.1080/19371918.2011.629856

Pettit, B., & Western, B. (2004). Mass imprisonment and the life course: Race and class inequality in U.S. incarceration. *American Sociological Review, 69*, 151–169.

Schwartz-Soicher, O., Geller, A., & Garfinkel, I. (2011). The effect of paternal incarceration on material hardship. *Social Service Review, 85*(3), 447–473. https://doi.org/10.1086/661925

Sykes, B. L., & Pettit, B. (2015). Severe deprivation and system inclusion among children of incarcerated parents in the United States after the Great Recession. *RSF.*

The Pew Charitable Trusts. (2010). *Collateral costs: Incarceration's effect on economic mobility* (pp. 1–40). The Pew Charitable Trusts.

Travis, J., & Western, B. (2017). Poverty, violence, and Black incarceration. In A. J. Davis (Ed.), *Policing the Black man: Arrest, prosecution, and imprisonment* (pp. 294–321). Vintage Books.

Wakefield, S., & Wildeman, C. (2016). *Children of the prison boom: Mass incarceration and the future of American inequality* (Reprint edition). Oxford University Press.

Western, B. (2006). *Punishment and inequality in America*. Russell Sage Foundation.

Western, B. (2018). *Homeward: Life in the year after prison*. Russell Sage Foundation.

Western, B., & Wildeman, C. (2009). The Black family and mass incarceration. *The Annals of the American Academy of Political and Social Science, 621*, 221–242. JSTOR.

U.S. Census Bureau. (2020). *2016–2020 American community survey 5-year estimates*. https://data.census.gov/cedsci/table?q=United%20States&g=0100000US&tid=ACSDP5Y2020.DP05

Index

J. L. Bellamy et al. (eds.), *Social Work Practice with Fathers*,
https://doi.org/10.1007/978-3-031-13686-3